Potiphar's Wife

The Vatican's Secret
and Child Sexual Abuse

Kieran Tapsell

Potiphar's Wife

The Vatican's Secret and Child Sexual Abuse

Kieran Tapsell

ATF Press
Adelaide

2014

Author: Tapsell, Kieran John, author.

Title: Potiphar's wife: the Vatican's secret and child sexual abuse/
            Kieran John Tapsell.

ISBN: 9781921511455 (paperback)
            9781921511462 (hardback)
            9781921511479 (ebook: epub)
            9781921511486 (ebook: pdf)

Notes: Includes index.

Subjects: Catholic Church--Government--History.
            Popes–Conduct of life.
            Papacy–Vatican city–History
            Secrecy–Religious aspects–Christianity.
            Sex crimes–Religious aspects–Catholic Church.
            Sex crimes–Vatican city–History.

Dewey Number: 262.13

First printed 2014
Reprinted 2014
Reprinted 2014

Artwork by Michael Mucci
Cover design by Astrid Scngkey
Layout by Anna Dimasi

Text Minion Pro Size 11

Published by:

An imprint of the ATF (Australia) Ltd
PO Box 504
Hindmarsh, SA 5007
ABN 90 116 359 963
www.atfpress.com

Dedicated to

Bert and Pat Watkins

I cannot accept your canon that we are to judge Pope and King unlike other men, with a favourable presumption that they did no wrong . . . There is no worse heresy than that the office sanctifies the holder of it.

Lord Acton: Letter to Bishop Mandel Creighton, April 5 1887.

Law functions as a teacher . . . It is capable of instigating great cultural change; it is capable of profoundly reinforcing a status quo . . . The law calls forth the ideology that defend(s) it, thus rationalizing and deepening the (ideology) that brought it into being in the first place.

Cardinal Francis George (2003)

CONTENTS

1

Acknowledgments

There are many people who have helped me with this book: Sharon Carleton, Ross Tapsell, Chris Geraghty, Mick and Jill Ryan, Bert and Pat Watkins, Dave Ward-Smith, Peter Aubourg, Penny Palmer, David McCann, Alan Bennett, Paul Wonnocott and Des Farmer for help and advice with the text. Friedrich Schwank, Merran Loewenthal, Stefan von der Beck, Torsten Bloch, Pierre Antoine Cals and Rafael Chalela were very helpful with their advice about Austrian, German, French and Colombian law. I would particularly like to thank Michael Mucci for the cover and Fr Tom Doyle for providing me with documents not available on the internet. In some areas, I have come to a slightly different opinion to some of the things that Tom has written. I would also like to thank some canon lawyers, members of the clergy, who have helped me understand some of the finer points of the canons. I also have to thank Brian Coyne and Amanda McKenna, and the many contributors to the web site Catholica (www.catholica.com.au) whose trawling of the internet for information about all manner of things affecting the Catholic Church, and particularly the abuse problem, turned them into an extraordinary virtual research team that allowed me to track down the pieces that make up the jigsaw. Finally, I have to thank the survivors of clerical sexual abuse whose doggedness in the face of institutional opposition led to the many inquiries that are slowly making sure that those responsible for the two cover-ups are indeed 'facing the truth'. The opinions I have expressed are my own, and any errors are entirely mine. The facts as known to me are current to 1 March 2014.

Pope Pius XI

2

Introduction

Sometimes you have to read a news report a second time to make sure you have read it correctly. That happened to me on 20 March 2010. No, it wasn't about another natural disaster or a terrorist bomb. It was a letter, the *Pastoral Letter* of Pope Benedict XVI to the people of Ireland, his response to the findings of the Murphy Commission about the cover up of clergy sexual abuse in the Archdiocese of Dublin.

As the new millennium was starting, the Irish Government had established a number of Commissions of Investigation, following continuous allegations of cover up of sexual abuse by institutions, and particularly the Church.[1] Similar inquiries in Australia and litigation in the United States revealed the same cover up.[2] Victims were taking their complaints to the police and priests were going to jail.

The sexual abuse of children is a serious crime in anyone's laws and language, but the Church was not reporting well-founded allegations against its priests to the police for investigation. These priests were never excommunicated, and rarely dismissed from the priesthood. They were often shifted around to other parishes or dioceses where

---

1. Unless otherwise stated, references to 'the Church' means the Roman Catholic Church, whose head is the pope, the Bishop of Rome.
2. The *Victorian Parliamentary Inquiry* in its Report of 13 November 2013 found: 'There has been a substantial body of credible evidence presented to the Inquiry and ultimately concessions made by senior representatives of religious bodies, including the Catholic Church, that they had taken steps with the direct objective of concealing wrongdoing.' See https://s3-ap-southeast-2.amazonaws.com/family-and-community-development-committee/Executive+summary+%26+recommendations.pdf (Accessed 13 November 2013).

they continued to prey on children. The striking thing is that the pattern of behaviour by bishops in covering up clergy sexual assaults on children seemed to be the same everywhere.[3]

Around 2007 I found out that in 1994, a former seminary professor of mine, Bede Heather, who became Bishop of Parramatta in the Sydney region, had allegedy refused to hand over to the police a report from a canon lawyer about the sexual abuse of children by a group of priests in his diocese. The end result was that a search warrant was issued, and his presbytery searched.[4] The priests were convicted and sent to jail. Bishop Heather was, in my experience, an admirable and honourable man. Why would he have done that? The Australian Jesuit, Fr Frank Brennan SJ expressed the same surprise about Archbishop Little of Melbourne who did not keep any notes of complaints of sexual abuse by priests, and routinely shifted them around where more children were abused. Brennan said this was devastating news 'for those of us who thought Frank Little to be a kind, compassionate, considerate, prayerful leader of his flock. And he was'.[5] Why did this otherwise admirable man do that?

This could not have been a conspiracy—there were too many people involved—and it could not have been universal incompetence or bad faith. There had to be some reason why a bishop in Dublin, one in Los Angeles, another in Sydney and another in Melbourne acted in the same way—and you could multiply that by just about

---

3. Fr Thomas Doyle in Sex Crimes and the Vatican at 20.02 mins, ' . . . the priests when they are discovered, the systemic response has been not to investigate and prosecute, but to move them . . . this is not just in the United States where this is happening. This is all over the world. You see the same pattern and practice no matter what country you go to', http://vimeo.com/654677 (Accessed 12 September 2013), Professor Patrick Parkinson: 'The Smith Lecture 2013: Child Sexual Abuse and the Churches—a Story of Moral Failure?', http://smithlecture. org/sites/smithlecture.org/files/downloads/lecture/smith-2013-transcript.pdf (Accessed 25 October 2013).

4. Various aspects of the case were reported in some newspapers: *Sydney Daily Telegraph* 19/7/1997, 13/11/1997, *Sydney Morning Herald* 13/11/1997, 3/3/1998, 4/3/1998, 28/3/1998; *The Australian*, 23/12/1994:13, *Sydney Sun-Herald* 16/11/1997: 56 http://brokenrites.alphalink.com.au/nletter/page12.html (Accessed 16 July 2013).

5. 'Church-State Issues and the Royal Commission', in *Eureka Street*, 3 September 2013,   http://www.eurekastreet.com.au/article.aspx?aeid=38146#.Ui5vaKt-8 (Accessed 10 September 2013).

every city in the world. There had to be some sort of legal, cultural or theological framework, and perhaps a combination of all three, behind these patterns of behaviour.

Out of curiosity, and without having any intention of writing a book, I started collecting information about what I thought might be the prime suspect, canon law, the law of the Church, a subject I had studied for about three years in the 1960s, while a student for the priesthood in that great gothic pile overlooking Sydney's Manly beach, St Patrick's Seminary, now used as a hospitality training centre.

My curiosity led me to buying books on the topic and, after trawling through the internet with a newly acquired commentary on the *1983 Code of Canon Law,* I came to the tentative conclusion that the legal framework for the cover up was what was called 'the secret of the Holy Office'. In 1974 it changed its name to ' the pontifical secret', the only significant difference being that excommunication for breach was not automatic. This was the Church's 'Top Secret' classification, and it applied to all allegations, Church investigations and trials of child sexual abuse by clergy. It prevented bishops and clergy investigating these allegations from reporting them to the police. But canon law also set the bar so high for dismissing a priest for sexual abuse of children that the only way it would be achieved was with the consent of the criminal himself. As time went by and there were more revelations and more leaks, the tentative nature of my conclusion disappeared.

On 26 November 2009, the Report of the Irish Commission of Investigation, headed by Judge Yvonne Murphy on sexual abuse by clergy in the Archdiocese of Dublin was published by the Irish government (*Murphy Dublin Report*).[6] It was a damning condemnation of the cover up of clergy sexual abuse in the Archdiocese, of the failure of its bishops to report these crimes to the police and to use canon law to dismiss sex-abusing priests from the priesthood. It also criticised the Irish State for being complicit in some cases. But it also went into a detailed examination of canon law and of the practice of the Vatican, finding that 'the structures and rules of the Catholic Church facilitated that cover-up'.[7]

6. http://www.justice.ie/en/JELR/DACOI%20Part%201.pdf/Files/DACOI%20 Part%201.pdf (Accessed 25 April 2013).
7. *Murphy Dublin Report,* Part 1 http://www.justice.ie/en/JELR/DACOI%20 Part%201.pdf/Files/DACOI%20Part%201.pdf (Accessed 25 April 2013), 1.113.

On 11 December 2009, the Vatican announced in a press release that His Holiness, Pope Benedict XVI had given the *Murphy Dublin Report* 'careful study', and that he was 'deeply disturbed and distressed by its contents'[8]

It is customary within the Church for bishops and popes to write 'Pastoral Letters' which provide advice and admonition on various matters of importance that might affect the faithful, and the same press release announced that Pope Benedict would be writing a *Pastoral Letter* to the people of Ireland in response to the *Murphy Dublin Report.*[9]

On 19 March 2010, the *Pastoral Letter* was released to the press.[10] I was expecting Pope Benedict to apologise to the victims, not only for the behaviour of the priests who sexually assaulted children, but also for all the problems that he and his predecessors had caused, by enshrining in canon law a system of cover up that allowed these priests to continue sexually abusing children. This book would never have been written had he done that.

I was more than surprised when I read the *Pastoral Letter.* Of course, Benedict condemned the crimes of the priests, and apologised to the victims, but he blamed some of the Irish bishops (the *Murphy Dublin Report* was only about that Archdiocese) for not applying 'the long-established norms of canon law to the crime of child abuse'. He mentioned nothing about the significant role that canon law, the Popes and the Vatican Curia played in protecting sex abusing priests from civil prosecution and from being dismissed from the priesthood, for the reasons spelt out in chapter and verse in the *Murphy Dublin Report.*

I was expecting Benedict to admit that the imposition of pontifical secrecy on the Church internal investigations of child sexual abuse was a dreadful mistake, and that he was going to change it to allow unrestricted reporting to the police by bishops and those investigating such allegations on their behalf. I thought he would apologise on

---

8.   Vatican Press release 11 December 2009. http://www.vatican.va/resources/resources_irish-bishops-dec2009_en.html (Accessed 19 May 2005).

9.   Ibid, and see also the announcement by Archbishop Martin of Dublin http://www.rte.ie/news/2010/0217/127689-abuse/ (Accessed 9 July 2013).

10. http://www.vatican.va/holy_father/benedict_xvi/letters/2010/documents/hf_ben-xvi_let_20100319_church-ireland_en.html (Accessed 16 July 2013).

behalf of himself, his predecessors as pope, and the Roman Curia for pontifical secrecy, and for the shambles that they had created within the Vatican's own disciplinary system under canon law which made it almost impossible to dismiss a priest from the priesthood without the priest's consent. But there was none of that. Benedict put the blame for the cover up on the bishops and their 'failures of leadership'. According to the *Pastoral Letter*, it was their fault, and these increased attacks on children had nothing to do with canon law and those ultimately responsible for it, the six popes who had set up and maintained the system enshrined in canon law for some ninety years since 1922.

On 16 November 2012, a documentary film, *Mea Maxima Culpa: Silence in the House of God*, by Alex Gibney was released. It was a gut wrenching indictment of the cover up in the United States of sexual abuse of as many as 200 deaf mute boys, and more covering up in Ireland and elsewhere. An Irish reporter in the documentary, Mick Peelo, said that after the publication of the *Pastoral Letter*, he spoke to an Irish bishop who was very angry. 'How dare he blame us', the bishop said. 'Show me where we didn't follow canon law. Canon law was the problem.' Indeed it was. It had provided the legal framework for the cover up that allowed far more children to be abused than if these priests had been reported to the police, and weeded out the moment they had offended.

Benedict XVI's *Pastoral Letter* also wrote the script for a second cover up—shielding the popes and the Vatican from any criticism over child sexual abuse. That cover up had started a few years earlier in about 2006 when newspaper articles and television programs, like the 2006 BBC Panorama Program, *Sex Crimes and the Vatican*, directly accused the Vatican, and particularly Pope Benedict XVI, of ordering and maintaining a policy of cover up through canon law. Benedict put his *imprimatur* on the second cover up with his *Pastoral Letter*: blame the bishops and don't mention canon law or the Vatican. This cover up gathered steam in Ireland and in Rome through Vatican spokesmen. I suspected that the same might happen in Australia, and those suspicions have now been confirmed by the submission of 21 September 2012, made by the Church in the State of Victoria to the Victorian Parliamentary Inquiry into the Handling of Child Abuse by Religious and Other Organizations (*Victorian Parliamentary Inquiry*), and by the *Australian Church Submission* of 30 September

2013 (*Australian Church Submission*) on behalf of the Australian bishops to the Australian Federal Government's Royal Commission into Institutional Responses to Child Sex Abuse (*Australian Royal Commission*).

The Church in the State of Victoria, consisting of the Archdiocese of Melbourne, and the dioceses of Ballarat, Sandhurst and Sale, and representatives of the Religious Orders, Congregations and Societies submitted a 155 page document, called *Facing the Truth* to the *Victorian Parliamentary Inquiry*.[11] Despite its name, it is a typical defence lawyer's submission, trying to put the best possible gloss on the client's case by exaggerating the positives and playing down or ignoring the negatives.

It repeated the claim that the Church, like the rest of society, was only just coming to grips with the sexual abuse of children, as if that provided some sort of excuse for not reporting these crimes to the police, and having an internal disciplinary system that was all but useless. The extent of sexual abuse and knowledge about its psychological damage to children might be something new, but the fact that it was a crime punishable by the State was not new, and had been accepted by the Church for some 1500 years—until 1922 when *Crimen Sollicitationis*, the decree that imposed 'the secret of the Holy Office', was promulgated by Pope Pius XI.

The Victorian Church submission has a chronology of 150 pieces of legislation, both civil and canonical, and references to inquiries, reports and Commissions from all over the world from 1961 to the present. But the central document in the cover up, when clergy sexual abuse was at its height in the 1960s and 1970s, the reissue of *Crimen Sollicitationis* in 1962, is never mentioned, nor is pontifical secrecy, imposed by later decress. There were acknowledgments of the inadequacies of past practices but there was no mention that these past practices were underpinned by canon law. The *Australian Church Submission* to the *Australian Royal Commission* follows the same script.

When it came to giving evidence at the *Victorian Parliamentary Inquiry*, the current and former bishops of Ballarat and Melbourne

---

11. http://www.parliament.vic.gov.au/images/stories/committees/fcdc/ inquiries/57th/Child_Abuse_Inquiry/Submissions/Catholic_Church_in_ Victoria.pdf (Accessed 6 April 2013).

poured the bucket over their predecessors for the cover up of a number of serial sexual abusers. These bishops were following Pope Benedict's lead: blame the bishops, and don't mention canon law and the Pope's responsibility for it. Their stance is understandable. Every bishop prior to his ordination has to take a special oath of loyalty, not to God, or to the Church, but to the pope.[12] One of the bishops, on whom the bucket was poured, was Bishop Ronald Mulkearns, who had a doctorate in canon law, was a founding member of the Canon Law Society of Australia and New Zealand, and the initial chairman of the Special Issues Committee set up by the Australian Catholic Bishops Conference to find a better way of dealing with sex abusing priests than through canon law.[13] Everything Mulkearns did as Bishop of Ballarat, misguided as it was, followed canon law.

So long as Benedict did not apologise for the role of the Vatican and canon law in the cover up, this matter would continue to fester, because nothing festers like falsehoods. Indeed that is what has happened. The festering has now resulted in continuous and damaging inquiries into the Church throughout the world, and significantly for Australia, the setting up of the *Victorian Parliamentary Inquiry*, the Special Commission of Inquiry into Matters Relating to the Police Investigation of Certain Child Sexual Abuse Allegations in the Catholic Diocese of Maitland-Newcastle (*Maitland-Newcastle Inquiry*) and the *Australian Royal Commission*.

The Australian story about the sexual abuse cover up is no different to the rest of the world. Its legal system is relevant to other countries, because canon law imposed pontifical secrecy on the Church's internal investigations of clergy sexual abuse, with no exception for reporting

---

12. Bishop Geoffrey Robinson: 'Before they are ordained, all bishops are required to take a special oath of loyalty to the pope (not to God, not to the church, but to the pope). This oath is a symptom of the constant and severe pressure on all bishops to protect all levels of papal authority at all costs and in all circumstances. A very high value is put on a bishop being "a pope's man". http://bishopgeoffrobinson. org/usa_lecture.htm (Accessed 23 August 2013). Similar comments have been made by Sipe, Benkert and Doyle: Spirituality and the Culture of Narcissism: http://www.awrsipe.com/reports/2013/Spirituality%20and%20the%20 Culture%20of%20Narcissism%20-%20Complete%20article%20-%208-30-2013. pdf at 6(Accessed 30 September 2013).

13. *Australian Church Submission,* 73/26 http://dev.childabuseroyalcommission.gov. au/wp-content/uploads/2013/10/14.-Truth-Justice-and-Healing-Council.pdf (Accessed 12 October 2013).

that information to the police. In 2010, the Vatican announced that it will provide an exception to pontifical secrecy where the local civil law required reporting, and in the meantime it announced that it would give an instruction to bishops in those terms. However, on the recommendation of Law Reform Commissions, many countries, including Australia, abolished most of their laws requiring reporting of serious crimes (other than where there are children currently at risk) more than thirty years ago, in the mistaken belief that the moral sense in the community to report serious crimes to the police was so strong that there was no need for the criminal law to back it up. It must come as a surprise to the Law Reform Commissioners to discover that the leaders of the Church did not share that moral sense when it came to its priests sexually assaulting children.

The Church claims that it has rectified the problems of the past. It has changed many of its attitudes to victims for the better, but on the most serious issue of the cover up it has been moonwalking. It has fiddled around the edges of pontifical secrecy and created a modern rendition of the famous line of the Sicilian aristocrat in Giuseppe de Lampedusa's novel, *The Leopard*: 'If you want things to stay as they are, things will have to change.' Pontifical secrecy for clergy crimes against children, the cornerstone of the cover up, stays the same. It is still writ large in canon law with a limited exception that is useless in most countries.

3

Chronology of Church Response
to
Clergy Sexual Abuse of Children

DATE CE	EVENT	DESCRIPTION
153	The *Didache*	Prohibition on adult men having sex with boys.
306	The Council of Elvira	First Church law against the sexual abuse of boys.
312	Emperor Constantine	Decreed 'privilege of clergy', that is the right of clergy to be tried exclusively in Church courts. Church adopts the military practice of *degradatio* or dishonourable discharge to strip clergy of status as priests.
330–379	St Basil of Caesarea	Monastic rule of the Eastern Church. A cleric or monk who sexually molests youths or boys is to be publically whipped, his head shaved, he be spat upon, and kept in prison for six months in chains on a diet of bread and water, and after release is to be subject to supervision and kept out of contact with young people.
672–735	St Bede the Venerable	*'Penitentials'*. Sex abusing clergy were to be imprisoned, living on bread and water from three to twelve years.
6th–12th c	*The Penitentials*	The punishments meted out to clergy were more severe than for laymen.
1008	Burchard, Bishop of Worms, books of canon law	Repeated many of these earlier condemnations of canon law about clergy sexual abuse.

1051	St Peter Damian, *Book of Gomorrah*	Damian appealed to Pope Leo IX to take action against child sexual abuse by clergy. The pope's response was to dismiss only repeat offenders, ignoring the effect on the victims and emphasising the need for forgiveness of the perpetrator.
1140	Gratian, *The Concordance of Discordant Canons*	His 'decrees' are the most important source in the history of canon law. Supports the policy that clergy who rape young boys should also be punished by the civil law, which at that time meant execution.
29 Dec 1170	Thomas a'Becket	The Archbishop of Canterbury murdered in Canterbury Cathedral by knights of King Henry II with whom he had been in dispute over 'privilege of clergy'.
1179	Third Lateran Council, Pope Alexander III	Condemnation of unnatural acts of both laity and clergy, but in the case of clergy, they were to be kept indefinitely in a monastery or subjected to *degradatio*.
1189–1198	Pope Celestine III	Approved the punishment of clergy serial offenders by the secular power
1198	Pope Innocent III, decree c viii, *De Crimine Falsi*, X, v, 20.	Clerical sexual abusers of children, after *degradatio*, should be handed over to the secular power, to be punished according to the law of the land.
1514	Fifth Lateran Council, Pope Leo X	Sex abusing clerics are to be punished 'respectively according to the sacred canons or with penalties imposed by the civil law'.

1551	The Council of Trent	Clergy convicted of grievous crimes were to be 'defrocked' publically and then handed over to a lay judge, who was to be present during the trial, for further punishment according to the civil law.
1566	Pope St Pius V, *Constitution Romani Pontifici*	Clerics who committed sodomy to be first 'degraded' by a canonical court, and then handed over to the secular authorities for punishment.
1568	Pope St Pius V, decree, *Horrendum Illud Scelus*	Decree condemning clerics who 'sinned against nature' with children. They were to be cast out of the clergy to be deterred by 'the avenging secular sword of civil laws'.
1570	Priest named Fontino charged before a canonical court of sodomy with a choirboy.	He was defrocked, and then handed over to the secular authority for punishment according to the civil law. He was executed by beheading.
1726	Sacred Congregation of the Council	A priest who sodomized boys was sentenced to work in a hospital. The Council refused to reinstate him as a priest after serving his sentence. An example of eighteenth century zero tolerance.
1741	Pope Benedict XIV, decree *Sacramentum Poenitentiae*	Canonical procedures for dealing with cases of priests soliciting sex in the confessional. Such cases come under jurisdiction of The Holy Office (later called Congregation for the Doctrine of the Faith).
1790	The United States	All vestiges of privilege of clergy abolished in federal courts.
1827	The United Kingdom and its colonies	All vestiges of privilege of clergy abolished by the U.K. Parliament. The abolition applies to Australia, Canada and other colonies.

1846	Pius IX	Giovanni Maria Mastai-Ferretti elected pope.
1866	Pius IX	The Holy Office issues a decree that all cases involving soliciting sex in the confessional to be subject to absolute secrecy because of the seal of confession.
1904	Pope St Pius X	Sets up commission to codify canon law under Cardinal Gasparri and Monsignor Pacelli, later Pope Pius XII.
1905	Beatification of John Vianney	John Vianney taught, 'After Christ, the priest is everything'. Clericalism within the Church surges.
1917	Pope Benedict XV	Code of Canon Law promulgated. Decrees requiring sex abusing priests to be handed over to the civil authorities not included in the Code. However, they were to be declared 'infamous'.
1920	First Commercial Radio licence granted	First commercial radio licence in the world granted to Westinghouse in the United States.
1922	The British Broadcasting Corporation	BBC established. The Church recognizes the propaganda benefits of radio, but also its disadvantages in spreading 'scandal' and its effect on Church membership. Secrecy is the solution.
6 Feb 1922	Pope Pius XI	Achille Ratti elected pope.

1922	Pope Pius XI decree *Crimen Sollicitationis*	Applies to soliciting sex in the confessional, homosexuality, bestiality and abuse of children by clerics. Bishops to conduct preliminary investigation of such allegations, to notify the Holy Office, and to conduct a penal trial. Dismissal from the priesthood was only permitted when there was 'no hope, or almost no hope of amendment'. The proceedings were to be subject to 'the secret of the Holy Office', the breach of which was automatic excommunication that could only be lifted by the Pope personally. There were no exceptions for reporting to the civil authorities. The results of any such trial were to be sent to the Holy Office. Any requirement under the Code for such priests to be declared 'infamous' dropped.
1925	Pope Pius XI	Canonizes St John Vianney.
1922–1933	Treaties between the Vatican and Latvia, Poland, Italy, Austria and Germany.	The treaties with Latvia (1922), Poland (1925) and Italy (1929) provided for modified forms of privilege of clergy: they would be treated by civil authorities with due regard to their level in the hierarchy and any jail sentence would be served in a 'place separated from lay people' or in a monastery. The Lateran Treaty with Italy (1929) and the treaty with Nazi Germany (1933) provided for privilege in the clergy's 'pastoral ministry' communications, that is, the State is denied access to them.

1931	Pope Pius XI	Engages Marconi to set up the Vatican Radio.
2 March 1938	Pope Pius XII	Eugenio Pacelli elected Pope.
1946	Aurelio Yanguas	The noted Spanish canon lawyer says that the purpose of *Crimen Sollicitationis* was to preserve the Church's reputation by taking 'swift, decisive and secret action' before these crimes reach the civil courts so that the Church would be spared the humiliation of having priests in the public dock as sexual offenders.
1947	Fr Gerald Fitzgerald	Fr Gerald Fitzgerald establishes *The Servants of the Paraclete* to deal with alcohol and sexual problems of clergy. Recommends zero tolerance approach to clergy child sexual abusers.
1953	Concordat between Spain and the Vatican	The Spanish dictator, General Franco restores many of the privileges of clergy that were abrogated by the 1931 Republic. He and the Vatican agree that a bishop can only be put on trial in a civil court with the consent of the Vatican. Criminal proceedings against clerics can only be brought with the consent of the bishop. Any deprivation of liberty was to be spent in a religious house, not in jail, and the proceedings were not to be publicised. Clerics and religious could be made to testify in court, but only with the consent of the bishop, and no cleric could be questioned about his knowledge of crimes of others that came to them while performing their ministry. Effectively, a bishop could not be questioned by the State about facts uncovered in canonical investigations about child abuse.

16 June 1954	Concordat between the Dominican Republic and the Vatican	Priests cannot be interrogated by judges or other authorities over things revealed to them in the exercise of their 'sacred ministry'. Priests would serve their sentences separate from lay persons.
28 Oct 1958	Pope John XXIII	Angelo Roncalli elected pope
1962	Pope John XXIII	Reissues *Crimen Sollicitationis* with some minor changes. Sets up Commission to revise the *1917 Code of Canon Law*.
21 June 1963	Pope Paul VI	Giovanni Batista Montini elected pope.
1963	Fr Gerald Fitzgerald	Recommends to Pope Paul VI a zero tolerance approach to sex abusing priests, and warns him about the repercussions of not acting to dismiss them.
1960–1980	Significant increase in sexual abuse of children worldwide by Catholic clergy and religious.	
1967	The United Kingdom	Misprision of felony abolished. Mere failure to report a serious crime is not itself a crime.
1971	Congregation for the Doctrine of the Faith (CDF)	Issues instruction that bishops may petition the CDF for an 'administrative laicization' or dismissal of a priest for living a 'depraved life', which includes the sexual abuse of children.

12 July 1973	Concordat between Colombia and the Vatican	Bishops cannot be tried by the state courts, but only by the Church courts. Priests can be tried in state courts but the proceedings are not to be publicised. This and other parts of the Concordat were declared unconstitutional by the Colombian Constitutional Court in 1993. Despite controversy over the matter, the Vatican was still insisting in 2007 that under the Concordat, Colombian bishops were entitled to impunity, and were above the law. The matter is still unresolved.
1974	Pope Paul VI, decree *Secreta Continere*	The 'Secret of the Holy Office' is renamed 'the Pontifical Secret', the only significant difference is that excommunication for breach is not automatic, but it could still be imposed. Pontifical secret applies to communications between the Vatican and its legates, and for 'delicts against faith and moral'. The pontifical secret not only applies to the investigation and trial of sexual abuse cases against children, but also applies to the allegation itself. Bishops cannot report any allegation of sexual abuse to the police without risking excommunication.
1974–1996	Archbishop Frank Little of Melbourne	Little kept no records of abuse allegations made against abusive priests and shifted them around. None of the allegations were reported by the Church to the police. At the *Victorian Parliamentary Inquiry* in 2012, Archbishop Hart of Melbourne said he assumed that Little was abiding by the confidentiality provisions of *Crimen Sollicitationis*. Little had also adopted the practice of keeping no notes of such matters.

1975	Fr Sean Brady, later Cardinal Brady	Then a thirty-six year old priest with a doctorate in canon law interviews a boy with a more senior member of the clergy about the boy's being abused by a serial paedophile, Fr Brendan Smyth. The boy's father was asked to remain outside, and the boy was sworn to secrecy. The report of the two priests was sent to the bishop and nothing was reported to the police. Brady was following the procedures laid down by *Crimen Sollicitationis*. The Irish canon lawyer, Maurice Dooley confirms that canon law prohibited Brady from reporting the matter to the police.
1976–1998	Fr Marcial Maciel	Numerous allegations of sexual abuse made against the founder of the Legion of Christ. Maciel has a budget of $650m and makes generous donations to the Vatican. No action is taken against him until 2006.
1978	Fr. Tony Walsh (Ireland)	First allegations of abuse of children by this serial paedophile.
26 Aug 1978	Pope John Paul I	Albino Luciani elected pope
16 Oct 1978	Pope John Paul II	Karol Wojtyla elected pope
1980	Pope John Paul II	Abolishes 'administrative laicisation'. The only method now available under canon law to dismiss a priest from the priesthood is through the judicial trial. The accused priest alone can apply for an 'administrative laicisation'.
1981	The State of Victoria, Australia.	Misprision of felony abolished. The States of Queensland and Western Australia, and the Northern Territory have similar formulations requiring a benefit of some kind for the concealment to be punishable. The State of Tasmania never adopted misprision in its criminal law.

1983	Pope John Paul II	The *1983 Code of Canon Law* promulgated. It continues and extends the 'pastoral approach' to sex abusing priests, requiring the bishop to try to reform the priest before subjecting him to a canonical trial for dismissal. It introduces a 'Catch 22' defence: a priest cannot be dismissed for paedophilia because he is a paedophile, that is he cannot help himself. It imposes, for the first time, a limitation period for child sexual abuse offences. If canonical proceedings are not commenced within five years of the abuse, the canonical crime is 'extinguished'.
1984	Congregation for Clergy to Archbishop Moreno	Archbishop Moreno writes to the Congregation for the Clergy about a womanising priest, and asked about whether he should hand over his files in the case of a subpoena. The Congregation said he should not, and should instruct lawyers to fight the matter because it involved 'an intolerable attack on the free exercise of religion in the United States.'
1987	Cardinal Roger Mahony, Archbishop of Los Angeles	Together with his advisers, concealed clergy sexual crimes from the police, and even warned priests who were wanted by the police not to return to California so as to avoid arrest.
1988	Cardinal Ratzinger	Writes to Cardinal Castillo Lara, the President of the Pontifical Council for Legislative Texts, asking for a more streamlined way of dealing with clergy who had sexually abused children, because the formal judicial trial was too unwieldy. Castillo Lara rejects the request because it would interfere with the 'priest's fundamental right of defence'.

1988	The American bishops ask for an extension to the limitation period.	The American bishops explain to the Vatican that the five year limitation period would mean very few canonical trials because abused children take some time to come to terms with what has happened to them. The negotiations continue for six years, and in 1994 an extension is granted for ten years from the victim's eighteenth birthday. The extension only applies to the United States.
1988	Australian Catholic Bishops Conference	Sets up a Special Issues Committee to establish a protocol where allegations of a criminal nature were made against priests and religious.
26 July 1990	Dr Nicholas Tonti-Filippini,	The Catholic ethicist advised the Australian bishops: 'For the sake of the Church, reasonable suspicion of a crime must be reported to the authorities. Any attempt to contain it within an in-house investigation and management risks bringing the Church into disrepute.' Advice ignored, except where there is a civil law requiring reporting, until 2010. Apart from New South Wales, no other State requires reporting of 'historic abuse' that accounts for more than 99% of all complaints.
25 Nov 1990	New South Wales	Misprision of felony abolished but replaced by a statutory form of it in S.316 Crimes Act 1900 (NSW).

1900–1995	Fr Brian Lucas	As member of the Special Issues Committee, Lucas was of the view that the canonical procedures for dismissing sex abusing priests were 'unworkable'. He then tried to convince accused priests to resign. He dealt with about thirty-five priests during that period. He kept no notes of any conversations he had with such priests. No reports made by the Church to the police. Only NSW had law requiring reporting historic abuse. Bishops and canonical investigators avoid breaching canon law by referring victims to counsellors who then arranged for the reporting. Counselling was not part of the canonical disciplinary procedure.
Sept 1992	The 'Father F' Case	Fr Brian Lucas, Fr John Usher and Fr Wayne Peters interviewed 'Father F', a serial paedophile with a view to convincing him to agree to voluntary laicisation. 'Father F' finally agrees to laicisation in 2005. In 2012 Antony Whitlam QC appointed to conduct a private Church enquiry and concludes that the admissions contained in Fr Peter's letter were not shared by his colleagues. Fr Peter's letter indicates that the main concern was the avoidance of scandal.
1992	Australian Catholic Bishops Conference	Special issues Committee drafts protocol that required bishops and religious superiors to abide by any laws relating to compulsory reporting.

1993 onwards	Australian States	Introduced mandatory welfare reporting laws requiring specific categories of professionals, such as teachers and doctors to report reasonable suspicions about the abuse or mistreatment of a child. The obligation to report ceases once the child turns eighteen years of age. Non-teaching clergy did not have to report in Victoria, and may not have to in Tasmania, Queensland and Western Australia, depending on their activities.
1993	Archdiocese of Melbourne	First attempts to discipline Fr Desmond Gannon. Gannon was convicted in a civil court in 1995, 1997, 2000, and 2009 for sexual crimes against children, but this was not enough to satisfy the 'absolute certitude' of the Vatican. The Archbishop was still trying to have him dismissed in 2012
1994	South Australia	Misprision of felony abolished.
1994	Archbishop Castrillón of Bucaramanga, Colombia	Proceedings started by the Colombian Attorney General, Gustavo de Grieff against certain bishops, including Archbishop Dario Castrillón Hoyos of Bucaramanga for complicity with the FARC guerrillas, contrary to Colombian law. He had to abandon the proceedings because of the immunity under the Concordat, which protected the bishops from any criminal proceedings.

1994	Bishop Bede Heather	Heather engages Dr Rodger Austin, a canon lawyer, to investigate allegations of sexual abuse amongst the St Gerard Majella religious congregation. Heather allegedly refuses to hand over Austin's report and other evidence to the police. Police issue search warrant and search his presbytery. Priests convicted and sent to jail.
June 1994	Fr Tony Walsh (Ireland)	In 1993, the Dublin Canonical Tribunal dismisses Fr Walsh, described by the *Murphy Dublin Report* as Ireland's worst serial paedophile priest, but his appeal is upheld by the Roman Rota, the Vatican's appeal court on the basis of the 'Catch 22' defence, the lack of 'full' imputability, that is, that Walsh could not be dismissed for paedophilia because he was a paedophile. Under this defence, the worse the paedophile, the more likely he will avoid dismissal.
1994	Australian Catholic Bishops Conference	Bishop Geoffrey Robinson asked to draw up a protocol to deal with sex abusing priests and victims.
1994	United States Catholic Bishops Conference	Extension of the limitation period from five years to ten years from the eighteenth birthday of the victim, but not to operate retrospectively. Limited to the United States
1995	Fr Denis McAlinden (Newcastle, NSW)/Fr Phillip Wilson	McAlinden was a serial paedophile. Fr Philip Wilson, now Archbishop of Adelaide, and a canon lawyer with a doctorate in canon law, interviews the victims. No report was made to the police.

1996	Fr Brian Lucas	Writes article for the Canon Law Society of Australia and New Zealand: 'Are Our Archives Safe: An Ecclesial View of Search Warrants', and concluded that no form of legal privilege attached to documents relating to investigations of sex abusing priests (as well as other matters) under the civil law. While he warned against selective destruction of documents, he wrote that there may be cases that appear so sensitive that it is in the best interest of the parties and of the Church that the documents not be created in the first place.
January 1996	Fr Tony Walsh	Dismissed from the priesthood by the Pope on petition by Cardinal Connell of Dublin, after the Roman Rota allowed his appeal on the basis of the 'Catch 22' defence.
15 June 1996	Archbishop Castrillón of Bucaramanga, Colombia.	Appointed Pro-Prefect of the Congregation for the Clergy and made Cardinal in 1998 and appointed full Prefect the same year.
7 Aug 1996	Bishop Geoffrey Robinson	Receives an official letter from the Congregation for Bishops rebuking him for criticism of the 'magisterial teaching and discipline of the Church', for saying that he was not happy with the levels of support from Rome. The only significant difference between *Towards Healing* and the *Melbourne Response* from the point of view of canon law was that *Towards Healing* required bishops to report allegations of sexual abuse where the law required it, in breach of canon law, and *The Melbourne Response* did not.

October 1996	Archbishop George Pell	Sets up the *Melbourne Response*. Pell was a member of the CDF from 1990 to 2000. The *Melbourne Response*, in contrast with Bishop Robinson's proposals for *Towards Healing* had no proposals for reporting to the police, although it stated that the victim would be encouraged to do so. This was in keeping with the policy expressed in the letters of Cardinal Castrillón, the Prefect of the Congregation of the Clergy to the Irish Bishops in 1997 and 1998. Pell tells *Victorian Parliamentary Inquiry* in 2013 that the CDF was 'pleased with' *The Melbourne Response*
1996	United States Canon Law Society has meeting with Archbishop Bertone of the CDF.	Bertone tells Society members that *Crimen Sollicitationis* was not repealed by the *1983 Code of Canon Law*, and that it can be used for dealing with sex abusing priests outside soliciting in the confessional.
1996	Congregation for the Doctrine of the Faith	The CDF extends limitation period for Ireland—ten years from the eighteenth birthday of the victim.
4 Jan 1996	Catholic Bishops Conference of Ireland	Forwards to the Vatican the *Framework Document* that has a provision for mandatory reporting of all complaints of clergy sexual abuse to the police.
31 Jan 1997	Archbishop Storero on behalf of Congregation of Clergy	Advises that their proposals for 'mandatory reporting gives rise to serious reservations of both a moral and a canonical nature'. Further advises that non-compliance with canon law on reporting could mean that any canonical action against a priest may fail on appeal to Rome.

March 1997	Australian Catholic Bishops Conference	Adopts the 1996 *Towards Healing* protocol.
24 Mar 1997	Archbishop Weakland of Milwaukee	Obtains the consent of Archbishop Bertone of the CDF to proceed with a judicial trial of Fr Lawrence Murphy for the sexual abuse of deaf mute boys.
6 April 1998	Archbishop Weakland/ Archbishop Bertone CDF	After receiving a letter from Fr Lawrence Murphy, Bertone instructs Archbishop Weakland to consider 'pastoral methods' again in his case.
13 May 1998	Archbishops Weakland/ Bertone	At a meeting in Rome, Bertone advises Weakland to withdraw the judicial action against Murphy, because Rome would allow an appeal.
1998	Congregation for the Doctrine of the Faith	CDF confirms extension of limitation period for the United States of ten years from eighteenth birthday of the victim. Only the United States and Ireland have this extension. The limitation period is still five years for the rest of the world.
1998	Fr Marcial Maciel	Eight former members of the Legion of Christ make allegations of sexual abuse against the Congregation's founder. Cardinal Ratzinger pressured by Curia Cardinals not to continue investigation.
Nov 1998	Cardinal Castrillón meets with Irish bishops in Sligo, Ireland.	Irish bishops again request permission to report clergy sexual abuse crimes to the police. Castrillón refuses. Castrillón writes to Irish bishops saying that any complaints to the police had to be by the victim, not by bishops.

1999	Irish Bishops and Cardinal Castrillón meet in Rome	Castrillón tells bishops to be 'fathers to your priests and not policemen'.
July 1999	Fr Patrick Maguire (Ireland)	Canonical proceedings for dismissal commenced against Maguire, a serial paedophile. In June 1998 he had been sentenced to eighteen months imprisonment for indecent assault on two boys. On release in March 1999, extradited to Ireland on twelve more charges and sentenced to six years imprisonment in January 2000.
Dec 1999	New South Wales Law Reform Commission Report on S.316 Crimes Act 1900 (NSW)	Recommends the abolition of S.316 on the ground (amongst others) that 'The Commission disapproves of substituting a legal duty which is enforced by a criminal sanction for a moral one unless there are overall substantial benefits to society in doing so'.
Sept 2000	Fr Patrick Maguire	Dublin Canonical Tribunal dismisses Maguire from the priesthood. Maguire appeals to the Roman Rota.

| 30 Apr 2001 | Pope John Paul II, *Motu Proprio Sacramentorum Sanctitatis Tutela* | Requires bishops to send results of their preliminary inquiries under canon 1717 in respect of child sexual abuse to the CDF which will then instruct them what to do. Restores the situation that existed before 1983 where the CDF could dismiss a priest on petition by the bishop. Pontifical secrecy applies to 'cases of this nature' under *Secreta Continere*. The *Motu Proprio* has an historical introduction that states that *Crimen Sollicitationis* was in force until then, despite the Vatican sending a clear message to all the world's bishops that it had been repealed by the *1983 Code of Canon Law* by its negotiations for an extension of the Code's limitation period. There was no limitation period under *Crimen Sollicitationis*. |
| 18 May 2001 | Cardinals Ratzinger and Archbishop Bertone | Writes a letter to the bishops explaining the changes and asserting, contrary to the Vatican behaviour over the previous eighteen years, that *Crimen Sollicitationis* was 'in force until now'. |

8 Sept 2001	Cardinal Castrillón writes to Bishop Pican	French Bishop Pican was given a three-month suspended prison sentence for concealing knowledge that a priest in his diocese, the Reverend René Bissey, had sexually assaulted a number of boys. Cardinal Castrillón, then Prefect of the Congregation for the Clergy wrote to him, congratulating him. 'You have acted wisely, and I am delighted to have a fellow member of the episcopate who, in the eyes of history and of other bishops, would prefer to go to prison rather than denounce his priest-son. For the relationship between priests and their bishop is not professional but a sacramental relationship which forges very special bonds of spiritual paternity.' Castrillón will write to all the bishops of the world to advise them to do the same—do not report clergy crimes to the police and be prepared to go to jail. He later says that he sent the letter with the approval of Pope John Paul II.
Nov 2001	Cardinal Billé, President of the French Catholic Bishop's Conference	Accuses those who demand that sex crimes by priests against children be reported to the police of being 'intellectual terrorists'. At the French Catholic Bishops Conference said he said that the conviction of Pican was an infringement by secular authorities of the norms of professional secrecy
17 Sep 2001	Lord Nolan Final Report to Catholic Bishops Conference of England and Wales	The effect of the Nolan reports was to recommend openness, reporting to the police, and prosecution of offenders, amongst other matters. Nolan trusted that any difficulties with canon law would be dealt with 'responsively'. That turned out to be wishful thinking.

February 2002	Archbishop Bertone, Secretary of the CDF	Interview with *30 Giorni* says that 'the demand that a bishop be obligated to contact the police in order to denounce a priest who has admitted the offense of paedophilia is unfounded.'
23 April 2002	Vatican and United States Bishops	Meeting in Rome to discuss sexual abuse crisis.
29 April 2002	Archbishop Herranz, President Pontifical Council for the Interpretation of Legislative Texts,	At a conference in Milan rejected the idea that there was any obligation for a bishop to report a paedophile priest to the police. He said there was a 'The rapport of trust and the secrecy of the office inherent to the relationship between the bishop and his priests', and it must be respected.
16 May 2002	Cardinal Rodriguez Maradiaga of Honduras	At a news conference says that paedophile priests should leave the priesthood, but rejects reporting to the police. 'For me it would be a tragedy to reduce the role of a pastor (bishop) to that of a cop. We are totally different, and I'd be prepared to go to jail rather than harm one of my priests . . . We must not forget that we are pastors, not agents of the FBI or CIA.'
18 May 2002	Fr Gianfranco Ghirlanda SJ, Dean of the Faculty of Canon Law at Rome's Gregorian University and a judge for the *Apostolic Signatura*	Writing in the quasi-official *La Civiltà Cattolica*, says it is not 'pastoral behaviour' for a bishop to report a priest to the police if the victim could do it. His reference to 'pastoral behaviour' is a reference to Canon 1341 of the *1983 Code of Canon Law* which requires a bishop to try to reform the priest before starting proceedings to dismiss him.

June 2002	Meeting of United States bishops in Dallas	Bishops wanted the right to report clergy sexual abuse crimes to the civil authorities, irrespective of whether or not the law required it, zero tolerance approach to sexual abuse, suspension of priests pending investigation, and the use of lay review boards. Proposal submitted to the Vatican.
June 2002	Fr Patrick Maguire	The Roman Rota (the Vatican Appeal Court) allows his appeal against dismissal on the grounds of the 'Catch 22' defence: he could not be dismissed for paedophilia because he was a paedophile. He lacked 'full' imputability, that is he could not restrain himself.
8 June 2002	Cardinal Schotte of Belgium	Says he has reservations about bishops cooperating with police over sexual abuse allegations against clergy, and that the Church should not have to hand over its documents as these are 'confidential to the Church'.
July 2002	Cardinal Lehmann, Chairman of the German Catholic Bishops Conference	Says it is not the bishops' role to report sex abusing priests to the police. Their only role is to try to convince the priest to hand himself in.
2002 and 2010	Monsignor Maurice Dooley, Senior Irish Canon Lawyer	Says a bishop swears allegiance to canon law, and if there is a conflict with civil law, he has to choose canon law, even if that means going to jail. He confirms that canon law prohibits the bishop from revealing to the police anything he has learned through his canonical investigations.

14 Oct 2002	Cardinal Re, Congregation for Bishops	Writes to United States bishops stating that it is difficult to reconcile their Dallas proposals with the *1983 Code of Canon Law* and the *2001 Motu Proprio*. The latter imposed 'pontifical secrecy', and the US bishops wanted to report accused priests to the police.
October 2002	Cardinal Ratzinger and United States Bishops	Meeting at the Vatican. Compromised reached on reporting—only allowable where there is a local civil law requiring it.
8 Dec 2002	*Recognitio* by the Vatican of amended Dallas proposals	New canon law for the United States, but restricted to that region.
2003	Cardinal Francis George	Writes an article: 'Law and Culture' for the *2003 Ave Maria Law Review* in which he says that laws are a reflection of a culture when they are made, but thereafter they reinforce, perpetuate, rationalize and deepen that culture. His remarks apply equally to canon law and its culture of clericalism.
2003	Professor Patrick Parkinson	Publishes *Child Sex Abuse and the Churches, Understanding the Issues*. The inconsistency between *Towards Healing* and canon law over the disciplining of priests is unacceptable. The priest could (and did) appeal to Rome and have the decision overturned.
19 Feb 2005	Pope Benedict XVI	Josef Ratzinger elected pope
2005	Irish Catholic Bishops Conference	Adopts a new set of guidelines called *Our Children, Our Church, 2005*, providing for all allegations of child abuse to be taken to the civil authorities, including historic abuse. It is inconsistent with canon law, and never receives the Vatican *recognitio* to make it canon law for Ireland.

2006	Fr Marcial Maciel	Pope Benedict suspends him from the priesthood and requires him to spend the rest of his days in 'prayer and doing penance'. Until his death in 2008 he lives in a house in a gated community in Florida that the Legion of Christ bought for him. He is not handed over to the police for child sexual abuse.
17 May 2006	A priest known as DS	Bishop Jarrett of Lismore receives a complaint of sexual abuse. Carries out preliminary inquiry and reports it to the CDF in accordance with the *2001 Motu Proprio*.
1 Oct 2006	BBC documentary: *Sex Crimes and the Vatican*	Accuses Benedict XVI, as Cardinal Ratzinger, of being in charge of enforcing secrecy about sex crimes of clergy on minors, as laid down in *Crimen Sollicitationis*
2 Oct 2006	Catholic Bishops Conference of England and Wales	Says it will make a formal protest to the BBC about the program. It said that according to Archbishop Nichols of Birmingham, *Crimen Sollicitationis* was 'not directly concerned with child abuse at all, but with the misuse of the confessional'. This statement was incorrect.
2007	John P Beal writes on *Crimen Sollicitationis*	'The 1962 Instruction: Crimen Sollicitationis: Caught Red Handed or Handed a Red Herring?' 41 Studia Canonica 199. Confirms that the 'secret of the Holy Office' (later known as the 'pontifical secret') prevents bishops and canonical investigators from revealing 'everything that they have learned as part of the penal process'.

2007	Bishop Geoffrey Robinson	Publishes *Confronting Power and Sex in the Catholic Church.* Says that 'creeping infallibility' in the Church prevents Popes from admitting mistakes.
2007	Cumberlege Report, United Kingdom	The Cumberlege Commission was established to report on the operation of the Nolan Report since its adoption by the British bishops in 2001. It criticised the lack of *recognitio* which would have made its provisions the canon law for England and Wales. It identifies the same problems outlined by Professor Parkinson about *Towards Healing,* where there is conflict between canon law and the protocols.
2008	A priest known as DS	The CDF advises Bishop Jarrett of Lismore that the penalty imposed on DS is to require him to say Mass for the victims every Friday and to live a life of 'prayer and penance'. He continues to live in a presbytery with other priests.
April 2008	BBC	Rejects complaint of the Catholic Bishops Conference of England and Wales, saying that 'The programme had accurately reported the effect of the 1962 and 2001 documents, in that the documents ensured that allegations of child sexual abuse by priests were bound by secrecy within the Catholic Church'.
Feb 2009	Irish Catholic Bishops Conference	*Safeguarding Children, Standards and Guidance Document for the Catholic Church in Ireland.* All allegations were to be referred to the Irish Police or the Health Board, irrespective of any legal requirement to do so. The document is inconsistent with canon law on reporting, and it does not receive the Vatican's *recognitio* to become canon law for Ireland.

Feb 2009	Irish Catholic Bishops Conference	*Safeguarding Children, Standards and Guidance Document for the Catholic Church in Ireland.* All allegations were to be referred to the Irish Police or the Health Board, irrespective of any legal requirement to do so. The document is inconsistent with canon law on reporting, and it does not receive the Vatican's *recognitio* to become canon law for Ireland.
20 May 2009	Ryan Commission Report	Report on widespread abuse of children in Irish institutions.
26 Nov 2009	The *Murphy Dublin Report* on the Archdiocese of Dublin	It criticized the Irish bishops, the Irish State, canon law and the Vatican for facilitating the cover up of child sexual abuse in the Archdiocese. It expresses concern about the letter of 31 January 1997 from Archbishop Storero that encouraged the non-implementation of the *Framework Document*, and criticizes the 'Catch 22' defence, and refers to two out of three cases where appeals went to Rome were allowed on this ground. It also criticised canon law for its lack of coherency and confusion on child sexual abuse. Some of that confusion arose from misleading statements made by Cardinal Ratzinger and Archbishop Bertone about the repeal of *Crimen Sollicitationis.*
7 Dec 2009	Fr Sean McDonagh, prominent Irish priest.	Writes to the *Irish Times*, commenting on calls for some Irish bishops to resign. Says that the *2001 Motu Proprio* had encouraged bishops to commit criminal offences by not reporting clergy crimes to the police, and, perhaps in a moment of prescience, wondered if Pope Benedict should also resign.

10 Dec 2009	Martin Long, on behalf of the Irish bishops.	In response to McDonagh, Long writes to the *Irish Times*, saying that the secrecy provisions of canon law only applied to the Church's 'internal disciplinary procedures', and were not intended to frustrate or undermine any civil investigation or prosecution. Nearly all information the Church had about child sexual abuse by clergy came from the Church's 'internal disciplinary procedures', and there would not be a police investigation to be frustrated if they did not know of the allegations.
11 Dec 2009	Vatican Press Release	Announces that Pope Benedict had given the *Murphy Dublin Report* 'careful study', and was 'deeply disturbed and distressed by its contents', and that he would respond with a *Pastoral Letter* to the people of Ireland.
19 Mar 2010	Benedict XVI: *Pastoral Letter to the People of Ireland*	Makes no mention of his own role, or the role of any other member of the Roman Curia or the role of canon law in the cover up. Blames the Irish bishops for failing to follow the 'long established norms of canon law'. He blames them for a 'misplaced concern for the reputation of the Church and the avoidance of scandal, resulting in failure to apply existing canonical penalties', when that was Vatican policy for some ninety years, since 1922. Benedict writes the script for the second cover up: blame the bishops and ignore any involvement of the Vatican and the popes in the cover up.

20 Mar 2010	Monsignor Scicluna, the Vatican prosecutor for the Congregation for the Doctrine of the Faith	In an interview with *The Tablet* he says: 'The norms on sexual abuse were never understood as a ban on denouncing [the crimes] to the civil authorities.' That statement was incorrect, as the canonical documents themselves and the historical record show. He also said that since 2001 the CDF had handled 3,000 cases. He makes no mention of any case where the CDF had instructed the bishop to report a case of child sexual abuse to the civil authorities.
25 Mar 2010	Fr Federico LombardiSJ, the Vatican spokesman	Issues a statement on the notorious Fr Lawrence Murphy who sexually assaulted some 200 deaf mute boys in the United States. ' . . . Indeed, contrary to some statements that have circulated in the press, neither Crimen nor the Code of Canon Law ever prohibited the reporting of child abuse to law enforcement authorities.' That statement was partly true in that the *Code of Canon Law* did not impose pontifical secrecy. It was imposed by *Secreta Continere* which is not part of the Code. His statement is contradicted by some of his later statements admitting that information obtained through a canonical investigation was subject to the strictest confidentiality.

12 April 2010	The Congregation for the Doctrine of the Faith	Issues a document called *A Guide to Understanding Basic CDF Procedures concerning Sexual Abuse Allegations*, which it said was 'an introductory guide which may be helpful to lay persons and non-canonists'. It explained the various procedures, and then said that: 'Civil law concerning reporting of crimes to the appropriate authorities should always be followed.' Such an instruction amounted to a dispensation from pontifical secrecy under canon 85, for those countries that have such laws. All Australian States, other than NSW do not have such laws for the vast majority of such complaints. Fr Lombardi's statement of 15 July 2010 casts some doubt as to whether the dispensation applies once a canonical investigation and trial starts.
21 May 2010	Pope Benedict XVI	Issues decree revising the *2001 Motu Proprio*. The historical introduction is rewritten, and corrects the 2001 historical introduction by conceding that the *1983 Code of Canon Law* did, in effect, repeal *Crimen Sollicitationis*. It reimposes pontifical secrecy under *Secreta Continere,* and expands it to cover the sexual abuse of persons who 'habitually lack the use of reason' and to priests who have child pornography in their possession.

25 June, 2010	Canon lawyer, Fr John P Beal, one of the authors of the *New Commentary on the Code of Canon Law*	Reported in the National Catholic Reporter to have said: 'Pontifical secrecy does not prevent Catholic officials from reporting sexual abuse to civil authorities. It applies only to internal church proceedings.' The vast bulk of all information the Church has about clergy sexual abuse comes from 'internal Church proceedings'.
15 July 2010	Fr Federico Lombardi, Vatican spokesman.	Explains the 2010 revision of the *2001 Motu Proprio* and he referred to cooperating with the civil authorities as provided for in the Guide for 'lay persons and non-canonists'. He said that such cooperation had to be done: '. . . in good time, not during or subsequent to the canonical trial'. This statement contradicts what he said on 25 March 2010 that canon law did not preclude reporting to the police. It also creates uncertainty as to the extent of the dispensation to report to the police where the civil law requires it. It could suggest that reporting is prohibited once a canonical investigation and trial starts even if there is a civil law requiring reporting.
19 July 2010	Fr Federico Lombardi, Vatican spokesman.	Through the Vatican Radio service, he says: 'The revised norms maintain the imposition of "pontifical secret" on the church's judicial handling of priestly sexual abuse and other grave crimes, which means they are dealt with in strict confidentiality.'

21 July 2010	Nicholas Cafardi, canon and civil lawyer and Professor of Law at Duquesne University	Writes in *Commonweal Magazine*: 'But that's all the secrecy requirement covers: the internal church legal process, not the crime itself. It does not prevent victims, their families, or even church officials from reporting a civil crime to the civil authorities or to the media.' The vast bulk of the information that the Church had about child sexual abuse by clergy came through its own 'internal legal processes'.
3 May 2011	The Vatican	Cardinal Levada of the CDF asks all Bishops Conferences to present it with guidelines for dealing with sexual abuse by clergy. Once approved under Canon 455, those guidelines then become canon law for the area covered by the Bishops Conference. Like the dispensation given in 2010, those guidelines only provide for an exception to pontifical secrecy where the local law requires reporting.
2 June 2011	Cardinal Castrillón, former Prefect of the Congregation for the Clergy	Interviewed by Patricia Janiot for Colombian CNN. He denies that there is such a thing as paedophilia, and says that priests who abuse children make 'mistakes', and are punished by canon law by being suspended. If they show "correction", canon law requires them to be reinstated and they are sent to another parish. He says that every priest who has been proven to have sexually abused children has been punished under canon law. When asked why Fr Marcial Maciel had not been punished, he refused to answer.

13 July 2011	The Murphy Commission the *Cloyne Report*	Found that Bishop Magee of Cloyne failed to report nine out of fifteen complaints that should have been reported to the police, that he had two different files on abusive priests, one for the Vatican and a sanitized version in answer to a subpoena or search warrant, and that the Storero letter of 31 January 1997 had cautioned against the implementation of the *Framework Document*, which required reporting of all child abuse allegations to the police.
14 July 2011	Irish Foreign Minister, Ian Gilmore	Calls in the Papal Nuncio to Ireland and gives him a note saying: 'it is unacceptable to the Irish Government that the Vatican intervened to effectively have priests believe they could in conscience evade their responsibilities under Irish law.'
20 July 2011	Fr Federico Lombardi	Says that the Storero letter 'did not object to any civil law (regarding the obligation to provide information to civil authority) . . . because it did not exist in Ireland at that time'. That statement was incorrect. Misprision of felony was repealed on 22 July 1997, six months after the Storero letter.

| 20 July 2011 | Irish Prime Minister, Enda Kenny | Speech in Parliament alleging that there was 'an attempt by the Holy See, to frustrate an Inquiry in a sovereign, democratic republic . . . the standards of conduct which the Church deems appropriate to itself, cannot and will not, be applied to the workings of democracy and civil society in this republic. Not purely, or simply or otherwise. Children . . . first'. The Irish Parliament passed a motion that it '. . .deplores the Vatican's intervention which contributed to the undermining of the child protection framework and guidelines of the Irish State and the Irish Bishops.' |
| 25 July 2011 | The Vatican | Recalls its Papal Nuncio for 'consultations'. |

3 Sept 2011	Vatican Response to *Cloyne Report*	The Response makes no mention of the 'secret of the Holy Office' or the 'pontifical secrect', and says that the *Framework Document* could not be given a *recognitio* under canon law because it was not a resolution of the Bishops Conference under canon 455. That statement was correct, but its assertion that the Storero letter did not have the effect of instructing the bishops to break Irish law was misleading. It said, 'In 1996, apart from cases relating to misprision of felony, the reporting of incidents of child sexual abuse to either the relevant health board or the Irish police was not mandatory. Furthermore, misprision of felony was removed from the Irish Statute Book by the Criminal Justice Act of 1997.' The letter failed to state that misprision of felony was repealed on 22 July 1997, six months after the Storero letter.
5 Sept 2011	Archbishop Martin of Dublin	Blames the Irish bishops for the cover up. Makes no mention of the role of canon law or the Vatican's responsibility and the finding of the *Murphy Dublin Report* that the rules and structures of the Catholic Church facilitated the cover up.

2012/2013	*Victorian Parliamentary Inquiry*, the Whitlam Inquiry into the 'Father F' case, and the Maitland-Newcastle Special Commission (*Maitland-Newcastle Inquiry*), and the *Australian Royal Commission*	The chances of dismissing a priest through a canonical trial were variously described in these inquiries as 'very difficult' (Cardinal Pell), 'close to hopeless' (Bishop Malone) 'very, very difficult' (Archbishop Hart) 'extraordinarily difficult' (Archbishop Coleridge), and the whole procedure was 'unworkable' (Fr Brian Lucas).
8 Feb 2012	Congregation for the Doctrine of the Faith	Announces that it has handled 4,000 child sexual abuse cases. No indication of the number of cases where an instruction was given by the CDF to report the matter to the police.
May 2012	The Italian Catholic Bishops Conference	Announces that under Italian law it has no obligation to report clergy sexual abuse to the civil authorities. It will cooperate with the civil authorities once criminal proceedings have commenced against a priest (under Italian law, this includes the investigation), but will otherwise not be volunteering any information. This is consistent with the bishops' obligations under the 2010 dispensation to pontifical secrecy, where reporting is only permissible where there is a local civil law requiring it.

12 June 2012	Monsignor Lynn (USA)	Convicted of child endangerment by not reporting sex abusing priests to the civil authorities. Sentenced to three to six year's imprisonment. Appeal subsequently allowed in December 2013 because the particular law only applied to persons who directly supervised children.
21 Sept 2012	The Victorian Church submission to the *Victorian Parliamentary Inquiry* entitled, *Facing the Truth*	Submission to the *Victorian Parliamentary Inquiry* by the Church in Victoria. It follows the script of Pope Benedict XVI in his *Pastoral Letter* to the people of Ireland. Its chronology of significant events starts in 1961 and contains a list of 150 reports, inquiries, legislation both civil and canonical, books and research. There is no mention of *Crimen Sollicitationis* of 1962, nor is there any mention of pontifical secrecy imposed by *Secreta Continere* and confirmed in the *2001 Motu Proprio* and its revision in 2010. It cherry picks passages from the *Murphy Dublin Report*, but ignores the criticism of canon law and the Vatican and the finding that the 'structure and rules of the Catholic Church facilitated the cover up'. It claims that the Church, like the rest of society has been on a 'learning curve' about sexual abuse and blames the bishops for the cover up.
Nov 2012	Bishop Geoffrey Robinson	Publishes *For Christ's Sake End Sexual Abuse in the Catholic Church for Good*, and writes, ' . . .the entire response of the Church to the scandal of sexual abuse has taken place in an atmosphere that the Pope cannot have been wrong in any matter that involved papal energy and prestige.'

12 Nov 2012	Australian Prime Minister, Julia Gillard	Announces the setting up of a *Royal Commission into Institutional Responses to Sex Abuse (Australian Royal Commision)*
12 Dec 2012	The Australian Catholic Bishops Conference	Announces the setting up of the *Truth, Justice and Healing Council* to represent the Church at the Royal Commission.
13 Mar 2013	Pope Francis	Jorge Bergoglio elected pope
3 April 2013	Francis Sullivan, CEO, *Truth Justice and Healing Council*	Interviewed on *7.30 Report*, and asked what steps the Church should take if one of its teachers reported to Church authorities that he suspected that a priest was sexually abusing children at their school. He said it was up to the teacher to report it, and not the Church authorities. This is consistent with the Vatican position that bishops should not be doing any reporting.
22 April 2013	Francis Sullivan	Addresses the St Thomas More Forum in Canberra. Admits cover ups, says Church on a 'learning curve', and that things are much better now than twenty years ago. He makes no mention of pontifical secrecy or of the current conflict between canon law and *Towards Healing* where there is no civil law obligation to report to the police, and no mention that the Vatican has not approved *Towards Healing* under Canon 455 to make it part of canon law for Australia

29 April 2013	*Victorian Parliamentary Inquiry*	Bishops Connors and Bird, criticise their predecessor, Bishop Ronald Mulkearns of Ballarat for being 'very naïve', for having 'effectively facilitated child sexual abuse' and for making 'terrible mistakes'. Mulkearns has a doctorate in canon law, was one of the founders of the Canon Law Society of Australia and New Zealand, and was the first chairman of the Special Issues Committee set up by the Australian Catholic Bishops Conference to find a better way of dealing with sex abusing priests. Everything he did was in accordance with canon law, as interpreted by the Vatican.
27 May 2013	*Victorian Parliamentary Inquiry*	Cardinal George Pell says the cover up was the bishops' responsibility and not 'Rome's'.
30 Sept 2013	Truth Justice and Healing Commission submission on *Towards Healing* to the Australian Royal Commission, Issues Paper Number 2	Section 10 entitled 'Dealing with the Accused' discusses canon law at length, but nowhere is there any mention of *Crimen Sollicitationis*. The *2001 Motu Proprio* is mentioned, but there is no mention of the 'pontifical secrect' applying to the cases of sexual abuse of children by clergy. It says: 'There is nothing in the 1983 Code that is in conflict with any applicable civil law obligations relating to the reporting of allegations of child sexual abuse.' That statement is correct, but the *1983 Code* is not the only source of canon law. The 'pontifical secret' is imposed by *Secreta Continere* which is not part of the Code. Until the dispensation given in 2010, reporting to the police of information obtained by the Church's internal procedures was prohibited by canon law. Under Canon 22, bishops were required to breach civil law.

3 Oct 2013	Francis Sullivan	Says that *Australian Church Submission* to the *Australian Royal Commission* was a 'warts and all' approach, but the main wart, the 'pontifical secret', is not mentioned either in his speech or in the *Australian Church Submission*.
12 Nov 2013	*Victoria Parliamentary Report, Betrayal of Trust*	Found that no representatives of the Church directly reported the criminal conduct of its members to the police, and that there was no justification for this. The probable explanation was the secrecy imposed by canon law. It rejected the claim that the Church was on a 'learning curve' about sexual abuse and notes that if there was a lack of awareness of it within society, the Church contributed to that by actively concealing it within its own ranks. It found: 'Various structures, laws and teachings of the Catholic Church contributed to the concealment of the issue from wider society and civil authorities. The manner in which the Catholic Church responded (or failed to respond) to complaints gave perpetrators the opportunity to commit further abuse.' In relation to the criticisms of Bishops Mulkearns and Archbishop Little by their successors, the Committee stated: ' . . . it is unfair to allow the full blame to rest with these individuals, given that they were acting in accordance with a Catholic Church policy.' It recommended: reinstatement of misprision of felony so far as sexual abuse is concerned and other law reform measures.

19 Dec 2013	*Australian Royal Commission*	Bishop Jarrett of Lismore agrees with Commissioner McLellan that the limitation period of ten years from the eighteenth birthday of the victim was too short because the 'overwhelming majority' of complaints would not be reported to the Vatican because 'many people don't report their abuse until well after a ten-year period'.
31 Jan 2014	United Nations Committee on the Rights of the Child hands down its Concluding Observations on the Second Periodic Report of the Holy See.	The Report notes that: Some of the rules of canon law are not in conformity with the Convention on the Rights of the Child. The Holy See had adopted policies and practices that led to the continuation of the abuse and impunity of perpetrators. The Holy See covered up known sex abusers, and shifted them elsewhere. The Holy See had declined to provide the Committee with information on the outcome of its canonical disciplinary procedures. The Holy See had allowed a vast majority of abusers to escape criminal prosecution by its confidential disciplinary proceedings. The code of silence imposed on clergy under penalty of excommunication meant that few cases of child sexual abuse were reported. The reporting to national law enforcement agencies has never been made compulsory, and while expressly rejected and the in the Storero letter of 1997. In many cases the Holy See has refused to cooperate with judicial authorities.

4

Potiphar's Wife

In the Book of Genesis, Joseph (of the technicolour dream coat) was taken to Egypt, and sold as a slave to Potiphar, the Captain of the Guard at the Pharaoh's palace. Potiphar's wife tried to seduce him, but Joseph declined the invitation. She then accused him of attempting to rape her. Potiphar had him thrown into prison.[1] And so we have the enduring myth that 'Hell hath no fury like a woman scorned'.[2]

Several thousand years later, in 2002, when the clerical abuse scandal was erupting in the United States, Catholic priests who sexually assaulted children were being prosecuted, and claims for damages were being made by the victims, Cardinal Obando y Bravo, the Archbishop of Managua in Nicaragua, likened some of the victims to Potiphar's wife:

> The reasons that drive Potiphar's wife to lie are pleasure, spite and unrequited love. I don't want to deny the drama of the authentic victims of sexual abuse . . . . . But one can't hide the fact that in some cases we are dealing with presumed victims who want to gain large pay offs on the basis of calumnious accusations . . . It seems to me that in this moment, the Church in the United States is living through a heroic moment, of bloodless martyrdom. Of persecution.[3]

1. Genesis chapter 39.
2. William Congreve (*The Mourning Bride*), Act III (1697).
3. Interview on 1 September 2002 with the Italian monthly, *30 Giorni*, quoted in John R Allen *All the Pope's Men: The Inside Story of How the Vatican Really Thinks* (New York: Doubleday, 2004).

It is not the only time that sexually abused children have been accused of lying, and of trying to seduce or even rape clergy. On 28 May 2003, Peter Hollingsworth, the former Anglican Archbishop of Brisbane who had been accused of covering up the sexual abuse crimes of his clergy, was forced to resign his position as Governor General of Australia after comments on national television about the case of an Anglican priest's relationship with an underage teenage girl:

> My belief is that this was not sex abuse. There was no suggestion of rape or anything like that. Quite the contrary. My information is that it was rather the other way around. [4]

In August, 2012, a prominent Catholic Franciscan priest from New York, with his own television show, Fr Benedict Groeschel, said in an interview that priests accused of child sexual abuse are often seduced by their accusers.[5]

On 6 October, 2013, the head of the Polish episcopate, Archbishop Jozef Michalik said divorced parents were partly to blame for clergy paedophilia because 'this inappropriate attitude manifests itself when a child is seeking love'.[6]

Nor is it the only time that Catholic clergy have claimed that when society was moving in a direction with which they disagreed, there was a return to the early Roman persecutions, of Christians being thrown into the lions' dens. Cardinal Francis George, the Archbishop of Chicago, complained about 'secularisation', and Western countries, 'making "laws" beyond their competence'. One of the things that he associated with this 'secularisation', which he described as 'communism's better scrubbed bed fellow', was the increasing public acceptance of same sex marriage.[7] The end result of the secularist slippery slope will be:

---

4. http://www.abc.net.au/austory/transcripts/s479623.htm (Accessed 15 June 2013). http://www.abc.net.au/7.30/content/2003/s864968.htm (Accessed 7 May 2013).
5. Interview with the *National Catholic Register*: http://www.huffingtonpost.com/2012/08/30/benedict-groeschel-sex-abuse-apology_n_1844947.html (Accessed 10 July 2013).
6. http://www.huffingtonpost.com/2013/10/08/polish-archbishop-jozef-michalik-sex-abuse-comments-_n_4065751.html (Accessed 11 October 2013).
7. http://www.catholicnewworld.com/cnwonline/2013/0609/cardinal.aspx (Accessed 9 July 2013).

I expect to die in bed, my successor will die in prison and his successor will die a martyr in the public square. His successor will pick up the shards of a ruined society and slowly help rebuild civilization, as the church has done so often in human history.[8]

These assertions by Cardinal Obando y Bravo and Cardinal Francis George reflect the culture of clericalism within the Church that has had disastrous consequences on the lives of children.

Clericalism in the Church arises out of a theology that says that priests are 'ontologically changed', that is, marked out by God through ordination as special people whose very nature has been changed, and who are divinely destined to change the world.[9] This has led them to believe that they deserve to be treated differently. As the famous nineteenth century Catholic historian, Lord Acton said: 'there is no worse heresy than that the office sanctifies the holder of it.'[10]

This culture of clericalism found its way into the law that governs the members of the Church, otherwise known as 'canon law', a set of rules that govern how the Church is set up, organised and managed.

---

8. http://www.catholicnewsagency.com/news/cardinal-george-warns-us-secularization-is-more-serious-than-elections/ (Accessed 2 May 2013). Even more bizarre, although on a different issue, is the Ugandan Cardinal Wamala's claim that women who refuse to allow their husbands to wear condoms to avoid HIV infection will be the new Christian martyrs. http://www.abc.net.au/foreign/content/2004/s1159065.htm (Accessed 7 May 2013).

9. http://www.vatican.va/holy_father/benedict_xvi/audiences/2009/documents/hf_ben-xvi_aud_20090624_en.html (Accessed 7 May 2013), and for a Vatican pronouncement on it: ' . . . ordination also inserts them into a Sacramental Order, which is universal and confers a new ontological participation to the "munera" of Christ, which makes them capable of implementing these duties in his name and in the name of the Church, in any place, after having first received a concrete mandate from a Bishop.' .http://www.vatican.va/roman_curia/congregations/cclergy/documents/rc_con_cclergy_doc_23111998_pvatican_en.html (Accessed 7 May 2013). See also Richard Sipe in *Mea Maxima Culpa* at 1:23.04. Christopher Geraghty: *Dancing with the Devil* (Melbourne: Spectrum Publications, 2012), 92

10. Lord Acton (1834–1902) is best known for the words that follow in his letter to Bishop Mandel Creighton, 'Power tends to corrupt and absolute power corrupts absolutely'. Letter to Bishop Mandell Creighton, April 5, 1887 published in *Historical Essays and Studies*, edited by JN Figgis and RV Laurence (London: Macmillan, 1907).

The name comes from the Greek word *kanon*, meaning a rule or a straight line.[11]

Canon law is like the laws and rules of any private organisation within a state, whether they are sporting or social clubs. It is different to most other private organisations because its rules are determined, not by the members themselves (perhaps with some obligatory rules imposed on them by the state), but by the Bishop of Rome, also known as the pope, the head of the Church, a foreign Head of State who is effectively an absolute monarch when it comes to canon law. His decrees apply to the Church in every part of the world. Canon law, like the rules of any other private organisation, has no status within the state. It cannot exempt any resident within the state from complying with the civil law.[12] But it can require them to break it.

The word 'scandal' in the Church has a technical meaning beyond the usual. It means the loss of faith amongst the faithful when those who are supposed to act in the place of Christ, namely priests, bishops and religious, do the opposite.[13] To avoid the loss of Church membership through 'scandal', arising from the public trials of priests who had sexually abused children, the Church decided on a course of action in 1922 that effectively revived the ancient practice known as 'privilege of clergy', whereby clergy were not tried for such crimes in the state courts, but only in its own Church or canonical courts in accordance with canon law. Such trials would themselves be held in secret, and anyone involved in them would be sworn to secrecy.

The Church in 1922 did not have the political power which it had in the Middle Ages, so it could not do this openly and directly.

---

11. Pennington: *A Short History of Canon Law from Apolstolic Times to 1917*: http://faculty.cua.edu/pennington/Canon%20Law/ShortHistoryCanonLaw.htm (Accessed 6 January 2014). Thomas Doyle *Affidavit Jane Doe v Omi of Texas* http://www.bishop-accountability.org/news2008/03_04/2008_03_03_Doyle_TomDoyle.htm paragraph 55 (Accessed 19 June 2013).

12. Ferns Report Chapter 3. http://www.bishop-accountability.org/reports/2005_10_Ferns/ferns_3_1_structures_church.pdf (Accessed 3 October 2013), Sir Matthew Hale, *History and Analysis of the Common Law of England 1713* (Chicago: University of Chicago Press, 1971), 28–29. See also *Reichel v Bishop of Oxford* (1889) 14 Appeal Cases 259.

13. Archbishop Hart of Melbourne at the *Victorian Parliamentary Inquiry* http://www.parliament.vic.gov.au/images/stories/committees/fcdc/inquiries/57th/Child_Abuse_Inquiry/Transcripts/Catholic_Archdiocese_of_Melbourne_20-May-13.pdf , 19 (Accessed 18 June 2013).

Modern civil society had fought very hard for the separation of Church and state, and for the principle that no one is above the law. But the Church could achieve the same result by the back door use of secrecy. If the State did not know about the sexual assaults by clergy on children there would be no State prosecutions. The Church could then treat the matter as a 'canonical crime', to be dealt with exclusively and secretly in its own courts.

In 1922, Pope Pius XI issued his decree *Crimen Sollicitationis,* which required all investigations by the Church of clergy sexual assaults on children to be carried out in strict confidentiality 'in all things and with all persons', with no exceptions for reporting such matters to the police.[14] The penalty for breaching the confidentiality was automatic excommunication, the Church's worst form of punishment, involving expulsion from the Church community, refusal of the sacraments and participation in the liturgy, refusal of burial in sacred ground and, if you take the Church's doctrine seriously, the eternal fires of Hell.

This was no ordinary excommunication which could be lifted by lesser mortals in the Church hierarchy. It could not even be lifted by the Sacred Penitentiary, the Vatican Tribunal that had jurisdiction to lift excommunications for more serious crimes, such as assaulting the pope or breaking the 'seal of confession'. The automatic excommunication for reporting to the police the evidence that the Church had uncovered about the sex crimes of its priests against children could only be lifted by the pope personally.[15] The penalties that could be imposed by canon law on priests who had sexually assaulted children did not even include excommunication. Sexual abuse of children could be forgiven with a slap on the wrist (and so often it was), but ratting on a fellow priest to the police was beyond the pale.

The secrecy did not simply apply to what the bishops discovered from their investigations. It also applied to the very process itself. *Crimen Sollicitationis* was not to be published anywhere, or commented on by canon lawyers. The few copies that were printed for bishops were to be kept in a locked safe where they and their chancellors alone had the key. The success of this venture depended on the outside world not knowing about it.

---

14. http://www.vatican.va/resources/resources_crimen-sollicitationis-1962_ en.html (Accessed 4 August 2013)
15. *Ibid,* clause 11.

Crimen Sollicitationis continued to be the Church's canon law until 1962 when it was reissued by Pope John XXIII, for limited distribution for bishops. It was during the next thirty years that there was an explosion of sex assaults on children by clergy.[16] *Crimen Sollicitationis* set the bar so high for dismissing a sexually abusive priest that it invariably could never happen without his consent. He could only be dismissed if there seemed to be 'no hope, humanly speaking, or almost no hope, of his amendment'. All he had to do was say he was sorry, and he would remain as a priest, in the same position of power and respect that made it easier for him to attack more children.[17]

Whatever the achievements of Pope John Paul II, his pontificate was marked by the continuation of the cover up, enshrined in canon law, that prevented bishops and their delegates investigating clergy sexual abuse from taking the matter to the police. But just as significant were his changes to canon law that rendered the Church's internal procedures for dealing with the problem virtually useless. These changes took place within the first five years of his pontificate.

The first change was in 1980 when he removed the capacity of bishops to ask the Vatican to dismiss an offending priest by the use of the simpler procedure known as 'administrative laicisation'.

---

16. According to the 2004 John Jay Report, commissioned by the American Conference of Catholic Bishops, the number of alleged abuses increased in the 1960s, peaked in the 1970s, declined in the 1980s, and by the 1990s had returned to the levels of the 1950s http://www.usccb.org/issues-and-action/child-and-youth-protection/upload/The-Nature-and-Scope-of-Sexual-Abuse-of-Minors-by-Catholic-Priests-and-Deacons-in-the-United-States-1950-2002.pdf (Accessed 29 April 2013). Similar figures for Australia are produced by the Victorian Church's submission to the *Victorian Parliamentary Inquiry*, *Facing the Truth*, except that the decline in the 1990s was more significant. *Facing the Truth*, page 4, http://www.parliament.vic.gov.au/images/stories/committees/fcdc/inquiries/57th/Child_Abuse_Inquiry/Submissions/Catholic_Church_in_Victoria.pdf (Accessed 6 April 2013).

17. Fr John Usher at the *Maitland-Newcastle Inquiry* said, '. . . our church is strong on forgiveness and reconciliation, and if someone said, "I'm terribly sorry, I won't do it again", there was a tendency to believe such people, to give them help and support and therapy and believe that they wouldn't do it again.' http://www.lawlink.nsw.gov.au/lawlink/Special_Projects/ll_splprojects.nsf/vwFiles/Day_22_-_9_September_2013.pdf/$file/Day_22_-_9_September_2013.pdf p.2350 (Accessed 11 September 2013).

The second was the promulgation of the *1983 Code of Canon Law* which repealed *Crimen Sollicitationis,* and had its own provisions for dealing with clergy sexual abuse of children.[18] The requirements of secrecy continued under the *Code* because another decree, *Secreta Continere* (1974) required 'pontifical secrecy' to apply to any allegation, investigation and trial of clergy accused of sexually abusing children.[19]

The most significant change was the ridiculously short limitation period (*prescription*) of five years from the time of the offense, imposed by the *1983 Code of Canon Law.*[20] Virtually all complaints of clergy sexual abuse were made by adults who had been abused as children, and so were outside the five year period.[21] The effect of the limitation period was to 'extinguish' the crime under canon law, so that no further action could be taken to dismiss the priest.

Limitation periods are imposed in civil society for claims for damages so as not to disadvantage a defendant because of the lapse of time. They also encourage a plaintiff to bring the claim quickly. But most civil societies accept that they have no place for serious crimes and for professional disciplinary matters. Prior to 1983, even the Church accepted that philosophy because *Crimen Sollicitationis* had no limitation period.[22] The imposition of such a limitation period in 1983 marks the apotheosis of clericalism in the Church where the paramount concern was not the abused child, but the priest.

---

18. Canon 1395, and see Chapter 9 below on the repeal of *Crimen Sollicitationis.*
19. *Secreta Continere* of 1974 imposed pontifical secrecy on a number of matters, including reports from papal legates. Papal legates are dealt with in Canons 362 to 377, and the Code does not deal with communications from legates or secrecy to be applied to them. Likewise communications on the appointment of bishops, Cardinals and members of the Curia are covered by the pontifical secrecy and there is no equivalent provision in the Code. The application of *Secreta Continere* in Article 25 and Article 30 of the norms of the *2001 Motu Proprio* and its 2010 revision confirm that it survived the *1983 Code of Canon Law.*
20. Canon 1362.
21. If the figures for the State of Victoria, mentioned in the *Victorian Parliamentary Inquiry* can be applied across the board to Australia, less than 1% of all complaints would have come within the five year limitation period.
22. Canon 1362§1 specifically excludes any limitation periods for matters 'reserved to the Congregation for the Doctrine of the Faith', and sexual abuse of children under *Crimen Sollicitationis* was so reserved.

Under the old *1917 Code of Canon Law*, a bishop could suspend a priest pending the outcome of an investigation into allegations against him. The new *Code* took away that right, and only allowed a suspension after the preliminary investigation was complete, and a formal canonical trial had commenced. But if there was no right to have a formal canonical trial, because of the five year limitation period, there was no right to suspend either.

Further, the bishop was required to attempt 'fraternal correction' or other 'pastoral methods' (such as sending him off for treatment) before commencing any penal processes under the *1983 Code of Canon Law*.[23] Even assuming that the five year limitation period had not expired at the time the complaint was made, it more than likely had expired by the time the bishop was satisfied that none of these remedies had worked.

The *1983 Code of Canon Law* continued with the tradition set by *Crimen Sollicitationis* of setting the bar impossibly high for dismissing a priest, and in fact, made the situation even more difficult for reasons I will explain.

The effect of these provisions was that canon law was virtually useless for dismissing clergy sexual abusers from the priesthood. That, coupled with the prohibition on reporting such allegations to the police explains why these priests were not thrown out of the priesthood, and were not prosecuted by the state. Canon law did have provisions allowing bishops to restrict a priest's ministry, but that was the only thing they could do.

By his *Motu Proprio, Sacramentorum Sanctitatis Tutela,* of 30 April, 2001, *(2001 Motu Proprio)* Pope John Paul II modified the *Code's* procedures. After carrying out his preliminary investigation under Canon 1717, the bishop was to send the information to the Congregation for the Doctrine of the Faith which would then instruct him how to proceed. Pontifical secrecy was again imposed, with no exceptions for reporting such crimes to the civil authorities. The simpler method of the Vatican dismissing a priest by 'administrative' action was restored by an authorisation to Congregation of the Doctrine of the Faith in 2003. There was no change to Canon 1341 that required the use of 'pastoral' methods to try to reform the priest prior to initiating any proceedings for dismissal.

---

23. Canon 1341.

The limitation period was extended to ten years from the victim's eighteenth birthday. Ten years from the victim's eighteenth birthday was still almost useless in the case of child sexual abuse where the victims often have difficulty coming to terms with it until much later in life.[24] In addition, the extension of the limitation period did not operate retrospectively so that if the abuse occurred prior to 30 April 2001 and five years had expired, the canonical crime was still 'extinguished'.[25]

By 2001, many victims had given up complaining to the Church, particularly in the United States, and had taken their grievances to the civil authorities, demanding prosecutions, and suing for damages. Local Churches were forced to produce their documents to civil courts. Given the widespread media coverage, the Vatican had given up on the idea that it could keep *Crimen Sollicitationis* under lock and key in the secret diocesan archives. It acknowledged its existence in the historical introduction to the *2001 Motu Proprio,* and published it on the Vatican website in 2003.[26]

---

24. Evidence of Bishop Jarrett, *Australian Royal Commission,* http://www.childabuseroyalcommission.gov.au/wp-content/uploads/2013/12/Transcript-RC_IRCSA_Day-032_19-Dec-2013_TBC_Public.pdf, 3396.14ff (Accessed 20 December 2013). Jarrett agreed with Commissioner McLellan that the period of ten years was too short because the 'overwhelming majority' of complaints would not be reported to the Vatican because 'many people don't report their abuse until well after a 10-year period.'

25. Elizabeth M Delaney sgs, *Canonical Implications of the Response of the Catholic Church in Australia to Child Sexual in Australia,* a doctoral dissertation of 2004 submitted to the Faculty of Canon Law, Saint Paul University, Ottawa, Canada, 189. If prescription is regarded as a 'substantive' matter, rather than a 'procedural' one, then it does not operate retrospectively. Delaney says: 'Writing in 1994, J Alesandro asserted that prescription is a matter of procedural law. In the 2001 CDF norms, the article on prescription is the last article in Part One, Substantive Norms, suggesting that the CDF viewed prescription as substantive rather than procedural law.' See JA Alesandro: *Dismissal from the Clerical State in Cases of Sexual Misconduct: Recent Derogations,* 37. Since the CDF is the 'legislature', and has the role of interpreting canon law, the extension of the limitation period could not operate retrospectively. See also Delaney *Canonical Implications of the Response of the Catholic Church in Australia:* ' . . . outside the United States of America, the change in the law concerning the period of prescription is applicable only to offences perpetrated after 30 April 2001. Hence, normally, for offences that occurred before this date, the period of prescription is five years', 229.

26. Delaney, *Canonical Implications of the Response of the Catholic Church in*

In 2010, Pope Benedict XVI modified the *2001 Motu Proprio* by including the sexual abuse of intellectually impaired adults, and priests who possessed child pornography in the list of canonical crimes that could be dealt with by the Church courts. He extended the limitation period to twenty years from the victim's eighteenth birthday. He continued to impose pontifical secrecy, but this time with a possible exception. If a particular country had civil laws that required the reporting of sex crimes against children and intellectually impaired adults, and the possession of child pornography, the bishops in that country were required to include in their child abuse protocols a provision requiring them to obey such laws. If the Vatican gave its approval to the protocols, that would become canon law for that particular country. On the other hand, if there were no such reporting laws in a country, pontifical secrecy still applied, and bishops and other clergy involved in the investigation of such crimes were forbidden to take the matter to the police, even if they wanted to.

On 19 July 2010, in explaining the new revised norms of the *2010 Motu Proprio*, the Vatican spokesman, Fr Federico Lombardi announced that the Congregation for the Doctrine of the Faith would be issuing instructions to bishops to comply with civil law.[27]

This instruction was effectively a dispensation from pontifical secrecy where there were such local civil laws.[28] But its terms were restricted to where there was a local civil law requiring reporting. Dispensations under canon law are subject to a strict interpretation.[29]

Australia,152, footnote 21.

27. http://www.catholicnews.com/data/stories/cns/1002901.htm   (accessed   21 February 2014).

28. Canons 85 and 87, and John P Beal, A Coriden and Thomas J Green, *New Commentary on the Code of Canon Law* (Mahwah, NJ: Paulist Press, 2000) 130–132. Canon 85 provides 'A dispensation, or the relaxation of a merely ecclesiastical law in a particular case, can be granted by those who possess executive power within the limits of their competence, as well as by those who have the power to dispense explicitly or implicitly either by the law itself or by legitimate delegation.' Canon 87 provides that a bishop: 'is not able to dispense, however, from procedural or penal laws nor from those whose dispensation is specially reserved to the Apostolic See or some other authority.' It follows that only the Vatican can give a dispensation from pontifical secrecy. See also the evidence of Dr Rodger Austin at the *Maitland Newcastle Inquiry* http://www.lawlink.nsw.gov.au/lawlink/Special_Projects/ll_splprojects.nsf/vwFiles/Transcript_Day_20_-_TOR_2_-_31_July_2013.pdf/$file/Transcript_Day_20_-_TOR_2_-_31_July_2013.pdf , 2233.

29. Canon 92.

This secrecy imposed by canon law came out of the clerical culture, but as the former President of the United States Conference of Catholic Bishops, Cardinal Francis George has pointed out, law and culture are intimately entwined, and once a law is passed it has the effect of reinforcing, perpetuating and deepening the culture that gave rise to it in the first place.[30] This is what happened to the Church through its canon law that demanded secrecy about clergy sexual abuse of children.

It was this culture that ultimately led to Cardinal Obando y Bravo's comparing some victims of clerical sexual abuse to Potiphar's wife and to the extensive use by Church hierarchy and spokesmen of 'mental reservation'.

Catholic theology says that it is permissible to use 'mental reservation' to avoid 'scandal' and to preserve 'professional secrets'.[31] Cardinal Desmond Connell, the former Archbishop of Dublin, explained 'mental reservation' to the Murphy Commission, as deceiving someone without telling a lie:

> ... there may be circumstances in which you can use an ambiguous expression realising that the person who you are talking to will accept an untrue version of whatever it may be ... [32]

The sexual abuse of children of priests was a 'scandal', and therefore it was permissible to use 'mental reservation' to avoid it becoming public. Likewise, as we shall see, the Vatican and its senior Cardinals regarded any communications between priests and bishops to be 'professional secrets' that should not even be produced on subpoena to a civil court. It was therefore permissible to use 'mental reservation' to preserve those secrets.

---

30. Francis George, *Ave Maria Law Review,* 1/1 (2003): 1 http://legacy.avemarialaw.edu/lr/assets/articles/v1i1.george.copyright.pdf (Accessed 7 May 2013).

31. *Catholic Catechism,* http://www.vatican.va/archive/ccc_css/archive/catechism/p3s2c2a8.htm, paragraph 2489 and 2491 (Accessed 7 May 2013) and *Catholic Encyclopaedia,* http://www.newadvent.org/cathen/10195b.htm (Accessed 7 May 2013).

32. *Murphy Dublin Report,* Part 2, http://www.justice.ie/en/JELR/DACOI%20Part%202.pdf/Files/DACOI%20Part%202.pdf paragraph 58.20 (Accessed 9 July 2013).

But an even greater cause for the loss of faith through 'scandal', justifying the use of 'mental reservation', is the involvement of six popes, canon law and the Vatican in setting up and maintaining a secret system to deal with complaints about sex abusing priests that inevitably led to more children being abused. In the chapters of this book, there are many examples of the Church using mental reservation to mislead.

From the time of the election of Pope Benedict XVI in 2005, the Church has misled the public about the involvement of the Vatican and six popes in establishing, maintaining and expanding the system of cover up of clergy sexual abuse. There is not just one cover up, but two, and the second, the responsibility of six popes and their advisers in the Roman Curia is still being covered up: Pius XI (who issued *Crimen Sollicitationis* in 1922); Pius XII (who maintained it); John XXIII (who reissued and expanded it); Paul VI (who expanded pontifical secrecy with his 1974 decree *Secreta Continere*) (it is unfair to count John Paul 1, who died thirty-three days after being elected); John Paul II (who imposed pontifical secrecy in his *2001 Motu Proprio*) and Benedict XVI (who confirmed and expanded pontifical secrecy in his 2010 revision of the *2001 Motu Proprio*). The first cover up was dictated by canon law. The second is dictated by theology.

5

Sex and the Confessional

The beginning of this story does not quite go back 3,000 or more years to Joseph and Potiphar's wife, but to 153 CE when Christianity started to spread, and the Church had its first experience of the sexual abuse of children within its ranks. The first century handbook for Christians, the *Didache*, has an explicit prohibition on adult men having sex with boys.[1] The Church's concern about sexual abuse by clergy also had an early history. The first Church law against the abuse of boys was passed at the Council of Elvira in 306 CE.[2]

In about 312 CE, the Emperor Constantine gave to the Church a number of privileges, including the 'privilege of clergy', the right to be tried exclusively in the Church courts.[3] Constantine recognised that such courts might act partially towards their brethren, but he considered that 'secret impunity would be less pernicious than public scandal'.[4] At the same time, if the secular magistrates considered that being dismissed from the clergy was not sufficient punishment, they ignored such immunities.[5]

---

1. Aaron Milevec, *The Didache, Text, Translation, Analysis and Commentary* (Collegeville: Liturgical Press ,2003), 54
2. Council of Elvira (306), Canon 18: 'Bishops and presbyters and deacons, if—once placed in the ministry—they are discovered to be sexual offenders shall not receive communion even at the end . . .' Canon 71 Coincil of Elvira: 'Men who sexually abuse boys shall not be given communion even at the end.' The reference to 'communion at the end' suggests that they will not be forgiven and therefore will be punished in hell. http://www.awrsipe.com/patrick_wall/selected_documents/309%20Council%20of%20Elveria.pdf (Accessed 15 February 2014).
3. Edward Gibbon: *Decline and Fall of the Roman Empire*, Volume 2, (New York: Everyman's Library 1993), 335.
4. *Ibid*, 335.
5. *Ibid*, 336.

St Basil of Caesarea, the fourth century Church Father (330–379 CE), the main author of monastic rule of the Eastern Church, wrote that a cleric or monk who sexually molests youths or boys is to be publically whipped, his head shaved, spat upon, and kept in prison for six months in chains on a diet of bread and water, and after release is to be always subject to supervision and kept out of contact with young people.[6] Leaving out such antiquated punishments as whipping, spitting and head shaving, St Basil seems remarkably modern in his understanding of the sexual abuse of children: the tendency to recidivism and the need for some sort of supervision.

The military's practice of dishonourable discharge was known as *degradatio,* and the Church adopted this practice to describe its dismissal of a priest. The first record of it being used by the Church is in the 83rd Novel of Justinian (527–565 CE). *Degradatio* at this time did not necessarily mean the loss of clergy privilege.[7]

The 'Penitentials', books of punishments for certain sins are often associated with St Bede the Venerable, who lived in England from 672 to 735 CE. They contain quite detailed lists of sexual sins and their punishments, and they were used from the sixth to the twelfth century. Punishments meted out to clergy were more severe than for laymen. Although they do mention sexual activity involving children, they are ambiguous when it comes to whether they are referring to adults having sex with children or children having sex with each other.[8] Nevertheless sexual abuse of children by adults comes within the general description of the various sexual sins.[9] The

---

6. St Basil of Caesarea, as quoted in St Peter Damien, *Liber Gomorrhianus,* cols. 174f. *Randy Engel, St Peter Damian's Book of Gomorrah: A Moral Blueprint for Our Times,* Part I: 'Other Church Fathers favoured defrocking the offending cleric and then turning him over to the State for punishment', footnote 5. http://www.ourladyswarriors.org/articles/damian1.htm (Accessed 6 May 2005). See also Nicholas Cafardi, *Before Dallas: The US Bishops' Response to Clergy Sexual Abuse* (Mahwah, NJ, Paulist Press, 2008), 3, who cites Burchard, the Bishop of Worms for this decree. Burchard wrote twenty books of Canon Law, and it was quite usual for compilers to incorporated decrees from older sources.

7. *Catholic Encyclopaedia,* http://www.newadvent.org/cathen/04677c.htm (Accessed 1 February 2014).

8. *The Penitentials of Cummean,* for example, refer to 'a small boy misused by an older one', *Medieval Handbooks of Penance,* translated by John T McNeill and Helena M Gamer (Chicago: Columbia University Press, 1938).

9. *Ibid.*

penitentials recognised that many of these sins required a form of imprisonment, and that the kinds of punishments which the Church could impose these days, such as restrictions on practising as a priest, were insufficient.

St Peter Damian in his *Book of Gomorrah* (1051 CE) was particularly harsh on clerics who had sex with young boys.[10] His final chapter is an appeal to Pope Leo IX to take action. But the pope's response was to dismiss only repeat offenders, ignoring the effect on the victims and emphasising the need for forgiveness of the perpetrator.[11] The seeds of clericalism, the idea that clergy were special and that the office sanctified the holder of it, had its origins as far back as Constantine, but they were always lying fallow beneath the surface.

Burchard, the bishop of Worms wrote a number of books on canon law around 1008, in which he repeated many of these earlier condemnations of canon law about clergy sexual abuse.

In Europe prior to the French Revolution in 1789, there was little separation between Church and state as we know it today. The separation began around the eleventh century, and in the twelfth century the dividing line between Church and state started to widen, as demonstrated by the celebrated clash between King Henry II of England and the Archbishop of Canterbury, Thomas a'Beckett. Canon law began to be systematized, and a trend developed requiring clergy sexual abusers to be 'degraded', and then handed over to the civil authority to be dealt with in accordance with the civil law.

In 1140 CE, the monk Gratian wrote a book called *The Concordance of Discordant Canons*, and his decrees, as they became to be known, were the most important source of the history of canon law.[12] His decrees have many sections dealing with the sexual transgressions of clerics. Punishments for clerics were to be more severe than for laymen, and he cites the ancient Roman law opinion that *stuprum pueri*, the sexual violation of young boys, should be punished by death.[13]

---

10. Fr Thomas Doyle: *Affidavit in the case of Jane Doe v Oblates of Mary Immaculate*, District Court Bexar County Texas, Cause No. 2006CI09725, January 2008, paragraph 18 http://reform-network.net/?p=1464 (Accessed 6 May 2013). *Ibid*, paragraph 20.
11. *Ibid*, paragraph 21.
12. *Ibid*, paragraph 16.
13. *Ibid*, paragraph 22. See also Cafardi, *Before Dallas*, 4, and *Catholic Encyclopaedia*

At the Third Lateran Council in 1179, Pope Alexander III introduced the euphemism of a 'crime against nature' in his decrees, and it was subsequently adopted by the Church's jurisprudence. The euphemism almost certainly included the sexual abuse of a minor by clergy. In the case of clergy, they were to be kept indefinitely in a monastery or subjected to 'degradation'.[14]

Pope Celestine III (1191–1198) approved the punishment of clergy serial offenders by the secular powers. In 1209 Pope Innocent III (1198–1216) ruled that the *degradatio* of a cleric should take place in the presence of someone of the secular authority who would then take custody of him. Innocent III took the view that the Church had to take the initiative in involving the 'secular arm' in the punishment of delinquent clergy.[15] At the Fourth Lateran Council in 1215, Innocent III continued the condemnation of 'crimes against nature'.[16]

At the Fifth Lateran Council in 1514, Pope Leo X decreed that clerics involved in 'crimes against nature' are to be punished 'respectively according to the sacred canons or with penalties imposed by the civil law'. [17]

The Council of Trent in 1551 accepted that some crimes committed by clerics were 'so grievous that on account of the atrocity thereof, they have to be deposed from sacred orders and delivered over to a secular court'.[18]

In 1566, Pope Pius V (1566–72) issued the Constitution *Romani Pontifici* requiring clerics who committed sodomy to be first 'degraded' by a canonical court and then handed over to the secular authorities for punishment.[19] Two years later, the same pope issued

http://www.newadvent.org/cathen/04677c.htm (Accessed 26 October 2013).

14. Cafardi, *Before Dallas*, 4, footnote 23. http://www.awrsipe.com/patrick_wall/ selected_documents/309%20Council%20of%20Elveria.pdf   (Accessed   15 February 2014).

15. Pope Celestine III, JL 17639, *Decretales Gregorii* referred to in the *New Cambridge Medieval History* (Cambridge: Cambridge University Press, 1995), parts 1-2. c 1024–c 1198, 440. Pope Innocent III, *decree c. viii, De Crimine Falsi, X*, v, 20, *(1198) Catholic Encyclopaedia,* http://www.newadvent.org/cathen/04677c.htm (Accessed 9 July 2013).

16. Cafardi, *Before Dallas*, 5.

17. *Ibid*, 5 and footnote 27.

18. *Catholic Encyclopaedia* http://www.newadvent.org/cathen/04677c.htm (Accessed 26 October 2013).

19. Pope Pius V, '*Romani Pontifices*, 1 April 1566 in P Gasparri, editor, *Codicem Iuris Canonici Fontes*, Volume 1 (Vatican: Typis Polygottis, 1926), 200.

a further decree, *Horrendum Illud Scelus* against clerics who 'sinned against nature' with children. They were to be cast out of the clergy to be deterred by 'the avenging secular sword of civil laws'.[20]

In Italy in 1570 a priest named Fontino was charged before a canonical court with sodomy of a choir boy. He was defrocked, and then handed over to the secular authority for punishment according to the civil law. He was executed by beheading. The choir boy was whipped and banned from the papal states. (R Sheer 'A Canon, A Choir Boy and Homosexuality in the late Sixteenth Century Italy: A Case Study', in *Journal of Homosexuality*, 21 (1991): 1–22

In 1726, a priest who had sodomized young boys was sentenced to the galleys, but it was never carried out, and he served his sentence working in a hospital. He petitioned the Sacred Congregation for the Council for permission to say Mass again, but it was refused.[21] The interesting thing is that the Church in this case applied a 'zero tolerance' approach to clergy sexual abuse of children, a stance that was gradually abandoned two hundred years later in 1922 with *Crimen Sollicitationis*, and reinstated in 2002 for the United States alone, at the insistence of its bishops. It still does not apply to the rest of the world.

From the twelfth century to the Reformation that started in 1517, the role of the Church was similar to that exercised now by the European Union, with the pope deciding disputes between the monarchies of the countries over which the Church had influence.[22]

---

20. http://www.eurekaencyclopedia.com/index.php/Category:15th-18th_ Centuries_Abuse (Accessed 6 May 2016), http://www.awrsipe.com/patrick_ wall/selected_documents/1568%20Horrendum.pdf (Accessed 4 August 2013).

21. Nicholas Cafardi, *Before Dallas*, 6. Nicholas Cafardi has a civil law degree from Pittsburgh University and is a doctor of canon law from the Angelicum. He is Dean Emeritus of the Faculty of Law at Duquesne University, a Catholic University in Pittsburgh, Pennsylvania. http://www.duq.edu/academics/faculty/nicholas-cafardi (Accessed 29 May 2013). He is a former general counsel of the Diocese of Pittsburgh and was chairman of the US bishops' National Review Board, which oversees their response to abuse complaints. He describes himself as an 'orthodox Catholic', http://www.post-gazette.com/stories/local/neighborhoods-city/duquesne-professor-cafardi-considered-for-vatican-ambassador-671890/ (Accessed 15 October 2013).

22. Pennington, *A Short History of Canon Law from Apolstolic Times to 1917*, http://faculty.cua.edu/pennington/Canon%20Law/ShortHistoryCanonLaw. htm (Accessed 6 January 2014). James Spigelman, http://www.abc.net.au/ classic/content/2013/07/09/3798528.htm (Accessed 12 July 2013). The religious

The Church in many places still had the sole right to punish its clergy, but these punishments were restricted to stripping them of their privileges as clergy or perhaps there was a requirement to 'do penance' in a monastery. But the Church recognised that it was a proper role of the secular power to punish child sexual abusers among the clergy for their crimes in accordance with whatever the civil law imposed at the time. The Church was conflicted over handing over its clerics to the civil authority but there is no doubt that where the crimes were regarded as serious enough it did so. For more on this see Mark D Jordan: *The Silence of Sodom: Homosexuality in Modern Catholicism* (Chicago: University of Chicago Press, 2000), 122. It was only when the separation between Church and state accelerated (and the extent of that varied in different countries), that this reluctance to hand over clerics for punishment by the civil authorities started to gather steam within the Church itself.

There was one thing that exacerbated the problem of sexual assaults on children amongst clergy by providing an excellent opportunity: the sacrament of penance or, as it came to be known, confession.

The sacrament of penance dates back to the earliest Christian Church, although its modern form of individuals confessing sins to a priest dates from the latter part of the sixth century in the Irish monasteries.[23] According to Catholic dogma, persons who have committed 'mortal' or very serious sins, like murder, rape, adultery and serious stealing, and who have not been absolved by a priest before they die, will go to hell to be punished for all eternity. For lesser 'venial' sins, like telling white lies, or petty theft, they have to suffer in 'purgatory' for a period of time before being allowed into Heaven.[24]

---

allegiance of Europe was divided by the Reformation, but clergy privilege was recognized for some centuries in England after Henry VIII's break with the Church. A typical instance of the role of the Pope is the Treaty of Tordesillas of 1494 when Pope Alexander VI settled the dispute between Spain and Portugal over the 'ownership' of the newly discovered lands of Latin America by drawing a line roughly down the middle of the continent, http://www.princeton.edu/~achaney/tmve/wiki100k/docs/Treaty_of_Tordesillas.html (Accessed 15 June 2014).

23. Fr Thomas Doyle, *Affidavit in Jane Doe Vs. Omi of Texas*, paragraph 17, http://www.bishop-accountability.org/news2008/03_04/2008_03_03_Doyle_TomDoyle.htm (Accessed 15 July 2013).

24. *Catholic Catechism*, paragraph 1031, http://www.vatican.va/archive/ccc_css/archive/catechism/p123a12.htm (Accessed 1 October 2013) and see the encyclical

The priest, by virtue of his ordination, has the power to wash away people's sins, and to 'absolve' them when they are 'confessed' to him.[25]

In 1215 the Fourth Lateran Council required all Catholics to go to confession to a priest at least once per year. There were some attempts after the Second Vatican Council (1962–1965) to bring back the older communal form of Confession, whereby the priest would absolve everyone present without their having to confess their sins individually to a priest. But it was generally frowned upon by Pope John Paul II who tried to encourage the practice of individual Confession in his 1984 encyclical *Reconciliatio et Paenitentiae*.[26]

One of the features of Confession is what is known as the 'seal' of the confessional. A priest is absolutely forbidden to reveal directly what has been told to him in the confessional, and incurs automatic excommunication from the Church if he does so.[27]

The confessional box was an obvious place where boys could be seduced, particularly in places where schools were attached to monasteries. The most complete historical records of this come from Spanish Canonical Tribunals revealing 3,775 cases of priests attempting to solicit sex in the confessional between 1723 and 1820.[28] That amounts to nearly forty such cases a year in Spain alone.

Various councils and popes made declarations to deal with this problem, the main document being Pope Benedict XIV's decree *Sacramentum Poenitentiae* (1741). Because the seal of confession was involved in any investigation of such a canonical crime, Pius IX in 1866, through a decree issued by the Holy Office, imposed absolute secrecy on the proceedings.[29]

Reconciliatio et Paenitentiae, http://www.vatican.va/holy_father/john_paul_ii/apost_exhortations/documents/hf_jp-ii_exh_02121984_reconciliatio-et-paenitentia_en.html (Accessed 1 October 2013).

25. *Catholic Catechism,* paragraph 1422ff http://www.vatican.va/archive/ccc_css/archive/catechism/p2s2c2a4.htm (Accessed 1 October 2013).

26. http://www.vatican.va/holy_father/john_paul_ii/apost_exhortations/documents/hf_jp-ii_exh_02121984_reconciliatio-et-paenitentia_en.html paragraph 32 (Accessed 1 October 2013).

27. Canon 1388.

28. Fr Thomas Doyle, *Affidavit in Jane Doe Vs. Omi of Texas,* http://www.bishop-accountability.org/news2008/03_04/2008_03_03_Doyle_TomDoyle.htm paragraph 36 (Accessed 15 July 2013).

29. *Ibid,* paragraph 36. See also P Gaspari, editor, *Codicem Iuris Canonici Fontes,*

This brief overview establishes that the problem of clergy sexually assaulting children was not something new for the Church, and it can be seen that for some 1500 years after Christianity became the official religion of the Roman Empire, around 380 CE, the Church recognised that sexually assaulting children was not just a sin, but a serious crime. Clerics who engaged in such activities were not just to be subjected to restrictions on their ministry or forms of prayer and penance that the Church could impose under its canon law. By the twelfth century, canon law decreed that they were to be stripped of their status as clerics and handed over to the civil authority for further punishment. And the Church had to disclose to the state the nature of his crime when it handed him over. That all changed slowly and radically in the latter part of the 19th century, and particularly with *Crimen Sollicitationis* in 1922.

Before dealing with canon law and how its modern formulation grappled with the problem of clergy sexual abuse, we have to backtrack to the twelfth century, because another event took place which was very significant in this story of how the Church came to be in such a mess over this issue. As Church and state (such as it was) started to drift apart in England and other countries, a power struggle began between them over whether or not clergy should be tried in the civil or Church courts for any kind of crime, and not just clergy sexual abuse. While clergy might well be punished by being stripped of their ecclesiastical privileges and then handed over to the state for further punishment, the Church was the one who decided if they would be handed over. Henry II of England wanted to abolish the 'privilege or benefit of clergy' *(Privilegium clericale)*, which effectively gave the Church a veto over state prosecutions of clergy. This struggle led to one of the most celebrated murders in English history.

Volume 1 (Vatican: Typis Polyglottis, 1926).

6

The Murder in the Cathedral

On 29 December 1170, four armed knights from the Court of King Henry II of England entered Canterbury Cathedral. They had previously heard the King complain about the Archbishop of Canterbury, Thomas a'Becket, who had long been in dispute with Henry over the power of Church and state, 'Will no one rid me of this turbulent priest?' Henry is reported to have said.[1] Four knights of his court took the hint, and went to Canterbury Cathedral with their swords and armour. At first they hid them in the grounds of the cathedral, and were ushered into the archbishop's private chambers. They made a number of demands, including that he lift his excommunication of the bishops who had supported Henry. A'Becket refused. They then went out to the cathedral grounds, and returned suited and with their weapons. A'Becket meanwhile was in the cathedral, walking towards the choir for vespers. The knights tried to drag him outside, but he grabbed onto a pillar. The first knight scalped him with his sword, and a second hit him again on the head. He fell to the ground. The third and fourth finished him off by taking off the top part of his skull. His brains, covered in blood, fell over the cathedral floor.

The confrontation between King Henry II and Thomas a'Becket was mainly over the privilege or benefit of clergy. Most of the bishops were prepared to acquiesce, and let Henry II have his way, but a'Becket was the thorn in his side. The dispute finally ended with the murder in the cathedral.

---

1. This expression is probably more legend than fact, as there are no contemporary accounts of his actually saying that, but it seems that he did say something that did give the hint to his knights. But playwrights have found this version irresistible: James Spigelman, *Becket & Henry, The Becket Lectures,* St Thomas More Society (2004): 249

Thomas a'Becket was venerated as a martyr, and was canonised by Pope Alexander III as a Catholic saint in 1173, a little more than two years after his death. His saintliness even survived the Reformation, and he is still revered by the Anglican Church. Public sentiment turned against Henry, and he backed down over the clergy privilege issue. But as the secular state became stronger, and the power of the Church declined, clergy privilege was gradually whittled away. In the thirteenth century it morphed into a strange fiction that allowed first offenders, even if they were not clerics, to receive a more lenient sentence. Persons who wished to claim the benefit had to appear in court wearing a monk's tonsure and robe. Later a literacy test was substituted, because the clergy, by and large, were those who could read and write.[2] The English dramatist, Ben Jonson avoided hanging by pleading benefit of clergy in 1598 when charged with manslaughter.[3] Any vestiges of it were abolished in federal courts in the United States in 1790, and in the United Kingdom of Great Britain and Ireland by two acts in 1823. The UK Parliament formally abolished it in 1827.[4]

But the privilege has survived in other parts of the world in different forms. The 1922 Concordat between Latvia and the Vatican provided that if a priest or religious monk is sentenced to imprisonment by a state court, he will be treated in accordance with his status in the hierarchy, and his sentence will be served in a monastery unless in the meantime he had been dismissed from the priesthood.[5] By this means the Church had control over whether a priest went to jail or not. The 1925 Concordat between Poland and the Vatican and the 1929 Lateran Treaty between Mussolini and the Vatican have similar provisions.[6] These treaties reflect the belief that priests are different and should be treated more leniently.

A variation of the Lateran Treaty between the Vatican and the Italian state in 1985 provides that clergy are not required to give judges or other authorities, information on persons or matters which

---

2. *Catholic Encyclopaedia*, http://www.newadvent.org/cathen/02476a.htm (Accessed 29 October 2013).

3. Sean McEvoy: *Ben Johnson* (Edinburgh: Edinburgh University Press, 2008), 4.

4. Crimes Act of 1790, chapter 9, 1 Statute 112. *Catholic Encyclopaedia*, http://www.newadvent.org/cathen/02476a.htm (Accessed 3 July 2013).

5. http://www.worldlii.org/int/other/LNTSer/1923/80.html (Accessed 13 January 2013).

6. http://www.racjonalista.pl/kk.php/s,1369/k,2 (Accessed 13 January 2014). Lateran Treaty 1929, Article 8, http://www.aloha.net/~mikesch/treaty.htm (Accessed 14 December 2013).

come to their knowledge by reason of their ministry.[7] This does not seem to be restricted to confession, and therefore bishops could not be interrogated about what priests have told them outside confession. A similar provision was included in the 1933 Concordat with Nazi Germany.[8]

Franco's 1953 Concordat (Treaty) between Spain and the Vatican restored many of the privileges that had been agreed to between the Vatican and the Spanish monarchs, and which were repudiated by the 1931 Republican government.[9] The 1953 Concordat provided that a bishop could only be put on trial in a civil court with the consent of the Vatican.[10] It allowed criminal proceedings against clerics but only with the consent of the bishop.[11] Any deprivation of liberty was to be spent in a religious house, not in jail, and the proceedings were not to be publicised—the first was a reflection of clericalism that the priest was someone special, to be treated more leniently than every other citizen, and the second reflected the Church's concern about the effects of 'scandal'. Clerics and religious could be made to testify in court, but only with the consent of the bishop, and no cleric could be questioned about his knowledge of crimes of others that came to them while performing their ministry. Effectively, a bishop could not be questioned by the state about facts uncovered in canonical investigations into the sex crimes of priests against children.[12] These privileges were abolished in Spain in 1985.[13]

---

7. Agreement 3 June 1985, Article 4(4).
8. Article 9, http://www.concordatwatch.eu/showkb.php?org_id=858&kb_header_id=752&kb_id=1211 (Accessed 13 January 2014).
9. The Republican government repudiated the 1851 Concordat between the Vatican and Queen Isabella that incorporated many clergy privileges, http://www.concordatwatch.eu/showtopic.php?org_id=845&kb_header_id=34511 (Accessed 13 January 2014).
10. http://www.vatican.va/roman_curia/secretariat_state/archivio/documents/rc_seg-st_19530827_concordato-spagna_sp.html (Accessed 7 May 2013) Article XVI (1.)
11. *Ibid,* Article XVI (4).
12. http://www.vatican.va/roman_curia/secretariat_state/archivio/documents/rc_seg-st_19530827_concordato-spagna_sp.html (Accessed 7 May 2013). Article XVI (1.) This says, 'In the case of arrest or detention, clergy and religious will be treated in accordance with their status and their position in the hierarchy. The penalty of deprivation of liberty will be spent in an ecclesiastical or religious house that, in the judgment of the bishop of the place and the judicial authority of the state offers the appropriate guarantees; or at least in local places different to where lay people are kept, unless the ecclesiastical authority has laicized the cleric.'
13. http://www.laicismo.org/data/docs/archivo_678.pdf, 58 (Accessed 7 May 2013).

There is a modified form of the privilege in Brazil, Argentina, Bolivia and Paraguay where military chaplains convicted under military law are to have their punishments determined by the bishop.[14] In Venezuela, their punishment is to be determined in agreement with the bishop.[15]

The 1954 Concordat between the Vatican and the Dominican Republic provides that priests cannot be interrogated by judges or other authorities over things revealed to them in the exercise of their 'sacred ministry'.[16] Priests would serve their jail sentences separate from lay persons.[17]

In Colombia, a form of privilege of clergy survived under the Concordat (Treaty) with the Vatican of 12 July 1973.[18] Bishops could not be tried by the state courts, but only by the Church courts. Priests on the other hand can be tried in state courts but the proceedings are not to be publicised, and again, we have the Vatican's concern about the effect of 'scandal'. The Church's objection by that time was not so much about priests being punished by the state under the law of the land, but that anyone should know about it. But bishops were another matter. Under the Concordat, they could not even be tried by the Colombian state, no matter what they did. They were above the law. In 1993, the Colombian Constitutional Court declared the Concordat

14. Agreement with the Vatican 3 October 1989, http://www.vatican.va/roman_curia/secretariat_state/archivio/documents/rc_seg-st_19891023_santa-sede-brasile_po.html (Accessed 14 December 2013). Agreement with the Vatican 28 Jun 1957, http://www.laicismo.org/detalle.php?pk=17718 (Accessed 7 May 2013) (Argentina) and http://www.vatican.va/roman_curia/secretariat_state/archivio/documents/rc_seg-st_19861201_santa-sede-bolivia_sp.html Art IX (Accessed 18 October 2013) (Bolivia), http://www.vatican.va/roman_curia/secretariat_state/archivio/documents/rc_seg-st_19601126_convenio-paraguay_sp.html Article XI (Accessed 18 October 2013) (Paraguay).

15. http://www.vatican.va/roman_curia/secretariat_state/archivio/documents/rc_seg-st_19941031_s-sede-venezuela_sp.html Article XIII(Accessed 18 October 2013).

16. Concordat 16 June 1954. http://www.vatican.va/roman_curia/secretariat_state/archivio/documents/rc_seg-st_19540616_concordato-dominicana_sp.html Art XI(2)(Accessed 18 October 2013).

17. Emilio Betances, *The Catholic Church and Power Politics in Latin America* (London: Roman and Littlefield, 2007), 38.

18. Article XIX and XX http://mre.cancilleria.gov.co/wps/portal/embajada_santasede/!ut/p/c0/04_SB8K8xLLM9MSSzPy8xBz9CP0os3gLUzfLUH9DYwOL4BAnAyMvVyM3IyPTAGNDU_2CbEdFAKVyXgk!/?WCM_PORTLET=PC_7_85F9UO1308STB02JE2F225P3H4_WCM&WCM_GLOBAL_CONTEXT=/wps/wcm/connect/WCM_EMBAJADA_SANTASEDE/embajada/relaciones+bilaterales/concordato+con+la+santa+sede (Accessed 19 October 2013).

inconsistent with the 1991 Constitution requiring equal treatment under the law.[19] Despite controversy over the matter, the Vatican was still insisting in 2007 that Colombia respect the Concordat: Colombian bishops were entitled to impunity and were above the law.[20] The matter is still unresolved.

In 1994 the Colombian Attorney General, Gustavo de Grieff started proceedings against certain bishops, including Archbishop Dario Castrillón Hoyos of Bucaramanga for complicity with the FARC guerrillas, contrary to Colombian law. But he had to abandon the proceedings because of the immunity under the Concordat, which protected the bishops.[21] Two years later Castrillón was called to Rome and appointed to head the Congregation for the Clergy, and was made a Cardinal in 1998. He remained in that post until 2006.

Cardinal Castrillón, who was saved by privilege of clergy from being tried in a Colombian Court, like any other citizen against whom an allegation of criminal conduct is made, had a pivotal role in the strange modern re-run of the struggle between Church and state for the privilege, some eight centuries after the clash between Henry II and Thomas a'Becket. Only this time, Castrillón was working to maintain a de facto privilege of clergy for priests who had been sexually assaulting children.

While the Church could retain some elements of the privilege through the use of treaties with sympathetic governments where the Church had influence, very few governments were sympathetic. But the Church could achieve the same thing everywhere by the use of

---

19. http://www.eltiempo.com/archivo/documento/MAM-217215 (Accessed 19 October 2013). It seems that there was some question about the jurisdiction of the Constitutional Court to issue judgments on international treaties: http://bibliotecanonica.net/docsad/btcadx.htm (Accessed 19 October 2013), http://www.usergioarboleda.edu.co/civilizar/revista8/concordato_jurisprudencia.pdf (Accessed 19 October 2013). There is currently no sign of any concordat with Colombia on the list of agreements with other countries on the Vatican website, http://www.vatican.va/roman_curia/secretariat_state/index_concordati-accordi_en.htm (Accessed 19 October 2013).

20. http://www.caracol.com.co/noticias/actualidad/concordato-en-colombia-impide-encarcelar-al-arzobispo-de-manizales/20070423/nota/418074.aspx (Accessed 19 October 2013).

21. http://www.eltiempo.com/archivo/documento/MAM-92041 (Accessed 30 May 2013). It seems that the action of the Constitutional Court is still a matter of some controversy.

secrecy in its own canonical investigations. And six popes and their Curia advisers were remarkably successful in preserving this de facto privilege in virtually every country in the world.

The practical effects of the Church's revival of the privilege through the back door of secrecy were very lenient sentences for clergy in the form of warnings, spiritual exercises, seeking some form of psychological treatment and perhaps spending some time "doing penance" in a monastery. Only in the most extreme cases were sex abusing priests dismissed from the priesthood—a punishment, as we shall see, that was so difficult to achieve under canon law that it effectively required the abusing priest's consent.

While in 1170, it was the secular state under Henry II and his courtly knights that acted abominably, in the modern re-run of this struggle that started in 1922 with *Crimen Sollicitationis*, it was the Church under its popes, cardinals and bishops. And its outcome was much worse than the death of one archbishop in a cathedral. It involved the suicide of many hundreds of people who had been sexually abused as children by serial sexual abusers whom the Church protected, and hid from the civil authorities for no other reason than that the abusers were priests.[22] The Church hierarchy was prepared to pay any price to avoid the 'scandal' of a public trial of these priests in a civil court. And the price was an unwanted but foreseeable increase in sex assaults on children.

The modern struggle between Church and state over this issue also had its 'turbulent priests', priests who, this time, were not bucking up against the state, but against their own Church. They were an American Dominican priest, Fr Thomas Doyle, an Australian bishop, Geoffrey Robinson, both of them canon lawyers, two other retired Australian bishops, Pat Power and William Morris, Bishop Michael Smith and Fr Sean McDonagh, in Ireland, and Archbishop Weakland and Bishop Tom Gumbleton in the United States.[23] Doyle has been ostracised by the Church hierarchy, and Robinson resigned

---

22. In the State of Victoria alone, the number is said to be forty, http://www.theage. com.au/victoria/inquiry-looms-as-more-suicides-linked-to-sexual-abuse-by-catholic-priests-20120413-1wz3h.html (Accessed 3 July 2013).

23. In June 2013, Bishops Robinson, Power and Morris called for a special Council of the Church to tackle the clerical sexual abuse problem, http://www.change.org/en-AU/petitions/pope-francis-the-vatican-for-christ-s-sake-stop-sexual-abuse-for-good (Accessed 15 July 2013).

his position as an auxiliary bishop of Sydney, and has criticized the way the Church has handled the issue of clergy sexual abuse.[24] Bishop Morris was dismissed from his post as Bishop of Toowoomba for suggesting that the Church should discuss the issue of women priests, but another likely factor, according to some, was his strong demand that the Church be honest about sexual abuse.[25] Bishop Gumbleton was removed from his post by the Vatican after speaking up for victims.[26]

These two factors, the sexual abuse of children by priests and the insistence by the Church that its courts alone should have the right to try such priests formed a toxic mix that infected canon law that governed the Church. But before we go into the detail of how that occurred, it is necessary to say something about canon law itself because canon law and its conflict with civil law are at the core of the problem.

---

24. Robinson has written two books on the subject, *Confronting Power and Sex in the Catholic Church* (Melbourne: John Garratt Publishing, 2007), and *For Christ's Sake End Sexual Abuse in the Catholic Church for Good* (Melbourne: Garratt Publishing, Melbourne, 2013). The Australian Catholic Bishops Conference issued a statement after the publication of the first: 'The book's questioning of the authority of the Church is connected to Bishop Robinson's uncertainty about the knowledge and authority of Christ himself. Catholics believe that the Church, founded by Christ, is endowed by him with a teaching office which endures through time. This is why the Church's Magisterium teaches the truth authoritatively in the name of Christ. The book casts doubt upon these teachings.' http://www.catholicculture.org/culture/library/view.cfm?recnum=8193 (Accessed 15 October 2013).
25. http://www.eurekastreet.com.au/article.aspx?aeid=26378 (Accessed 6 June 2013). *The Australian* 15 July 2010, http://www.theaustralian.com.au/news/catholic-church-must-aid-sexual-abuse-victims-despite-cost/story-e6frg6n6-1225891796453 (Accessed 12 August 2013).
26. Fr Thomas Doyle, *Thirty Years: What We've Learned and What I've Learned*, 27 July 2013, http://reform-network.net/?p=22122 (Accessed 1 August 2013).

Pope Pius XII

7

Canon Law

Canon law is the body of law and regulations adopted by Catholic Church authorities for governing the Church itself and its members.[1] Prior to the promulgation of the first *Code of Canon Law* in 1917, canon law was in all sorts of decrees from popes and councils of the Church, requiring the refined skills of a solver of jigsaw puzzles to find an answer to a problem.[2] In 1904, Pope Pius X set up the first Commission that took thirteen years to pull it all together into a single code of canon law.

The whole point of a code of canon law in any system of law is to have all the law on a particular subject in the one place, so that anyone can go to the Code and find something easily. A number of states in Australia have codes dealing with criminal law, and the United States has the *Uniform Commercial Code* dealing with commercial law. The aim of the *1917 Code of Canon Law* was to do the same thing.

Pope John XXIII is best known for having called the Second Vatican Council, but he also set up a commission in 1963 to revise

---

1. *Catholic Encyclopaedia,* http://www.newadvent.org/cathen/09056a.htm (Accessed 9 February 2013).
2. The first Council to issue decrees that bound the whole Church was that of Nicaea in 325, called by the Emperor Constantine. It created rules for Church governance, and defined the roles of bishops. It made laws relating to ecclesiastical discipline, such as clergy not being permitted to practice usury, or be eunuchs. It also came up with a statement of Christian belief, known as the Nicaean Creed. Papal decretal letters as a way of creating canon law started in the fourth and fifth centuries, but it was only in the twelfth century with Alexander III and Innocent III that the role of the Pope in declaring canon law became the normal practice: Pennington, *A Short History of Canon Law from Apolstolic Times to 1917*, http://faculty.cua.edu/pennington/Canon%20Law/ShortHistoryCanonLaw.htm (Accessed 6 January 2014).

the *1917 Code of Canon Law*. Twenty years later on 25 January, 1983, Pope John Paul II put his signature to the *1983 Code of Canon Law* to replace the *1917 Code of Canon Law*.

Canon law derives from Roman law, and its official language is Latin. Translations are available on the Vatican website.[3] The word 'norm' in English usually means a standard or level of behaviour, without it necessarily being legally binding, but general and particular laws are often referred to as 'norms' in canon law.

Canon law creates its own crimes, which it calls 'delicts'.[4] Some of those crimes are peculiar to the Church and do not constitute crimes under any civil law (a term used to cover both state criminal and civil law in this book). Examples are desecrating the Holy Communion wafer or breaking the seal of the confessional. But others overlap, and some matters are crimes under both canon law and civil law: homicide, kidnapping, mutilating or gravely wounding someone, fraud, and sexual assaults on minors.[5] Some crimes can be committed by any Catholic, both clerical and lay (for example homicide, kidnapping, assaulting the pope, etc), and some only by 'clerics', for example, the sex assaults against children under Canon 1395. A lay person who sexually assaults a child is still committing a mortal sin, but it is not a canonical crime that would see him brought before a canonical court.

Canon 22 deals with conflicts between canon and civil Law:

> Civil laws to which the law of the Church yields are to be observed in canon law with the same effects, insofar as they are not contrary to divine law and unless canon law provides otherwise.[6]

Canon 22 can be interpreted narrowly to mean that it only applies where canon law specifically 'yields' to civil law. Examples of this are

---

3. www.vatican.va.
4. The glossary attached to the Code provides: 'Delict: a crime in canon law, an external violation of a law or precept gravely imputable by reason of malice or negligence', http://www.vatican.va/resources/resources_glossary-terms_en.html (Accessed 12 March 2013).
5. Canons 1397 and 1395.
6. http://www.vatican.va/archive/ENG1104/__P3.HTM (Accessed 6 March 2013)

in relation to the age of minority, contracts and a number of other matters, and the priority of canon law only applies in those particular subject matters where canon law prescribes something different to what is in the civil.[7] On the other hand, *The New Commentary on the Code of Canon Law* says that Canon 22 expresses a more general principle whereby canon law has priority over civil law wherever there is a conflict.[8]

The position of office holders in the Church, however, is clear. Canon law requires all those taking on positions in the Church

---

7. Canon 98§2, and 1290.

8. 'For Catholics, two systems of law oblige simultaneously, canon law (including divine law) and legitimate civil laws. While both are binding within separate but parallel systems, the canon law prevails whenever there is conflict with the civil law', John P Beal, James A Coriden and Thomas J Green, *New Commentary on the Code of Canon Law* (Mahwah, NJ: Paulist Press, 2000), 85. Thomas J Paprocki in the same New Commentary at 1803 says: '. . . as long as civil laws are not contrary to divine law or unless canon law provides otherwise, canon law often defers to civil laws (c 22), especially civil contract law (c1290), labour laws (cc 231§2 and 1286), prescription (cc 197–199 and 1268–1270), the law of wills and inheritance (c1299§2), and probably also tort law (compensation for negligent and intentional harms and injuries: see c128).' He makes no mention of criminal law. Monsignor Green appears to have repeated this view of Canon 22 when discussing the Dallas Charter, *Critique of the Dallas Charter,* http://natcath.org/ NCR_Online/documents/Greencritique.htm paragraph K (Accessed 17 August 2013). Fr Langes Silva JCL, JCD in 'Canon Law and Secular Law: A Comparative Essay', *Intermountain Catholic News,* June 14, 2007 states: 'Where it applies, the civil laws are to be observed with the same effects in canon law. However, matters cannot be left to civil law if its prescriptions are contrary to divine law, or if canon law has made other provisions', http://www.freerepublic.com/ focus/f-religion/1850280/posts (Accessed 1 February 2013). At the *Maitland-Newcastle Inquiry,* Fr John Usher said that canon law required compliance with civil law unless the civil law is opposed to divine law. 'I don't know the exact wording. But we all felt obliged that we had to comply with the civil law as best we could in the circumstances of the time.' Fr Usher seems to have misunderstood the effect of the 'narrow' interpretation of Canon 22, which says nothing about a positive obligation to follow civil law, and requires disobedience to civil law in some situations where there is a conflict, http://www.lawlink. nsw.gov.au/lawlink/Special_Projects/ll_splprojects.nsf/vwFiles/Day_22_-9_ September_2013.pdf/$file/Day_22_-_9_September_2013.pdf 2375 (Accessed 11 September 2013). Delaney, *Canonical Implications of the Response of the Catholic Church in Australia,* 222 argues that respect for civil law, unless it conflicts with divine law is an essential aspect of Christian morality. However, she makes no mention of Canon 22 or what is the position where there is a conflict between canon law and civil law..

hierarchy, and those in religious orders to make a 'profession of faith' according to an approved formula which also requires them to swear that they will obey all ecclesiastical laws and especially the *Code of Canon Law*.[9]

The Pope as the Source of Canon Law

The source of all canon law is the pope. The pope is an absolute monarch in the political and legal sense. Canon 331 of the *1983 Code of Canon Law* provides that the pope possesses, by virtue of his office, supreme, full, immediate, and universal ordinary power in the Church, which he is always able to exercise freely. There is no appeal from the decision of the Roman pontiff, and the pope is to be judged by no one.[10]

The pope is the absolute monarch, both of the Vatican City State, and of the Church itself. The Church draws a distinction between the 'Vatican' which is the miniature state consisting of some forty-four hectares in Rome and 'the Holy See', which refers to the authority of the bishop of Rome to govern Church members all over the world. Many official documents referred to in the text will use the term 'Holy See'. In everyday language and media reports, the word 'Vatican' often refers to both, and that term will be used to include 'the Holy See' throughout this book.

General councils of the Church, a meeting of all the bishops of the Church, can pass decrees that become part of canon law, but they are called infrequently. The most recent general Councils were the Council of Trent (1563), the First Vatican Council (1870) and the Second Vatican Council (1965). Virtually all canon law creating specific rights or obligations derives from the pope at the time.

Theoretically the pope governs the Church with the bishops, but for practical reasons, he has his own 'cabinet ministers' called the

---

9. Canon 833, http://www.vatican.va/archive/ENG1104/__P2R.HTM (Accessed 3 March 2013), and http://www.vatican.va/roman_curia/congregations/cfaith/documents/rc_con_cfaith_doc_19880701_professio-fidei_en.html (Accessed 3 March 2013). 'I shall follow and foster the common discipline of the entire Church and I shall maintain the observance of all ecclesiastical laws, especially those contained in the Code of Canon Law.'

10. Canon 333§3 and Canon 1404http://www.vatican.va/archive/ENG1104/_INDEX.HTM (Accessed 9 February 2013).

'Roman Curia'. It consists of a number of departments that are known as 'dycasteries' or 'congregations' that are headed by a senior cardinal called a 'prefect'.

But ultimately it is the pope alone who makes canon law. Whereas the United States President, Harry Truman, once said 'The buck stops here', that was only partly true because he could always be inhibited by the United States Congress, the Senate, the Supreme Court or the United States Constitution itself. The pope is answerable to no person, court or institution, and the 'buck' for any policy expressed in canon law truly does stop with him.[11]

In his *Pastoral Letter* to the people of Ireland of 19 March 2010, Benedict XVI told the Irish bishops that they had to 'cooperate' with the civil authorities in matters of child abuse 'in their area of competence'.[12] He did not elaborate on what he meant by the 'area of competence' of the civil authorities, nor did he define what cooperation meant.

On 13 July 2011, the Murphy Commission handed down its report on the Cloyne diocese (*Cloyne Report*).[13] In a response to criticisms of the Vatican by the Irish Foreign Minister, Mr Ian Gilmore for interfering in Irish affairs, as revealed in the *Cloyne Report*, the Vatican published a response on 3 September 2011, in which it said:

> . . . canon law and civil law, while being two distinct systems, with distinct areas of application and competence, are not in competition and can operate in parallel.[14]

The problem is that canon law does not always keep its areas of application distinct. It also creates canonical crimes of homicide,

---

11. John P Beal, James A Coriden and Thomas J Green, *New Commentary on the Code of Canon Law* (New York: Paulist Press, 2000), 13: No laws or general decrees with the force of law or derogations from laws may be issued without the specific approbation of the Roman Pontiff.

12. http://www.vatican.va/holy_father/benedict_xvi/letters/2010/documents/hf_ben-xvi_let_20100319_church-ireland_en.html (Accessed 9 February 2013).

13. http://www.justice.ie/en/JELR/Cloyne_Rpt.pdf/Files/Cloyne_Rpt.pdf par 4.22 (Accessed 6 March 2013).

14. http://www.vatican.va/resources/resources_risposta-gilmore_20110903_en.html (Last accessed 30 March 2013).

kidnapping, causing serious bodily harm, fraud, sexual assaults on minors and more recently sexual assaults on intellectually disabled people and the possession by clerics of child pornography, all of which are crimes under civil law.

There is nothing wrong with that in principle. Rules of professional associations often provide for people to be de-registered or struck off the rolls for activities that are also crimes under civil law (doctors for drug dealing and lawyers for stealing money from trust accounts). The big difference is that canon law prevents those in the Church who are investigating those crimes to report the allegations and evidence to the police. If there is a requirement to report such crimes under the civil law, their oath of office requires them to follow canon law. Canon law and civil law have been in competition over clergy sex crimes against children since at least 1922, and the Church's supposedly 'parallel' line has crossed over into the legitimate area of competence of the state with disastrous consequences for children.

While the principle source of canon law is the pope, and occasionally general councils of the bishops of the Church, there is another way that canon law can be declared for a particular geographical area. This is through resolutions of bishops conferences that are approved by the Vatican.

Bishops Conferences

Although the Church is hierarchical with its pope, cardinals, archbishops, bishops, monsignors, and priests in descending order, it is not organised strictly like an international corporation where lower members of the hierarchy are answerable to the one higher in the pecking order. From about the fourth century, the Church organised itself into geographical regions, called dioceses, which derives from a Greek word, meaning 'group'. Each bishop is effectively the governor of his diocese, and controls it within the limits of canon law laid down by the popes.[15] But there were times in the past where the bishops

15. *Ibid* and http://www.parliament.vic.gov.au/images/stories/committees/fcdc/inquiries/57th/Child_Abuse_Inquiry/Submissions/Catholic_Church_in_Victoria.pdf (Accessed 6 April 2013) paragraph 4.4, Cardinal George Pell, evidence before the *Victorian Parliamentary Inquiry*, http://www.parliament.vic.gov.au/images/stories/committees/fcdc/inquiries/57th/Child_Abuse_Inquiry/Transcripts/Catholic_Archdiocese_of_Sydney_27-May-13.pdf, 3 (Accessed 22

came together, and agreed on laws to apply in their own regions. These councils or synods were usually named after the place where the meeting was held, such as Carthage, Basel etc.[16]

The authority of these regional councils was eventually formalised and incorporated into canon law which now recognises national conferences of bishops which can only be set up by the pope.[17] Australia, for example, has its Australian Catholic Bishops Conference. These conferences can pass resolutions which become canon law for the region if passed by a two thirds majority, and they receive the approval or *recognitio* of the Vatican.[18]

June 2013).

16. Thomas Doyle, *Affidavit, Jane Doe v Omi of Texas*, paragraph 15, http://www. bishop-accountability.org/news2008/03_04/2008_03_03_Doyle_TomDoyle.htm (Accessed 19 June 2013), *Catholic Encyclopaedia*, http://www.newadvent.org/ cathen/04423f.htm (Accessed 15 October 2013).

17. Canon 449.

18. Canon 455 §1: 'A conference of bishops can only issue general decrees in cases where universal law has prescribed it or a special mandate of the Apostolic See has established it either motu proprio or at the request of the conference itself.' §2: 'The decrees mentioned in §1, in order to be enacted validly in a plenary meeting, must be passed by at least a two thirds vote of the prelates who belong to the conference and possess a deliberative vote. They do not obtain binding force unless they have been legitimately promulgated after having been reviewed by the Apostolic See", http:// www.vatican.va/archive/ENG1104/__P1L.HTM (Accessed 6 March 2013) An example of a "special mandate" is when the Vatican directed Bishops Conferences to provide detailed guidelines for transfer of seminarians from one religious institution to another: http://www.catholicculture.org/culture/library/ view.cfm?recnum=5107 (Accessed 13 June 2013). In its response to the Irish Foreign Minister on 3 September 2011, the Vatican explained how Canon 455 operated: 'As canon 455 makes clear, the recognitio of the Holy See is required for any validly adopted decision of an Episcopal Conference which is to have binding force on all its members but it is not required for guidelines as such, nor is it required for the particular norms of individual Dioceses', http://www. vatican.va/resources/resources_risposta-gilmore_20110903_en.html (Accessed 6 March 2013). See also *Apostolos Solus* of Pope John Paul II, paragraph 18 http://www.vatican.va/holy_father/john_paul_ii/motu_proprio/documents/ hf_jp-ii_motu-proprio_22071998_apostolos-suos_en.html (Accessed 15 July 2013). See also Canons 455§4, 119§3. Nicholas Cafardi, *Another Long Lent The Abuse Crisis Resurfaces in Philadelphia,* http://www.commonwealmagazine.org/ another-long-lent (Accessed 4 June 2013). If there was no unanimity amongst the bishops, the Vatican could issue a 'special mandate'. In that case, only a two thirds majority was required.

The issue of a *recognitio* for Australia, Britain and Ireland whose bishops wanted to have the right to report clergy sexual abusers to the police is a significant matter in the saga of the cover up. As will be discussed in further detail in chapter 17, the Irish bishops in 1996 sent off to the Vatican for comment the *Framework Document* which provided for mandatory reporting of clergy crimes against children to the civil authorities. It was a document prepared by an advisory committee of the Irish Catholic Bishops Conference. The bishops received back a letter from the Congregation of the Clergy through the Papal Nuncio, Archbishop Storero, dated 31 January 1997, expressing concerns that its proposals for mandatory reporting gave rise to 'serious reservations of both a moral and a canonical nature'.[19]

The *Cloyne Report* criticised the letter because it cautioned against the implementation of the *Framework Document*.[20] The Vatican's response was legalistic. It said that it could not approve the document because it came from an advisory committee and, was not a validly passed decision of the Irish Catholic Bishops Conference. That was technically correct, but a very clear message was contained in the Papal Nuncio's letter that even if the formalities were followed, the proposal for mandatory reporting would not be approved. It was not just a question of it breaching the secrecy provisions of canon law. The letter suggested it was immoral for a bishop to report a priest to the police, even if the priest was a serial paedophile. And that message was subsequently repeated by the highest Vatican cardinals and officials in the years 2001 and 2002.

On 14 July 2010, after the publication of the *Cloyne Report*, the Irish Minister for Foreign Affairs, Ian Gilmore called in the Papal Nuncio and handed him a note accusing the Vatican of intervening in Irish domestic affairs by making priests believe that they could in conscience evade their responsibilities under Irish law. On 3 September, 2011, the Vatican responded, and explained that bishops were free to make their own laws and guidelines without the need

19. http://graphics8.nytimes.com/packages/pdf/world/Ireland-Catholic-Abuse. pdf?ref=europe, http://www.nytimes.com/2011/01/19/world/europe/19vatican. html?_r=0 (Accessed 9 July 2013). A Papal Nuncio is the diplomatic representative of the Holy See, holding ambassadorial status.
20. http://www.justice.ie/en/JELR/Cloyne_Rpt.pdf/Files/Cloyne_Rpt.pdf paragraph 4.22 (Accessed 6 March 2013).

to have approval from the Vatican, provided that such laws and guidelines were 'not contrary to canon law'.[21] But that was the problem, as Archbishop Storero's letter pointed out, with mandatory reporting.

There were many things such as education, awareness, behaviour protocols and counselling for victims that were not contrary to canon law, and could be adopted by individual bishops. But in relation to mandatory reporting to the police of the crimes of priests against children, the Congregation for the Clergy was quite specific: mandatory reporting by bishops conflicted with canon law. And it did. *Crimen Sollicitationis*, in force prior to 1983, required pontifical secrecy in the investigation of such matters, and there were no exceptions for reporting to the police. The same was true of Canon 1395 of the *1983 Code of Canon Law,* to which pontifical secrecy applied by reason of the decree *Secreta Continere* (1974).

The Australian bishops never received a *recognitio* from Rome for their 1996 proposals for mandatory reporting contained in their *Towards Healing* protocol for dealing with clergy sexual abuse. The bishops were not unanimous because Archbishop Pell of Melbourne declined to sign it, and set up his own protocol called *The Melbourne Response*. But given the attitude of the Vatican to the issue of reporting priests to the police at the time, there was little point in applying for it. The secrecy provisions of the *1983 Code of Canon Law* and the *2001 Motu Proprio* decrees still applied, and the proposals for reporting in *Towards Healing* conflicted with canon law. The Australian bishops were in the same position as their Irish brethren. *Towards Healing*, like the *Framework Document*, also dealt with matters such as counselling, care of the victims, education etc, none of which conflicted with canon law. Each bishop was free to adopt the guidelines on those matters, but they were not free to report to the police the information that they had gained in their investigations.

In 2001, a distinguished Catholic lawyer and former member of the United Kingdom's highest court, the judicial committee of House of Lords, Lord Nolan, advised the British bishops that they had to have a form of mandatory reporting. The Catholic Bishops Conference of England and Wales adopted his proposals. The Vatican

---

21. http://www.vatican.va/resources/resources_risposta-gilmore_20110903_en.html (Accessed 6 March 2013).

did not provide a *recognitio* for the proposals so as to make them canon law for the area covered by the Bishops Conference.[22]

The American Catholic Bishops Conference, however, did receive a *recognitio* for its proposals, but not for what they originally wanted— the right to report sex abusing priests to the police irrespective of whether there was a local law requiring reporting. The Vatican would only approve an exception to pontifical secrecy where the local law required it.[23]

On 18 October 2012, the Victoria Deputy Police Commissioner, Graham Ashton told the *Victorian Parliamentary Inquiry* that of the 620 cases of clergy sexual abuse dealt with internally by the four Victorian dioceses since 1996, none had been reported by the Church to the police.[24] The Victorian Church's submission to the *Victorian Parliamentary Inquiry* did not dispute that figure, but a later submission on behalf of the Archdiocese of Melbourne said it was 611 in total, with 304 dealt with by the Melbourne Archdiocese's *The Melbourne Response* protocol and the balance of 307 by the *Towards Healing* protocol of the other three Victorian dioceses.[25] Mr Peter O'Callaghan QC, *The Melbourne Response*'s Independent Commissioner who handled 304 complaints said that the majority

---

22. Cumberlege Review of the Nolan Report, paragraph 2.17, http://www.cathcom.org/mysharedaccounts/cumberlege/report/downloads/CathCom_Cumberlege2.pdf. Nor is there any indication on the Vatican website that it has been subsequently approved.(Accessed 9 February 2013).
    Geoffrey Robertson QC, *The Case of the Pope,* chapter 2 paragraph 45.

23. http://www.vatican.va/roman_curia/congregations/cbishops/documents/rc_con_cbishops_doc_20021216_recognitio-usa_en.html (Accessed 9 February 2013)
    See also Ladislas Orsy SJ, *Bishops Norms: Commentary and Evaluation,* http://www.bc.edu/dam/files/schools/law/lawreviews/journals/bclawr/44_4/04_FMS.htm (Accessed 9 February 2013).

24. For the terms of reference and the submissions, see http://www.parliament.vic.gov.au/images/stories/committees/fcdc/inquiries/57th/Child_Abuse_Inquiry/Final_FCDC_CAinROs_Submission_Guide.pdf (Accessed 3 July 2013), http://www.parliament.vic.gov.au/images/stories/committees/fcdc/inquiries/57th/Child_Abuse_Inquiry/Right_of_Reply/Right_of_Reply_Francis_Moore.pdf (Accessed 10 August 2013).

25. http://www.parliament.vic.gov.au/images/stories/committees/fcdc/inquiries/57th/Child_Abuse_Inquiry/Submissions/Catholic_Church_in_Victoria.pdf (Accessed 6 April 2013), 3, and http://www.parliament.vic.gov.au/images/stories/committees/fcdc/inquiries/57th/Child_Abuse_Inquiry/Right_of_Reply/Right_of_Reply_Francis_Moore.pdf (Accessed 10 August 2013).

of them had been reported by the victims.[26] He said that he had 'effectively' referred complaints to the police by making appointments for victims who were willing to go to the police to do so.[27] But the whole point that Ashton was making, and *Victorian Parliamentary Inquiry* accepted, was that *the Church* had never reported any of these incidents to the police.[28]

The continued existence of pontifical secrecy over the Church's internal investigations and the existence of punishments under canon law for breaching that secrecy, go a long way to explaining why the Church authorities failed to report.

On 3 May 2011, Cardinal Levada, the Prefect of the Congregation for the Doctrine of the Faith, sent out a circular letter to all bishops providing guidelines to assist bishops' conferences write their protocols for dealing with clerical sexual abuse of minors, and required that all such guidelines contain a provision that 'the prescriptions of civil law regarding the reporting of such crimes to the designated authority should always be followed.'[29]

Once the guidelines of bishops conferences have been approved by the Vatican under Canon 455, this conflict between canon and civil law over child sexual abuse should disappear, provided there is a civil law reporting. Canon law will then 'yield' to civil law under Canon 22. In the meantime, bishops were effectively given a dispensation from the pontifical secrecy requirements to enable them to report sexual abuse to the police where the local civil law required it.[30] However, there

---

26. http://www.parliament.vic.gov.au/images/stories/committees/fcdc/inquiries/57th/Child_Abuse_Inquiry/Right_of_Reply/Right_of_Reply_P._OCallaghan_Part_1.pdf (Accessed 3 July 2013).

27. http://www.parliament.vic.gov.au/images/stories/committees/fcdc/inquiries/57th/Child_Abuse_Inquiry/Right_of_Reply/Right_of_Reply_P._OCallaghan_Part_1.pdf page 3(c) (Accessed 25 June 2013).

28. *Betrayal of Trust*, Report of the *Victorian Parliamentary Inquiry*, paragraph 7.3.6, 170, https://s3-ap-southeast-2.amazonaws.com/family-and-community-development-committee/Inquiry+into+Handling+of+Abuse_Volume+1_FINAL_web.pdf (Accessed 14 November 2013).

29. http://www.vatican.va/roman_curia/congregations/cfaith/documents/rc_con_cfaith_doc_20110503_abuso-minori_en.html (Accessed 9 February 2013).

30. Canons 85 and 87, and Beal, Coriden and Green, *New Commentary on the Code of Canon Law*, 130–132and Dr Rodger Austin at the *Maitland-Newcastle Inquiry*, http://www.lawlink.nsw.gov.au/lawlink/Special_Projects/ll_splprojects.nsf/vwFiles/Transcript_Day_20_-_TOR_2_-_31_July_2013.pdf/$file/Transcript_Day_20_-_TOR_2_-_31_July_2013.pdf , 2233.

were comments by the Vatican spokesman, Fr Federico Lombardi SJ on 15 July 2010 that suggest that reporting to the police cannot take place once the canonical investigation and trial starts.[31]

Because of the terms of the Vatican's guidelines, there are still systemic problems because of its continued insistence that the canonical investigation be subject to pontifical secrecy. As will be shown below, the not so 'parallel' system of justice, which has been so destructive to children, will in many places continue, simply because there are no civil laws requiring reporting, and for a very good reason.

Civil society in much of the English speaking world decided more than thirty years ago, that the moral sense in the community about reporting serious crimes to the police was so strong that there was no need for there to be laws to make it criminal not to report.[32] The crime of not reporting serious crimes to the police, known as 'misprision of felony', was abolished in most jurisdictions.

Unfortunately, and no doubt to the surprise of many, the Church at its highest levels did not share this moral sense when it came to its priests' sex crimes against children. Priests, in its view, were special, and needed to be treated differently and more leniently to the common herd, and bishops had a moral obligation not to report their crimes to the police. The clericalism that is so obvious in the concordats that the Vatican has negotiated with a few sympathetic countries is still reflected in canon law as it applies everywhere.[33]

The Interpretation of Canon Law

The *1983 Code of Canon Law* has rules of interpretation which are generally the same as in our English system of law.[34] Canon law is

---

31. http://www.vatican.va/resources/resources_lombardi-nota-norme_en.html (Accessed 21 July 2013).
32. See New South Wales Law Reform Commission, http://www.lawreform.lawlink. nsw.gov.au/agdbasev7wr/lrc/documents/pdf/report_93.pdf paragraph 3.58 (Accessed 16 July 2013).
33. See chapter 6: The Concordats or treaties between the Vatican and Latvia, Poland, Italy, the Dominican Republic, Franco's Spain, Colombia and to a lesser extent Venezuela, Argentina, Bolivia and Paraguay give clergy a privileged status under the law. The most extreme form of it is in Colombia under the 1973 Concordat where bishops are effectively above the law, and cannot be tried for crimes in the state courts.
34. There are some differences of interpretation, the most significant being that if there is reasonable doubt about the meaning of a text (a 'doubt of law'), the

to be understood according to the proper meaning of the words considered in their text and context, and if there is any ambiguity, resort can be had to other sources, such as to 'parallel places . . . to the purposes and circumstances of the law, and to the mind of the legislator' to determine their meaning.[35] But if the meaning is clear, there is no need to resort to these other sources.[36]

There are some other differences between canon law, and the English common law system. The ultimate authority for the meaning of the law in the English common law system rests with the courts, whereas in canon law, it rests with the legislature.[37] Likewise, in canon law, there is no system of precedent, and a decision made in a particular case only binds those parties to it.[38]

Lawyers in the common law system consult the decisions of courts to determine what a particular law might mean. On the other hand, canon lawyers consult statements by the legislature and scholarly commentaries to clarify the meaning.[39]

---

ordinance has no binding force, which has no equivalent in Australian civil law: Ladislas Orsy SJ, *Bishops Norms: Commentary and Evaluation,* http://www. bc.edu/dam/files/schools/law/lawreviews/journals/bclawr/44_4/04_FMS.htm (Accessed 9 February 2013).

35. See Canon 17.

36. Edward Peters:, 'Lest Amateurs Argue Canon Law: A Reply to Patrick Gordon's brief against Bp Thomas Daily', in *Angelicum* 83 (2006): 121–142.http://www. canonlaw.info/a_gordon.htm (Accessed 3 July 2013), internet copy, between footnotes 30 and 31.

37. Canon 16§1 'The legislator authentically interprets laws as does the one to whom the same legislator has entrusted the power of authentically interpreting'. And see Peters *ibid*, 'Common law is a system of judicial supremacy; canon law is a system of legislative supremacy', Doyle, *Canon Law: What is It?*, *http://www. awrsipe.com/doyle/2006/2006-02-Canon_Law-What_Is_It.pdf* (Accessed 24 July 2013).

38. Canon 16§3. Delaney, criticises this aspect of canon law because it prevents a jurisprudence being developed to allow consistency of decision making in canonical courts: Delaney, *Canonical Implications of the Response of the Catholic Church in Australia to Child Sexual in Australia*, 263ff.

39. Edward Peters 'Lest Amateurs Argue Canon Law: A reply to Patrick Gordon's brief against Bp. Thomas Daily', in *Angelicum,* 83 (2006): 121–142, http://www. canonlaw.info/a_gordon.htm (Accessed 3 July 2013), internet copy between footnotes 34 and 35. In common law systems, it has become much more common to cite academic writings than it used to be as authority for particular interpretations. German continental law has diverged from canon law and is now closer to the common law system. While the German courts will consult

Canon 20 distinguishes between general laws that apply to the whole Church and particular laws which apply to the Church in a specific region.[40] The particular law or 'norm' created by the *recognitio* of the proposals arising from the Dallas Charter in 2002 became the particular law, that is, canon law for the United States requiring Church authorities to comply with reporting laws on child sexual abuse.

The universal law contained in *Crimen Sollicitationis*, the *1983 Code of Canon Law*, with the 1974 decree *Secreta Continere*, and the *2001 Motu Proprio* requiring secrecy for the Church's investigations applied to all other regions of the Church covered by Bishops Conferences which did not have the benefit of such an exception. Australia was one of them.

In 2010, the Vatican granted the same limited exception enjoyed by the United States by way of a dispensation with an instruction from the Congregation for the Doctrine of the Faith. Church authorities are now entitled to report allegations of sexual abuse to the civil authorities where there is a local law requiring reporting. In Australia, apart from mandatory reporting of 'children at risk', only the State of New South Wales has a law requiring reporting of 'historic' abuse, that is, where the victims are no longer children. In the other states, pontifical secrecy prevents Church authorities from reporting historic abuse to the police, even if they wanted to.

---

scholarly commentaries, which are not binding on them, they do not consult the legislature to determine the meaning. That is left to the courts, not the legislature. The decisions of the German Federal Constitutional Court are legally binding. On the other hand the decisions of other courts—even the highest federal courts— do not have the same legally binding effect. But the German State supreme courts have to enforce the federal courts decisions in order to ensure the consistency of jurisdiction. They will reverse decisions of the country and local courts which are out of line. The European Court of Justice in Luxembourg interprets the law of the European Union and their decisions are legally binding. Advice of Dr Stefan von der Beck, Chief Judge, Suprme Court, Oldenburg (Lower Saxony), Germany in private correspondence with the author in January 2014.

40. John P Beal, James A Coriden and Thomas J Green, *New Commentary on the Code of Canon Law* (Mahwah, NJ: Paulist Press, 2000), 83.

8

The Canonical System of Trials

Canon law is based on Roman law, and therefore its trial method is the European continental inquisitorial system, rather than the common law adversarial one.

In the common law system, investigations take place outside the court system, through police, public prosecutors or district attorneys. Charges are then laid, and the matter goes to trial where the judge or judge and jury listen to the evidence presented by both sides. The court then makes a decision. The 'trial' only starts once the investigation by the prosecution and defence has been completed. The judge in the common law system is more like a football referee, making sure the rules of the game are observed, rules of evidence applied, and everyone has a fair go at presenting their case. Judges decide cases on the evidence presented. It is not the judge's role in the common law system to advise the parties about what evidence they should produce. Their role is to blow the whistle if they find that, for example, one of the parties is trying to introduce material which is contrary to the laws of evidence or breaches some other procedural rules.

The European continental system, like canon law, gives the judge a much more active role, and the important difference with the common law system is that the trial begins as soon as complaint is made. That does not mean that the judge will personally carry out the investigation. In the German system, for example, this will be done by the state's public prosecution department. The judge will be there to assist with matters such as search warrants and for signing arrest warrants at the prosecutor's request. The process for finding facts and listening to testimony takes place in a series of hearings that are normally conducted over a long stretch of time rather than in a single trial as in the common law system.[1]

There is a certain amount of cross over in the two systems. Coronial inquiries in the common law system, where the coroner investigates the cause of death or a fire, are similar to the inquisitorial system. The coroner has police assisting him, and perhaps a counsel assisting. They will have continuous discussions about where the investigation is leading. And as further pieces of evidence start trickling in, the coroner might well direct further investigations along some other paths.

Royal commissions and state tribunals, like the New South Wales Independent Commission Against Corruption (ICAC), are set up in the same way. And likewise, in the European continental system, defence lawyers still have plenty to do in gathering their own evidence to counter the case that they expect will be made against their client. They will not leave that entirely to the judge.

There are many arguments as to which system is 'better'. The fear amongst those in the common law system is that the judge might become too closely associated with the case of one of the parties to be seen as impartial. The fear amongst European continental lawyers about the common law system is that the 'truth' may not come out in a system where the evidence to be presented is at the discretion of the opposing litigants. The reality is that in modern times the two seem

---

1. The same is true of canon law: Rev Kevin E McKenna, JCD, *Canon Law Seminar for Media*, May 25, 2010, Canon Law Society of America, "The complaint is sometimes made about the confidentiality that is imposed on a canonical trial when an allegation of sexual abuse has been made. In the canonical system it is the role of the judges (or those delegated by the judges) rather than the representatives (or lawyers) of the parties, to gather oral and written evidence. The process for finding facts and testimony takes place in a series of hearings that are normally conducted over a long stretch of time rather than in a single trial as in a civil case. Because in the canonical system of law evidence is normally to be accumulated and assembled over time, judges typically impose "confidentiality" restrictions upon witnesses and their testimony to prevent the possible contamination of other witnesses who may appear later before the court", http://www.docstoc.com/docs/83976670/USCCB-CANON-LAW-SEMINAR-2010-MCKENNAdoc---Welcome---The-Catholic (Accessed 24 July 2013). Edward N Peters, http://www.themediareport.com/wp-content/uploads/2012/08/Peters-reply-to-Wall-and-Doyle.pdf, paragraph 73, footnote 116 (Accessed 9 February 2013).

to be coming closer together with elements of both systems being used where they appear to be more appropriate.[2]

Where an allegation of child abuse is made against a cleric, Canon 1717 of the *1983 Code of Canon Law* requires a bishop to undertake a 'preliminary investigation', and under the *2001 Motu Proprio*, he is to send off the results of his investigation to the Congregation for the Doctrine of the Faith in Rome which will then instruct him on how to proceed. The Congregation may then order a penal trial. If that occurs, then the proceedings start to look more like the common law adversarial system, with canon lawyers appearing for the prosecution and the defence. The same occurs if the Congregation itself decides to conduct the trial. The Congregation has its own 'Promoter of Justice', and for many years it was Monsignor Scicluna who has a cameo role in this story. His function certainly has all the hallmarks of a common law prosecutor with which those in the English-speaking world will be familiar, the main difference being that witnesses are only allowed to be questioned by the judges.[3]

The importance of this discussion on the difference between the two systems relates to the time when the secrecy provisions apply. If, for example, the secrecy provisions only applied when a formal canonical trial was ordered after the results of the preliminary investigation went to Rome, then there was nothing to stop a bishop from going to the police with the results of his preliminary investigation. On the other hand, if secrecy applies from the time the allegation is made and the preliminary investigation commenced, then bishops are not free to go to the police—not even to report the allegation.

The decree *Secreta Continere,* discussed below, imposes pontifical secrecy on 'extrajudicial allegations' and 'trials', but the trial in the broad sense in the canon law system (as it does in the European continental system) commences the moment the complaint is made and the investigation starts.[4]

---

2. Marfolding and Eylandt: *Civil Litigation in New South Wales: Empirical and Analytical Comparisons with Germany*, University of New South Wales Faculty of Law Research Series 2010, Paper No. 28, 8.
3. Cafardi, *Before Dallas*, 42.
4. Thomas Doyle, http://reform-network.net/?p=3006 (Accessed 3 July 2013), paragraph 23, John P Beal 'The 1962 Instruction: Crimen Sollicitationis: Caught Red Handed or Handed a Red Herring?', in 41 *Studia Canonica* 199 at 228ff, http://www.vatican.va/resources/Beal-article-studia-canonica41-2007-pp.199-236.pdf (Accessed 3 July 2013).

Pope John XXIII

9

Canon Law on Clergy Sexual Abuse of Children

At least since the time of Pope Innocent III in 1198, the cleric found guilty of the sexual abuse of children, homosexuality or bestiality was first to be dismissed from the priesthood, and he was to be handed over to the civil authorities to be dealt with according to the civil law.

The canonical term for dismissing a priest is 'laicisation', but that term can also cover the situation where a priest who wants to get married applies to be 'laicised' so as to be released from his obligations of celibacy. The word 'defrocking' is more often associated with the dismissal of Protestant ministers, but it was used in the *1917 Code of Canon Law*, meaning the deprivation of the clerical garb. That code referred to the dismissal of a priest as a *degradatio*, the Church's equivalent of a dishonourable discharge in the military.[1] Under the *1983 Code of Canon Law*, only dismissal from the clerical state (formerly *degradatio*) remains.[2] To avoid confusion, the word 'dismissal' will be used to cover the situation where a priest is 'laicised' against his will.

In 1917, the Church promulgated the first *Code of Canon Law*. The work of creating the Code involved using, modifying or discarding decrees that the Church thought were relevant or irrelevant for the time. Cardinal Gasparri led the Pontifical Commission for the Codifcation of Canon Law, and its assistant from 1904 to 1916 was Monisgnor Eugenio Pacelli, the future Pope Pius XII. The Commission discarded the decress of Pope Celestine III, Innocent III, Leo X, Pope

---

1. *Catholic Encyclopaedia,* http://www.newadvent.org/cathen/04677c.htm (Accessed 9 July 2013).
2. John P Beal, James A Coriden and Thomas J Green, *New Commentary on the Code of Canon Law* (Mahwah, NJ: paulist Press, 2000),382.

St Pius V, the Fourth and Fifth Lateran Councils and the Council of Trent, requiring priests guilty of sexually assaulting children to be handed over to the civil authorities. The canon law and practice of handing over the priest for punishment in accordance with the civil law had been abandoned. The code provided that those who sexually abused children were to be suspended, 'declared infamous', 'deprived of any office' and in more 'more serious cases' shall be dismissed.[3]

Five years later, by 1922, when *Crimen Sollicitationis* was published, these requirements were watered down. There would be no more declarations of infamy, and the requirement to dismiss for 'more serious cases' had become one where dismissal was available only where there was an impossibility of reform. These crimes were now to be kept secret, and the priests could be transferred to another territory to avoid 'scandal'.[4] These provisions reflected the twin concerns of the Vatican: the avoidance of 'scandal' and treating priests differently because they had been 'ontologically changed' when they were anointed by God at ordination. The revival of privilege of clergy through the back door of secrecy had begun.[5]

As indicated earlier, the whole point of having a code for any system of law is so that people can go to a single document to find out the law on a particular matter. It does not always work that way with canon law. When a state wants to change one of its codes, the changes it makes are incorporated into the code. The Church, on the other hand generally retains the code in its original form, but the Pope creates supplementary decrees. That was the case with *Crimen Sollicitationis*. The first *Code of Canon Law* was promulgated in 1917, and *Crimen Sollicitationis* became part of canon law in 1922. The process is sometimes analogous to the common law system where regulations, consistent with the Act authorising them, provide further detail, but sometimes the new decree in canon law will provide for something completely inconsistent, such as the *2001 Motu Proprio*.[6]

---

3. Canon 2359 §2 *1917 Code of Canon Law.*
4. *Crimen Sollicitationis,* Clauses 64(d), 68 & 69. http://www.vatican.va/resources/resources_crimen-sollicitationis-1962_en.html (Accessed 4 August 2013).
5. http://reform-network.net/?p=3006 paragraph 27 (Accessed 3 July 2013).
6. Edward N Peters, http://www.themediareport.com/wp-content/uploads/2012/08/Peters-reply-to-Wall-and-Doyle.pdf, paragraphs 141–143 (Accessed 9 February 2013). Peters argues that *Crimen Sollicitationis* was more by way of providing further detail, in the manner of a regulation in civil law. But the

The Vatican prefers to change the interpretation of the canons rather than the canons themselves.[7] The difficulty of coming to grips with such changes was one of the things that the *Murphy Dublin Report* criticised about canon law, accusing it of lacking one of the basic features of a coherent legal system.[8]

Crimen Sollicitationis continued in force until 1962 when it was reissued, with some minor changes. The only real difference between the two was that the 1962 document applied the procedures to clerics who were also members of religious orders.[9] In 1983, it was repealed by the promulgation of the new *Code of Canon Law* which had its own canon to deal with the sexual abuse of minors by clerics.[10] Its language about priests who committed sex crimes against children was much milder than that used in the *1917 Code*. But worse than that, it severely weakened the capacity of canon law to protect children by making it much more difficult to dismiss child sexual abusers from the priesthood. Canon law under *Crimen Sollicitationis* and the *1917 Code* was bad enough, but after the *1983 Code* came into force, it was hopeless.

---

analogy breaks down because it went much further than the rule making power normally granted under civil law, by imposing automatic excommunication for breach of the secrecy provisions.

7. Archbishop Coleridge at the *Australian Royal Commission,* http://www. childabuseroyalcommission.gov.au/wp-content/uploads/2013/08/Transcript-RC_IRCSA_Day-026_11-Dec-2013_Public.pdf p 2740 (Accessed 13 December 2013).

8. http://www.justice.ie/en/JELR/DACOI%20Part%201.pdf/Files/DACOI%20 Part%201.pdf (Accessed 25 April 2013), paragraphs 4.88–4.89

9. *Murphy Dublin Report,* Part 1 http://www.justice.ie/en/JELR/DACOI%20 Part%201.pdf/Files/DACOI%20Part%201.pdf paragraph 4.20 (Accessed 25 April 2013), John P Beal: 'The 1962 Instruction: Crimen Sollicitationis: Caught Red Handed or Handed a Red Herring?', 41 *Studia Canonica,* 199 at 201, http:// www.vatican.va/resources/Beal-article-studia-canonica41-2007-pp.199-236.pdf (Accessed 16 July 2013). However, Fr Thomas Doyle says that the only difference was in relation to formularies to be used in the proceedings, http://reform-network.net/?p=3006, paragraph 12 (Accessed 2 October 2013). Clause 4 of *Crimen Sollicitationis* says that the local bishop is a judge for cases involving priests who are also members of religious orders, but that does not prevent the religious Superior to discipline them and to remove them from any ministry. Clause 74 provides that exempt religious can proceed either administratively or judicially, and Superiors of non-exempt religious can proceed only administratively. Where the decision is to expel the guilty party from religious life, the expulsion has no effect until approved by the Holy Office.

10. Canon 1395.

Crimen Sollicitationis

Crimen Sollicitationis contains an introduction, followed by five parts or 'titles'.[11] The first four titles deal with the crime of soliciting sex in the confessional, the procedures to be followed, and the penalties to be imposed. Title five has the heading *Crimen Pessimum*, (Latin for 'the worst crime'), namely homosexuality, bestiality and sexually assaulting children. Somewhat unusually for a legal document in any language or system, it contains an exclamation: '. . . should some cleric (God forbid) happen to be accused of it . . .'

However, when you read the penalties imposed by *Crimen Sollicitationis* for clerics who engaged in (God forbid) such activities, none of them seem to have been regarded as so shocking after all.

On the front page of the document, in bold letters is this:

**TO BE KEPT CAREFULLY IN THE SECRET ARCHIVE
OF THE CURIA FOR INTERNAL USE.
NOT TO BE PUBLISHED OR AUGMENTED WITH COMMENTARIES**

The 'curia' referred to in this heading to the document is the central office of the bishop's diocese. The *1917 Code of Canon Law* required every bishop to have a 'secret archive of the curia' under the care of the chancellor, who alone was to have the key.[12] No one was to have access to this safe without the consent of the bishop, the vicar general or the chancellor.[13]

---

11. http://www.vatican.va/resources/resources_crimen-sollicitationis-1962_en.html (Accessed 4 August 2013).

12. *Code of Canon Law: Latin-English Edition* (Washington: Canon Law Society of America, 1984) Canon 379 and Canon 372.4, http://cssronline.org/CSSR/Archival/1997/1997_303.pdf (Accessed 15 October 2013). Canon 377 provides that only the chancellor is to have the key. Canon 379 also provides: 'Promptly, once a year, documents in criminal cases are to be burned in moral cases, or in which the defendant has died or ten years have passed since the condemnatory sentence, retaining only a brief summary of the facts, with the text of the definitive sentence', http://books.google.com.tr/books?id=2XbtF6Y21LUC&pg=PA148&lpg=PA148&dq=1917+Code+of+Canon+law+diocesan+archives&source=bl&ots=onqWZGzhHf&sig=qAYDuBKJFhEQgJadpIb2zbeeVwI&hl=en&sa=X&ei=z8VdUojvB-jb4QSwjoHADw&redir_esc=y#v=onepage&q=1917%20Code%20of%20Canon%20law%20diocesan%20archives&f=false (Accessed 16 October 2013).

13. Canon 377.

The requirement to keep a written law in a locked safe with very few people having access to it is strange, because generally a very important feature of any coherent legal system is that it be published, and to be available for anyone to consult it, especially those who are governed by it. But a critical feature of the whole policy of cover up was that no one outside select members of the clergy should know about this system of secret investigations and trials. The success of the de facto revival of the 'privilege of clergy' depended on secular society not knowing about it. The bishops who had to deal with the matter had to know the procedures, but it was better that as few people as possible knew about them.

Although one can now find *Crimen Sollicitationis* on the Vatican website, this publication only occurred in 2003.[14] Bishops and clergy involved in Church investigations were allowed to know, but the rest of the world was not. This was a deliberate policy, and not something that simply happened as a sort of side effect of a clumsy attempt to protect the good names of participants in the Church investigation. It reflects the Church's obsession with 'scandal', a word which appears twenty-eight times throughout the *1983 Code of Canon Law*. The words 'secrecy' or 'secret' appear thirty-five times, three times more than 'Scripture'. The avoidance of 'scandal' is an expression that appears frequently in the Church's internal documents on child sexual abuse matters. A concern about 'scandal' was understandable because that meant the loss of faith, and therefore, membership of the Church.

The first part of *Crimen Sollicitationis,* dealing with soliciting sex in the confessional required the Catholic faithful who had been 'solicited', to report the matter to the bishop, who would then carry out an investigation.[15] The document then describes, in fairly convoluted

---

14. It was referred to in Cardinal Ratzinger's letter of 18 May 2001 and became common knowledge after that, with several commentators in 2003 claiming it was the 'smoking gun' on the cover up of sexual abuse, http://www.natcath.org/NCR_Online/archives2/2003c/081503/081503n.htm (Accessed 15 July 2013). It was referred to in some court cases in the United States in 2005 and 2008: Fr Thomas Doyle, http://reform-network.net/?p=3006 paragraphs 6–14ff (Accessed 3 July 2013). It was published on the Vatican website in 2003, Delaney, *Canonical Implications of the Response of the Catholic Church in Australia,* 152, footnote 21.

15. Clauses 5–28, http://www.vatican.va/resources/resources_crimen-sollicitationis-1962_en.html (Accessed 4 August 2013).

language the procedures that are to apply. All those involved in the investigation, the bishop, the complainant, witnesses, note takers and canon lawyers are bound by the 'secret of the Holy Office'.

> All those persons in any way associated with the tribunal, or knowledgeable of these matters by reason of their office, are bound to observe inviolably the strictest confidentiality, commonly known as the secret of the Holy Office, **in all things and with all persons,** under pain of incurring automatic excommunication, ipso facto and undeclared, reserved to the sole person of the Supreme Pontiff . . . . [16] (my emphasis).

The confidentiality applies to 'all persons', including those who know about what went on inside the tribunal 'by reason of their office'. That includes the people involved in the proceedings themselves, and the bishop or religious superior to whom they have to report. Significantly, there is no exception for reporting to the police.

The person conducting the investigation on behalf of the bishop is to forward all documents and findings to the bishop, without keeping a copy for himself.[17]

Title V which includes sexual abuse of children under the rubric of *crimen pessimum* provides that the same procedures are to apply to canonical investigations of sex crimes against children with appropriate changes as the nature of the case requires.[18] The Latin phrase is *mutatis mutandis*, a term which is also used in civil law. It means that one can make more or less superficial modifications to procedure to suit the case.[19]

---

16. *Ibid,* Clauses 11, and see also on secrecy, clauses 13, 23 and 70.
17. *Ibid*, Clause 22.
18. *Ibid*, Clause 72 and 73.
19. There were matters relevant to soliciting in the confessional that were not relevant to sexual abuse of children outside the confessional, for example, that the penitent had the obligation to 'denounce' the priest to whom the confession was made. Such matters were ignored under mutatis mutandis. John P Beal in 'The 1962 Instruction*, Crimen Sollicitationis:* Caught Red Handed or Handed a Red Herring?' 41 *Studia Canonica* 199 at 228ff, http://www.vatican.va/resources/Beal-article-studia-canonica41-2007-pp.199-236.pdf , 233 (Accessed 4 March 2013). See also Edward N Peters deposition, http://www.themediareport.com/wp-content/uploads/2012/08/Peters-reply-to-Wall-and-Doyle.pdf (Accessed 3 July

If the allegations are found to be false, all the evidence is to be destroyed. If the evidence is found to be vague and indeterminate, the evidence is to be archived, in case another allegation is made in the future.[20]

If the evidence of a crime is considered grave enough, but not yet sufficient to file a formal complaint, the bishop is to 'admonish' the accused priest 'paternally' and 'gravely' with a first or second warning and is to threaten him with a trial if a new accusation is brought.[21]

If it is decided to have a formal trial against the priest, he can be suspended from exercising his 'sacred ministry' until the conclusion of the trial.[22]

Graduated penalties are imposed including suspension from saying Mass, administering the sacraments, spiritual exercises in a religious house, etc. However, the penalty of dismissal, is available

> . . . only when, all things considered, it appears evident that the Defendant, in the depth of his malice, has, in his abuse of the sacred ministry, with grave scandal to the faithful and harm to souls, attained such a degree of temerity and habitude, that there seems to be no hope, humanly speaking, or almost no hope, of his amendment.[23]

This formed the canonical basis before 1983, for what came to be

---

2013). The Vatican's lawyer in America, Jeffrey Lena has claimed that bishops had a discretion to dispense with pontifical secrecy where there was conflict with civil law, http://www.nbcnews.com/id/37182162/ns/world_news-europe/ (Accessed 6 March 2013). There is some suggestion of this in Beal's *Studia Canonica* article at 223, but it contradicts what he had earlier written about *mutatis mutandis* being confined to superficial changes to procedure. Dispensing with pontifical secrecy to allow reporting to the police with a penalty of automatic excommunication is hardly a superficial change of procedure. Whatever may have been the position prior to 1983, there is no such *mutatis mutandis* provision in the *1983 Code of Canon Law.* Canon 87 reserves dispensations in penal procedural matters to the Vatican. In its response to the Irish Foreign Minister, the Vatican did not suggest there was such a discretion. If the bishops did have this discretion it would have provided a complete defense to the claim that the Vatican had interfered in Irish affairs.

20. Clause 42(b), http://www.vatican.va/resources/resources_crimen-sollicitationis-1962_en.html (Accessed 4 August 2013).

21. Clause 42 (c), http://www.vatican.va/resources/resources_crimen-sollicitationis-1962_en.html (Accessed 4 August 2013).

22. *Ibid*, Clause 51.

23. *Ibid*, Clause 63.

known as the 'pastoral approach' to clergy sex crimes. In other words, efforts would be made to 'cure' him, and only if there was no hope, or almost no hope of being cured, was he to be dismissed. Significantly, there was no 'pastoral approach' to victims, other than to give them a right to claim damages in the course of a canonical trial, which was never likely to happen.

Crimen Sollicitationis also envisaged that the abusing priest might be shifted around. If he is 'admonished' or 'convicted', and transfers to another diocese, the new bishop is to be informed of 'the priest's record and his legal status'.[24]

Repeal of Administrative Dismissal

The *1917 Code of Canon Law* had allowed a bishop to suspend a priest on the basis of an 'informed conscience' if he was satisfied that he had sexually abused children. There was no trial or dismissal as such, and the bishop still had the obligations to support him.[25] However, in 1971, the Congregation for the Doctrine of the Faith issued new instructions for 'administrative laicisation', allowing for the bishop to petition the Congregation for a decree of dismissal on the basis of his living a 'depraved life'.[26]

In 1980 Pope John Paul II, two years after becoming pope, introduced changes to the role of the Congregation for the Doctrine of the Faith in relation to the simpler form of dismissal. The 1970s saw many priests leaving the priesthood, and Pope John Paul II, on his election as pope in 1978, decided to make it harder for them to be 'laicised'. On 14 October, 1980 he brought in new rules that not only achieved that, but also abolished the right of the bishop to petition the Congregation for 'administrative laicisation'. Only the priest himself could request to be laicised.[27]

The removal of this measure was disastrous because it became virtually impossible to dismiss a priest from the priesthood without his consent, and not all of them consented, because while they were

---

24. Clauses 68–69.
25. Nicholas Cafardi, *Before Dallas*, 58.
26. Nicholas Cafardi, *Before Dallas,* 62, Congregation for the Doctrine of the Faith, October 14 1980, *Acta Apostolicae Sedis*, 72 (1980): 1132–37.
27. Nicholas Cafardi, *Before Dallas*, 62.

still not dismissed, they were entitled, under canon law, to receive an income and support from the Church.

The *1983 Code of Canon Law*

The *1983 Code of Canon Law* had an even more disastrous effect on the capacity of bishops to deal with priest sexual abusers, because it not only entrenched Pope John Paul II's changes to administrative dismissal, but it also introduced limitation periods that did not exist under *Crimen Sollicitationis*. It marks the *apotheosis* of clericalism, where the rights and privileges of clergy became far more important than the rights of the victims of clerical sexual abuse.

Sexual abuse of children under the *1983 Code of Canon Law* is a canonical crime if committed by clerics, but not if committed by lay people.[28] Under canon law, religious brothers and nuns are regarded as lay people because they do not administer the sacraments, the rituals whereby God's grace is received by believers. However, canon law does have special rules governing them, and they can be dismissed from their religious Congregations or Orders for sexual abuse of children.[29] To that extent, it continued in the tradition of the *1917 Code of Canon Law* which had similar provisions.

Dismissal from the priesthood under the code could only take place through the more formal judicial process with three judges who were priests with doctorates, or licentiates, in canon law sitting on the tribunal.[30] In other words, the *1983 Code* entrenched the position that Pope John Paul II had decreed in 1980, that the administrative procedure could only be used where the priest consented. The 'judicial' procedure of dismissal is, according to the *New Commentary on the Code of Canon Law*, a penalty 'rarely inflicted because of the complexity of the process'.[31]

---

28. Canons 1395 §2, and 207.
29. Canons 694–704.
30. Canon 1421§3. By a decree of Pope John Paul II in 2003, the requirement that all judges have doctorates could be dispensed with by the Congregation for the Doctrine of the Faith, Delaney, *Canonical Implications of the Response of the Catholic Church in Australia,* 75
31. John P Beal, James A Coriden and Thomas J Green, *New Commentary on the Code of Canon Law*, 383.

While no one had any doubt that the *1983 Code of Canon Law* repealed and replaced the *1917 Code of Canon Law,* an issue arose at the *Murphy Dublin Inquiry* in 2009 as to whether or not *Crimen Sollicitationis* had also been repealed by the code. Canon lawyers were confused about it.[32]

The commission went on to say:

> Even the best attempts of competent people to discover the norms which, according to canon law, should be applied to cases of sexual abuse were in vain . . . There seems to have been a total absence of any straightforward, easily verifiable system for ascertaining which decrees or statements had the force of canon law and which had not, and what the effects of new canonical instruments, such as the code of 1983, or the 2001 procedural rules, had on previous instruments which had been treated as having the force of law . . . It is a basic feature of every coherent legal system that there is a firm, simple and unmistakeable procedure for the promulgation of a law. The absence of any such procedure within Church law, in the Commission's view, makes that law difficult to access, and very difficult to implement and to monitor compliance.[33]

The commission's criticism of the general absence of such a procedure in canon law is a valid one. But in the case of *Crimen Sollicitationis* and the *1983 Code of Canon Law*, there appeared to be such a provision. Canon 6 of the *1983 Code of Canon Law* repealed all previously existing penal laws, unless they were incorporated into the *1983 Code of Canon Law* itself.[34]

The repeal of *Crimen Sollicitationis* depended on whether it was a penal law (which meant it had been repealed) or a procedural law

---

32. http://www.justice.ie/en/JELR/DACOI%20Part%201.pdf/Files/DACOI%20 Part%201.pdf (Accessed 25 April 2013) paragraph 4.16.
33. *Ibid*, paragraphs 4.87–4.89.
34. http://www.vatican.va/archive/ENG1104/__P2.HTM and see Article by Bishop Arrieta Secretary of the Pontifical Council for Legislative Texts, http://www. vatican.va/resources/resources_arrieta-20101204_en.html (Accessed 21 June 2013).

(which meant it had not).[35] From 1983 until about 1996, the Vatican took the view that *Crimen Sollicitationis* had been repealed because it was a penal law.

Cardinal Ratzinger's own behaviour after 1983 would suggest that he himself believed that *Crimen Sollicitationis* had been repealed by the Code. In 1988, he wrote to the Church's then chief canon lawyer, Cardinal Castillo Lara, the President of the Pontifical Council for Legislative Texts, asking for a change to canon law to have a more streamlined way of dealing with clergy who had sexually abused children, because the formal judicial trial was too unwieldy. At that time, Cardinal Ratzinger's Congregation for the Doctrine of the Faith had no role in canonical trials for sexual abuse except where there had also been soliciting sex in the confessional. His Congregation was also involved in dealing with applications by priests to be laicised so that they could marry. He was finding that coming across his desk were many applications for voluntary laicisation from clergy who had been sexually assaulting children—that being the only feasible way for a priest sexual abuser to be dismissed.[36] Ratzinger thought that this was inappropriate and those priests should be put on trial and dismissed from the priesthood.[37]

There is no suggestion in this correspondence that Cardinal Ratzinger believed that his Congregation still had jurisdiction to deal with clergy sexual abuse of minors as provided by *Crimen Sollicitationis*. Cardinal Castillo Lara rejected the request saying that any change to canon law would endanger the priest's 'fundamental right of defence'.[38] Cardinal Castillo Lara's reply smacks once again of extreme clericalism. He was more concerned about the 'rights' of the

---

35. Delaney, *Canonical Implications of the Response of the Catholic Church in Australia,* 211, footnote 10.
36. See evidence of Cardinal Pell http://www.parliament.vic.gov.au/images/stories/committees/fcdc/inquiries/57th/Child_Abuse_Inquiry/Transcripts/Catholic_Archdiocese_of_Sydney_27-May-13.pdf, 21.8, and Report of Antony Whitlam QC, http://www.parra.catholic.org.au (Accessed 9 February 2013), paragraph 58.
37. Article by Archbishop Arrieta, the Secretary of the Pontifical Council for Legislative Texts in *La Civiltà Cattolica* on 4 December 2010 http://www.vatican.va/resources/resources_arrieta-20101204_en.html (Accessed 21 June 2013). *Pastor Bonus* reorganised the Roman Curia in 1988 and from 1989 onwards requests for voluntary laicization were handled by the Congregation for Divine Worship and Discipline of the Sacraments (Article 68), Beal, Corriden & Green: *New Commentary on Code of Canon Law,* 385.
38. *Ibid*, Arrieta article in *La Civiltá Cattolica.*

accused priest than the possibility that the difficulties of the canonical procedures were increasing the attacks on children.

The worst impediment that the *1983 Code of Canon Law* created for dealing with child sex abusing priests was the five year limitation period from the time of the offence. After five years the canonical crime of abuse was 'extinguished', and then no action could be taken against the priest.[39] On the other hand these crimes that had previously been reserved to the Congregation for the Doctrine of the Faith under *Crimen Sollicitationis* had no limitation period at all.[40]

In 1988, the American bishops approached the Vatican with a view to extending the five year limitation period because, in just about every case, it precluded them from prosecuting clergy sexual abusers because children take some time to come to terms with what has happened to them. These six year negotiations from 1988 to 1994 were a very clear indication from the Vatican that the *1983 Code of Canon Law* had replaced *Crimen Sollicitationis*—because otherwise, they were totally unnecessary. In 1994, an extension was granted to ten years from the eighteenth birthday of the victim, but limited to the United States. The same extension was given to Ireland in 1996, and confirmed again on 4 December 1998 for the United States.[41]

However, despite that, it seems that around the late 1990s, the Congregation for the Doctrine of the Faith, headed by Cardinals Ratzinger and Archbishop (later Cardinal) Bertone started to claim that *Crimen Sollicitationis* had not been repealed by the *1983 Code of Canon Law*, and that it was still in force for clergy sexual abuse that did not involve soliciting in the confessional. The basis upon which it could be argued that it was still in force was that it was really a 'procedural' law and not a 'penal law' but that ignored the

---

39. Canon 1362§2, Ladislas Orsy SJ, says that the canonical 'prescription' is different to civil law statutes of limitation because the former extinguishes the cause of action, but the latter only prevent reliance on it (estoppel). That may be the situation in the United States, but many limitation statutes in Australia provide for extinguishment. http://www.bc.edu/dam/files/schools/law/lawreviews/journals/bclawr/44_4/04_FMS.htm (Accessed 2 October 2013).

40. Canon 1362§1, http://www.vatican.va/archive/ENG1104/__P51.HTM (Accessed 29 May 2013).

41. Letter of the Secretariat of State, 4 December 1998, Prot. N. 445.119/G.N, quoted in Delaney, *Canonical Implications of the Response of the Catholic Church in Australia*, 72.

interpretation that the Vatican had placed on the effect of Canon 6 on *Crimen Sollicitationis* for a period of some eighteen years between 1983 and 2001, with an attempt by the Congregation for the Doctrine of the Faith in 1996 to say otherwise.

In the meantime most senior clergy from 1983 onwards either did not know about *Crimen Sollicitationis*, or had forgotten about it.[42] Civil lawyers do not bother learning about or remembering procedural laws that are no longer in force, and there is no reason to think that their canonical brethren would be any different.

This ignorance extended even to Australia. Monsignor Dolan, the Dublin Chancellor told the Murphy Commission that he was unaware of the 1962 document until an Australian bishop told him that he had received a letter from the Vatican stating that *Crimen Sollicitationis* was still in force.[43] The Australian bishop was probably Bishop Wilson of Wollongong, now the Archbishop of Adelaide who stumbled across the old instruction as a canon law student in Rome in the early 1990s. He found that canonists were divided as to whether the *1983 Code of Canon Law* had repealed *Crimen Sollicitationis*. In

---

42. http://www.justice.ie/en/JELR/DACOI%20Part%201.pdf/Files/DACOI%20 Part%201.pdf (Accessed   25 April 2013), paragraphs   1.89, 4.21–4.24. The evidence before the Murphy Commission was that Archbishop McQuaid of Dublin (1940–1971) had used the 1922 document in the case of Fr Edwards in 1960 (paragraph1.89), and that during his time as Archbishop, the document was well known to senior Church figures and was 'well thumbed', but there was no evidence that the Archdiocese had received a copy of the 1962 document (paragraph 4.21). In the United States, Cardinal Francis George of Chicago in court evidence said that the 1962 document was taught to him in the seminary, and Bishop Madera said that it was discussed at a meeting of clergy with Archbishop Manning of Los Angeles in the early 1960s, http://reform-network. net/?p=3006, paragraph 14 (Accessed 5 December 2013). According to Fr John P Beal, the general nature of the procedures were dealt with in manuals of moral theology and canon law taught in seminaries, for continuing formation after ordination, certainly from the late 1930s onwards. The Spanish canon lawyer, Aurelio Yanguas in 1947 said it was 'universally known' amongst clerics. Beal says that not long after the 1962 document was disseminated, the study of canon law in seminaries declined, and it then 'gathered dust' in the archives until it was mentioned in the *2001 Motu Proprio*, John P Beal 'The 1962 Instruction: Crimen Sollicitationis: Caught Red Handed or Handed a Red Herring?', 41 *Studia Canonica*, 199 at 229–231: http://www.vatican.va/resources/resources_introd-storica_en.html (Accessed 5 August 2013).
43. *Ibid*, paragraph 4.23.

the late 1990s, he discussed the matter with Cardinal Ratzinger's office and was told that it had not been repealed and was the applicable canon law.[44] This is consistent with Archbishop Hart's evidence at the *Victorian Parliamentary Inquiry* that the first time he heard about *Crimen Sollicitationis* was in about 1996/1997 when he became Vicar General of the Archdiocese of Melbourne.[45]

In 1996, officers of the Canon Law Society of America had a meeting with the secretary of the Congregation for the Doctrine of the Faith, the then Archbishop Bertone. In its 1996 Newsletter, the Canon Law Society of America reported on the visit and said that although *Crimen Sollicitationis* was being 'reviewed', it was, in the meantime, to be applied.[46]

The year 1996 is interesting because in that very same year, the Vatican extended the limitation period for Ireland from five years to ten years after the eighteenth birthday of the victim, as it had done for the United States two years earlier. And then in 1998, the Vatican renewed the extension for the United States. Such extensions were unnecessary if *Crimen Sollicitationis* was still in force. Did the left hand of the Vatican know what the right was doing? The *Murphy Dublin Report* stated that:

> It is not easy to provide a coherent description of the relevant parts of canon law because, since the 1960s, canon law itself has been in a state of flux and considerable confusion, making it difficult even for experts to know what the law is or where it is to be found. This is the case, not only with local canonists, but also, it appears, even with spokesmen for the Holy See itself. A Vatican spokesman believed the 1962 instruction, *Crimen Sollicitationis,* had been superseded by the *1983*

44. *New York Times,* 1 July 2010, http://www.nytimes.com/2010/07/02/world/europe/02pope.html?pagewanted=all&_r=1& (Accessed 15 June 2013).

45. http://www.parliament.vic.gov.au/images/stories/committees/fcdc/inquiries/57th/Child_Abuse_Inquiry/Transcripts/Catholic_Archdiocese_of_Melbourne_20-May-13.pdf, 13 (Accessed 18 June 2013).

46. Thomas Doyle *The 1922 Instruction and the 1962 Instruction Crimen Sollicitationis promulgated by the Vatican,* http://www.bishop-accountability.org/news2010/03_04/2010_03_12_Doyle_VeryImportant.htm **paragraph 10** (Accessed 2 October 2013).

Code of Canon Law when its existence in the late 1990s was being referred to by others.[47]

That confusion was evident in April 2000, when Bishops Robinson and Wilson went to Rome on behalf of the Australian Catholic Bishops Conference for a four day meeting of bishops under the direction of the Congregation of the Clergy whose members seem to have regarded the whole issue of sexual abuse by clergy as a modern re-enactment of Joseph being falsely accused of rape by Potiphar's wife, and something that was peculiar to the Anglo-Saxon world.[48] The limitation period was there to protect priests from people following the example of Potiphar's wife. The issue of *Towards Healing* and canon law was raised at that meeting.

Bishop Robinson reported back to the Australian Bishops that very few cases could be dealt with under the judicial process because of the limitation period.[49] Cardinal Castrillón's Congregation took the view that *Crimen Sollicitationis* had been repealed, something that was consistent with the protracted negotiations over the limitation period. Robinson's companion, Bishop Wilson, who had been told in 1996 by Cardinal Ratzinger's Congregation that *Crimen Sollicitationis* was still in force, said about the meeting, 'There was confusion everywhere'.[50]

---

47. *Murphy Dublin Report,* Part 1 http://www.justice.ie/en/JELR/DACOI%20 Part%201.pdf/Files/DACOI%20Part%201.pdf par 4.6 (Accessed 25 April 2013).
48. The *New York Times* reported on the meeting: '. . . many at the meeting grew dismayed as, over four long days in early April 2000, they heard senior Vatican officials dismiss clergy sexual abuse as a problem confined to the English-speaking world, and emphasize the need to protect the rights of accused priests over ensuring the safety of children, according to interviews with ten church officials who attended the meeting. Cardinal Darío Castrillón Hoyos, then the head of the Congregation for the Clergy, set the tone, playing down sexual abuse as an unavoidable fact of life, and complaining that lawyers and the media were unfairly focused on it, according to a copy of his prepared remarks. What is more, he asked, is it not contradictory for people to be so outraged by sexual abuse when society also promotes sexual liberation?', *New York Times*, 1 July 2010, http:// www.nytimes.com/2010/07/02/world/europe/02pope.html?pagewanted=all&_ r=0 (Accessed 12 October 2013).
49. NCPS Meeting Minutes 10 May 2000, *Australian Church Submission*, 90, paragraph 50–54, http://dev.childabuseroyalcommission.gov.au/wp-content/ uploads/2013/10/14.-Truth-Justice-and-Healing-Council.pdf (Accessed 12 October 2013).
50. *New York Times*, 1 July 2010, http://www.nytimes.com/2010/07/02/world/

The Vatican's left hand did know what the right was doing, but they were involved in an unbecoming cat fight over which congregation was to be in charge of clergy sexual abuse.

The *1983 Code of Canon Law* imposed a further obstacle to dealing with sex abusing priests. It took away the right to suspend an accused priest pending the outcome of the investigation. This paralysis of the canonical disciplinary system, coupled with the prohibition on reporting these crimes to the police gave clergy sexual abusers a free ticket to continue their attacks on children.

Then in 2001, Pope John Paul II issued the *2001 Motu Proprio,* and the Congregation for the Doctrine of the Faith then sent out a letter that not only created further confusion, but undermined the integrity and coherence of canon law, the oldest continuing functioning legal system in the Western world.[51]

The *2001 Motu Proprio* Decree

On 30 April 2001, Pope John Paul II issued the *2001 Motu Proprio.*[52] It retained many of the features of *Crimen Sollicitationis*, requiring *delicts* against the sacraments to be referred to that Roman congregation. These are purely a matter for the Church and do not involve any infringement of civil laws.

But included amongst those matters to be referred were:

> Delicts against morality:
> 1. The violation of the sixth commandment of the Decalogue, committed by a cleric with a minor under the age of eighteen.[53]

---

europe/02pope.html?pagewanted=all&_r=0 (Accessed 12 October 2013).

51. http://www.canonlaw.info/ (Accessed 21 June 2013).

52. http://www.documentcloud.org/documents/243690-10-sacramentorum-sanctitatis-2001-with-2003.html (Accessed 4 August 2013).

53. http://www.vatican.va/resources/resources_introd-storica_en.html (last accessed 18 February 2013) and http://www.documentcloud.org/documents/243690-10-sacramentorum-sanctitatis-2001-with-2003.html Art 4 (Accessed 4 August 2013). http://www.bishop-accountability.org/resources/resource-files/churchdocs/EpistulaEnglish.htm (Accessed 4 August 2013) and the 2010 Revision, http://www.vatican.va/resources/resources_norme_en.html (Accessed 5 August 2013).

In plain English, that means sexual abuse of children. The most significant requirement relating to the sexual abuse of children by clergy was Article 25:

'Cases of this kind are subject to the pontifical secret.'[54]
Unlike *Crimen Sollicitationis*, the *2001 Motu Proprio* did not impose secrecy on accusers or witnesses.[55]

The requirement of pontifical secrecy is repeated in the letter of explanation from the Congregation for the Doctrine of the Faith, of 18 May 2001, signed by Cardinal Ratzinger and Archbishop Bertone to the bishops of the world.[56]

Like the *1983 Code of Canon Law*, the *2001 Motu Proprio* decree required the bishop to carry out a 'preliminary investigation' either personally or through a delegate. Under the *1983 Code of Canon Law* It was then up to the bishop to decide if he had sufficient evidence for a formal trial.[57] However, the *2001 Motu Proprio* provided that in the case of the sexual abuse of children, the results of that investigation had to be sent to the Congregation for the Doctrine of the Faith in Rome, headed by Cardinal Ratzinger. The congregation would then instruct the bishop on how to proceed. That might involve a formal trial by the bishop or by the congregation itself, or some other action.[58]

Cardinal Ratzinger finally had his 1988 wish for a more simplified procedure for dismissing sex abusing priests. While the judicial process was still retained for dismissal, the Congregation for the

---

54. http://www.documentcloud.org/documents/243690-10-sacramentorum-sanctitatis-2001-with-2003.html Article 25 and footnote 31 specifically referring to *Secreta Continere* (Accessed 4 August 2013).

55. Thomas Doyle, *A Very Short History of Clergy Sexual Abuse in the Catholic Church,* http://www.crusadeagainstclergyabuse.com/htm/AShortHistory.htm (Accessed 5 May 2013).

56. http://www.bishop-accountability.org/resources/resource-files/churchdocs/EpistulaEnglish.htm (Accessed 5 August 2013).

57. http://www.vatican.va/archive/ENG1104/__P6V.HTM (Accessed 3 July 2013).

58. A more detailed description of the alternatives is contained in the article by the former Vatican prosecutor Monsignor Scicluna at the Annual Canon Law Conference of the Canon Law Society of Australia and New Zealand, Canberra, 2006 in a paper called 'The Procedure and Praxis of the Congregation for the Doctrine of the Faith regarding *Graviora Delicta*', http://www.vatican.va/resources/resources_mons-scicluna-graviora-delicta_en.html (Accessed 14 June 2013).

Doctrine of the Faith could dispense with that requirement when so requested by the bishop, and the congregation could dismiss the priest by decree. Alternatively the Congregation for the Doctrine of the Faith could refer the matter to the pope to do so.[59]

On 18 May 2001, Cardinal Ratzinger and Archbishop Bertone sent out a letter to the bishops of the world explaining the changes made by the *2001 Motu Proprio*.[60] The strange thing about the historical introduction to the *2001 Motu Proprio,* and the letter of 18 May 2001 from the Congregation for the Doctrine of the Faith, was their Orwellian attempt to rewrite history.

The historical introduction referred to the reissue of *Crimen Sollicitationis* in 1962, and then asserted that the Congregation for the Doctrine of the Faith had jurisdiction under its provisions to deal with priests through the 'administrative' or 'judicial' process.[61] There

---

59. http://www.documentcloud.org/documents/243690-10-sacramentorum-sanctitatis-2001-with-2003.html Article 17 (Accessed 4 August 2013). In the case of a dismissal *ex officio* by the pope, the Vatican required that the case was 'beyond doubt and well documented': Monsignor Scicluna, 'The Procedure and Praxis of the Congregation for the Doctrine of the Faith Regarding *Graviora Delict'*, http://www.vatican.va/resources/resources_mons-scicluna-graviora-delicta_en.html (Accessed 22 October 2013), and see Delaney, *Canonical Implications of the Response of the Catholic Church in Australia*, 84. The administrative dismissal procedure was authorised by an amendent to the *2001 Motu Proprio* in 2003, see *Facing the Truth*, 33.

60. http://www.bishop-accountability.org/resources/resource-files/churchdocs/EpistulaEnglish.htm (Accessed 23 August 2013).

61. *Crimen Sollicitationis* in Clause 74 says that proceedings could be taken administratively or judicially, but it seems to be confined to cases of clergy who are exempt or non exempt religious, and any action taken was only valid if approved by the Holy Office. On the other hand, the historical introduction to the *2001 Motu Proprio* said that 'judicial competence had been attributed exclusively' to the Congregation for the Doctrine of the Faith, 'which competence could be exercised either administratively or through the judicial process'. That would seem to indicate that the supreme interpreter of canon law, the pope, had regarded Clause 74 as applying generally to all clerics. On the other hand, when the historical introduction was rewritten in 2010, this statement was omitted. Indeed, in that rewritten historical introduction, Benedict XVI said 'In 1962, Blessed Pope John XXIII authorised a reprint of the 1922 Instruction, with a small section added regarding the administrative procedures to be used in those cases in which religious clerics were involved'. He seemed to be referring to Clause 74, because it is the only part of *Crimen Sollicitationis* in its 1962 version that referred to an administrative procedure. The right of bishops therefore to deal administratively under *Crimen Sollicitationis* with priests who are not members of religious orders is not clear.

was no mention of the effect of the *1983 Code of Canon Law*, and particularly Canon 6. Indeed, one would have to assume from the above, that the Vatican was saying that it had no effect at all, and *Crimen Sollicitationis* continued to be the law to be applied until 2001. If there was any doubt about that, the 18 May 2001 letter said so expressly. It went on to describe how the Congregation for the Doctrine of the Faith had set up an ad hoc commission because:

> . . . the instruction Crimen Sollicitationis . . . **in force until now**, was to be reviewed when the new canonical codes were promulgated[62] (my emphasis).

For some eighteen years, it seems that most, if not all canon lawyers considered that the *1983 Code of Canon Law* had repealed *Crimen Sollicitationis*. Such a conclusion was hardly surprising, because Canon 6 expressly repealed all prior penal laws, and the conduct of the Vatican itself in negotiating an extension of the limitation period under the Code was consistent with it holding the view that *Crimen Sollicitationis* was a penal law and therefore repealed. Then in 2001, the canon lawyers and bishops of the world were told that *Crimen Sollicitationis* had been 'in force' all along, (presumably because it was now regarded as a procedural law) until the changes introduced by the *2001 Motu Proprio*.

After the *1983 Code of Canon Law* was promulgated, canon lawyers in the United States were advising their bishops that Canon 1362 imposed a limitation period of five years from the date of the offence for taking proceedings against accused priests.[63] This effectively ruled out most canonical trials. But the *2001 Motu Proprio* and the 18 May 2001 letter said that *Crimen Sollicitationis* was 'in force until now', which would mean that there was no statute of limitations, and the simplified administrative procedure was available because the historical introduction said the jurisdiction to dismiss a priest could also be exercised 'administratively' under *Crimen Sollicitationis*.

---

62. http://www.bishop-accountability.org/resources/resource-files/churchdocs/ EpistulaEnglish.htm (Accessed 23 August 2013).
63. Nicholas Cafardi, 'The Scandal of Secrecy: Canon Law and the Sexual-abuse Crisis', in *Commonweal*, 21 July 2010 http://commonwealmagazine.org/scandal-secrecy (Accessed 27 May 2013), and Bishop Robinson from Australia had told the Australian bishops this, after his meeting with Bishop Wilson at the Congregation for the Clergy in Rome in April 2000.

The confusion created by this statement cannot be underestimated. In 1988, the American bishops asked the Vatican to extend the limitation period because it effectively meant there would be no canonical trials of sex abusing priests. The Vatican was reluctant to agree, but finally did so six years later in 1994. The period was extended to ten years after the victim turned eighteen. Nicholas Cafardi says:

> While Vatican officials were discussing a longer statute of limitations, they undoubtedly believed that canon 1362's five-year statute applied. Whatever can be said about the labyrinthine thought processes that occur within the halls of the Apostolic Palace, those people aren't stupid—and they aren't careless. If they felt a need to negotiate a longer statute with the US bishops, they must have been convinced that the shorter five-year statute of the 1983 Code of Canon Law applied.[64]

And that conviction was hardly surprising, because *Crimen Sollicitationis* had all the markings of being a penal law, because of the punishments it imposed. Another noted canon lawyer, Fr John P Beal made a similar observation to Cafardi:

> It makes no sense to me that they were sitting on this document. Why didn't they just say, 'Here are the norms. If you need a copy we'll send them to you?'[65]

Bearing in mind that in the canonical system, questions of interpretation are determined not by some independent court, like the United States Supreme Court or the High Court of Australia, but by the legislature, namely, the Vatican, the American bishops and their colleagues in other countries were quite justified in thinking that the *1983 Code of Canon Law* with its five years limitation period applied. Any possible ambiguity about whether *Crimen Sollicitationis* was a penal or procedural law had disappeared with the negotiations being conducted with the Vatican to extend the limitation period.[66]

---

64. *Ibid.*
65. http://www.nytimes.com/2010/07/02/world/europe/02pope.html?pagewanted=all&_r=1& (Accessed 21 June 2013). Fr John P Beal is Professor of Canon Law at the Catholic University of America.
66. Cafardi, *Before Dallas*, 30. And see Edward Peters 'Lest Amateurs Argue Canon

What John Paul II and the Vatican Curia did in 2001 is the equivalent of the Supreme Court of the United States now saying that it never did decide *Brown v The Board of Education,* which ended segregation in the United States, or the High Court of Australia declaring that it never did decide *Mabo v Queensland (2)* about the existence of aboriginal native title in Australia. Those courts could preserve their coherency and integrity by subsequently declaring that those cases were wrongly decided, but *never* that they had not made those decisions. By asserting in 2001 that *Crimen Sollicitationis* was 'in force until now', Pope John Paul II, and the Roman Curia cardinals were saying that the Vatican had never regarded it as having been repealed by the *1983 Code.* That was incorrect. The integrity of the system could have been preserved if the pope, in 1996, had stated that he had decided to reinstate *Crimen Sollicitationis.* That did not happen.

For some eighteen years at least, during the height of the complaints about clergy sexual abuse, bishops were following procedures under the *1983 Code.*[67] Why did the Vatican not admit the truth in the historical introduction to the *2001 Motu Proprio* and in the letter of 18 May 2001 sent out by the Congregation for the Doctrine of the Faith that the *1983 Code of Canon Law* had repealed *Crimen Sollicitationis?*

Law: A reply to Patrick Gordon's brief against Bp. Thomas Daily', in *Angelicum,* 83 (2006): 121–142, http://www.canonlaw.info/a_gordon.htm Accessed 3 July 2013), text between footnote 20 and 21, where says that in the canonical system: 'Desirous of bringing about a norm for conduct in a "civil law" society, the legislator drafts a provision and enacts it. But in so doing, again probably without conscious advertence to his thinking, he knows he need not spend nearly as much time trying to anticipate potential interpretive difficulties in his law because, he knows, all such questions will eventually be referred to him (or a delegate[21]) for settlement.' The 'legislator' in this case, the Vatican, was giving two contradictory messages signals on the effect of the *1983 Code of Canon Law* on *Crimen Sollicitationis,* one between 1983 and about 1996, that it had been abrogated, and another, after 1996, and only by one Congregation, that it had not been.

67. *Murphy Dublin Report,* Part 1 http://www.justice.ie/en/JELR/DACOI%20 Part%201.pdf/Files/DACOI%20Part%201.pdf paragraph 4.30 (Accessed 16 July 2013). Monsignor Stenson of the Dublin Archdiocese only ever dealt with the clergy abuse matters under the Code, and only became aware of *Crimen Sollicitationis* around 1997: par 4.22, and see Nicholas Cafardi, 'The Scandal of Secrecy: Canon Law and the Sexual-abuse Crisis', in *Commonweal,* 21 July 2010, http://commonwealmagazine.org/scandal-secrecy (Accessed 27 May 2013).

Nicholas Cafardi says that the explanation is in *bella figura*.[68] Bishop Geoffrey Robinson explains that in Italian culture *bella figura* (literally 'beautiful figure'), means presenting a good external appearance to the world, while *bruta figura* (literally 'ugly figure') means doing the opposite. He says that it pervades the Vatican: mistakes can be pardoned, but the unpardonable sin is to make them public.[69] Cafardi says that the fib was told to cover up a turf fight between Cardinals Ratzinger and Castrillón over who was to be in charge of the sexual abuse issue. The *2001 Motu Proprio* really did give jurisdiction back to Ratzinger's Congregation for the Doctrine of the Faith, but *bella figura* demanded that it appear that he had it all along.

This not only created confusion. It led to a finding by the Murphy Commission that canon law lacked one of the basic features of a coherent legal system.[70]

There is another explantion that is still infected with *bella figura*. The advice given by Ratzinger and Bertone in the late 1990s about using *Crimen Sollicitationis* was canonically dubious, and actions done under their instructions could have been null and void. Legal systems have a transparent way of dealing with this by legislating to validate the actions taken. But that means admitting a mistake. Rather than do that, the Vatican preferred the Orwellian solution of rewriting history.

But there is another more Machiavellian explanation that goes beyond *bella figura*. If bishops were not hampered by these provisions under the code, then they could be more easily blamed for any failure to dismiss paedophile priests, because there was no limitation period under *Crimen Sollicitationis* and the historical introduction also said that the simpler administrative was available.[71] And this is exactly what Ratzinger did in 2010 after becoming Pope Benedict XVI, when in his *Pastoral Letter* to the Irish people, he blamed the Irish bishops

---

68. http://www.commonwealmagazine.org/scandal-secrecy (Accessed 27 May 2013).
69. Geoffrey Robinson, *For Christ's Sake: End Sexual Abuse in the Catholic Church for Good* (Melbourne: John Garratt Publishing, 2013), 122.
70. http://www.justice.ie/en/JELR/DACOI%20Part%201.pdf/Files/DACOI%20Part%201.pdf (Accessed 25 April 2013), paragraphs 4.88–4.89.
71. Clause 74, *Crimen Sollicitationis*.

for not using the 'long established norms of canon law' to dismiss these priests.

Whatever the explanation, the Vatican provided cogent support for Sir Walter Scott's axiom:

'Oh, what a tangled web we weave . . . when first we practice to deceive.'[72]

The tangled web caused confusion for the witnesses at the Murphy Commission in Ireland, and for the Murphy Commission itself as to what really was canon law over child sexual abuse. The Murphy Commission stated that 'even the best attempts by competent people to discover the norms which, according to canon law, should be applied to cases of sexual abuse were in vain'.[73]

The web became even more tangled with Benedict XVI's *Pastoral Letter* to the people of Ireland, of 19 March 2010, blaming bishops for not applying the 'long-established norms of canon law'. Which 'norms' was he talking about? *Crimen Sollicitationis,* which he said in his 2001 letter was 'in force' until then? If that was what he meant, then he and Pope John Paul II, and their colleagues in the curia had for some eighteen years misled the world's bishops and canon lawyers into thinking that there was a five year limitation period for taking action to dismiss a sex abusing priest, when in fact it did not exist, and that the simpler administrative procedure was not available, when, according to the historical introduction, it was.

If Benedict was referring to the *1983 Code of Canon Law*, then there was a five year limitation period that effectively prevented any canonical trial for nearly all child sexual abuse by priests. The Vatican begrudgingly extended the period for the United States in 1994 and Ireland in 1996, but left the rest of the world with it until 2001. And further, the simpler administrative procedure was not available, leaving the bishops with no other alternative than to use the impossibly complicated judicial one.

On 1 October 2006, the BBC Panorama Program, *Sex Crimes and the Vatican* alleged that for twenty years, Pope Benedict XVI, as

---

72. Sir Walter Scott, *Marmion.*
73. http://www.justice.ie/en/JELR/DACOI%20Part%201.pdf/Files/DACOI%20 Part%201.pdf (Accessed 25 April 2013), paragraph 4.87.

Cardinal Ratzinger, was in charge of enforcing secrecy about the sex crimes of clergy on minors, as laid down in *Crimen Sollicitationis*.[74] In fact he had only been in charge of enforcing it for two years, not twenty. It had been repealed by the *1983 Code of Canon Law*, two years after he had become Prefect of the Congregation for the Doctrine of the Faith. But the BBC was not to blame. This was Ratzinger's own fault, because of what his congregation claimed in its letter of 18 May 2001 to the Church's bishops. It was not until 2010 that Pope Benedict XVI, 'corrected' the Orwellian rewrite of history long after the program went to air. The tangled web had come back to bite him, giving the impression that he was personally far more culpable than he really was.

The web became even further tangled for the poor unfortunate canon lawyers who were giving evidence in the trials that were starting up in the United States. How were they going to explain the anomaly that the Vatican was negotiating from 1988 to 1998 to extend a period of limitation in the *1983 Code of Canon Law*, when the pope was telling everyone in 2001 that there was no limitation period to extend? The solution that Monsignor Brian Ferme, former Dean of the School of Canon Law at Catholic University of America, took in an affidavit submitted in a California civil case in 2005 was to say 'technically' *Crimen Sollicitationis* was in force until the *2001 Motu Proprio*.[75] In other words, it wasn't really, but technically it was—or vice versa. After all, the final interpreter of canon law, the Supreme Pontiff himself had spoken, and declared something to be true when in fact it wasn't. *Bella figura* had crossed the Atlantic.

The 2010 Revision of the *2001 Motu Proprio*

On 12 April, 2010, the Vatican issued a document called *A Guide to Understanding Basic CDF Procedures Concerning Sexual Abuse Allegations,* which it said was 'an introductory guide which may be helpful to lay persons and non-canonists'. It explained the various procedures, and then said that:

---

74. http://vimeo.com/654677 (Accessed 12 September 2013).

75. Thomas Doyle 'The 1922 Instruction and the 1962 Instruction "Crimen Sollicitationis" promulgated by the Vatican', http://www.awrsipe.com/Doyle/2008/2008-10-03-Commentary%20on%201922%20and%201962%20documents.pdf paragraph 5 (Accessed 19 June 2013).

Civil law concerning reporting of crimes to the appropriate authorities should always be followed.[76]

There is nothing in canon law that suggests that it can be changed by issuing a guide 'for lay persons and non-canonists', and indeed, the Vatican spokesman, Fr Lombardi admitted as much in his explanatory statement on 15 July 2010, published on the Vatican website.[77] Fr Lombardi said that reporting such crimes where the civil law required it was a 'practice suggested by the Congregation for the Doctrine of the Faith'. He repeated this on 19 July 2010. That was news to everyone because, as we shall see in chapter 16, all the public statements issued by the Vatican prior to 2010 were to the effect that such a 'practice' of reporting by Church authorities was contrary to canon law or was in some way immoral. And two cardinals had said that bishops should be prepared to go to jail rather than do that.

On 21 May 2010, Pope Benedict XVI issued his decree revising the *2001 Motu Proprio*. The changes involved some slight change of wording, but it also added a number of canonical crimes to be dealt with by the procedure: the attempted ordination of women,[78] sexual abuse of mentally disabled people[79] and possession of child pornography.[80]

The 'pontifical secret' was also retained:

Article 30 §1. Cases of this nature are subject to the pontifical secret. [81]

---

76. http://www.vatican.va/resources/resources_guide-CDF-procedures_en.html (Accessed 17 July 2013).

77. Fr Lombardi said 'An initial clarification–especially for use by the media - was provided recently with the publication on the Holy See website of a brief *Guide to Understanding Basic CDF Procedures concerning Sexual Abuse Allegations*'. The publication of the new Norms is, however, quite a different thing, providing us with an official and updated legal text which is valid for the whole Church', http://www.vatican.va/resources/resources_lombardi-nota-norme_en.html (Accessed 21 July 2013).

78. Article 5, http://www.vatican.va/resources/resources_introd-storica_en.html (Accessed 3 July 2013).

79. *Ibid*, Article 6 §1.

80. *Ibid*, Article 6 §2.

81. http://www.vatican.va/resources/resources_norme_en.html (Accessed 5 August 2013), Article 30, footnote 41.

There is no exception in the revised *2001 Motu Proprio* to allow reporting to the civil authorities. The words in the Guide to 'lay persons and non-canonists' about reporting crimes to the appropriate authorities were not incorporated into the revision. It would have been a simple thing to do, by adding the words 'except for reporting such matters to the civil authorities where the civil law requires it', to Article 30 §1, but they are not there.

As we have already seen, canon law can be changed for a particular region when a proposal from a bishops conference receives the approval or *recognitio* from the Vatican. On 3 May 2011, Cardinal Levada from the Congregation for the Doctrine of the Faith sent out a circular letter calling for bishops conferences to send in their guidelines for dealing with sexual abuse, and advising that those guidelines should include a clause to the effect that the civil Law requirements on reporting should always be followed.[82] When each country's guidelines are approved under Canon 455, those guidelines will become canon law for that particular region.

So, apart from announcing to the world that the Vatican would dispense with pontifical secrecy to allow reporting where the civil law required it, what was the point of this guide for 'lay persons and non-canonists'? We have another example of *bella figura*. Just as the Vatican cardinals wanted to give the impression that *Crimen Sollicitationis* was in force until the *2001 Motu Proprio*, when in fact it wasn't, now it wanted to create the bureaucratic illusion for 'lay persons and non-canonists', that canon law has always allowed bishops to report clergy sex crimes to the civil authorities, when, for the last ninety or so years, it had strictly forbidden it. It could not use the word 'dispensation' because that would amount to a concession that canon law did forbid bishops reporting to the police, but a 'dispensation' is effectively what the Vatican was giving.

The spin did not stop there. The revision included another, much longer historical introduction. The misleading statement about *Crimen Sollicitationis* being 'in force until now' in the 2001 history must have been apparent, especially in the United States whose bishops and canon lawyers had been negotiating with the Vatican for six years to extend a limitation period that did not even exist if *Crimen Sollicitationis* was still 'in force'. Professor Cafardi could not

---

82. http://www.vatican.va/roman_curia/congregations/cfaith/documents/rc_con_cfaith_doc_20110503_abuso-minori_en.html (Accessed 9 February 2013).

have been the only person to notice this Orwellian attempt to rewrite history.

On 26 November 2009, the *Murphy Dublin Report* criticised the state of confusion in canon law over clergy sexual abuse of children in the period it was examining from 1975 to 2004, effectively accusing it of being incoherent. One can only speculate as to whether or not this was the catalyst for writing the longer and corrected historical introduction, but it hardly seems coincidental that it happened just five months after publication of the Report.

One of the inexorable rules of Sir Walter Scott's 'tangled web' is that deceit has to be piled upon deceit to cover up the earlier one. And an equally inexorable rule of *bella figura* is that one never admits to making a mistake. And both things happened with the 2010 attempt to correct the 2001 Orwellian rewrite.

The new and revised historical introduction to the *2001 Motu Proprio* said that the *1983 Code of Canon Law*, 'updated the whole discipline' for dealing with sexual abuse of minors, and its reference to the appeal processes leaves no doubt that it was admitting that *Crimen Sollicitationis* had been repealed by the Code.[83]

What was the Vatican going to do about the 'in force until now' statement in the 2001 version of history? *Bella figura* dictated that a mistake could never be admitted, let alone a fib. The Vatican composed a marvellous piece of confusing prose, designed to restore the *bella figura* and hide the *bruta* by even more misrepresentation. In referring to the letter from the Congregation of the Doctrine of the Faith on 18 May 2001, the revised historical introduction said:

> This letter informed the bishops of the new law and the new procedures which replaced the Instruction *Crimen Sollicitationis.*

Having admitted that *Crimen Sollicitationis* had been repealed, the Vatican then muddies the waters by repeating what the 18 May 2001 letter said. The letter's statement that *Crimen Sollicitationis* was 'in force until now' was incorrect, but this could be overcome by 'mentally reserving' the falsity of the facts stated in the letter, and simply repeating what the letter said—without making any comment

---

83. Cafardi, http://commonwealmagazine.org/scandal-secrecy (Accessed 27 May 2013).

about whether it was true or not. It was another exquisite piece of 'mental reservation' designed to correct the Orwellian rewrite of history, and at the same time to preserve the *bella figura*. As Cardinal Connell explained mental reservation, 'you can use an ambiguous expression realising that the person who you are talking to will accept an untrue version'. In this new, ambiguous historical introduction, the Vatican was talking to the whole world.

On 20 March 2010, two months prior to the publication of this longer historical introduction, and the day after Benedict XVI's *Pastoral Letter* to the people of Ireland was published, Monsignor Scicluna, the Vatican's chief prosecutor attached to the Congregation for the Doctrine of the Faith, gave an interview with the English Catholic magazine, *The Tablet*. It was put to him that some people had used *Crimen Sollicitationis* to accuse Pope Benedict of being involved in the cover up when he was Prefect of that Congregation. Scicluna denied it, praised his old boss, and said that it was only with the *2001 Motu Proprio* that paedophilia came within the exclusive jurisdiction of his Congregation, confirming that it was not before.[84]

Sydney's Cardinal Pell, who was a member of the Congregation for the Doctrine of the Faith from 1990 to 2000, told the *Victorian Parliamentary Inquiry* in 2013 something similar, when he was asked about the Vatican's handling of the sexual abuse by clergy. He said that the Congregation for the Clergy 'did not get it', and so Pope John Paul II was persuaded by the American bishops to transfer the whole issue of clergy sexual abuse to the Congregation for the Doctrine of the Faith.[85]

The web had become hopelessly tangled, and the *bella figura* terminally *bruta*, pushed along by the Vatican's chief prosecutor, and confirmed some three years later by an Australian Cardinal, both of whom were telling the truth. As will be shown in chapter 21, it is not surprising that the Vatican involved itself in such obfuscation and the use of 'mental reservation' because there are theological problems about admitting that popes had ever made mistakes, let alone had been telling fibs.

---

84. http://www.thetablet.co.uk/article/14451 (Accessed 4 April 2013).
85. http://www.parliament.vic.gov.au/images/stories/committees/fcdc/ inquiries/57th/Child_Abuse_Inquiry/Transcripts/Catholic_Archdiocese_of_ Sydney_27-May-13.pdf, 21.8 (Accessed 3 July 2013).

If *Crimen Sollicitationis* had indeed been *in force* between 1983 and 2001 to deal with clergy sex crimes against children, then practically every bishop and canon lawyer in the world had been misled by the Vatican into thinking that the five year limitation period applied and that the 'judicial' procedure was the only way to dismiss child sex abusing priest. This was certainly Bishop Geoffrey Robinson's view after his meeting at the Vatican in April 2000. On 10 May 2000, he reported to the Australian Catholic Bishops Conference that due to the statute of limitations under canon law, 'only a very small proportion of cases would be able to proceed to the judicial process'.[86] In other words, in Australia and other countries without the benefit of the extension given to the Americans in 1994 and the Irish in 1996, the canonical procedures for dismissing clergy sexual abusers from the priesthood were all but useless.

Quite apart from any confusion about the law that applied, the really extraordinary thing is that the Vatican finally agreed to extend the limitation periods for the Americans and Irish, because their bishops were telling the Roman Curia cardinals that children take some time to come to terms with what has happened to them, and are unlikely to complain within five years of their being abused. Were the Vatican cardinals so out of touch that they thought that children in other parts of the world, such as Australia, would not be similarly affected, and as a result their priest abusers would also escape dismissal under canon law?

It took thirteen years from the time the Vatican was first told about this problem in 1988 until 2001 before it finally agreed to extend the limitation period for the rest of the world. There was only one beneficiary of a limitation period: the accused priest. A limitation period cuts off any redress at the door of the court. The court is precluded from even considering whether the abuse took place, because the crime has been 'extinguished' by the lapse of time. If the curia cardinals were convinced that the adults who were complaining about sexual abuse as children were making false claims of rape, like Potiphar's wife, then there was a guillotine solution to the problem:

---

86. NCPS Meeting Minutes 10 May 2000, *Australian Church Submission*, 90, paragraph 53 (a)http://dev.childabuseroyalcommission.gov.au/wp-content/ uploads/2013/10/14.-Truth-Justice-and-Healing-Council.pdf (Accessed 12 October 2013).

introduce a limitation period that made it virtually impossible for there to be a canonical trial. That seems to be the only feasible explanation for the introduction for the five year limitation period in 1983, and why it took eighteen years for an extension to be granted to the whole world. It had finally dawned on the cloistered cardinals that those alleging sexual abuse against priests were not like Potiphar's wife. They were, in fact, telling the truth.

But there were further misrepresentations in the 2010 attempt to correct history when revising the *2010 Motu Proprio*. The revision discussed how canon law dealt with clergy sexual abusers in the period between the end of the Second Vatican Council in 1965 and 1983 when the new *Code of Canon Law* came into force. It said:

> The reforms proposed by the Second Vatican Council required a reform of the 1917 Code of Canon Law and of the Roman Curia. The period between 1965 and 1983 ... was marked by differing trends in canonical scholarship as to the scope of canonical penal law and the need for a de-centralized approach to cases with emphasis on the authority and discretion of the local bishops. [87]

The 'decentralised approach' was not something invented by 'canonical scholarship' after the Second Vatican Council in 1965. It was enshrined in *Crimen Sollicitationis* in 1922 with the local bishops conducting the trials. The only involvement of the Vatican under *Crimen Sollicitationis* was for it to be notified of the allegation and the outcome of the trial, to deal with any procedural difficulties and to handle appeals.[88] By 2013, according to the former Vatican Promoter of Justice, Monsignor Scicluna, the Vatican still uses that decentralised approach.[89] The revised historical introduction then continued:

---

87. http://www.vatican.va/resources/resources_introd-storica_en.html (Accessed 5 August 2013).

88. *Crimen Sollicitationis*, Clause 66, 67 and 74, 45, 54, 58, 59. Clause 74 required a dismissal from the religious life to be approved by the Holy Office in the case of 'exempt religious'.

89. http://ncronline.org/news/accountability/canon-lawyers-hear-church-prosecutor-sex-abuse-cases (Accessed 27 October 2013) 'Although all sexual abuse cases are referred to Rome, few cases are resolved directly by the Congregation for the Doctrine of the Faith. The general practice is to allow the local church to exercise its jurisdiction under the supervision of CDF.'

> A 'pastoral attitude' to misconduct was preferred and canonical processes were thought by some to be anachronistic. A 'therapeutic model' often prevailed in dealing with clerical misconduct. The bishop was expected to 'heal' rather than 'punish'. An over-optimistic idea of the benefits of psychological therapy guided many decisions concerning diocesan or religious personnel, sometimes without adequate regard for the possibility of recidivism.[90]

The 'pastoral attitude' and 'therapeutic model' were not invented after the Second Vatican Council either. They were written into *Crimen Sollicitationis* in 1922 by its secrecy provisions, preventing reporting to the police, and by only allowing the dismissal of a priest where he shows 'no hope, humanly speaking, or almost no hope, of his amendment'. Pope John Paul II and his Roman Curia continued the 'pastoral approach' towards child sex abusing priests, because the *1983 Code of Canon Law* required it before even commencing a formal trial—it even uses that word.[91]

They even strengthened this requirement because under *Crimen Sollicitationis* the 'pastoral approach' was a matter to be taken into account on sentence.[92] Under the *1983 Code of Canon Law*, it was a matter to be taken into account in deciding if the priest should be subjected to a formal trial at all. If there is any doubt about the meaning of the 'pastoral' approach, one only has to look at the way the Congregation for the Doctrine of the Faith handled the Fr Lawrence Murphy case in 1998, just three years before the issue of the *2001 Motu Proprio*.[93]

Pope John Paul II and his curia must also have thought that 'canonical processes' were 'anachronistic', because the *1983 Code of Canon Law* made it virtually impossible to use them to dismiss a priest. This was yet another attempt at *bella figura*, blaming 'canonical scholars' and 'diocesan or religious personnel' when the attitudes that Benedict now criticised were enshrined in canon law by Pope John Paul II himself.

---

90. http://www.vatican.va/resources/resources_introd-storica_en.html (Accessed 5 August 2013).
91. Canon 1341.
92. Clause 63.
93. The case of Fr Lawrence Murphy is discussed in detail in chapter 15.

Nicholas Cafardi writes that, after the promulgation of the *1983 Code of Canon Law,* there was 'nearly unanimous' agreement amongst canon lawyers in the United States that the proper approach, required by canon law was 'the therapeutic and pastoral approach', that is, sending off these priests to treatment centres rather than having them prosecuted either under civil law or canon law.[94] The Vatican did not think any differently. The end result, Professor Cafardi is reported to have said:

> When it came to handling child sexual abuse by priests,
> our legal system fell apart.[95]

Canon law's collapse was predictable. It became a house of cards in 1922 when the Church's leaders went up to the temple to pray and thanked God that they were not like the rest of men, that they had been ontologically changed, so that even if some of their brethren were sexually assaulting children, there was no need for them to be reported to the police and to spend time in jail. The Church's internal disciplinary system was so hopeless, that the only way to dismiss a paedophile priest was to beg him to sign a request to be laicised. As we shall see, bishops even visited these priests in jail when the civil law finally caught up with them, begging them to consent to laicisation. A priest, who had not been dismissed or laicised, was still entitled to be supported financially by his bishop.[96] The wheels have really fallen off a legal system when it needs the consent of criminals to strike them off the rolls of their profession, and to deprive them of the income paid by the very institution they betrayed.

---

94. Cafardi, *Before Dallas,* 20–21.
95. http://www.nytimes.com/2010/07/02/world/europe/02pope.html?pagewanted=all&_r=2& (Accessed 21 June 2013). Fr Frank Brennan SJ made a similar comment in 'Church-State Issues and the Royal Commission', in *Eureka Street,* 3 September 2013: 'The church processes and canonical procedures for dealing with child sexual abuse have in the past been highly deficient', http://www.eurekastreet.com.au/article.aspx?aeid=38146#.Ui5vaKt-8qQ (Accessed 10 September 2013).
96. Canon 281, Delaney, *Canonical Implications of the Response of the Catholic Church in Australia,* 198: ' . . . c 1350 specifies 'except in the case of dismissal from the clerical state, care must always be taken that he does not lack what is necessary for his worthy support.'

10

The Secrecy Provision of Canon Law

The Secret of the Holy Office

The 'secret of the Holy Office' under *Crimen Sollicitationis* applied to canonical investigations and trials against clerics for the matters set out in *Crimen Sollicitationis*: soliciting sex in the confessional, homosexuality, bestiality and sex assaults on children. The breach of this secrecy incurred automatic excommunication that could only be lifted by the pope personally.

The 'strictest confidentiality' was imposed at the start of the investigation into an allegation of a cleric sexually assaulting a child.[1] Before he started an investigation, the bishop, theoretically, was free to go to the civil authorities to report allegations against a priest.[2] That all changed in 1974.

The Pontifical Secret

In 1974, Pope Paul VI abolished 'the secret of the Holy Office' and replaced it with the 'pontifical secret', which extended the secrecy to the allegation itself. The pontifical secret is the subject of the instruction *Secreta Continere* of 4 February 1974 issued by the

---

1. Clause 33. 'Once the Ordinary has received any denunciation of the crime of solicitation, he will . . . summon two witnesses . . . who know well both the accused and the accuser. In the presence of the notary . . . he is to place them under a solemn oath to tell the truth and to maintain confidentiality, under threat, if necessary, of excommunication reserved to the local Ordinary or to the Holy See . . ', http://www.vatican.va/resources/resources_crimen-sollicitationis-1962_en.html (Accessed 4 August 2013).
2. Fr Thomas Doyle, http://reform-network.net/?p=3006 paragraph5(d) (Accessed 3 July 2013). 'The highest degree of secrecy, the Secret of the Holy Office, was imposed on everyone involved in the process from the time it started'.

Vatican Secretariat of State.[3] Pontifical secrecy in that instruction is described as one with a more 'serious obligation'.[4] The Church's 'Top Secret' classification covers matters such as the preparation of papal documents, notifications from the Congregation for the Doctrine of the Faith about teachings, reports of papal legates covered by pontifical secrecy, information on the appointment of bishops and naming of cardinals, papal legates and officers of the Roman Curia. It also covered the allegations, evidence and judgment in a canonical trial for canonical crimes against faith and morals, which includes sexual abuse of minors.[5]

The term 'pontifical secret' is not used in the *1983 Code of Canon Law* itself, and it was imposed by the decree *Secreta Continere* of 1974. The *2001 Motu Proprio* and its revision in 2010 specifically incorporated the pontifical secret into the *Substantive Norms* in Article 25 and Article 30 respectively. *Secreta Continere* provides:

> Article 1. Included under the pontifical secret are:
> 4. **Extrajudicial denunciations received regarding delicts against faith and against morals,** and regarding delicts perpetrated against the sacrament of Penance; likewise **the trial and decision** which pertain to those denunciations, with due regard for the right of the one who has been reported to the authorities to know of the denunciation, if such knowledge is necessary for his own defense . . . (90)[6] (my emphasis).

The term 'extrajudicial denunciation' is not a technical term in canon law, and it simply means 'an allegation' outside any formal court

---

3. The text is published in *Acta Apostolicae Sedis,* 1974, 89–92, shttp://www.documentcloud.org/documents/243690-10-sacramentorum-sanctitatis-2001-with-2003.html Footnote (31) (English), http://www.vatican.va/resources/resources_norme_en.html Footnote 41 (Latin)(Accessed 4 August 2013).

4. http://www.iuscanonicum.org/index.php/documentos/70-discursos-del-romano-pontifice/380.. (Accessed 25 June 2013) http://www.tutorgigpedia.com/ed/Pontifical_secret (Accessed 25 June 2013).

5. *Ibid.*

6. http://www.documentcloud.org/documents/243690-10-sacramentorum-sanctitatis-2001-with-2003.html (Accessed 4 August 2013). Footnote (31) (English), http://www.vatican.va/resources/resources_norme_en.html , Footnote 41 (Latin).

processes.[7] The terms of Article 1§4, that require secrecy, are very tight. A specific exception is made so that the accused is allowed to know about the allegation (the 'denunciation') against him, but there is no exception for reporting to the police.[8]

---

7. It is referred to in the documents of the Spanish Inquisition where informers accused people in their community of heresy: Andrew Dixon White: *Records of the Spanish Inquisition* (2012) Goodrich, 267. Canon 1537 deals with 'extra-judicial confessions', which Beal in the *New Commentary of the Code of Cannon* law, 1673 says refers to a confession 'made out of the context of the trial. The statement is later brought to the attention of the court, often by a witness who heard the confession.' The word 'confession' in Canon 1535 seems to be the same as an 'admission' in civil law. The Canon Law Centre has this definition of *extrajudicial evidence*: 'Evidence which is presented outside of a judicial process. The term applies to evidence which is introduced before the judicial process has begun. After the process has begun, it applies to evidence which is not given to a judge or duly appointed delegate, auditor or the like. Such evidence can be admitted into the acts by judicial decree and thereby obtain probative force'. http://www.canonlawcentre.com/glossary-of-canonical-terms/ (Accessed 9 August 2013). The Catholic Encyclopaedia defines a 'denunciation' as 'denunciation (Latin denunciare) is making known the crime of another to one who is his superior.' http://www.newadvent.org/cathen/04733b.htm (Accessed 9 August 2013). Likewise, the role of the fiscal procurator is 'in preventing crime and safeguarding ecclesiastical law. In case of notification or denunciation it is his duty to institute proceedings and to represent the law. His office is comparable to that of the state attorney in criminal cases'. http://www.newadvent.org/cathen/06082b.htm (Accessed 9 August 2013). The term 'extrajudicial denunciation' in canon law therefore refers to an allegation made against someone to his superior, outside the context of any trial. The English word, 'denounce' still has the meaning of reporting a crime to the police or other civil authority, but the word 'report' is more commonly used. Spanish still uses the term *denunciar* to refer to reporting a crime to the police. Cardinals Castrillón and Bertone, and Monsignor Scicluna in arguing that bishops should not report paedophile priests to the police also used (or their translators did) the word 'denounce' to the police. Fr John Beal considered that the secrecy applied to the allegations themselves: John P Beal 'The 1962 Instruction: Crimen Sollicitationis: Caught Red Handed or Handed a Red Herring?', 41 *Studia Canonica*, 199 at 231–233, http://www.vatican.va/resources/resources_introd-storica_en.html (Accessed 5 August 2013).

8. Edward Peters in his article, 'Lest Amateurs Argue Canon Law: A reply to Patrick Gordon's brief against Bp. Thomas Dail', in *Angelicum* 83 (2006): 121–142. http://www.canonlaw.info/a_gordon.htm (Accessed 3 July 2013), refers to the differences between the canonical and common law systems, pointing out that the canonical draftsman may not be as precise as his common law counterpart because he knows that if difficulties of interpretation come up, then the legislature can make it clear what the law means. Civil lawyers in Australia are familiar with this kind of system with 'rulings' given by the Australian Taxation

When Pope Benedict XVI revised the *2001 Motu Proprio* in 2010, the Vatican spokesman, Fr Lombardi, explained the changes on 15 July 2010 and mentioned 'collaboration with the civil authorities':

> It must be borne in mind that the Norms being published today are part of the penal code of canon law, which is complete in itself and entirely distinct from the law of states.[9]

Canon law is not complete in itself because it specifically incorporates parts of civil law, such as the law of contract for the particular region where the Church is operating. Nor it is 'entirely distinct' from the law of states, because its canonical crimes include such things as homicide, kidnapping, mutilating or gravely wounding someone, fraud, and sexual assaults on minors, and more recently, sexual abuse of people with intellectual disabilities and the possession of child pornography, all of which are crimes under civil law. Canon law provides for entirely different punishments for them.[10] Fr Lombardi then went on to discuss the secrecy requirements for the canonical procedures, and referred to the *Guide to Understanding Basic CDF Procedures concerning Sexual Abuse Allegations*, published on the Vatican website, which stated that 'civil law concerning the reporting of crimes to the appropriate authorities should always be followed':

> This means that in the practice suggested by the Congregation for the Doctrine of the Faith it is necessary to comply with the requirements of law in the various

---

Office. However, in the case of pontifical secrecy, as will be seen below, there were statements from the highest levels in the Vatican from 1997–2002 that reporting to the police conflicted with canon law one way or another. And even if the Levada guidelines of 3 May 2011 can now be regarded as an authoritative interpretation, reporting only applies where there is a local law requiring it. However, even that argument is untenable, because the whole purpose of the guidelines was not to create some definitive ruling on the interpretation of canon law, but for canon law to be changed on a regional basis by approval of protocols of Bishops Conferences pursuant to Canon 455.

9. http://www.vatican.va/resources/resources_lombardi-nota-norme_en.html (Accessed 21 July 2013).
10. Canons 1395–1397.

countries, **and to do so in good time, not during or subsequent to the canonical trial** (my emphasis).[11]

As I have explained earlier, the 'trial' in the canonical and continental system of law includes the investigation, and in the case of canon law, this means the 'preliminary investigation' under Canon 1717, which the bishop is required to undertake where the allegation 'at least seems to be true'. The allegation itself is subject to pontifical secrecy under *Secreta Continere*, and so is any preliminary investigation under Canon 1717, because it involves obtaining proof of the allegations.[12] Likewise, in the *2001 Motu Proprio* and its 2010 revision, pontifical secrecy is not just imposed on 'trials'. The decrees say that 'cases of this kind' and 'cases of this nature' are subject to pontifical secrecy. So, when is 'in good time' under canon law? Never, because the allegation itself is subject to pontifical secrecy.[13] It is part of the 'case'. The Canadian canon lawyer, Fr Francis G Morrissey suggested that

11. http://www.vatican.va/resources/resources_lombardi-nota-norme_en.html (Accessed 21 July 2013). Amongst the documents produced by the Archdiocese of Milwaukee the decision of the judicial tribunal in the case against Fr Knighton, the following note appeared at the bottom of the definitive sentence of 27 July 2007: 'Be it known to all that this case is explicitly subject to the pontifical secret (Article 25, *Graviora Delicta*); this applies to all information, processes and decisions associated with this case (*Secreta Continere*, February 4, 1974 (AAS 66 1974, 89–92)'. http://www.andersonadvocates.com/documents/Key_Milwaukee_Documents/Lacization_All.pdf (Accessed 2 July 2013).

12. John G Proctor: 'Clerical Misconduct: Canonical and Practical Consequences', *Canon Law Society of American Proceedings*, 49 (1988): 227–244. 'It is imperative that the good name of the accused or of the accuser not be placed in jeopardy. Thus, the investigation is confidential, even to the point of placing any acta in the secret archive of the chancery. Having completed the investigation (or having decided that it is superfluous), the bishop must make three determinations: ... If something further should be done, should the penal process be employed? If the penal process is seen as an adequate response to the situation, should the bishop then proceed administratively or judicially?' The author is obviously talking about the preliminary investigation and not the formal judicial trial, as being 'confidential'.

13. Delaney, *Canonical Implications of the Response of the Catholic Church in Australia,* 232, referring to Article 25 of the *2001 Motu Proprio*: 'Accordingly, not only the acts of the process, including the judgment, but also the denunciation itself are subject to pontifical secrecy. This article follows the requirement of Crimen sollicitationis that all who participate in cases to which it applies should observe the strictest secrecy, the secrecy of the Holy Office.'

the diocesan authorities make discreet inquiries within twenty-four hours of being notified, and then if there is a civil law requirement to report, to do so immediately, before any preliminary investigation that entails taking statements of witnesses etc, occurs.[14]

Even if one ignores the words 'extrajudicial denunciations' in *Secreta Continere*, and confines pontifical secrecy to the formal judicial trial after the preliminary investigation, that means that if the preliminary investigation comes up with evidence of two sexual assaults on children, but the priest admits to twenty two at the judicial trial, and even admits to murdering one of the children, no one involved with the tribunal, and the bishop to whom they report, can take that information to the police without breaching canon law, and risking excommunication. It is useless for the Church to say that no bishop or tribunal judge would hide that from the police, because the whole point of any law—civil or canonical—is that it should be obeyed. A system of law, whether civil or canonical that does not mean what it says has lost its integrity.

On 19 July 2010, Fr Lombardi expanded on these comments on the revised norms on the Vatican website through the Catholic News Service, and said that judicial trials for sexual abuse by clergy were 'dealt with in strict confidentiality', and that the reason was: 'to protect the dignity of everyone involved'. He said that while the Vatican norms:

> . . . do not directly address the reporting of sex abuse to civil authorities, it remains the Vatican's policy to encourage bishops to report such crimes wherever required by civil law. These norms are part of canon law; that is, they exclusively concern the church. For this reason they do not deal with the subject of reporting offenders to the civil authorities.[15]

---

14. Morrissey 'Procedures to be Applied in the case of Sexual Misconduct by a Priest', in *Studia Canonica* 26 (1992): 39–73 at 49 & 56, http://www.attorneygeneral.jus. gov.on.ca/inquiries/cornwall/en/hearings/exhibits/Frank_Morrisey/pdf/06_ Morrisey_Procedures.pdf (Accessed 30 June 2013). Morrissey later says that the reporting laws should also be complied with if, after the preliminary inquiry, it is found that there are reasonable grounds to believe that the crime against minors has been committed (at 57). He makes no mention of pontifical secrecy. This opinion conflicts with the plain words of *Secreta Continere*, and the views expressed by John G Proctor and by senior Vatican Cardinals and canon lawyers.

15. http://www.catholicnews.com/data/stories/cns/1002901.htm (Accessed 6 March

This is another example of the Vatican's use of 'mental reservation'. Part of his statement is true and part is false. Breaches of Church rules regarding the sacraments and the ordination of women do 'exclusively concern the Church'. But the sexual abuse of children and people with intellectual disabilities, and the possession of child pornography do not 'exclusively concern the Church'. They are serious crimes under the civil law of practically every country in the world. When the norms imposed 'strict confidentiality' on any information obtained through the Church investigation and trial of such matters, it is incorrect to assert, that they 'do not directly address' reporting of sexual abuse to civil authorities. They prohibit any allegation or information obtained from the Church investigation and trial being reported to anyone except the accused priest and his bishop. Reporting to the civil authorities could not have been more directly addressed. The only dispensation to that prohibition, from 2010 onwards, is when the civil law required reporting.

Other Secrecy Provisions in the *1983 Code of Canon Law*

There are other secrecy provisions throughout the *1983 Code of Canon Law*, including the requirements for judges and tribunal personnel:

> Judges and tribunal personnel are always bound to observe secrecy of office in a penal trial . . .[16]

2013) http://en.radiovaticana.va/storico/2010/07/16/vatican%E2%80%99s_revised_rules_on_sexual_abuse_of_children/in2-408723 (Accessed 25 August 2013).

16. Canon 1455§1, §2. Canon 1455 §1:
Judges and tribunal personnel are always bound to observe secrecy of office in a penal trial, as well as in a contentious trial if the revelation of some procedural act could bring disadvantage to the parties. §2. They are also always bound to observe secrecy concerning the discussion among the judges in a collegiate tribunal before the sentence is passed and concerning the various votes and opinions expressed there, without prejudice to the prescript of Canon 1609, §4. §3. Whenever the nature of the case or the proofs is such that disclosure of the acts or proofs will endanger the reputation of others, provide opportunity for discord, or give rise to scandal or some other disadvantage, the judge can bind the witnesses, the experts, the parties, and their advocates or procurators by oath to observe secrecy. In the case of a 'contentious trial', that is, the canonical equivalent of a civil claim for damages or other remedy, the secrecy of office is to be observed, 'if the revelation of some procedural act could bring disadvantage to the parties' http://www.vatican.va/archive/ENG1104/__P5H.HTM (Accessed 6 October, 2013). See also, Delaney, *Canonical Implications of the Response of the*

A penal trial only begins after the preliminary investigation is completed under Canon 1717. It therefore does not prevent reporting to the civil authorities before the penal trial begins. The prohibition on reporting to police at any time after the receipt of the allegation is imposed by *Secreta Continere*, not by Canon 1717.

Likewise, where there a risk of 'scandal' (as there always will be in the case of sexual abuse of children), the judges can make the witnesses take an oath of secrecy.[17] Clergy who hold diocesan offices, such as vicars general are required to observe secrecy.[18]

All the documentary evidence created during the preliminary trial under Canon 1717 is to be kept in the secret archive of the diocese.[19] There are no exceptions for communicating either that information or documents to the civil authorities.

The Australian canon lawyer, Dr Rodger Austin expressed the view to the Maitland-Newcastle Inquiry that if a civil court required the disclosure of material revealed to a Church tribunal, the appropriate thing would be to seek a dispensation to reveal it. He did not indicate who could 'dispense' with such secrecy, but canon law says that it would have to come from the Vatican.[20] The fact that

---

Catholic Church in Australia, 165
17. Canon 1455§3.
18. Canon 471/2, Delaney, *Canonical Implications of the Response of the Catholic Church in Australia,*165.
19. Canon 1719.
20. Canon 87, and Beal, Coriden and Green, *New Commentary on the Code of Canon Law*, 130–132. Canon 85 provides 'A dispensation, or the relaxation of a merely ecclesiastical law in a particular case, can be granted by those who possess executive power within the limits of their competence, as well as by those who have the power to dispense explicitly or implicitly either by the law itself or by legitimate delegation'. Canon 87 provides that a bishop: 'is not able to dispense, however, from procedural or penal laws nor from those whose dispensation is specially reserved to the Apostolic See or some other authority.' See also Delaney, *Canonical Implications of the Response of the Catholic Church in Australia,* 182, and Dr Rodger Austin at the *Maitland-Newcastle Special Inquiry,* http://www.lawlink.nsw.gov.au/lawlink/Special_Projects/ll_splprojects.nsf/vwFiles/Transcript_Day_20_-_TOR_2_-_31_July_2013.pdf/$file/Transcript_Day_20_-_TOR_2_-_31_July_2013.pdf , 2233. Austin's assertion at 2230 that there are no restrictions under canon law on reporting allegations of sexual abuse to the civil authorities seems to be contradicted by his later evidence that if a civil court required the disclosure of material before a canonical tribunal, the witness would have to seek a 'dispensation' from the Church to reveal it.

a person involved in the tribunal would have to get a 'dispensation' because they had been subpoenaed to appear in a civil court is further evidence that canon law prohibited the voluntary disclosure of such matters to the civil authorities.

Delicts against Morals

The *1983 Code of Canon Law* defined a number of 'delicts against morals'. The decree *Secreta Continere* of 4 February 1974 provides that pontifical secrecy is also to apply to all investigations and trials for 'delicts against . . . morals', and that goes well beyond homosexuality, bestiality and clergy sexual abuse of minors covered by *Crimen Sollicitationis.*

Canon 1397 includes in its list of 'delicts against morals', homicide, kidnapping, mutilating or seriously wounding someone and fraud. Any Catholic can be tried for these crimes in a Church court, and pontifical secrecy will apply to those proceedings from the time the allegations are made, throughout the investigation and to the conclusion of any trial, with no exceptions for reporting these matters to the civil authorities. The chances of hiding murder, kidnapping or serious bodily harm from the police are fairly small. But the chances of hiding a sex assault by a priest on a child are very high. And in that, the Church was remarkably successful.[21]

The Justification for Pontifical Secrecy

Edward N Peters, an American canon lawyer argued that *Crimen Sollicitationis* was simply a more detailed instruction on how to proceed under the *1917 Code of Canon Law*. He points out that the *1917 Code* also dealt with sexual abuse of minors, as well as homosexuality, bestiality etc. and that confidentiality was already part of the inquiry based system based on Roman law.[22]

But *Crimen Sollicitationis* took secrecy to new levels. The *1917 Code of Canon Law* imposed confidentiality on matters involving

---

21. In *Sex Crimes and the Vatican*, the Benedictine priest, Patrick Wall had the job in the United States of covering up the sex crimes of priests with a $7m budget : 'Most of the cases never saw the light of day. Hence we were successful'. He said that the Church had to have a confidentiality order. 'The biggest thing you have to do is to absolutely shut down the scandal.'
22. 1917 Code cc.364 § 2 n 3, 1623 § 1.

Church tribunals in terms similar to the *1983 Code of Canon Law*.[23] *Crimen Sollicitationis*, however, imposed 'the secret of the Holy Office' the breach of which carried automatic excommunication, the same punishment that was applied to breaking the seal of confession. Further, the excommunication could only be lifted by the Pope personally and not even by the Sacred Penitentiary which normally handled such matters.[24] Further, when Pope Paul VI modified the 'secret of the Holy Office' and renamed it the 'pontifical secret', he referred to various levels of secrecy required, and in some matters of major importance, a special secret with a much more serious obligation, called the 'pontifical secret' is applied.[25] It is the Church's 'Top Secret' classification.

Peters talks about the secrecy provisions in *Crimen Sollicitationis* as if they were no more than the confidentiality required by the continental European system to prevent the contamination of evidence.[26] Whatever may be the situation in other European countries, German law does not impose any such confidentiality.[27] In the common law adversarial system, witnesses under cross examination may be asked not to speak to other witnesses until the trial is over to avoid this 'contamination' that Peters talks about. But then their evidence is usually given in open courts with access to the public, and afterwards, there is nothing to stop anyone involved in the process from talking about it in the pub, to the press, or over the back fence. Further, except in some rare cases, the transcript of evidence is available, as are the reasons for judgment. The secrecy imposed by *Crimen Sollicitationis*, and *Secreta Continere* was of an entirely different character.

Fr John P Beal, another eminent canon lawyer also argues that there was nothing sinister about such a requirement of secrecy, because it is

---

23. 1917 Code 1623, and 1983 Code of Canon Law 1455.
24. http://www.catholicculture.org/culture/library/dictionary/index.cfm?id=31912 (Accessed 10 July 2013).
25. 'Pero en ciertos asuntos de mayor importancia se requiere un secreto particular, que es llamado secreto pontificio y que debe ser custodiado con obligación grave.' (Spanish translation of *Secreta Continere*) http://www.iuscanonicum.org/index.php/ documentos/70-discursos-del-romano-pontifice/380 (Accessed 10 July 2013).
26. http://www.themediareport.com/wp-content/uploads/2012/08/Peters-reply-to-Wall-and-Doyle.pdf , paragraph 73, footnote 116 (Accessed 3 July 2013).
27. Dr Stefan von der Beck, Chief Judge, Supreme Court, Oldenburg (Lower Saxony), Germany, in private correspondence with the author in January 2014.

standard practice in law enforcement agencies, such as the CIA and the FBI to protect the confidentiality of their sources and investigative manuals.[28] Fr Beal's reference to law enforcement agencies such as the FBI and CIA in the common law system emphasises the difference between the common law system and the canonical system. In the latter, the 'trial' starts with the allegation and investigation, and not subsequent to it, as in the common law system.[29] The same is true of the European continental system.[30]

The secrecy required by *Crimen Sollicitationis* went well beyond the requirements to prevent contamination of evidence, because everyone involved in the process, witnesses, prosecutors, defence canon lawyers and judges were sworn to secrecy for the rest of their lives.[31]

Fr Beal concedes that the oath of secrecy may have been interpreted beyond what, in his opinion, were its strict terms, that is, it only prevented witnesses disclosing the questioning in the tribunal, and not about what happened to them when they were abused. But then, he concedes that ordinary people may not be expected to make such 'casuistic distinctions', and the effect of the oath was to prevent witnesses from reporting the crime to the civil authorities.[32]

The *1983 Code of Canon Law* did not require victims and witnesses to be sworn to secrecy as did *Crimen Sollicitationis*, except at the discretion of the judge to avoid 'scandal', but the whole rationale of avoiding the contamination of evidence makes no sense when applied

28. John P Beal in 'The 1962 Instruction: Crimen Sollicitationis: Caught Red Handed or Handed a Red Herring?', 41 *Studia Canonica* 199 at 228ff. http://www.vatican. va/resources/Beal-article-studia-canonica41-2007-pp.199-236.pdf (Accessed 3 July 2013).

29. Another canon lawyer, Fr Kevin E McKenna JCD expressed a similar view in his 2010 paper to the Canon Law Society of America: May 25, 2010, Canon Law Society of America.http://www.docstoc.com/docs/83976670/USCCB-CANON-LAW-SEMINAR-2010-MCKENNAdoc---Welcome---The-Catholic (Accessed 24 July 2013).

30. Dr Stefan von der Beck, Chief Judge, Supreme Court, Oldenburg (Lower Saxony), Germany, in private correspondence with the author in January 2014.

31. Fr Thomas Doyle in *Mea Maxima Culpa* at 54.20.

32. John P Beal: 'The 1962 Instruction: Crimen Sollicitationis: Caught Red Handed or Handed a Red Herring?', 41 *Studia Canonica*, 199 at 231. http://www.vatican. va/resources/Beal-article-studia-canonica41-2007-pp.199-236.pdf (Accessed 3 July 2013).

to the judges of the tribunal and the bishop to whom they report. They were also bound by pontifical secrecy not to disclose anything that they had discovered in their investigations even after the whole process has been completed.

On 16 July 2010, the Vatican spokesman Fr Federico Lombardi also used the justification that secrecy was necessary to protect the 'dignity' of the people involved in the investigation.[33]

The big difference between European continental civil law system and canon law, not mentioned by Peters, Beal and Lombardi, is that in European continental civil law, it is **the state** that is doing the investigating, not a private organization like the Church. The Court **is** the state. So any confidentiality imposed on witnesses, court staff and investigators is not going to have the effect of keeping the information from the state. That has been the effect of imposing the same confidentiality in canon law proceedings. The state was not allowed to know about it. And *Crimen Sollicitationis* made sure the state did not know about it by requiring the victim and witnesses to observe the same secrecy.

Fr Beal also concedes that this kind of strict secrecy is pointless, and indeed harmful to preserving the reputations of the accuser and accused. He points out that after the case is concluded, the bishop is barred by pontifical secrecy from telling anyone that the accused was either found guilty or not guilty.[34]

The Vatican spokesman, Fr Federico Lombardi confirmed that pontifical secrecy went well beyond preventing contamination of evidence, in his comments on the 2010 revision of the *2001 Motu Proprio*. He said that any reporting to the civil authorities had to be done 'in good time, not **during** or **subsequent** to the canonical trial'[35] (my emphasis). That can only mean that judges, canon lawyers and staff involved in the process are forbidden to reveal the evidence given

---

33. http://www.vatican.va/resources/resources_lombardi-nota-norme_en.html (Accessed 21 July 2013).

34. John P Beal, 'The 1962 Instruction: Crimen Sollicitationis: Caught Red Handed or Handed a Red Herring?', 41 *Studia Canonica,* 199 at 233. http://www.vatican.va/resources/Beal-article-studia-canonica41-2007-pp.199-236.pdf (Accessed 3 July 2013).

35. http://www.vatican.va/resources/resources_lombardi-nota-norme_en.html (Accessed 21 July 2013).

in the proceedings, even to the police. In 2010, Fr Beal referred to the requirements of secrecy after the conclusion of a trial: 'it's canon law, but it's a stupid law'.[36]

On 27 May 2013, Cardinal George Pell, the Archbishop of Sydney gave evidence before the *Victorian Parliamentary Inquiry*. He was asked about *Crimen Sollicitationis* and its requirements of 'strict confidentiality'. He said the original requirement of secrecy was because of the seal of confession, and another reason was to protect the privacy of the person making the allegations. He then said that 'we regard those restrictions now as inappropriate'.[37]

Secrecy was imposed on canonical trials for soliciting sex in the confessional by Pope Pius IX in 1866.[38] In 1922 *Crimen Sollicitationis* applied the 'secret of the Holy Office' to any allegations of sexual abuse of children where there was no connection with confession. That continued until 1974 when *Secreta Continere* replaced the secret of the Holy Office with the pontifical secret, and then expanded that 'Top Secret' classification to include the allegation itself. Then Pope Benedict XVI in 2010 extended it further to cover cases of sexual abuse of people who 'habitually lack the use of reason'. Cardinal Pell might now regard this kind of secrecy as inappropriate, but the Vatican does not.

It was put to Cardinal Pell by one of the parliamentarians, Frank McGuire, that the crime of sexually assaulting children used to be a capital offence in the State of Victoria, and has always had a serious term of imprisonment attached to it. Pell agreed it was a reprehensible crime, and then conceded that the primary motivation for secrecy was the 'fear of scandal' and to protect the reputation of the Church.[39]

In other words, secrecy wasn't just to 'protect the dignity of everyone involved'. Nor could it have been to protect the 'integrity of

---

36. http://ncronline.org/news/vatican/vatican-secrecy-keeps-victims-accused-dark (Accessed 22 July 2013).

37. http://www.parliament.vic.gov.au/images/stories/committees/fcdc/inquiries/57th/Child_Abuse_Inquiry/Transcripts/Catholic_Archdiocese_of_Sydney_27-May-13.pdf page 12.1 (Accessed 3 July 2013).

38. Fr Thomas Doyle, 'The 1922 Instruction and the 1962 Instruction, 'Crimen Sollicitationis' promulgated by the Vatican', http://reform-network.net/?p=3006 (Accessed 10 August 2013).

39. http://www.parliament.vic.gov.au/images/stories/committees/fcdc/inquiries/57th/Child_Abuse_Inquiry/Transcripts/Catholic_Archdiocese_of_Sydney_27-May-13.pdf page 12.8 (Accessed 3 July 2013).

evidence', because once the investigation and trial was over, there was no evidence to be contaminated by witnesses talking to each other. It is pretty obvious that the main motivation was the avoidance of 'scandal', and it still is.

Pontifical Secrecy and the 2010 Revision of the *2001 Motu Proprio Decree*

In 2010, Pope Benedict XVI had an opportunity to abolish pontifical secrecy once and for all, or at least to provide an exception to it, applicable everywhere in the world, that would allow bishops to report clergy sexual abusers to the police, irrespective of what the civil law required. There were no excuses arising from some dreamed up Vatican power struggles. He had been top dog for five years, the absolute monarch who could abolish it with the stroke of a pen. But instead of abolishing the backdoor privilege of clergy through the use of pontifical secrecy, he expanded it to cover clerics having sex with those who 'habitually lack the use of reason', and to priests' possessing child pornography. He thus ensured that civil authorities would be further deprived of evidence about clergy sex crimes.[40]

Pope Benedict's new idea of 'cooperating' with civil authorities had strings attached to it. Reporting would only be permitted where the civil law required it. As we will see, in most parts of the world, with few exceptions, that requirement to report in the majority of cases of sexual abuse does not exist.

---

40. See also Geoffrey Robertson, *The Case of the Pope*, 83. http://www.vatican.va/resources/resources_norme_en.html (Accessed 19 February 2003).

11

Misprision of Felony

The word 'felony' is an old English word that means a serious crime that generally required a jury trial. It contrasted with a 'misdemeanour', a minor crime normally dealt with by Justices of the Peace or Magistrates. They were archaic distinctions that tended to cause procedural problems.

In *Sykes v The Director of Public Prosecutions*[1], Lord Denning, one of judges in the House of Lords that heard the case, said that the crime of 'misprision of felony' had been part of the common law of '700 years or more'.[2] The elements of the crime were 'knowledge' of a felony (a serious crime), and 'concealment' from the civil authorities.[3] He also said that non-disclosure may sometimes be justified if there was a duty to keep the information confidential. Examples are the relationship between lawyer and client, doctor and patient. He also said that an employer who catches an employee involved in petty stealing (which could still be a felony) might be justified in giving him another chance. But where the crime was of a serious nature, even close family ties were no excuse. The other members of the House of Lords agreed. Lord Goddard added that there was no obligation to disclose mere rumours and gossip, but citizens are bound to disclose facts within their knowledge that might assist in arresting the felon.[4]

The decisions of the House of Lords in England are not strictly speaking binding on courts in other common law countries, like Australia, New Zealand, Canada, India and the United States etc, but

---

1. (1962) AC 528, http://www.uniset.ca/other/cs5/1962AC528.html (Accessed 3 July 2013).
2. *Ibid,* 555.
3. *Ibid,* 564.
4. *Ibid,* 570.

they will often be followed unless there seems to be a good reason not to do so.

Australia

In the 1980s there were a number of recommendations of Law Reform Commissions to abolish the archaic distinction between felonies and misdemeanours from the criminal law, and to abolish the common law offence of misprision of felony. It was argued that the crime was necessary when there were no police forces. If someone had committed a serious crime, known as a 'felony', ordinary citizens had the obligation to raise the 'hue and cry', get the posse together, and go and arrest the delinquent. Just like in the old westerns.

Some jurisdictions, such as NSW, abolished the offence in 1990, but replaced it with a statutory form in S.316 *Crimes Act (1900) NSW* where it was an offence not to report a serious crime, unless there was a reasonable excuse—a provision designed to include the confidential relationships outlined by Lord Denning in *Sykes*.[5] But

---

5. Misprision of felony was abolished and Section 316 was inserted into the *Crimes Act 1900 (NSW)* by the *Crimes (Public Justice) Amendment Act (1990)* (NSW), which was proclaimed on 25 November 1990: New South Wales Government Gazette No 141 of 9 November 1990 at 9816. The consent of the Attorney General to a prosecution is required for a prosecution of persons in prescribed professions, such as lawyers, doctors, etc: S.316(4) See S.316(1) provides: 'If a person has committed a serious indictable offence and another person who knows or believes that the offence has been committed and that he or she has information which might be of material assistance in securing the apprehension of the offender or the prosecution or conviction of the offender for it fails without reasonable excuse to bring that information to the attention of a member of the Police Force or other appropriate authority, that other person is liable to imprisonment for 2 years' There is one unreported decision in NSW that deals with the section. In *R v Crofts*, Meagher JA observed: 'The section is a comparatively new section and this is the first case, so far as one knows, which has been brought under it. It is a section which has many potential difficulties, the chief of which is the meaning of the words 'without reasonable excuse', difficulties which are magnified when one endeavours to contemplate how those words would apply to the victim of the crime.' Gleeson CJ added: '. . . depending upon the circumstances of an individual case, it may be extremely difficult to form a judgment as to whether a failure to provide information to the police was "without reasonable excuse"', http://www.judcom.nsw.gov.au/publications/ benchbks/sentencing/public_justice_offences.html#d5e25503. In his evidence before the *Maitland-Newcastle Inquiry*, Fr Brian Lucas took the view that if the victim specifically requested that the matter not be reported to the police, this

the relationship of confidentiality does not exist where a bishop is carrying out a canonical investigation of clergy sex crimes. Such people are investigators, not counsellors. And an employer's wish to avoid bad publicity as a result of a crime by an employee was not regarded as a reasonable excuse where serious crime was involved.[6]

The State of Victoria abolished misprision of felony in 1981 and replaced it with a formulation that did not match the common law one, requiring some positive impediment to a police investigation or some benefit being received for concealing the crime.[7] Merely not reporting it was no longer a crime. The other states have similar formulations.[8]

---

would amount to a 'reasonable excuse'. There is some merit in that argument. http://www.lawlink.nsw.gov.au/lawlink/Special_Projects/ll_splprojects.nsf/vwFiles/Transcript_Day_15_-_TOR_2_-_24_July_2013.pdf/$file/Transcript_Day_15_-_TOR_2_-_24_July_2013.pdf , 1599–1604, http://www.austlii.edu.au/au/legis/nsw/num_act/cjaa1990n51326.pdf (Accessed 3 July 2013), http://www.austlii.edu.au/au/legis/nsw/consol_act/ca190082/notes.html, (Accessed 3 July 2013), http://www.lawlink.nsw.gov.au/lrc.nsf/pages/DP39CHP2 (Accessed 10 February 2013).

6. http://www.lawreform.lawlink.nsw.gov.au/agdbasev7wr/lrc/documents/pdf/report_93.pdf paragraph 3.30. (Accessed 16 July 2013).

7. *S.322B Crime (Classification of Offences Act) (Vic)* 1981 http://www.austlii.edu.au/au/legis/vic/hist_act/cooa1981292.pdf. See also advice of Nicholas Pappas SC to the *Victorian Parliamentary Inquiry,* http://www.parliament.vic.gov.au/images/stories/committees/fcdc/inquiries/57th/Child_Abuse_Inquiry/Submissions/COIN_9.pdf (Accessed 10 February 2013).

8. *Crimes Act 1958 (Vic)* S.325, Schedule 11 of the South Australian *Criminal Law Consolidation Act* abolished misprision of felony in 1994. S.241 creates an offence to impede the investigation or prosecution of an offence but it requires some positive act rather than simply knowing about a crime and doing nothing. S.326 provides for an offence of concealment if there was some 'gain' in return: http://www.austlii.edu.au/au/legis/sa/consol_act/clca1935262/s241.html (Accessed 10 February 2013). The *Victorian Parliamentary Inquiry* in its final Report recommended the removal of the 'gain' provision: https://s3-ap-southeast-2.amazonaws.com/family-and-community-development-committee/Executive+summary+%26+recommendations.pdf, XXVIII. Queensland, Northern Territory and Western Australia have similar formulations of the Victorian legislation, and Tasmania has no general obligation to report, except for treason: http://www.lawlink.nsw.gov.au/lrc.nsf/pages/r93chp3 (Accessed 10 February 2013) See also *Crimes Act 1958* (Vic) s 326; *Criminal Code (Qld)* s 133; *Criminal Code (WA)* s 136; *Criminal Code (NT)* s 104; *Criminal Code (Tas)* s 102; *Crimes Act 1914 (Cth)* s 44, *Criminal Law Consolidation Act 1935 (SA)* s 241. For a summary of the position in other states, see http://www.lawreform.lawlink.nsw.gov.au/

NSW Law Reform Commission Proposal to Abolish S.316 Crimes Act 1900 (NSW)

The NSW Law Reform Commission Report 93 (1999)—*Review of Section 316 of the Crimes Act 1900 (NSW)* recommended, by a majority, that S.316 be abolished. A minority wanted it retained but suggested some amendments. The majority accepted a number of submissions in favour of abolition, but the most telling reason for abolition was because they disapproved of substituting a legal duty, backed up by criminal sanction, for a moral one, unless there are 'overall substantial benefits to society'. [9]

It must come as a surprise to the Law Reform Commissioners that the leaders of the Church did not share this moral sense in the community of reporting serious crimes when it came to the sex assaults of its priests on children.

In 2010, the Australian Church (other than the Melbourne Archdiocese) rectified that by amending *Towards Healing* so as to require all Church personnel to report, even though there is no legal obligation to do so. But this is contrary to canon law, as it presently stands, where the information is obtained through a canonical investigation. The Vatican still does not share this civic morality with the rest of the Australian population when it comes to reporting the sex crimes of priests.

The State of NSW has not acted on this recommendation of the Law Reform Commission. In the light of the cover up of clergy sexual abuse, the secrecy provisions of canon law, and the oath of office that requires Catholic clergy to follow canon law, there are not only 'overall substantial benefits' in retaining it or something like it, but there is now a pressing need. [10]

---

agdbasev7wr/lrc/documents/pdf/report_93.pdf par 3.73 (Accessed 1 August 2013). A similar summary is contained in the Victorian bishops' submission to the *Victorian Parliamentary Inquiry, Facing the Truth* at paragraph 16.2.

9.   New South Wales Law Reform Commission http://www.lawreform.lawlink. nsw.gov.au/agdbasev7wr/lrc/documents/pdf/report_93.pdf   paragraph   3.58 (Accessed 16 July 2013).

10. The Victorian Police and Catholics for Renewal submissions have called for similar laws to those in NSW to be enacted Victoria, http://www. catholicsforrenewal.org/Reports/CFR%20Submission%20on%20handling%20 Religious%20and%20other%20NGO%20Child%20Abuse.pdf   at paragraph 79 (Accessed 3 July 2013). http://www.parliament.vic.gov.au/images/stories/

Other Countries

New Zealand

Misprision of felony is not part of New Zealand law, and there is no duty to inform on others.[11]

Ireland

On 22 July 1997, the Irish Parliament also repealed misprision of felony, and replaced it with statutory offences similar to those in the United Kingdom and the State of Victoria.[12] The *Criminal Justice (Withholding of information on offences against children and vulnerable persons) Act* 2012 came into effect on 18 July 2012. It effectively restores misprision of felony to the Irish law in so far as 'vulnerable persons' are concerned. They are defined as children and those suffering from physical or intellectual disability restricting their capacity to guard against exploitation or abuse. The offence applies to historic abuse. There is a defence available where the victim or guardian has made it known to the person who has the information that he or she does not want it reported.[13]

The United Kingdom

Misprision of felony was abolished in the United Kingdom in 1967, and the failure to report only becomes a crime when some benefit is received as a result.[14] All Australian states, other than New South Wales, have followed that formulation.

France

The French Penal Code has a form of misprision of felony that applies to the deprivation or abuse of children or vulnerable people, and it applies to knowledge of historic abuse and not just those who are children or under a disability at the time the person becomes aware

---

committees/fcdc/inquiries/57th/Child_Abuse_Inquiry/Submissions/Victoria_ Police at p.10(Accessed 3 July 2013).

11. http://www.teara.govt.nz/en/1966/freedom-of-speech.

12. http://www.irishstatutebook.ie/1997/en/act/pub/0014/print.html#sec1 (Accessed 16 July 2013), http://www.independent.ie/opinion/analysis/change-in-the-law-means-there-is-now-no-criminal-offence-for-failure-to-report-crime-26031940.html (Accessed 16 July 2013).

13. http://www.irishstatutebook.ie/2012/en/act/pub/0024/print.html (Accessed 19 May 2013).

14. *Criminal Law Act* 1967. *A v Hayden ('ASIS case')* [1984] HCA 67; (1984) 156 CLR 532 (6 November 1984) per Mason J paragraph 7.

of it.[15] In September 2001, Bishop Pierre Pican was convicted under this section of the Code which does provide for certain exceptions in cases of professional secrecy, but which the Court found did not apply in his case.

Austria

In general, there is no general duty to report serious crimes, but there is an exception for public servants. Failure to report may result into the criminal act of abuse of office.[16] The obligation is extended to some specific categories, like doctors who are required to notify where it appears that death, injury or damage to health has been inflicted on the patient. This also applies to tormenting or neglecting of minors, youth, or helpless persons.[17]

There is an express exception from the duty to report for family members and for recognized professional confidentiality of doctors, lawyers, social workers, psychotherapists and for clerics in respect of knowledge acquired in confessions.[18]

Germany

There is no equivalent of misprision of felony in German law, other than the requirements of mandatory welfare reporting about children at risk.[19]

---

15. Article 434–3. Translation: 'The fact for anyone who has knowledge about deprivation, abuse or sexual abuse inflicted on a minor under fifteen years of age or a person who is not able to protect themselves because of age, a disease, disability, physical or mental disability or pregnancy, not to inform the judicial or administrative authorities is punished by three years imprisonment. Except where otherwise provided by law, are excepted from the foregoing persons permanently bound to secrecy under the conditions provided for in Article 226-13 provisions.' The section also provides for a fine of E45,000. The crime of failing to disclose the abuse is committed even though the accused became aware of it after the victim was an adult. In other words, it applies to 'historic' abuse. In the case of Bishop Pican, it did not matter that the abused person was no longer a child at the time Pican became aware of it. Translation and advice by French lawyer, Pierre-Antoine Cals.

16. The Austrian Code of Criminal Procedure (§ 84 StPO).

17. § 27 Medical Practitioners' Act.

18. Advice to the author by Dr Friedrich Schwank, Vienna, in private correspondence with the author, January 2014.

19. Advice of Dr Stefan von der Beck, Chief Judge, Supreme Court, Oldenburg (Lower Saxony), Germany, in private correspondence with the author in January 2014.

The United States

Misprision of felony is not a common law offence in the United States, but it has been put into statutory form in the *United States Code*.[20] However the requirement has been narrowly interpreted to mean that simply saying nothing is not itself a crime. It requires some form of active concealment which seems to suggest that the requirement is more like the UK and Victorian one.[21]

Some states in the United States also have misprision type statutes, and others require reporting in specific situations.[22] Overall, however, it seems that there is no general duty to report. The prominent American lawyer and Law Professor, Alan Dershowitz has written:

> Unlike many European countries, most American states place no affirmative duty on citizens to report even crimes they have themselves seen, and certainly no duty to report crimes that others have told them about.[23]

Canada

The position in Canada is generally the same as in the United States, and all Australian states, other than NSW. There is no general obligation to report under the Canadian *Criminal Code*, although there are welfare reporting laws in most Provinces that generally only apply to children at risk, but not to historic abuse.[24]

---

20. http://www.law.cornell.edu/uscode/text/18/4 (Accessed 15 July 2013). Whoever, having knowledge of the actual commission of a felony cognizable by a court of the United States, conceals and does not as soon as possible make known the same to some judge or other person in civil or military authority under the United States, shall be fined under this title or imprisoned not more than three years, or both. *(Title 18, §4).*

21. http://heinonline.org/HOL/LandingPage?collection=journals&handle=hein.journals/kentlj84&div=27&id=&page= (Accessed 15 July 2013).

22. http://www.sfu.ca/~palys/ICJR2001.pdf, Cafardi *Before Dallas*, 52, Gerard E Lynch, 'The Lawyer as Informer', in *Duke Law Journal* (1986): 491–548 http://scholarship.law.duke.edu/cgi/viewcontent.cgi?article=2948&context=dlj&sei-redir=1&referer=http%3A%2F%2Fwww.google.ca%2Furl%3Fsa%3Dt%26rct%3Dj%26q%3D%2522Duty%2Bto%2Breport%2Bcrimes%2522. Monsignor Lynn was convicted under 18 Pa.C.S. §4304 (relating to endangering welfare of children). http://law.onecle.com/pennsylvania/crimes-and-offenses/00.043.004.000.html (Accessed 26 September 2013).

23. http://www.huffingtonpost.com/alan-dershowitz/is-paterno-getting-a-bum-_b_1101933.html (Accessed 15 July 2013).

24. http://www.victimsofviolence.on.ca/rev2/index.php?option=com_content&task

Colombia

Colombia has a form of misprision of felony which makes it a crime not to report a serious crime to the civil authorities.[25]

The misprision of felony offence, at common law or in its statutory form, and similar offences in continental law countries, such as France and Colombia, created a direct conflict with the secrecy provisions of canon law at least until the dispensation granted in 2010. The evidence over the last 50 years shows the bishops and clergy did follow canon law, and many of them committed a criminal offence under the civil law by doing so. Bishop Pican was given a suspended sentence in France for failing to report, and there are charges pending against a priest in the State of New South Wales for the same thing.

=view&id=404&Itemid=284 (Accessed 15 July 2013).

25. Article 441, *Colombian Penal Code*. Article 446 also provides for an offence of cover up by a person who knows about a crime. The Colombian Constitution however, preserves the right not to have to incriminate oneself, and does not oblige reporting crimes of spouses or family relatives, http://www.secretariasenado. gov.co/senado/basedoc/ley/2000/ley_0599_2000_pr017.html (Accessed 15 July 2013).

12

Mandatory Welfare Reporting

The John Jay Study of 2004, commissioned by the American Catholic Bishops Conference, stated that virtually every published empirical study shows that victims delay reporting sexual abuse, and do so many years after it occurred.[1]

The *Cloyne Report* examined forty complaints of sexual abuse. Only two of them involved children at risk, and thirty-eight were cases of historic abuse.[2] The Commissioner for *The Melbourne Response* stated to the *Victorian Parliamentary Inquiry* that he investigated 304 complaints of sexual abuse, and only two involved victims who were still children at the time.[3] If those figures apply generally that represents less than one per cent of all complaints.

The significance of this is that virtually all countries have some form of mandatory reporting of sexual abuse of children 'at risk'. But where complaints are made by adults to the Church about being sexually abused by priests as children, (the vast majority of complaints, and possibly more than ninety-nine per cent) the mandatory reporting laws don't apply, even if clergy are included amongst those listed as having the obligation to report.

Australia

Laws passed by all Australian states and territories from 1997 onwards require people working with children to report to civil authorities

---

1. http://johnjay.jjay.cuny.edu/churchstudy/_pdffiles/response1.pdf par 5.1 (Accessed 15 July 2013).
2. The *Cloyne Report,* paragraph 1.8 http://www.justice.ie/en/JELR/Cloyne_Rpt. pdf/Files/Cloyne_Rpt.pdf (Accessed 9 February 2013).
3. http://www.parliament.vic.gov.au/images/stories/committees/fcdc/ inquiries/57th/Child_Abuse_Inquiry/Right_of_Reply/Right_of_Reply_P._ OCallaghan_Part_1.pdf paragrph 7(b) (Accessed 15 July 2013).

any kind of child abuse. The categories of people who are required to report vary from state to state, as does the definition of when the duty to report arises. In general, it arises when there is a reasonable belief or suspicion that a child is being abused or is at risk of significant harm, and the belief or suspicion arises from the person's employment or profession.[4]

In addition to state and territory laws, there are provisions under the *Family Law Act 1975* (Cth), requiring personnel from the Family Courts to report where they have reasonable grounds for suspecting that a child has been abused, or is at risk of being abused.[5]

How all this legislation affects a bishop who has been carrying out an investigation under canon law depends on the state in which his diocese is situated. The table produced by *The Australian Institute of Family Studies*, current to July 2013 for mandatory reporting of child abuse, including sexual abuse, provides a summary of the law and practice throughout Australia.[6]

---

4. http://www.aifs.gov.au/cfca/pubs/factsheets/a141787/index.html (Accessed 15 July 2013).

5. Section 67ZA of the *Family Law Act 1975* www.austlii.edu.au/au/legis/cth/consol_act/fla1975114/s67za.html (Accessed 16 July 2013).

6. http://www.aifs.gov.au/cfca/pubs/factsheets/a141787/index.html (Accessed 5 August 2013). Only South Australia and Northern Territory specifically require clergy to report child abuse. Queensland and Tasmania may require reporting depending on the priest's activities and whether the Church supplies health, welfare and educational services (Qld) or receives funding for them (Tas). S.25A *Ombudsman Act 1974* (NSW) applies to clergy where they are volunteers providing services to schools and organizations providing for the care of children, and the *Children and Young Persons (Care and Protection) Act 1998* (NSW) would only apply if clergy's services were regarded as 'welfare'. In regard to historic abuse, that is, where the victim is now an adult, some state legislation is fairly clear that their legislation applies only to children at risk, for example, the *Children and Young Persons (Care and Protection) Act 1998 (NSW)* refers to 'child . . . at risk', and therefore does not apply to historic abuse. However Part 3A of the *Ombudsman Act 1974* requires reporting of historic abuse. In Victoria, the *Children, Youth and Families Act 2005* (Vic) refers to where 'a child is in need of protection', and therefore does not apply to historic abuse. Other states and Territories (Queensland, South Australia, Western Australia, Tasmania, the Australian Capital Territory and the Northern Territory) refer to a child who 'has experienced or is experiencing' abuse or similar expressions. As these are sections involving criminal sanctions, the normal rule of interpretation is that the stricter interpretation is to be preferred.

In short, only one Australian state, New South Wales, provides for mandatory reporting of historic sexual abuse.[7] The New South Wales *Ombudsman Act 1974* in Part 3A requires reporting of all sexual abuse but only where the priest can be said to be engaged 'to provide services to children'. It is difficult to know whether or not this includes 'pastoral work', such as visiting families. Some of the worst cases of clergy sexual abuse of children have occurred during this activity.[8]

In the other states and territories, it is possible that there might be a requirement to report because of knowledge of a person's history of sexually abusing children, and where he is still in contact with children, therefore there are children 'at risk'. However, if the accused person is no longer in contact with children, it is hard to see where there is a requirement to report historic abuse.

Other Countries

New Zealand
New Zealand currently has no mandatory reporting of child abuse. In October 2012 the government issued a White Paper for discussion on the issue.[9] There is provision for the protection of people who voluntarily report.[10]

The United Kingdom
The United Kingdom currently has no mandatory reporting laws on child abuse in the sense referred to here, other than in Northern Ireland, where there is a statutory form of misprision of felony which would include child abuse.[11]

---

7. *Crimes Act* (NSW) 1900 S.316(1) and *Ombudsman Act* (NSW) 1974 Part 3A
8. A particularly disturbing account is given by Patricia Feenan in her book *Holy Hell*, about the sexual abuse of her son Daniel by Fr James Fletcher who died in jail. http://books.google.com.au/books?id=pn09PgggTAoC&printsec=frontcove r&dq=Holy+Hell+Patricia+Feenan&hl=en&sa=X&ei=sRWXUcqvJsSriAeQ44G ADQ&redir_esc=y (Accessed 15 July 2013).
9. http://www.childrensactionplan.govt.nz/the-white-paper/reporting-child-abuse (Accessed 15 July 2013).
10. *Children, Young Persons and Their Families Act 1989*, S15 and 16 http://www. legislation.govt.nz/act/public/1989/0024/latest/whole.html (Accessed 15 July 2013).
11. http://www.guardian.co.uk/society/2012/nov/09/uk-ireland-report-child- abuse (Accessed 15 July 2013), http://www.change.org/en-GB/petitions/

France

The French Penal Code requires reporting of deprivation or abuse or sexual abuse of children and vulnerable people.[12]

Austria

Certain professions including doctors are required to report cases of tormenting or neglecting minors, youth, or helpless persons.[13]

Germany

It is an offence for a person to fail to render assistance if a child is in actual or permanent danger of being sexually abused.[14]

Ireland

As at October 2012, there was no mandatory reporting in the sense described above, but there are proposals to introduce it following on a proposed Constitutional amendment.[15] The legal situation has been affected by the *Criminal Justice (Withholding of information on offences against children and vulnerable persons) Act* 2012, making it an offence not to report information about the exploitation of 'vulnerable persons'.[16]

The United States

As at August 2012, many states of the United States had clergy as mandatory reporters, and some of them provided privilege for

---

educationgovuk-introduce-law-requiring-adults-working-with-children-to-report-alleged-abuse-mandatenow (Accessed 21 August 2013).

12. Article 434–3, and see details above under Misprision of Felony, chapter 11.

13. § 27 Medical Practitioners' Act, Dr Friedrich Schwank Vienna in personal correspondence with the author, January 2014..

14. § 323 c German Penal Code, Dr Stefan von der Beck, Chief Judge, Supreme Court, Oldenburg (Lower Saxony), Germany, in private correspondence with the author in January 2014

15. http://arrow.dit.ie/cgi/viewcontent.cgi?article=1173&context=ijass (Accessed 15 July 2013) 'S 5 of the Protections for Persons Reporting Child Abuse Act, 1998 provides protection from civil liability for those who report such concerns reasonably and in good faith, while s 4 provides protection for employees who report child abuse concerns. Nevertheless, debate continues as to whether the current, "discretionary" . . . system for the reporting of child abuse provides sufficient protection for children who have already suffered or are at risk of harm . . .' See also *Facing the Truth*, at 5.6.6 on the progress of the *Children First Bill*. http://www.resilience.ie/international-expert-calls-for-mandatory-reporting-on-child-abuse-and-neglect-cases (Accessed 15 July 2013).

16. http://www.irishstatutebook.ie/2012/en/act/pub/0024/print.html (Accessed 19 May 2013).

communications in pastoral situations.[17] Likewise both federal and state laws, as in Australia, seem to be directed to protecting children at risk, and do not relate to complaints of historic abuse. Some states do have statutes dealing with child endangerment. Monsignor Lynn was convicted under such a statute.[18]

Canada

The general situation seems to be the same as in Australia and the United States, and each state has its own particular laws.[19] There is some research which suggests that in some Provinces there is a requirement to report historic abuse.[20]

In the countries surveyed above, the 'welfare' reporting laws generally do not require the reporting by the Church of historic abuse. Likewise, as we have seen from the abolition of misprision of felony, there is no general requirement to report. As will be shown later, this has great significance for the exception to pontifical secrecy that the Vatican proposed in 2010/2011.

17. https://www.childwelfare.gov/systemwide/laws_policies/statutes/clergymandated.pdf#Page=4&view=Fit (Accessed 15 July 2013).

18. Monsignor Lynn was convicted under 18 Pa.C.S. § 4304 (relating to endangering welfare of children). http://law.onecle.com/pennsylvania/crimes-and-offenses/00.043.004.000.html (Accessed 26 September 2013), but his conviction was overturned on appeal on the grounds that the particular statute (since amended) only applied to people who were direct supervisors of children, such as a parent or guardian http://www.pacourts.us/assets/opinions/Superior/out/J-A23005-13o%20-%201016613421853550.pdf?cb=1 (Accessed 26 December 2013).

19. http://cwrp.ca/faqs#Q10 (Accessed 15 July 2013), http://www.children.gov.on.ca/htdocs/English/topics/childrensaid/reportingabuse/abuseandneglect/abuseandneglect.aspx http://www.victimsofviolence.on.ca/rev2/index.php?option=com_content&task=view&id=404&Itemid=284 (Accessed 15 July 2013) 'Persons in a professional capacity are not legally obligated to report cases of child abuse in cases of historical abuse if the victim is now an adult. This means, for example, that if a twenty-five-year-old man tells his doctor that his parent(s) abused him when he was a child, that doctor is not obligated to report that information to the police or other agency', http://www.haltnow.ca/abuse/child-abuse/191-child-abuse-and-the-law.html (Accessed 15 July 2013).

20. https://www.nspcc.org.uk/Inform/publications/downloads/mandatoryreportingNI_wdf51133.pdf at 11(Accessed 15 July 2013).

Pope Paul VI

13

Law and Culture

Before dealing with the practical effects of the policy of secrecy, and how senior members of the hierarchy dealt with the conflicts between canon and civil law, we should look at the interplay of law and culture, because they are inextricably linked. Law is part of culture and it cannot be divorced from it.[1]

Laws will reflect the culture in which they are made. But, in addition to that, they will reinforce that culture once made. Law shapes culture as much as culture shapes law. It is a two way interactive process, with both influencing each other.[2]

The Influence of Law on Culture

The Church is a strong believer in the influence of law on culture. Mary Ann Glendon, one of America's most prominent conservative Catholics, and Harvard Law Professor says that law influences the way people interpret the world around them and it indicates that certain values have a privileged place in society.[3] Cardinal Francis George, the former President of the United States Bishops Conference is also a strong believer in the connection between the two. In his paper 'Law and Culture', he discussed the famous US Supreme Court case of *Brown v The Board of Education,* which ended legal segregation in the

---

1. Naomi Mezey, *Law as Culture,* http://scholarship.law.georgetown.edu/cgi/viewcontent.cgi?article=1310&context=facpub (Accessed 15 July 2013).
2. James L Nolan Jnr *Legal Accents, Legal Borrowing* (Princeton: Princeton University Press,)37. Nolan is Professor of Sociology at Williams College, and David Glandon, quoted by Nolan, is Professor of Law and Sociology at New York University. Mary Ann Glendon, quoted by Nolan is Professor of Law at Harvard University, and at one time US ambassador to the Vatican.
3. *Ibid.*

United States. He pointed out that law, whether just or unjust, acts as a teacher, and the Supreme Court knew that if racial discrimination was to end, the law had to be changed. The segregation laws were a reflection of the culture at the time when they were passed, but their very existence deepened and entrenched that culture.[4] He uses this argument to oppose things like gay marriage. But the principle he enunciated is correct, even if one disagrees with the kinds of things that he thinks should be prohibited or allowed under law. Justice Ronald Sackville, formerly of the Australian Federal Court has made a similar point about the connection between law and social change when applied to the decisions by superior courts.[5]

Indeed, the laws against homosexuality are a good example of the application of this principle. Exactly the same thing happened to homophobia as occurred with segregation after the decision of the United States Supreme Court in *Brown v The Board of Education.* The criminal laws targeting homosexual behaviour were the result of a culture of homophobia in Victorian times. But their very existence on the statute books meant that homophobia continued, and, to use Cardinal Francis George's words, it was 'reinforced and perpetuated . . . rationalized and deepened'. Once these laws were repealed the levels of homophobia decreased significantly. The converse is also the case. It is not surprising that there has been a reported increase in physical assaults on gays and lesbians following the recent anti-homosexual laws in Russia.

Canon law within the Church is no different in terms of its influence on the behaviour of people governed by it, and even more so when it comes to the clergy who are taught canon law in seminaries. It is even arguable that the influence of canon law is stronger in a closed society like the clergy than civil law is in the broader society.

Fr Thomas Doyle has correctly stated that canon law did not create the culture of secrecy.[6] But then the other side of the culture/ law equation cannot be ignored. *Crimen Sollicitationis* may have been

---

4. Francis George, *Ave Maria Law Review*, 1/1 (2003): 1, http://legacy.avemarialaw. edu/lr/assets/articles/v1i1.george.copyright.pdf (Accessed 15 May 2013).

5. http://flr.law.anu.edu.au/sites/flr.anulaw.anu.edu.au/files/flr/Sackville.pdf (Accessed 16 July 2013). Sackville points out that the courts role in creating social change is much more limited but accepts that court decisions often do reflect social change that has occurred through other means.

6. http://reform-network.net/?p=3006, paragraph 35 (Accessed 19 June 2013).

a product of the culture of secrecy, rather than its cause, but then by remaining in canon law, by being followed and obeyed, it served to 'reinforce and perpetuate' and to 'rationalise and deepen' (to use Cardinal Francis George's terms) the culture of secrecy. When you have bishops, who have taken an oath to follow canon law, being threatened with excommunication if they go to the civil authorities, it is pretty obvious what they are going to do. But you also have the influence of the fact that the belief system says that these laws derive from six Vicars of Christ: Pius XI, Pius XII, John XXIII, Paul VI, John Paul II and Benedict XVI, all of whom, with the exception of Pius XII, confirmed in one way or another the requirement of pontifical secrecy. When the Vicars of Christ repeat such canonical decrees, they take on a religious and spiritual dimension, particularly since Catholic doctrine teaches that the Church is inspired by the Holy Spirit.

You can transpose 'canon law' for 'law', 'hierarchy' for 'whites', and 'clericalism' and its practices for 'racism' and its practices, in a passage from Cardinal George's article, and his comments are equally valid when applied to canon law:

> Canon law, whether just or unjust, functions as a teacher. It is capable of instigating great cultural change; it is capable of profoundly reinforcing a status quo.... clericalism, as a cultural practice, would not end so long as canon law testified, and thus taught, in season and out, that clergy were different, that they were ontologically changed by God, and that the faithful should be protected from 'scandal' that would occur if priests were prosecuted in the civil courts for sexual assaults on children . . .
>
> *Crimen Sollicitationis* of 1922 was, in the beginning, the effect of clericalism rather than its cause. Its secrecy manifested cultural prejudices, the widespread belief among the hierarchy that clergy ought not to be tried as criminals in the ordinary courts for sexual abuse of children because of the loss of faith that it might cause. Does anyone doubt for a second, however, that canonically required secrecy—with bishops refusing to hand over documents to police, refusing to notify police

about complaints of child sexual abuse, shifting clergy
sexual abusers around, relying on treatment programs
to solve the problem, and being reluctant to dismiss
them except in the most extreme cases—reinforced,
perpetuated, and over time helped to create that culture?
. . .

Clergy and lay people involved in the Church's
institutions, tended to internalize the norms of canon
law protecting patterns of behaviour. Canon law called
forth the ideology that defended it, thus rationalizing
and deepening the clericalism that brought it into being
in the first place.

Canon law and the clerical culture stand in a complex
dialectical relationship. Neither comes first; neither
comes last. Canon law contributes massively to the
formation of the clerical culture. Culture influences and
shapes canon law. Inescapably, inevitably, canon law
and the clerical culture stand in a mutually informing,
formative, and reinforcing relationship.[7]

A Persistent Pattern

The same pattern of behaviour by bishops all over the world can only
be explained by a strong legal framework, underpinning the culture.[8]

Professor Patrick Parkinson, Professor of Law at Sydney University
and an acknowledged expert on child protection law, carried out
two reviews for the Australian Catholic Bishops Conference of the
Towards Healing protocol for dealing with sexual abuse.[9] He had
previously chaired a review of child protection laws in the State of
New South Wales. His submission to the *Victorian Parliamentary
Inquiry* on the Church's handling of sexual abuse allegations, both

---

7. Francis George, *Ave Maria Law Review,* 1/1 (2003): 1, at 6, http://legacy.
    avemarialaw.edu/lr/assets/articles/v1i1.george.copyright.pdf (Accessed 15 May
    2013).

8. Geoffrey Robertson, *The Case of the Pope,* chapter 2 where the author goes into
    some detail on the persistent pattern.

9. http://www.parliament.vic.gov.au/images/stories/committees/fcdc/
    inquiries/57th/Child_Abuse_Inquiry/Submissions/Parkinson_Patrick.pdf
    (Accessed 29 April 2013).

before and after 1996, is critical of the Church, and particularly of the Salesian Congregation of Catholic priests.[10]

He told the *Victorian Parliamentary Inquiry* into sexual abuse that the culture of the Church is weakly committed to obedience to state law because it has its own legal system, and when local bishops tried to develop their own protocols (for example, Ireland), they were countermanded by the Vatican:

> The real authority lies in the Vatican and the pope. That structure of an international church with hierarchy and law and disciplinary procedures in canon law means that somehow things are dealt with internally as a culture rather than through the state as a culture . . .[11]

In his 2013 Smith Lecture, Parkinson expanded on that by saying that the culture of international Catholicism is that the Church has its own jurisdiction and legal system, and the proper place for judging clergy is through canon law. It is no part of canonical thinking that child sexual abuse is a crime and should be routinely reported to the police and be dealt with by the criminal courts.[12] As the Concordats with Franco's Spain and with Colombia show, the Church culture still harks back to the days of Constantine and the 'privilege of clergy'.

Christopher Geraghty, as a former Catholic priest and seminary professor at the Sydney Archdiocesan seminaries, describes his experience inside the Church:

> . . . the Church has for centuries presumed that it can police its own borders, that it is an independent empire, not answerable to any secular power. It has had its own language, its own administration and training programmes, its own schools and universities, its own system of laws and regulations, its police force

10. *Ibid*, 7.
11. http://www.parliament.vic.gov.au/images/stories/committees/fcdc/ inquiries/57th/Child_Abuse_Inquiry/Transcripts/Prof_Patrick_Parkinson_19-Oct-12.pdf, 8 (Accessed 10 February 2013).
12. Patrick Parkinson: 'The Smith Lecture 2013: Child Sexual Abuse and the Churches: A Story of Moral Failure?' http://smithlecture.org/sites/smithlecture. org/files/downloads/lecture/smith-2013-transcript.pdf (Accessed 25 October 2013).

and lawyers, a developed list of penalties and its own courts and processes. A law unto itself—an organisation founded by God and answerable only to God.[13]

The attitude that canon law has always been adequate to deal with child sexual abuse was reflected by the Vatican's most senior canon lawyer, Archbishop (now Cardinal) Julian Herranz, President of the Pontifical Council for the Interpretation of Legislative Texts, at a conference in Milan in April 2002. He criticized attempts by some Church leaders (notably in Australia, Ireland and the United States) to change canon law to allow reporting of all abuse accusations to civil authorities, and to hand over to them relevant documents. He also said in December 2002 that church law 'provides all the trial and punishment tools necessary' to deliver justice and protect the community in clerical sexual abuse cases.[14] Cardinal Herranz seems blissfully unaware of his own Church's history. The Church never did have those tools, and up until 1922, it recognized that it did not have them. That is why for virtually its whole history, the Church required clergy sexual abusers to be handed over to the civil authorities.

When Pope Benedict XVI revised the *2001 Motu Proprio* in 2010, the Vatican spokesman, Fr Federico Lombardi SJ expressed a similar view that canon law was 'complete in itself and entirely distinct from the law of states', as if there was never any cross over with civil law.[15]

As Cardinal George said, in his *Ave Maria Law Review* article, the Justices of the Supreme Court of the United States in *Brown v The Board of Education* knew that segregation would continue unless the legal framework justifying it was removed. The problem for civil society is that there are no indications from the Church that it has any intention to abolish pontifical secrecy in relation to its canonical proceedings against clergy sexual abusers. This is predictable, because there is a strong theological culture behind its liking for secrecy.

---

13. Christopher Geraghty, 'Sexuality and the Clerical Life', in *Interface: A Forum for Theology in the World*, 16/1 (2013).

14. www.cf.americamagazine.org/content/article.cfm?article_id=1953 (Accessed 11 June 2013), since removed, but the citation is found in 'America staff, Signs of the Times: Vatican Official Says Church Has Legal Tools to Address Sex Abuse', in *America* (20 May 2002),4-5, at 4, and cited by Cafardi, *Before Dallas*, 46.

15. http://www.vatican.va/resources/resources_lombardi-nota-norme_en.html (Accessed 21 July 2013).

The Theological Culture Behind Secrecy

All organisations have a tendency to protect themselves and their reputations, whether they are the military, the police force or volunteer fire-fighters. The innate tribalism of the human species comes to the surface, and every member decks themselves out in their team colours to come to its defence.

Two of the major religions, Islam and Christianity have added on a layer to this natural tendency because of the teachings of their founders. One of the central instructions of Jesus Christ to his followers was to go out into the world and to preach the 'Gospel', the 'Good News' of salvation.[16] All Christian Churches take this instruction seriously because salvation in the next life only comes from faith in Jesus Christ. They might differ in what they mean by faith in Jesus Christ, but they all take seriously the injunction to convert others to the faith as they interpret it.

The Church is no different with its 'New Evangelization' programs, designed to win new converts.[17] As we have seen, the word 'scandal' has a technical meaning in the Church, and it means the loss of faith arising from bishops and priests not acting in accordance with the teachings of Christ. There is little point in bringing people in through the front door of the Church through evangelization programs, if they are fleeing out the back as a result of 'scandal'. The scandal of sexual abuse not only affected the reputation of the Church, but it attacked one of its core values and missions, namely bringing in converts to Catholicism, and keeping them.

The odd thing is that this core mission of evangelization has been around since the Church was founded, and the acceptance of the need to hand over sex abusing priests to the civil authorities had been around almost as long—until 1922. So, for some 1500 years, from the fourth to the twentieth century, the Church could live with the bad publicity coming from public punishment of priests who sexually assaulted children. In the late nineteenth century something changed. There may be many reasons for this, including the gradual separation of Church and state and the decline of Church influence, the spread

---

16. Mark 16:15.
17. http://articles.washingtonpost.com/2013-06-07/local/39815655_1_catholics-new-evangelization-vatican (Accessed 15 July 2013).

of secular education, or simply the recognition that 'scandal' could be spread so rapidly with modern radio technology.

The Vatican was not slow to take advantage of radio's propaganda benefits. The Vatican Radio was set up by Marconi in 1931 for Pope Pius XI, just twelve years after commercial and public radio stations started to appear around the world.[18] Three years after they had started to appear, Pius XI had imposed 'the secret of the Holy Office' on allegations of child sexual abuse by clergy. This new technology could just as easily spread 'scandal'. One solution was to cut off the information at its source.

Another factor in the change of attitude was the culture of clericalism, the theology that a priest is someone special. While the idea reaches back to before St Augustine, it seems to have reached a peak around the early 1900s, and was personified in the 1925 canonization by the same Pope Pius XI of the French priest, John Vianney, who proclaimed, 'After God, the priest is everything!'[19] Pope Benedict XVI in his letter to priests in 2009 quoted these words with approval.[20] It seems that the Church had accepted as orthodoxy, Lord Acton's worst heresy that 'the office sanctifies the holder of it'.

---

18. http://www.vatican.va/news_services/radio/multimedia/storia_ing.html (Accessed 30 October 2013). The first radio broadcast, as we know it today, is said to have come from PCGG in the Netherlands, but it soon spread to the United States where the first licence was granted to Westinghouse in 1920, and others quickly followed: James Wood, *History of International Broadcasting* (Peregrinus, 1992), 14. The BBC was set up in 1922: http://www.bbc.co.uk/historyofthebbc/resources/in-depth/reith_1.shtml (Accessed 30 October 2013).

19. http://www.vatican.va/holy_father/benedict_xvi/letters/2009/documents/hf_ben-xvi_let_20090616_anno-sacerdotale_en.html (Accessed 15 May 2013). The idea, at least as it applies to bishops, can also be traced earlier to St Ignatius of Antioch, in *Catholic Catechism,* paragraph 1549: http://www.vatican.va/archive/ccc_css/archive/catechism/p2s2c3a6.htm (Accessed 26 October 2013). Gary Macy argues that this concept of the priest having a special power, rather than being called to perform a particular role in the Christian community only dates from the twelfth century. http://scu.edu/ic/publications/upload/scl-0711-macy.pdf (Accessed 6 September 2013). But there seems little doubt that this culture of clericalism reached a peak at the beginning of the twentieth century. Pope Pius X in a 1906 encyclical insisted that the Church was made up of two divisions, the hierarchy that led and the flock whose only duty was to obey: http://www.vatican.va/holy_father/pius_x/encyclicals/documents/hf_p-x_enc_11021906_vehementer-nos_en.html. (Accessed 1 October 2013).

20. http://www.vatican.va/holy_father/benedict_xvi/letters/2009/documents/hf_ben-xvi_let_20090616_anno-sacerdotale_en.html (Accessed 3 October 2013).

Whatever the reason for the change in attitude, by 1922, the culture of secrecy and its felt need to hide clergy sex crimes against children, had become so strong that it found its way into canon law, and the Church quietly abandoned its centuries old practice of handing over such priests to the civil authorities after stripping from them their status as clerics.

Deepening the Culture from the Secrecy in Canon Law

Within a strictly hierarchical structure like the Church, the influence of canon law on culture is likely to be even more profound, if for no other reason than the 'trickle-down effect'. Lower ranks of the clergy look up to the higher ones for guidance.

Crimen Sollicitationis started off as a law dealing with soliciting in the confessional, that is, it was only dealing with priests, and not religious brothers and nuns who do not hear confessions. Indeed Title VI of *Crimen Sollicitationis* which extends the procedures for dealing with solicitation in the confessional to homosexuality, bestiality and paedophilia refers throughout to 'clerics'. The same is true of the *2001 Motu Proprio*, its revision in 2010 and the revised *Delicta Graviora* or *Substantive Norms*. Likewise Canon 1395 §2 dealing with sex assaults on minors, also only refers to 'clerics'.

Canon 207 reserves the word 'cleric' to those in Holy Orders, while acknowledging those who are not priests, and have taken vows in the religious life are important in the life of the Church.[21] Canon 695 does provide for the dismissal of nuns and religious brothers for breach of their vow of chastity, including sex assaults on children.

The *1983 Code of Canon Law* does not apply to sex crimes of lay teachers at Catholic schools—they are neither clerics nor religious. Quite apart from the 'trickle-down effect', canon lawyers were advising that canon law served as a guide for how to deal with such lay people accused of abusing minors, even though it did not apply to them.[22] One of the significant features of canon law is pontifical secrecy. There have been cases in the State of New South Wales, where

---

21. http://www.vatican.va/archive/ENG1104/__PT.HTM (Accessed 15 July 2013).
22. Morrissey, 'Procedures to be Applied in the Case of Sexual Misconduct by a Priest', in *Studia Canonica*, 26 (1992): 39–73 at 42, http://www.attorneygeneral.jus.gov.on.ca/inquiries/cornwall/en/hearings/exhibits/Frank_Morrisey/pdf/06_Morrisey_Procedures.pdf (Accessed 30 July 2013).

charges have been laid agaínts priests for allegedly not reporting such matters to the police. One priest died before the hearing and the other matter is being defended.[23]

But a more serious deepening of the culture occurs when people adopt practices that go beyond what the law itself provides. The United States laws on segregation did not allow lynching, but as Cardinal George points out in his article, the law called forth the ideology that gave rise to it, thus rationalising and deepening the racism that brought it into being in the first place. One might also apply that to the criminalising of homosexuality. The laws never justified 'poofter bashing', but it happened, and was encouraged by the existence of the law which reflected a view that homosexuals were inferior, dirty criminals and animals to be beaten.

And we can see exactly the same pattern in the Church. *Crimen Sollicitationis,* the *1983 Code of Canon Law* with *Secreta Continere,* and the *2001 Motu Proprio* prohibited reporting to the civil authorities. These laws did not sanction protecting clergy sexual abusers from the police in other ways. They did not of themselves sanction the protection of those involved in covering up clergy sexual abusers. Those who covered up were obeying canon law and doing 'the right thing'. They too needed to be protected from the civil law that threatened to prosecute them, but there was no requirement in canon law to do so.

- Cardinal Bernard Law was Archbishop of Boston, against whom allegations were made of covering up clergy child sexual abuse. On 13 December 2002, while in Rome, he resigned his position as Archbishop of Boston, and was appointed as Archpriest of the Basilica of Santa Maria Maggiore.[24] Whatever the truth of the allegations against Law, his new position ensured that he would not have to answer the allegations.

---

23. http://www.abc.net.au/radionational/programs/religionandethicsreport/priest-charged-with-concealing-sex-offences/4244662 (Accessed 25 June 2013). Fr Brennan died shortly after being charged, http://www.theherald.com.au/story/1266748/priest-aided-crime-police/ (Accessed 13 July 2013).
24. http://www.nytimes.com/2004/05/28/us/cardinal-law-given-post-in-rome.html (Accessed 23 June 2013). John L Allen, *All the Popes Men* at 71%.

- According to the 1929 Lateran Treaty, the basilica, located in Italian territory, is owned by the Vatican, and enjoys extraterritorial status similar to that of foreign embassies.[25] Cardinal Law was therefore protected by diplomatic immunity, and while he resides in the Vatican, he is also protected because the Vatican has no extradition treaty with any other state.[26] Here you have an extension of clericalism that went right up to Pope John Paul II, now canonised: clergy are special people, above the civil law, and the only law that should apply to them is canon law because they have sworn to obey canon law.
- In 2013, the Los Angeles Archdiocese finally agreed to hand over its documents in some long standing litigation, after losing case after case trying to withhold their production on the grounds of a 'privilege' that the civil law has never recognised. According to reports, the documents showed that not only did Cardinal Mahony not report clergy sexual abusers to the police, but he encouraged them to stay interstate to avoid being arrested.[27] Canon law did not authorise that, but it is exactly the sort of thing that you would expect in accordance with the principles laid down by Cardinal Francis George about the effect of law—this time, canon law. The existence of the law 'rationalises and deepens' the clericalism.
- Geoffrey Robertson QC refers to a Canadian case in 1993 where the Papal Nuncio's assistance was sought for ferretting clergy sexual abusers out of the country to take up positions overseas where they would be beyond the reach of the Canadian courts.[28] The same comments apply.

---

25. Lateran Treaty, Articles 13 and 15 http://spcp.prf.cuni.cz/dokument/lateran.htm (Accessed 23 June 2013).
26. See http://www.ucanews.com/news/vatican-denies-lack-of-cooperation-in-nuncio-abuse-case/70074 (Accessed 15 January 2013).
27. http://m.thetablet.co.uk/article/163741 (Accessed 9 February 2013), Michael D'Antonio, *Mortal Sins*, 344.
28. Geffrey Robertson, *The Case of the Pope*, chapter 2, paragraph 44.

- In Australia, Salesian priests accused of sexual abuse were shifted to Samoa and to Rome. Professor Patrick Parkinson told the *Victorian Parliamentary Inquiry* that when the Australian Provincial of the Salesians, tried to bring back a priest from Rome to face his accusers, the second in charge of the Salesians, who is now the Bishop of Ghent in Belgium, suggested that he be sent to another country without an extradition treaty with Australia.[29] Professor Parkinson gave other examples of where Australian priests accused of sex crimes against children were kept overseas by their religious orders.[30]
- On 12 November 2011, the Australian Jesuit and Professor of Law at the Australian Catholic University, Fr Frank Brennan, was interviewed on the ABC's *Lateline* program. He was asked about the clergy abuse problem.

FRANK BRENNAN: If I may say, I think the real problem with the Catholic Church is the sort of unaccountable clericalism . . . I'd been in Rome two years ago. I attended a meeting. I went across with two of my brother Jesuits from the United States. I attended a splendid concert that the Vatican put on and there was Pope Benedict and as the symphony played, an American priest turned to me and said, 'That man beside the Pope, that's Cardinal Law'. He said, 'If he was back home, he'd be in jail'.

I was very ashamed at that moment and I thought there is a structural problem, but it's not in terms as you've discussed. I think it's more the sort of unaccountable clericalism of a male celibate hierarchy and I think there are fundamental challenges for the Church in the 21st Century.

29. http://www.parliament.vic.gov.au/images/stories/committees/fcdc/ inquiries/57th/Child_Abuse_Inquiry/Transcripts/Prof_Patrick_Parkinson_19- Oct-12.pdf, 7 (Accessed 29 April 2013).
30. http://www.parliament.vic.gov.au/images/stories/committees/fcdc/ inquiries/57th/Child_Abuse_Inquiry/Submissions/Parkinson_Patrick.pdf   17 (Accessed 29 April 2013).

EMMA ALBERICI: He'd been in jail for what?
FRANK BRENNAN: Well, for things to do with failure to deal adequately with priests who'd been proven to be engaged in child abuse.
EMMA ALBERICI: So the accountability or the lack of accountability goes that high up within the Church?
FRANK BRENNAN: Sadly it does.[31]

And sadly, it goes even further than Cardinal Law. It goes to the man that Cardinal Law was sitting next to at the concert, now *emeritus* Pope Benedict XVI, the man in charge of the Congregation for the Doctrine of the Faith for twenty-five years before becoming pope in 2005—and even then, in 2010 still insisting on pontifical secrecy to prevent reporting to the police unless there is a local law requiring it.

But the cultural effects of canon law go even further than the actions and words of senior clergy protecting clergy sexual abusers and those who covered them up. It also affected the way that the hierarchy treated the victims.

Victims generally felt that they were seen by the Church as dishonest, greedy people out to make false accusations against clerics, like Potiphar's wife, for the sake of monetary gain. A particularly disturbing example of this was the way the Foster family felt they were treated by Archbishop Pell of Melbourne.

In our interactions with the now Cardinal Archbishop Pell, we experienced a sociopathic lack of empathy typifying the attitude and responses of the Church hierarchy.[32]

Claims by victims were met with every legal device possible, if they did not agree to go along with the Church's protocols for limited compensation.[33] In this modern version of the parable of the Good

---

31. http://www.abc.net.au/lateline/content/2012/s3631260.htm (Accessed 15 July 2013) Fr Brennan made similar comments about clericalism in 'Church-State Issues and the Royal Commission', in *Eureka Street*, 3 September 2013 www.eurekastreet.com.au (Accessed 4 September 2013).
32. http://www.parliament.vic.gov.au/images/stories/committees/fcdc/inquiries/57th/Child_Abuse_Inquiry/Transcripts/Foster_Family_23-Nov-12.pdf, 3–8.
33. David Marr, 'The Prince, Faith, Abuse and George Pell', in *Quarterly Essay*, 51

Samaritan, the man was left in the ditch not by robbers, but after being sexually assaulted by colleagues of the priests and bishops who passed him by. Some sections of the Church have improved their attitudes towards victims, but others are still playing hard ball.

The *1983 Code of Canon Law*, oddly enough, did say something about the rights of victims: Canon 1729 provided that a party who has suffered harm can bring a 'contentious action' for damages in the course of the penal case against a priest, but as the Murphy Commission noted, victims were never told about this right.[34] And, in any event, the *1983 Code of Canon Law* made such penal cases virtually impossible.

Cultural Inertia

Once a law is changed by the emergence of a new culture (racial integration in the United States, tolerance of homosexuality etc) the reinforcing of the new culture does not happen overnight. There is a certain cultural inertia which might be manifested in some resistance to the new way of thinking.[35] Cardinal Francis George, the leader of the delegation that went to Rome to convince Cardinal Ratzinger that he should allow the American bishops to report clergy sexual abusers to the police, is living proof of this.

In 2005 his archdiocese of Chicago was receiving complaints of sexual assault by a priest, Fr Dan McCormack, who was been investigated by the police. George did not act on the Independent Board of Review Recommendation for his removal. George eventually did, but in March 2006, after McCormack was arrested a second time. George publicly apologised for not acting earlier.[36] His was a case of cultural inertia and the continuing influence of the cultural effects of the old canon law before the Dallas amendments.

(September 2013): 30.

34. *Murphy Dublin Report*, Part 1 http://www.justice.ie/en/JELR/DACOI%20 Part%201.pdf/Files/DACOI%20Part%201.pdf paragraphs 4.17–4.28 (Accessed 25 April 2013) paragraph 4.73.

35. Juan D Carrillo, 'Cultural Inertia and Uniformity in Organizations', in *Journal of Law, Economics, & Organization* http://www-bcf.usc.edu/~juandc/PDFpapers/ wp-cult.pdf (Accessed 15 July 2013).

36. http://www.npr.org/templates/story/story. php?storyId=16235278 (Accessed 11 March 2013), http://www. bishoaccountability.org/news2006/01_02/2006_02_19_CBS2_ CardinalApologizes.htm (Accessed 11 March 2013), http://www.catholic newsagency.com/news/cardinal_george_apologizes_to_disgruntled_chicago_ parishioners/ (Accessed 11 March 2013).

But cultural inertia did not only affect Cardinal Francis George. It was widespread across the United States. The BBC Panorama Program, *Sex Crimes and the Vatican* in 2006 referred to the independent body called the National Review Board set up by the American Catholic Bishops Conference to monitor the 2002 Dallas Charter.[37] The Chairman of the Board was former Oklahoma governor, Frank Keating, but he resigned after a year in the job in June 2003. He compared some Church leaders to the Cosa Nostra. In his resignation letter, Keating said

> To resist Grand Jury subpoenas, to suppress the names
> of offending clerics, to deny, to obfuscate, to explain
> away. That is the model of a criminal organization, not
> my Church.[38]

The program also interviewed Judge Anne Burke, a Judge of the Illinois Appeals Court, who was vice-chairman of the Board and who took over as interim chairman from Keating, and continued to sit on the National Review Board until 2005. She said that despite the change of policy in the American Church in 2002, nothing much seemed to have changed, and there was a continual watering down of the Charter. Priests were not stood down when allegations were made, and it seemed to her that every month something indicated that bishops had not learned from their mistakes.[39]

These critics are not anti-Catholic bigots, but practising Catholics, and who in good faith took on these positions in order to assist the Church hierarchy overcome what was an obvious problem.

The Panorama program also interviewed a District Attorney from Phoenix Arizona, Rick Romley, who said that he never got any cooperation from the Church, only obstruction, including instructions to bishops to ship all their documentation to the Papal Nuncio who would be entitled to oppose the production of documents on subpoena because of his diplomatic status.[40]

Likewise, after the Bishops Conference of England and Wales adopted the Nolan Report 2001 recommendations (without a *recognitio* from the Vatican), the Cumberlege review committee

---

37. http://vimeo.com/654677 at 18 minutes (Accessed 12 September 2013).
38. See also http://richgibson.com/abuse.html (Accessed 15 July 2013),
39. http://vimeo.com/654677 (Accessed 12 September 2013).
40. *Ibid*, at 32.47 minutes.

found in 2007 that there was opposition from a 'strong and vocal lobby of priests'.[41]

The same thing happened in Ireland, where the *Cloyne Report* found that while the Bishop John Magee of the Cloyne diocese ostensibly supported child protection procedures, it was 'never genuinely committed to their implementation'.[42]

The evidence given by Professor Patrick Parkinson and Deputy Commissioner Ashton to the *Victorian Parliamentary Inquiry* would seem to suggest that the same attitude applied in Australia after the adoption by the Australian Catholic Bishops Conference of *Towards Healing* in 1996. Bishop Michael Malone in his evidence to the Maitland-Newcastle Inquiry said that he encountered resistance amongst both priests and bishops from other dioceses to his measures to deal with child sexual abuse.[43]

Even if canon law were to change, and pontifical secrecy abandoned, or civil laws changed to make reporting compulsory in all circumstances, there is always the problem of cultural inertia.

Clericalism in the Lower Ranks of the Church

Christopher Geraghty entered a Catholic seminary at the age of twelve. He was ordained a priest, obtained a Doctorate in Theology, and taught at Sydney seminaries. He subsequently left the priesthood, married, became a barrister and ultimately a District Court judge in the State of New South Wales. In his book, *Dancing with the Devil,* he described how the Catholic culture affected him when a seminary student advised him in confidence of his sexual relationship with the director of vocations for his diocese Fr Vincent Kiss, who was eventually jailed for his crimes.[44] The relationship had started when he was a young adolescent.

---

41. http://www.cathcom.org/mysharedaccounts/cumberlege/report/downloads/CathCom_Cumberlege2.pdf paragraph 2.17 (Accessed 15 July 2013).

42. http://www.justice.ie/en/JELR/Cloyne_Rpt.pdf/Files/Cloyne_Rpt.pdf (Accessed 6 March 2013) paragraph 4.88.

43. http://www.lawlink.nsw.gov.au/lawlink/Special_Projects/ll_splprojects.nsf/vwFiles/Transcript_Day_9_-_TOR_2_-_12_July_2013.pdf/$file/Transcript_Day_9_-_TOR_2_-_12_July_2013.pdf, 1011.28ff (Accessed 16 July 2013).

44. Christopher Geraghty, *Dancing with the Devil* (Melbourne: Spectrum Publications, 2012), 88–92

My night visitor had spoken to me in confidence, but I was wondering what other scandals might be bubbling under the cover of hymns and incense . . . Despite my failure to explore the intimate details of Father Kiss's 'missionary' activities, from the little I was told, I knew in my bones that what he had been doing constituted a grave sin . . . At that stage, the criminal law was well outside my clerical purview. My points of reference were heaven and hell, virtue and sin, especially sins of the flesh. One of my ingrained and principal concerns was loyalty to the institution founded by Jesus and his Apostles. Its reputation had to be protected—at all costs . . . I should add, knowing now full well how incomprehensible and abhorrent it is for any reasonable person outside the tight system of the ecclesiastical world, that I understand how it happened here in Australia, in the United States and throughout the world, that cardinals, bishops, senior priests, even a pope, covered up the sexual scandals of some of the clergy, moved them from parish to parish, hid their criminal deeds from the civil authorities, protected the culprits and hoped, prayed the victims would simply go away . . . It was inevitable that the system would come unstuck.[45]

There are many Catholics who had hoped that this form of inbred clericalism would have disappeared in the aftermath of the Second Vatican Council. But the pontificates of Pope John Paul II and Benedict XVI have been seen by many as an attempt to turn the clock back to the sixteenth century Council of Trent, and with the clericalism that it encouraged. An attempt was made to change this culture in 1996 when the Australian bishops, recognising the link between it and clerical sexual abuse, produced a report that tried to provide an alternative. It was called 'Towards Understanding: A

---

45. *Ibid.* The Marist Brother Provincial, Brother Crowe, told the *Australian Royal Commission* on the 24 January 2014, that he did not regard another Brother's touching a student's genitals was a crime. http://childabuseroyalcommission. gov.au/wp-content/uploads/2014/01/Transcript-RC_IRCSA_Day_036A_24-Jan-2014-2013_Public.pdf, 3766 (accessed 31 January 2014).

study of the factors specific to the Catholic Church which might lead to sexual abuse by priests and religious'.[46] This attempt was knocked on the head by the Vatican.[47] It would seem that the current crop of seminarians is being trained in that clericalism preferred in Rome.

In the Archdiocese of Sydney, there is a group of young Catholics who hold public forums in pubs, called *Theology on Tap*. At one such meeting, some young priests and seminarians were invited to speak about their experiences.[48] One of them, ordained just fifteen months, spoke about what a privilege it was for him to 'unite heaven and earth' by celebrating Mass, and then said:

> What a tremendous gift it is to be called 'Father' . . . By virtue of my ordination, I have the capacity to change lives forever . . . I wake up every single day thinking you really do have the greatest life in the world, because no one knows what you see. No one sees what you see. By virtue of being a priest, you see the world in a completely different light. In your homilies and in your preaching, you can change people's beliefs. One person said I was like Adolph Hitler. I said, 'what do you mean'. She said 'I mean in a good way'. I said, 'a good way of being Adolph Hitler?' She said, 'Yes, I'll believe everything you tell me."

And he seemed immensely proud of that power. He then went on to describe how at a celebration for his first anniversary of ordination a silent but 'very holy man' said to him:

> 'How wonderful it must be to be loved in the way that we love you'. And he went on to qualify that and said, 'And it is not because of what you say, not because of

46. See comments in *Betrayal of Trust*, Report of the *Victorian Parliamentary Inquiry*, Box 7.1, 159, https://s3-ap-southeast-2.amazonaws.com/family-and-community-development-committee/Inquiry+into+Handling+of+Abuse_Volume+1_FINAL_web.pdf (Accessed 14 November 2013).

47. http://ncronline.org/news/accountability/response-abuse-has-been-slow-stymied-vatican (Accessed 15 July 2013).

48. 'Our Young Fathers: What They Think of Their Lives and the Church' http://www.youtube.com/watch?v=0sgcRJu_iIs&list=PLB217DF7F0E5B3D28 (Accessed 15 July 2013). The quotations following are from that program.

what you do, but because of who you are. You are Christ
. . . Priests are other Christs'.

Richard Sipe, formerly a priest for eighteen years and then a
sociologist and researcher into offending priests, has often drawn
attention to the connection between power and the sexual abuse of
children. It makes it easier if people inclined that way are in positions
of power in the kinds of ways just described by this young priest.[49]
The *Victorian Parliamentary Inquiry* Report made the same point.[50]
There have been so many cases where the victim 'believed everything
he told me', and that the priest was 'another Christ'. A very good
example of the respect for priests that allowed sexual abuse to take
place was the case of Fr Michael Glennon, referred to in the Victorian
Church submission to the *Victorian Parliamentary Inquiry*, *Facing
the Truth*.[51] The *Murphy Dublin Report* made the same point about
the importance of dismissing clergy sexual abusers to prevent further
attacks on children.

> There is also the fact that a priest is still a priest and by
> his very status, if he wishes to commit child sexual abuse,
> he will find it easier to do so than if he were a layman.[52]

Bishop Geoffrey Robinson has written about the problem of the
'messiah complex' amongst recently ordained priests in Australia,

49. http://www.richardsipe.com/Comments/2012-05-11-sexual-abuse-by-priests.
htm (Accessed 15 July 2013). See also *Mea Maxima Culpa* where Sipe says, 'The
higher you go, the more they know. The system of the Catholic clergy, for which
I have great respect and to which I have given many years of my life, selects,
cultivates, protects, defends and produces sexual abusers'. http://www.abc.net.
au/lateline/content/2013/s3716097.htm (Accessed 15 July 2013).
50. *Betrayal of Trust*, Report of the *Victorian Parliamentary Inquiry*, chapter 7,
paragraph 7.3.4, 166, https://s3-ap-southeast-2.amazonaws.com/family-and-
community-development-committee/Inquiry+into+Handling+of+Abuse_
Volume+1_FINAL_web.pdf (Accessed 14 November 2013).
51. *Facing the Truth* paragarph 6.1.
52. http://www.dacoi.ie paragraph 1.75 (Accessed 9 February 2013), see also
evidence of Fr Brian Lucas at the *Maitland-Newcastle Inquiry*, http://www.
lawlink.nsw.gov.au/lawlink/Special_Projects/ll_splprojects.nsf/vwFiles/
Transcript_Day_15_-_TOR_2_-_24_July_2013.pdf/$file/Transcript_Day_15_-_
TOR_2_-_24_July_2013.pdf ,1571, 1608.

where they believe that they are on a special mission from God, and therefore above the rules of ordinary mortals:

> One of the saddest sights in the Church today is that of some young, newly-ordained priests insisting that there is an 'ontological difference' between them and laypersons, and enthusiastically embracing the mystique of a superior priesthood. Whenever I see young priests doing this I feel a sense of despair, and I wonder whether we have learned anything at all from the revelations of abuse.[53]

The 'messiah complex' is still being taught in Sydney seminaries. The former auxiliary bishop of Sydney, and now Archbishop of Hobart, Julian Porteous, a former rector of the Sydney seminary has even written a book about the ontological change that comes about on ordination, and when a priest acts, he 'acts as Christ'.[54]

This is a systemic problem arising from the doctrine and theological culture of the Church. It may not be a cause of child sexual abuse, but it is one of the matters that make it easier to occur because Catholic children are also taught to have this kind of respect for priests.

Another speaker, a nineteen year old seminarian, spoke about celibacy, repeating the common justification that it opened up the possibility of loving more people.

> Now, it is commonly held that celibacy is an archaic, oppressive burden placed on unwilling men, which only brings misery or, as we hear in the media, paedophilia, or other horrendous things. Take a look around you. How many miserable criminals do you see wearing collars or habits? The world is being sold a lie . . .

Unfortunately, more 'miserable criminals' than this young seminarian thinks. The level of paedophilia amongst Catholic priests in Australia,

---

53. Geoffrey Robinson, *For Christ's Sake: End Sexual Abuse in the Catholic Church for Good*, (Melbourne: John Garratt Publishing, 2013), 83–84.
54. Julian Porteous, *The Life and Ministry of Priests at the Beginning of the New Millenium* (Ballan Vic. Modetti Press, 2009), 57–59.

according to Professor Patrick Parkinson's evidence to the *Victorian Parliamentary Inquiry*, is more than six times the total of every other religious denomination.[55] Then the seminarian said:

> When you see a priest, pray for him because celibacy is not an easy life. Only through God's grace and the support of your prayers is such a life possible.

There is no reason to think that there has been any less quantity or quality of prayers in the past by the Catholic faithful for their priests. In view of much greater participation rates at Sunday Mass in the past (74% in 1954, decreasing to 10.6% in 2013[56]) one would have thought that there would have been a corresponding greater amount of praying for priests at the height of the sex assaults during the 1960s and 1970s than there is now. God's grace seems to have been in much shorter supply for Catholic priests than for Protestant ministers, Jewish rabbis and Muslim imams.

A third speaker, a seminarian, about to be ordained, spoke about the special relationship between priests, bishop and the pope, that senior Vatican cardinals used to justify not reporting sex abusing priests to the police. He said the relationship was 'much more powerful than a brother/sister relationship or husband and wife'.

The fourth speaker, a young priest, explained that every priest says both the Divine Office and the Mass every day, the 'most powerful prayer in the world'—and at Mass, 'at my finger tips is Almighty God'. But it would seem that both the daily prayers of priests and the prayers for them by the faithful have not, on Professor Parkinson's statistics, shown any comforting results. Bishop Michael Malone

---

55. http://www.parliament.vic.gov.au/images/stories/committees/fcdc/inquiries/57th/Child_Abuse_Inquiry/Transcripts/Prof_Patrick_Parkinson_19-Oct-12.pdf, 2 (Accessed 24 June 2013). See also Parkinson, 'Suffer the Teenage Children', in *Sydney Law School, Legal Studies Research Paper* 13/09 http://papers.ssrn.com/sol3/papers.cfm?abstract_id=2216264.

56. http://www.catholicsforministry.com.au/uploads/28737/ufiles/wilkinsontext1a1_copy.pdf http://www.pro.catholic.org.au/pdf/ACBC%20PRO%20Catholic%20profile%202013.pdf (Accessed 9 July 2013). According to Peter Wilkinson the participation rate reached 10.6% in 2013. http://www.theswag.org.au/2013/09/who-goes-to-mass-in-australia-in-the-21st-century/ (Accessed 9 September 2013).

at the *Maitland-Newcastle Inquiry* was asked about a letter sent by a serial sex abusing priest, Fr McAlinden, in which he refused to consent to laicisation:

> ... he was also claiming that his aberration or tendency to sexual abuse was somehow controlled by prayer and the sacraments, which is quite ridiculous. It's a psychological condition ... [57]

Sexual abuse is also a sin for which God's grace through prayer is supposed to be the remedy. Alfred Lord Tennyson once wrote 'More things are wrought by prayer than this world dreams of'.[58] But the statistics, and Bishop Malone's professional opinion, would suggest that at least in relation to preventing sex assaults on children by Catholic clergy, Tennyson was dreaming.

This young priest explained how some of his colleagues in Rome come from countries where there was a possibility of their becoming martyrs.

> 'I must imitate Christ by laying down my life ... It may not be happening in Australia, but we might be getting there ... Christ redeemed us by suffering and death, and that is how he saved souls. And that is how priests save souls.

This hopeful expectation of one day being a martyr has overtones of Cardinal Francis George, expecting his successor as Archbishop of Chicago to be martyred because of the slippery slide of secularism that, for example, allows gays to marry. These young men did not make this up. This is what they are being taught right now in seminary hot houses—and that is where the word 'seminary' comes from, a hot house. And in that hot house, they have been exposed to Pope Benedict XVI's fertilizer when he held up to them as an ideal to

---

57. *Maitland-Newcastle Inquiry,* http://www.lawlink.nsw.gov.au/lawlink/Special_Projects/ll_splprojects.nsf/vwFiles/Transcript_Day_8_-_TOR_2_-_11_July_2013.pdf/$file/Transcript_Day_8_-_TOR_2_-_11_July_2013.pdf , 878.3-5 (Accessed 14 July 2013).
58. *The Idylls of the King.*

be followed, a neurotic, self-flagellating French priest, John Vianney who thought that after God, the priest was everything.

And Christopher Geraghty candidly admits that he would have said the same sorts of things after he was ordained. That was what he was taught to think, and he accepted it. The reality was far different, and after some fifteen years as a priest, watching and observing, he says.

> However much we pretended that priests were above the common herd, that we were different, that we were all, as a group, unusually holy, that we were in the world, working in the world, ministering unselfishly to others, but that we were not of the world, the truth has always been that we were merely men, just human beings. Many of us were generous indeed, and committed to doing good. Some few were really holy, but they were truly the exception, and often a real pain in the arse. Others were weak and inadequate—some really crazy. Some a danger on the loose. And some few were truly evil. It does no good to the Church or to the priests to pretend otherwise.

But the Church is pretending otherwise. There are some dissident voices objecting to this clerical culture, like Bishop Geoffrey Robinson, and Fr Frank Brennan SJ and more recently Archbishop Martin of Dublin.[59] Even Pope Francis has made mention of the problem.[60] But while this sort of clericalism is being taught to young seminarians as part of Church doctrine, it is going to take a lot of effort to turn around the juggernaut.

In modern secular society, religions have the right, within certain limits, (like racial vilification), to preach and believe whatever they

---

59. Frank Brennan, 'Church-State Issues and the Royal Commission', in *Eureka Street*, 3 September 2013, http://www.eurekastreet.com.au/article.aspx?aeid=38146#.Ui5vaKt-8qQ (Accessed 10 September 2013) and on Archbishop Martin, http://www.catholicbishops.ie/2013/04/24/address-archbishop-diarmuid-martin-russo-family-lecture/ (Accessed 15 May 2013).
60. http://cathnews.co.nz/2013/04/23/clericalism-criticised-by-future-pope-francis/ (Accessed 15 May 2013).

like—Jehovah's Witnesses can believe that blood transfusions are sinful, Catholics that contraception is sinful—and that priests are 'special' in the way these young men describe. All civil society can do is to protect itself against the fall out of such doctrines. So adult Jehovah's Witness can refuse a blood transfusion, and let themselves die rather than have one, but society will not let that happen to their children who are not old enough to make an informed decision. Likewise the Church can have as much clericalism as it wants, but society has to protect its children against the fallout, the sexual assaults on children, and the covering up by the hierarchy that has been the outcome of this culture expressed in and deepened by canon law over the last ninety years. That can only mean strict civil laws on reporting to protect children.

These young Australian seminarians and priests have very similar clericalist ideas about the relationship between priests, and between priests and bishops to those of Cardinal Castrillón from Colombia.

Clericalism at the Top

Cardinal Dario Castrillón Hoyos, former Archbishop of Bucamaranga in Colombia, was Pro-Prefect from 1996 to 1998 and then Prefect of the Congregation for Clergy from 1998 to 2006. Castrillón has long preached this idea of the special, sacramental relationship between clergy, and particularly between priests and bishops. And yes, he too thought highly of the idea of being a 'martyr', preferring to go to jail rather than report a priest who had been sexually assaulting children. In his case, however, even a 'bloodless' martyrdom by jailing is highly unlikely to be fulfilled.

Colombia is one of the few countries on earth where bishops do enjoy a *de iure* privilege of clergy, recognised by the civil law. As a bishop, he can only be tried by a Church court. And on past performance the most that Church courts seem to hand out are slaps on the wrist and admonitions not to do it again. Even bloodless martyrdom by jailing is out of the question for him.

Before moving to Rome to head the Congregation for the Clergy, Castrillón had a colourful ecclesiastical career in Colombia. He once boasted that he had heard the confession of the notorious Colombian drug lord, Pablo Escobar who is reputed to have ordered the assassination of tens of thousands of people, including three

Colombian presidential candidates, an Attorney General, a Justice Minister, more than 200 judges, dozens of journalists, and over 1,000 police officers.[61] To gain access to Escobar, Castrillón is said to have disguised himself as a milkman. The confession, presumably, must have been a very long one, and Escobar's resolve never to sin again did not seem to have lasted.[62]

Castrillón once rode on horseback into the Colombian jungles for a meeting with the FARC guerrillas for peace talks, although in a later attempt in 1994 to prosecute him, the prosecution alleged that his connections with the FARC were also about other things. He used to be a keen water-skier and horse rider, and in Rome he drove a red Maserati coupe at 140 kph through Italy's highways, while singing *La Donna e Mobile (Women are fickle)* from *Rigoletto*.[63] He always had with him the laptop that Bill Gates gave him, and he was able to speak seven other languages apart from his native Spanish.[64] He achieved more notoriety in September 2001 with his letter to the French Bishop Pican, congratulating him for not reporting a paedophile priest to the civil authorities.

At the end of 2006 he tried to learn Arabic in a week, and flew off to calm down the Islamic Ayatollahs who were furious about the pope's citing the Byzantine Emperor, Manuel II Paleologo, which the pope had slipped into his speech, attacking Islam.[65]

In 2009, on his recommendation, Pope Benedict XVI lifted the excommunication against the schismatic bishops who were followers of Archbishop Lefebvre who believed that the Second Vatican Council was a pact with the devil. It was then discovered that one of them, Richard Williamson had given an interview on Swedish TV in which he said that not one Jew died in the gas chambers, and the holocaust was a Hollywood invention.[66] Castrillón was left with egg

---

61. http://www.biography.com/people/pablo-escobar-9542497 (Accessed 30 October 2013).
62. http://www.time.com/time/magazine/article/0,9171,1044740-3,00.htm (Accessed 2 April 2013).
63. http://www.elespectador.com/columna199791-canor-necat (Accessed 12 April 2013).
64. http://www.elespectador.com/columna117870-el-papa-y-el-paisa (Accessed 12 April 2013).
65. *Ibid.*
66. http://www.youtube.com/watch?v=k6C9BuXe2RM (Accessed 12 April 2013).

on his face, but blamed his colleague Cardinal Re, the Prefect of the Congregation for Bishops for the debacle.[67]

Castrillón was a strong supporter of the Latin Mass and the great leap forward to the sixteenth century Council of Trent, dressing himself up in the *Cappa Magna*, the cloak of the Renaissance Princes that was originally designed to cover incontinent horses' bottoms, but which the Church's cardinals had made from watered red silk with an ermine cape for winter, and lengthened to fifteen metres to be carried by acolytes in solemn procession. Pope Pius XII in 1952 ordered it to be shortened from fifteen to seven metres.[68] Pope Paul VI discouraged its use, perhaps in an attempt to rid the hierarchy of its image of dressing up as if they were on their way to a Gay Mardi Gras.[69]

In March 2008, Castrillón, who was so adamant that bishops obey canon law when it came to not reporting priests' sexual abuse crimes to the police, seemed quite unconcerned about ignoring Pope Pius XII's 1952 instruction about the length of his *Cappa Magna*. He officiated at a Latin Mass at Westminster Cathedral in England dragging his fifteen metre, red watered silk *Cappa Magna* behind him, looking like Priscilla Queen of the Desert with altar boys.[70] In 2010, he was invited to Washington to put on a repeat performance, but was forced to bow out after protests were threatened by sexual abuse victims, angered by his letter to Bishop Pican.[71]

In 1984 Castrillón admitted accepting money from Pablo Escobar's drug cartel. Most Colombian bishops refused to accept such money, often seeing it as nothing more than money laundering. Castrillón said it was for 'charitable purposes', and that he had accepted it to stop it being used for prostitution. He said that he had warned the donors

67. http://www.catholicculture.org/news/headlines/index.cfm?storyid=4142 (Accessed 12 April 2013).
68. *Valde solliciti, motu proprio*, http://www.vatican.va/holy_father/pius_xii/motu_proprio/documents/hf_p-xii_motu-proprio_19521130_valde-solliciti_lt.html (Accessed 16 April 2013).
69. http://www2.fiu.edu/~mirandas/instruction69.htm (Accessed 16 April 2013).
70. http://uvcarmel.wordpress.com/tag/westminister-cathedral/ (Accessed 16 April 2013).
71. http://ncronline.org/news/faith-parish/cardinal-who-praised-cover-bows-out-dc-latin-mass (Accessed 12 April 2013).

that simply giving money to the Church 'would not save their souls'.[72] He is, as they say, a 'character'.

But his repeated utterances over not reporting paedophile clergy to the police reflect a strong streak of clericalism—as if he needed words to add to the symbolism of his ecclesiastical fashions.

On 2 June 2011, Cardinal Castrillón had an interview with CNN's Patricia Janiot in Colombia. He denied that there was any such thing as a paedophile, and said that it was simply a matter of priests 'making a mistake', and if the priest acknowledges his crime the bishop punishes him in accordance with canon law. Castrillón said:

> He is suspended and taken away from his parish. If he shows correction, then he is sent to another parish. That is not a crime. It is not covering it up. It is following the law, like society does in the case of doctors and lawyers. They are not struck off for all eternity.

Janiot asked him whether or not the Church regarded sexual abuse of children as a crime, but Castrillón could only think in terms of canonical crimes and started to describe to her the procedures under canon law. It was as if a civil law was completely irrelevant confirming Professor Patrick Parkinson's view that it is no part of canonical thinking that child sexual abuse is a crime that ought to be dealt with by the criminal courts.

Castrillón denied that any priest had gone unpunished where the crime had been proved in a canonical court. And then the Vatican's high priest of clericalism could not resist the comparison with Potiphar's wife:

> ' . . . when . . . you have enormous sums of money that are benefiting a large number of people all of us have the right to cast doubt on the honesty of the claims about these kinds of crimes.'

---

72. Allen, John L, Jr, 'These Paths Lead to Rome', in *National Catholic Reporter*. 2 June 2000, http://natcath.org/NCR_Online/archives2/2000b/060200/060200a. htm (Accessed 2 April 2013).

Janiot put to Castrillón that if Pope John Paul had acted more decisively on the scandal of child sexual abuse then there would not have been this problem.

> **Castrillón:** Patricia, Pope John Paul did everything he had to do. He did it through the clearest norms of justice, charity, equity and maintaining the purity of the law. He did exactly what he had to do . . . I witnessed his concern, his sorrow. It is very easy for the world's press to latch onto unproven cases in which an unreal image of the clergy is projected. There are no cases within the Church which are known, and have not been punished. Show me just one . . . in any part of the world that is known and proved that has not been punished.
>
> **Janiot:** In the case of Fr Marcial Maciel, he was never brought to justice. The priest died, and his case was in the Vatican during the nineties and it was never heard by the judicial processes, while his own companions in his Order actually accepted that he had committed serious crimes.
>
> **Castrillón:** I don't want to answer that.[73]

Bella figura had turned *bruta* in Colombia, and this time on CNN television. This doctor of canon law, the prefect of the Congregation of the Clergy from 1996 to 2006, confirmed in his retirement what Bishop Michael Smith had said about his meeting with the Irish bishops in Sligo in 1998. That is, that for Castrillón child sexual abuse was just a moral issue, and that the Vatican's role was to defend accused priests against unfounded allegations. Castrillón had ignored the fact that Pope John Paul II had effectively destroyed any possibility that these allegations could even be investigated and tried under canon law because any crimes were 'extinguished' by the five year limitation period. As Cardinal Pell said at the *Victorian Parliamentary Inquiry,*

---

73. The author's translation, http://www.youtube.com/watch?v=gnIwp_d3Ue8 (Accessed 12 April 2013).

the former Prefect of the Congregation for Clergy 'did not get it'.[74] But neither did so many others, and not just in the Vatican.

74. http://www.parliament.vic.gov.au/images/stories/committees/fcdc/ inquiries/57th/Child_Abuse_Inquiry/Transcripts/Catholic_Archdiocese_of_ Sydney_27-May-13.pdf , 21.8 (Accessed 3 July 2013).

Pope John Paul II

14

The Ineffectiveness of the Church Processes

The Complicated Procedure for Dismissal

The de facto privilege of clergy from civil prosecution that the secrecy provisions of canon law created may not have been so disastrous if the Church's own tribunals were equipped to deal adequately with the problem of clergy sexual abusers. But they were not, because of the terms of *Crimen Sollicitationis* and the *1983 Code of Canon Law*.

Once a bishop received a complaint of sexual abuse by a priest, he was required by canon law to undertake a preliminary investigation. This was the requirement both of *Crimen Sollicitationis* and the *1983 Code of Canon Law*. The language of both documents did not give him any discretion in the matter.[1] Under the *1983 Code of Canon Law*, if, after the preliminary investigation, there appeared to be substance in the allegations, then he had to decide if a penal process is to be initiated.

The *1983 Code of Canon Law* had two kinds of penal processes that a bishop could take against a priest. The first was a simpler method, called an administrative process where the accused priest was notified of the charges and allowed to respond. The bishop, with two assessors then decides if guilt has been proved and sentence passed.[2] However, the more formal judicial process could only be

---

1. *Crimen Sollicitationis,* clause 29, 30–41, http://www.vatican.va/resources/resources_crimen-sollicitationis-1962_en.html (Accessed 4 August 2013) and in relation to the Code Nicholas P Cafardi, *Before Dallas* (Mahwah, NJ: Paulist Press, 2008), 16.
2. Canons 1342, 1720. There are also various options open to the priest to have the decision overturned: Canons 1733, 1734 and 1737. Although this simpler process was called an 'administrative' one, it has all the hallmarks of what would be regarded as a judicial process in the common law system, because there is the gathering of evidence and the right of defence before a decision is made. Judicial

used to dismiss a priest, and this involved a complicated process with a court of three judges, which sometimes took as long as seven years to be finalised.[3] In the United States, canon lawyers did not think that the process was likely to end in dismissal, or if it did, an appeal to Rome would be successful.[4]

One of the senior canon lawyers for the Dublin Archdiocese, Monsignor Sheehy considered that the penal aspects of canon law to dismiss a priest should rarely be invoked. This was understandable because canon law made it the absolute last resort.[5] The 1992 Canadian *ad hoc* committee to the Canadian Catholic Bishops Conference, in their report, *From Pain to Hope,* noted that canonical proceedings against clergy sexual abusers were rare.[6] And the same occurred in the United States.[7]

At the various inquiries in Australia, the chances of dismissing a priest through a canonical trial were variously described as 'very difficult' (Cardinal Pell), 'close to hopeless' (Bishop Malone) 'very, very difficult' (Archbishop Hart) 'extraordinarily difficult' (Archbishop Coleridge) and the whole procedure was 'unworkable' (Fr Brian Lucas).[8]

---

review within the common law system is the review by a court of a decision already made by an administrator. While natural justice may be a reason for setting aside the decision, the more common challenge is that the administrator did not exercise his or her decision in accordance with the law.

3. Cafardi: *Before Dallas*, 57 and John P Beal: 'Doing What We Can', in *The Jurist*, 52 (1992): 642–83 at 677, quoted in Cafardi: *Before Dallas,* 192, footnote 25, Cafardi, 'Loose Canons: Ratzinger, Church Law & the Sexual-Abuse Crisis', http://www.commonwealmagazine.org/loose-canons (Accessed 17 July 2013).

4. Cafardi, *Before Dallas*, 37ff..

5. *Murphy Dublin Report,* Part 1 http://www.justice.ie/en/JELR/DACOI%20Part%201.pdf/Files/DACOI%20Part%201.pdf, paragraph 1.26 (Accessed 25 April 2013)

6. http://www.cccb.ca/site/Files/From_Pain_To_Hope.pdf paragraph 14 (Accessed 19 May 2013)

7. Cafardi *Before Dallas*, 26.

8. Cardinal Pell, *Victorian Parliamentary Inquiry* http://www.parliament.vic.gov.au/images/stories/committees/fcdc/inquiries/57th/Child_Abuse_Inquiry/Transcripts/Catholic_Archdiocese_of_Sydney_27-May-13.pdf, 21.8 (Accessed 3 July 2013), Bishop Malone:, *Maitland-Newcastle Inquiry,* http://www.lawlink.nsw.gov.au/lawlink/Special_Projects/ll_splprojects.nsf/vwFiles/Transcript_Day_8_-_TOR_2_-_11_July_2013.pdf/$file/Transcript_Day_8_-_TOR_2_-_11_July_2013.pdf , 873.43ff (Accessed 14 July 2013); Archbishop Hart, *Victorian Parliamentary Inquiry,* http://www.parliament.vic.gov.au/images/

Apart from issues of jurisdiction and the complexity of the process, the bar for dismissal was set impossibly high.

The Grounds for Dismissal

Crimen Sollicitationis provided that dismissal was only possible when

> . . . it appears evident that the Defendant, in the depth of his malice, has, in his abuse of the sacred ministry, with grave scandal to the faithful and harm to souls, attained such a degree of temerity and habitude, that there seems to be no hope, humanly speaking, or almost no hope, of his amendment.

All a priest had to do was to promise not to do it again and no further action could be taken. There was always the possibility of his being 'amended', if he promised hard enough. Another factor that had to be taken into account for dismissal was if there had been 'grave scandal to the faithful'. If the faithful did not know about the sexual abuse, then the priest was less likely to be dismissed. And the secrecy provisions were designed so that the faithful did not know about it anyway. Secrecy and the lack of dismissal fed off each other.

Even after 1983, when bishops throughout the world understandably thought that the *1983 Code of Canon Law* had replaced *Crimen Sollicitationis*, the end result was the same, because Canon 1341 stated that the bishop could only initiate the administrative or judicial process to impose a penalty:

> . . . after he has ascertained that fraternal correction or rebuke or other means of pastoral solicitude cannot sufficiently repair the scandal, restore justice, reform the offender.

stories/committees/fcdc/inquiries/57th/Child_Abuse_Inquiry/Transcripts/ Catholic_Archdiocese_of_Melbourne_20-May-13.pdf, 9 (Accessed 18 June 2013); Archbishop Coleridge, *Australian Royal Commission,* http://www. childabuseroyalcommission.gov.au/wp-content/uploads/2013/08/Transcript-RC_IRCSA_Day-026_11-Dec-2013_Public.pdf p.2733 (Accessed 12 December 2013), Fr Lucas, *Newcastle-Maitland Inquiry,* http://www.lawlink.nsw.gov.au/ lawlink/Special_Projects/ll_splprojects.nsf/vwFiles/Transcript_Day_15_-_ TOR_2_-_24_July_2013.pdf/$file/Transcript_Day_15_-_TOR_2_-_24_ July_2013.pdf, 1570 (Accessed 18 August 2013).

The *Murphy Dublin Report* pointed out:

> This canon was interpreted to mean that bishops are required to attempt to reform the abusers in the first instance. In the Archdiocese of Dublin, significant efforts were made to reform abusers. They were sent to therapeutic facilities, very often at considerable expense. In a number of the earlier cases in particular, the Archdiocese seems to have been reluctant to go beyond the reform process even when it was abundantly clear that the reform process had failed.[9]

That criticism of the Irish bishops was legitimate, but their behaviour is understandable because of the difficulties imposed by canon law to taking the matter further. Canon 1341 was not the only hurdle.

Another example of the 'pastoral' attitude towards child sex abusing priests appears in the 2010 Vatican *Guide to Understanding Basic CDF Procedures*. If the priest 'has admitted to his crimes and accepted to live a life of prayer and penance', the bishop can issue a decree prohibiting or restricting the priest's public ministry. It is only if he violates those conditions that he can then be dismissed.[10] Restrictions on ministry were penalties imposed on Fr Marcial Maciel by Pope Benedict XVI in 2006, and on a serial abuser in the Lismore diocese by the Congregation for the Doctrine of the Faith in 2008.[11]

The Vatican 'Catch 22'

But even where the dismissal process was commenced against a priest, there was an extraordinary defence available. Canon 1321 has a kind of 'diminished responsibility' defence, and paedophilia itself was a canonical defence to a charge of sexual abuse of minors. The *Murphy Dublin Report* quotes a commentary on Canon 1395 (dealing

---

9. *Murphy Dublin Report*, Part 1 http://www.justice.ie/en/JELR/DACOI%20 Part%201.pdf/Files/DACOI%20Part%201.pdf paragraph 4.17-4.28 (Accessed 25 April 2013) paragraph 4.53.

10. http://www.vatican.va/resources/resources_guide-CDF-procedures_en.html (Accessed 24 December 2013).

11. *Australian Royal Commission* http://www.childabuseroyalcommission.gov.au/ wp-content/uploads/2013/12/Transcript-RC_IRCSA_Day-032_19-Dec-2013_ TBC_Public.pdf p. 3392.36 (Accessed 20 December 2013).

with sex assaults on minors) by the Canon Law Society of Great Britain and Ireland, which said that a priest who sexually assaulted a child might well be guilty and liable to imprisonment under civil law, but might not be guilty under canon law because of 'diminished imputability', or, if he is found guilty, the sentence might be no more than a warning.[12]

The *Murphy Dublin Report* commented:

> This is a major point of difference between the Church and the state law. In the former, it appears that paedophilia may be an actual defence to a claim of child sexual abuse just as insanity would be in the law of the state. [13]

The commission also noted that even where three priests were dismissed after local Church trials, their appeals against dismissal in two cases were upheld in Rome on this ground:

> This Commission finds it a matter of grave concern that, under canon law, a serial child sexual abuser might receive more favourable treatment from the Archdiocese or from Rome by reason of the fact that he was diagnosed as a paedophile.[14]

The Vatican 'Catch 22': the priest cannot be dismissed for paedophilia because he is a paedophile.

The British canon lawyers were not the only ones to think that the Vatican 'Catch 22' was a valid defence. In 1996, the American canon lawyer, John A Alesandro said that the prevalent opinion in 1992 in relation to paedophilia was that such priests were almost automatically exempted from dismissal because dismissal required not merely

---

12. Canon Law Society of Great Britain and Ireland, *Canon Law: Letter & Spirit: A Practical Guide to the Code of Canon Law* (London: Geoffrey Chapman, 1995), 805, *Murphy Dublin Report*, Part 1 http://www.justice.ie/en/JELR/DACOI%20 Part%201.pdf/Files/DACOI%20Part%201.pdf, paragraph 4.59 (Accessed 25 April 2013).
13. *Ibid*.
14. *Ibid*, 4.60.

'grave' imputability, but 'full' imputability.[15] Another noted American Canon lawyer, Thomas J Reese, the editor of *America* magazine, in a report to the 1992 United States Catholic Bishops Conference wrote that the *1983 Code of Canon Law* makes it 'almost impossible for bishops to dismiss priests for sexual abuse'.[16]

Canon lawyers in the United States also considered that the Vatican 'Catch 22' defence was another reason for not using the canonical processes. It was pointless, because the main reason for starting the judicial process was to dismiss the priest, and because of the diminished mental capacity defence available under Canon 1321, it was highly unlikely that he would be.[17] The irony is that the more the priest was a serial abuser the more likely the defence would succeed—he couldn't help himself. The cases referred to by the Murphy Commission, where appeals had gone to Rome, show that these canon lawyers were not just theorising.

Despite the fanfare claiming that everything had been improved by the *2001 Motu Proprio*, Canon 1321 is still there, unaffected by the changes. Whoever decides a case under the new procedures, whether it is the Congregation for the Doctrine of the Faith or the bishop, they are still obliged to apply the 'Catch 22' defence.

The Limitation Period

The *1983 Code of Canon Law* imposed a five year limitation period (*prescription*) after the alleged offence. The effect of the expiry of the limitation period is that the canonical crime is 'extinguished', that is, it is as if it never occurred, no matter how strong the case is against the priest.[18]

Nicholas Cafardi points out that American canon lawyers during the whole clergy abuse crisis thought and advised that if the abuse had taken place more than five years previously, they could do nothing under canon law.[19] And it seems that at least until the late 1990s, every

15. JA Alesandro, 'A Study of Canon Law: Dismissal from the Clerical State in Cases of Sexual Misconduct', in *The Catholic Lawyer*, 36 (1996): 262, quoted in Delaney, *Canonical Implications of the Response of the Catholic Church in Australia,* 194.
16. *Ibid*, 36 and *America* (December 5 1992): 443–44 at 444.
17. Cafardi, *Before Dallas,* 35.
18. Cafardi *Before Dallas*, 29, and footnote 75.
19. *Ibid*, 30.

Vatican Congregation thought that to be the case. The short limitation period meant that there was very little possibility of taking canonical proceedings to dismiss a priest because very few children came to terms with what happened to them until well into adulthood.[20]

The *2001 Motu Proprio* decree of Pope John Paul II extended the limitation period to ten years running from the eighteenth birthday. And in 2002 a further concession was made whereby the Congregation for the Doctrine of the Faith could extend the limitation period on a discretionary basis.[21] However, the Congregation was unable to deal with the vast number of referrals and instructed the bishops to 'apply disciplinary measures' to priests where the cases were outside the limitation period, thus ensuring that there would be no dismissals in the case of those priests, because only the Vatican could dismiss a priest.[22] In other words, the power to extend became useless.

In 2010, under the further 'reforms', the period was extended to twenty years from the date of the victim's eighteenth birthday, making the age of thirty-eight the cut-off point. But none of these extensions of the limitation period operated retrospectively.[23] There were no such time limitations under *Crimen Sollicitationis*. The retention of any limitation period in the revised norms of the *2001 Motu Proprio* is still a step backwards in solving the problem of sexual abuse in the Church.

Administrative Leave

A further problem arose from the inability to suspend a priest pending the preliminary investigation. A priest could only be suspended once

---

20. Nicholas Cafardi/Gallicho, *New York Times,* 'The CDF & Church Law–a Canonist Responds', http://www.commonwealmagazine.org/blog/nyt-cdf-church-law-canonist-responds (Accessed 27 May 2013), and Nicholas Cafardi, 'The Scandal of Secrecy: Canon Law and the Sexual-abuse Crisis', in *Commonweal*, 21 July 2010 http://commonwealmagazine.org/scandal-secrecy (Accessed 27 May 2013).

21. *Ibid*, at 4.63 and Charles Scicluna, 'The Procedure and Praxis of the Congregation for the Doctrine of the Faith regarding *Graviora Delicta*' (2006) http://www.vatican.va/resources/resources_mons-scicluna-graviora-delicta_en.html (Accessed 14 June 2013).

22. *Murphy Dublin Report*, Part 1, paragraph 4.29 http://www.justice.ie/en/JELR/DACOI%20Part%201.pdf/Files/DACOI%20Part%201.pdf (Accessed 16 July 2013).

23. Delaney, *Canonical Implications of the Response of the Catholic Church in Australia*, 189.

the preliminary investigation is complete—and this may take some time.[24] Further, suspension was regarded as a canonical penalty, and it can only be given after a warning, and the offender has time to mend his ways.[25]

In 1985, Fr Thomas Doyle who was then attached to the Papal Nuncio's Office in Washington DC, with a group of colleagues, put together a manual for dealing with the growing sexual abuse crisis in the Church in the United States. It was common practice in secular society for persons in positions of authority, against whom allegations had been made concerning their duties, to stand aside from their position pending the outcome of any hearing or inquiry. Doyle and his team proposed something similar for priests against whom allegations were made. They would go on 'administrative leave'.[26]

The difficulty with this idea was that it was a concept unknown to canon law, at least in those terms. The closest thing was suspension under Canon 1722, but that was only authorized after the preliminary investigation was over, and the canonical trial had commenced. In 1991, the noted canon lawyer, Fr John P Beal, in a flourish of hyperbole that should have won him a prize, described the whole idea of 'administrative leave' as:

> chillingly reminiscent of Stalin's use of mental institutions.[27]

In 2000, he was a bit more moderate, and described it as:

> a canonically flawed attempt to expand the circumstances in which the restrictions that can be imposed on the accused in the course of the penal process (c 1722) to include situations where no penal process is in prospect.[28]

---

24. Cafardi, *Before Dallas* , 41.
25. Canon 1347§1, and *ibid,* 191, footnote 14.
26. Cafardi, *Before Dallas,* 51.
27. John P Beal, 'To Be or Not To Be, That is the Question: The Rights of the Accused in the Canonical Penal Process', in *Canon Law Society of America Proceedings,* 53 (1991): 77–97, at 87, quoted in Cafardi, *Before Dallas,*117. See also J Alesandro, 'Dismissal from the Clerical State in Cases of Sexual Misconduct: Recent Derogations', in *Canon Law Society of America Proceedings,* 56 (1994): 54.
28. John P Beal: 'At the Crossroads of Two Laws', in *Louvain Studies* 25 (2000)

The canonical justification for 'administrative leave' was the interpretation of Canon 1722 that allowed a priest to be stood down 'to prevent scandals, to protect the freedom of witnesses and to guard the course of justice', but as indicated previously, this could only occur once the preliminary investigation was over, and the canonical trial commenced.[29] What Doyle and others tried to do was to justify the suspension *before* the preliminary investigation, but this was not justified by Canon 1722.[30] This issue over 'administrative leave' became a matter of contention between the American bishops and the Vatican when the Dallas proposals were submitted to it. The Vatican insisted on the *1983 Code of Canon Law* being followed before granting the *recognitio* in 2002. However, with the 2010 revision of *2001 Motu Proprio*, it relented to allow a priest to be stood down pending the preliminary investigation.[31]

Removal of Faculties

The bishop has the right under canon law to impose restrictions on priests in terms of how they operated as priests. Because of the difficulties of dismissing a priest, this was how bishops tried to 'control' them. But the Murphy Commission pointed out:

quoted in Cafardi, *ibid*, 191, footnote 14. As will be shown below, this was one of the problems with the 1996 *Towards Healing* document: if there is a finding by an assessor under that protocol, or a finding of guilt by a civil court then the priest was to go on 'administrative leave' pursuant to Canon 1722. But canon law only authorized a 'suspension' during the course of a canonical trial. That situation changed in 2010 with the revision of the *2001 Motu Proprio*, under which the bishop can stand the priest down pending the preliminary inquiry. The conflicts between such protocols and canon law were matters that concerned both Professor Parkinson in his reviews of *Towards Healing*, and the Cumberlege Commission in England in its reviews of *Lord Nolan's Report*. While the issue of 'administrative leave' has now been resolved for *Towards Healing* by a change in canon law, the problem of pontifical secrecy remains.

29. Delaney, 219: 'In terms of processes, the imposition of administrative leave during a preliminary investigation, while its use may be wise, does not have the support of universal law'. And see also page 156.
30. Cafardi, *Before Dallas*, 119.
31. The 'Substantive Norms' of the *Motu Proprio Sacramentorum Sanctitatis Tutela*, as revised in 2010, Article 19, http://www.vatican.va/resources/resources_norme_en.html (Accessed 5 August 2013), *Australian Church Submission*, 134, paragraph 35 http://dev.childabuseroyalcommission.gov.au/wp-content/uploads/2013/10/14.-Truth-Justice-and-Healing-Council.pdf (Accessed 12 October 2013).

> The Commission does not consider that an order to stay
> away from children, or to minister only to adults, or to
> meet children only when accompanied by another adult,
> is adequate. It is virtually impossible for such orders to
> be enforced.[32]

The only practical way of controlling people who sexually abuse
children is through the criminal justice system, which is not perfect
either, but it is better than the secret system imposed by canon law.

Canonical Proceedings against Religious

As previously explained, religious brothers and sisters are not 'clerics'
under canon law. However, there are parallel provisions under canon
law dealing with them if they sexually abuse children. They can only
be described as perverse. The code deals more leniently with those
who sexually abuse children than with those who have consensual
sex with adults. A religious who lives in 'concubinage' or who 'assists
with scandal in another external sin against sixth commandment'
(that is as a continuous sexual relationship with an adult) must be
dismissed (Canon 695).

A religious brother or nun can be dismissed from their religious
order or congregation for having sex with children but it says that the
superior does not have to dismiss him or her if the superior of the
order decides that:

> . . . dismissal is not completely necessary and that
> correction of the member, restitution of justice, and
> reparation of scandal can be resolved sufficiently in
> another way.

The same 'pastoral' approach, the Catch 22 and the limitation
period are applied to them as with priests.[33]

---

32. *Murphy Dublin Report*, Part 1, http://www.justice.ie/en/JELR/DACOI%20Part%201.
    pdf/Files/DACOI%20Part%201.pdf, paragraphs 4.17–4.28, 4.90 (Accessed 25
    April 2013).
33. Canon 695 §1, Beal, Coriden & Green, *New Commentary on the Code of Canon
    Law*, 865

The Appeal Process

Appeals to the Vatican were long drawn out processes, where procedural correctness seemed to be more important than matters of substance.[34] A good illustration of this is Cardinal Castrillón's advice to the Irish bishops through the Storero letter of 31 January 1997, that reporting allegations of sexual abuse to the police could be sufficient to allow a priest's appeal against dismissal.[35] The priest has every reason to appeal because unless he is dismissed, he is entitled to his salary from the Church.[36] The history of successful appeals to Rome seems to have been one of the factors impeding American bishops from pursuing the canonical course.[37]

The Discoverability of Documents in Canonical Proceedings

Another reason for American bishops not using the canonical process is that under American civil law, the documents produced by the Church tribunal could not resist a subpoena to produce. They were advised by their own civil lawyers that if they did not want material that came before the canonical court being made public, it would be better to avoid the canonical process.[38] In 1992, the Canadian canon lawyer, Francis G Morrissey advised bishops that while reporting laws had to be complied with, all documentation should be drawn up so as to be identified as a document prepared for legal advice by a civil lawyer so as to attract solicitor/client privilege. Likewise, it would be preferable that such documents be kept at the lawyer's office rather than in the chancery safe. He accepted that such a claim to privilege might not be recognised.[39] Such an attempt in Australia was doomed to failure.[40]

---

34. Cafardi, *Before Dallas,* 38.
35. See chapter 17.
36. Cardinal Pell at the *Victorian Parliamentary Inquiry,* http://www.parliament.vic. gov.au/images/stories/committees/fcdc/inquiries/57th/Child_Abuse_Inquiry/ Transcripts/Catholic_Archdiocese_of_Sydney_27-May-13.pdf, 40.8 (Accessed 22 June 2013).
37. Cafardi, *Before Dallas,* 38–39.
38. *Ibid,* 45.
39. Morrissey 'Procedures to be Applied in the case of Sexual Misconduct by a Priest', in *Studia Canonica,* 26 (1992): 39-73 at 47 http://www.attorneygeneral. jus.gov.on.ca/inquiries/cornwall/en/hearings/exhibits/Frank_Morrisey/pdf/06_ Morrisey_Procedures.pdf (Accessed 30 July 2013).
40. Fr Brian Lucas suggested that documents relating to preliminary investigations

In the 1990s, the Australian bishops shared the opinion of their American counterparts that it was virtually impossible to use the canonical processes to dismiss a sexually abusing priest. They appointed Fr Lucas to make informal approaches to the accused priests to convince them to resign. In 1994, the New South Wales Police had issued a search warrant against the presbytery of the Bishop of Parramatta, Bede Heather after he allegedly refused to hand over his files in relation to his inquiry about sexual abuse of minors by the members of the St Gerard Majella Society in his diocese. Any such refusal was in accord with requirements of pontifical secrecy under canon law.

In October 1996, Fr Lucas wrote a paper for the Canon Law Society of Australia and New Zealand, 'Are Our Archives Safe: An Ecclesial View of Search Warrants'. He described it as an 'academic paper raising questions for canon lawyers to further reflect on and discuss', and he was not making 'authoratative recommendations'. He discussed the problem where parties to canonical proceeedings might have been assured of confidentiality, and may have made admissions that they might otherwise not have made. He concluded that no form of privilege attached to such documents produced in Church tribunal proceedings under the civil law.[41] While he warned against selective destruction of documents, he said

> . . . the creation of such documents connected with internal Church investigations that could be linked to likely litigation should only happen in consultation with the legal advisers of the Church agency. Advice should be taken as to how the document will be created, who

---

might be kept in solicitor's offices on the grounds that they might be the subject of future litigation. But he seemed to concede that this would not work because: 'In order to attract legal professional privilege the document must have been brought into existence solely for purpose of obtaining legal advice', 'Are Our Archives Safe? An Ecclesial View of Search Warrants', referred to at http://www.lawlink.nsw.gov.au/lawlink/Special_Projects/ll_splprojects.nsf/vwFiles/Transcript_Day_15_-_TOR_2_-_24_July_2013.pdf/$file/Transcript_Day_15_-_TOR_2_-_24_July_2013.pdf , 1621. This reference and subsequent quotes are taken from a paper given by Fr Lucas at the Thirteenth Annual Conference of the Canon Law Society of Australia and New Zealand, at St Vincent's College, Potts Point, NSW, 7–11 October 1996.

41. *Ibid.*

will have custody of it and what status it will have in relation to legal professional privilege.

He said that 'there may be cases that appear to be so sensitive that it is in the best interest of the parties or one of them, and of the Church, that the documents not be created in the first place'. Fr Lucas dealt with about thirty-five priests in trying to convince them to agree to voluntary laicisation, in the period 1990–1995/96, and he regarded what he was doing as being outside the canonical system.[42] He kept no notes of any conversations he had with the priests, saying had he done so the priest would not agree to talk to him. When asked why he did not take notes afterwards, he said that in fairness, the priest 'ought to see them and endorse them as accurate'.[43]

Archbishop Little of Melbourne kept no notes of his inquiries about sex abusing priests.[44] Bishop Mulkearns admitted in a 1993 interview that 'he did not want to keep much in writing'.[45] Fr Brian Lucas's article was not published until 1995, just before Little's and Mulkearn's retirements, but it seems that they had both adopted the policy long before. Had they consulted civil lawyers about whether documents created in the course of their canonical inquiries had to be produced to a civil court, the answer would have been the same as that provided by Lucas: the only way to avoid the production of such documents was not to have any. The only real inference one can draw from Little and Mulkearns failure to take notes was a desire to protect the Church from 'scandal', or to protect priests, or both. And indeed, one of Little's successors, Archbishop Hart, accepted that by

---

42. *Ibid*, 1563 and 1632.
43. *Ibid*, 1563. Lucas's colleague, Fr John Usher had the practice of taking notes after a meeting with a priest or a victim. http://www.lawlink.nsw.gov.au/lawlink/Special_Projects/ll_splprojects.nsf/vwFiles/Day_22_-_9_September_2013.pdf/$file/Day_22_-_9_September_2013.pdf 2360 (Accessed 11 September 2013).
44. http://www.parliament.vic.gov.au/images/stories/committees/fcdc/inquiries/57th/Child_Abuse_Inquiry/Transcripts/Catholic_Archdiocese_of_Melbourne_20-May-13.pdf p. 11 (Accessed 18 June 2013)
45. *Betrayal of Trust*, Report of *Victorian Parliamentary Inquiry*, paragraph 7.4.1, 183 https://s3-ap-southeast-2.amazonaws.com/family-and-community-development-committee/Inquiry+into+Handling+of+Abuse_Volume+1_FINAL_web.pdf (Accessed 14 November 2013).

doing so, Little had covered up the 'foulest crime'.[46] Canon law did not prohibit Archbishop Little and Bishop Mulkearns from taking and keeping notes, but this is another example of Cardinal Francis George's principle that the very existence of pontifical secrecy under canon law rationalises and deepens the culture that gave rise to it in the first place.

Other Effects of Secrecy

Secrecy not only had an effect on preventing clergy sexual abusers to be prosecuted under the civil law. The *Murphy Dublin Report* found that secrecy imposed by canon law on the Church's investigations and trials created serious problems for its own administration. It meant that often people within the Church administration who needed to know were frequently not told.[47] The same thing occurred in Australia where Cardinal Pell, as auxiliary bishop to Archbishop Little of Melbourne, did not know about allegations against priests within the diocese.[48] Antony Whitlam QC found the same thing occurred in the 'Father F' case.[49]

The Lack of Resources and Personnel

The sad history of the Church's attempts to deal with clergy sexual abuse is sufficient proof of its inadequacy. But the systemic problems from which it suffers are obvious from canon law itself. The Church does not have any jails to keep clergy sexual abusers. It has no trained police force or powers of search and arrest. It has no access to DNA and scientific testing, an independent judiciary and public hearings. Nor does it have parole and supervision facilities.

The Victorian Church in its submission to the *Victorian Parliamentary Inquiry* and the *Australian Church Submission* to the *Australian Royal Commission* acknowledges that the police are more experienced and better resourced to be able to investigate criminal

---

46. *Ibid*, 12–13 and 35.
47. http://www.dacoi.ie paragraph1.64 (Accessed 9 February 2013).
48. Cardinal Pell at the *Victorian Parliamentary Inquiry* http://www.parliament.vic. gov.au/images/stories/committees/fcdc/inquiries/57th/Child_Abuse_Inquiry/ Transcripts/Catholic_Archdiocese_of_Sydney_27-May-13.pdf pages 7 & 13 (Accessed 22 June 2013).
49. http://www.parra.catholic.org.au/ paragraph 168 (Accessed 9 February 2013).

behaviour.[50] *Towards Healing* makes the same acknowledgment and accepts that Church penalties are inadequate for these kinds of crimes.[51] Bishop Malone at the *Maitland-Newcastle Inquiry* admitted that dismissing the priest from the priesthood did not stop him assaulting children, and that was a further reason for such crimes to be reported to the police.[52]

It is therefore highly surprising that the Vatican retains pontifical secrecy that will still apply to the majority of complaints about sex crimes against priests, because the 2010 dispensation only applies where there is a local law requiring reporting, and historic abuse generally does not have to be reported. That can only have the effect of continuing to protect offending priests from being dealt with under the civil law.

Not only did the canonical system not have the resources of the state available to it, but even within its own system it lacked experienced canon lawyers to deal with the dismissal process. That was a necessary consequence of the *1983 Code of Canon Law* making it virtually impossible to have a canonical trial because of the limitation period and the *1983 Code's* insistence on the adoption of the 'pastoral and therapeutic' approach. The end result was that there were virtually no canonical trials, and if there were no canonical trials, there were no canon lawyers with experience in the trial procedures.[53]

Conflicts of Interest

A further problem was the theological attitude to the priesthood and to the relationship between a priest and his bishop. Both Pope

50. *Facing the Truth*, paragraph 16.1 http://www.parliament.vic.gov.au/images/stories/committees/fcdc/inquiries/57th/Child_Abuse_Inquiry/Submissions/Catholic_Church_in_Victoria.pdf (Accessed 6 April 2013), *Australian Church Submission*, 115, paragraph 8.1, http://dev.childabuseroyalcommission.gov.au/wp-content/uploads/2013/10/14.-Truth-Justice-and-Healing-Council.pdf (Accessed 12 October 2013).
http://dev.childabuseroyalcommission.gov.au/wp-content/uploads/2013/10/14.-Truth-Justice-and-Healing-Council.pdf (Accessed 12 October 2013).
51. *Towards Healing*, pargraph 37.3.
52. *Maitland-Newcastle Inquiry* http://www.lawlink.nsw.gov.au/lawlink/Special_Projects/ll_splprojects.nsf/vwFiles/Transcript_Day_8_-_TOR_2_-_11_July_2013.pdf/$file/Transcript_Day_8_-_TOR_2_-_11_July_2013.pdf , 872.33-39 (Accessed 14 July 2013).
53. Cafardi, *Before Dallas*, 25–28.

John Paul II and Pope Benedict XVI have spoken about priests on ordination becoming 'ontologically changed', that is they have been specially marked out by God in a way that changes their very nature.[54]

Further, there are numerous instances where senior clerics have stated that the relationship between a bishop and a priest is a 'sacramental' one, and one like 'father and son'. Cardinal Castrillón, for example, in his letter to Bishop Pican after his conviction for covering up a French paedophile priest said,

> For the relationship between priests and their bishop is not professional but **a sacramental relationship** which forges **very special bonds of spiritual paternity** . . . But a bishop cannot be required to make the denunciation himself. In all civilised legal systems it is acknowledged that close relations have the possibility of not testifying against a direct relative (my emphasis).

At Bishop Pican's trial, Bishop Fihey told the Court that there was a special 'fraternal and paternal' relationship that unites a priest to his bishop—the implication being that he should not be expected to report a paedophile priest to the police.[55]

In his 2010 interview with *The Tablet*, the Vatican Prosecutor, Monsignor Scicluna, said,

> We're dealing with an onerous duty because these bishops are forced to make a gesture comparable to that of a parent who denounces his or her own son.[56]

These statements reflect what is in the Catholic Catechism, that there is 'an intimate sacramental brotherhood' between priest and his bishop.[57]

---

54. http://www.vatican.va/holy_father/benedict_xvi/audiences/2009/documents/ hf_ben-xvi_aud_20090624_en.html (Accessed 16 July 2013). See also Richard Sipe, in *Mea Maxima Culpa*, at 1:23.04.

55. http://www.thetablet.co.uk/article/5114 (Accessed 16 July 2013).

56. http://www.thetablet.co.uk/article/14451 (Accessed 4 April 2013).

57. http://www.vatican.va/archive/ccc_css/archive/catechism/p2s2c3a6.htm

Yet, under canon law, the person who is to conduct the preliminary investigation is the bishop or his delegate, and it is the bishop who is to decide if the priest is to be subjected to a canonical trial. This 'theology' creates a conflict of interest, and it is hardly surprising that recidivist clergy sexual abusers were treated leniently.

In cases of purely canonical crimes, like desecrating Holy Communion or ordaining women, such a conflict of interest is a matter for the Church. They are not matters that concern or affect wider society. But where the issues are serious breaches of the civil law, particularly involving the welfare of children and canon law prohibits reporting the results of the bishop's investigations to the civil authorities, it is inevitable that justice will never be achieved in a Church trial.

The *Cloyne Report* refers to a letter of June 2002 from Monsignor O'Callaghan, the canon lawyer for the Cloyne diocese that indicated a curious conflict not only arising from the relationship between the bishop and the priest, but between the priest and those investigating his alleged criminal behaviour on behalf of the bishop. He wrote to a friend outlining his opposition to the requirement to report such crimes to the police and said that it seriously 'compromised' the investigators relationship with the priest they were investigating.[58] One would have thought that the only 'relationship' that a canon law investigator should have is objectivity, the application of canon law to the facts, and to report the allegations to the police.

Disciplinary tribunals in secular professions have also had to face perceptions of conflicts of interest and allegations of being lenient with their own members. In larger professions where the members are not in frequent contact with each other, this is more a matter of perception. But perception is also important, and for this reason there are often 'lay' members appointed to those tribunals. There is no reason why the Church could not adopt similar practices, and some of their protocols have done so. However, because these bodies can only be advisory bodies for the bishop in the current state of canon law, the problem will never go away. The conflict problem has been

(Accessed 5 April 2013).

58. http://www.justice.ie/en/JELR/Cloyne_Rpt.pdf/Files/Cloyne_Rpt.pdf paragraph 1.23 (Accessed 5 April 2013).

alleviated to some extent by the *2001 Motu Proprio* which requires the bishop to receive instructions from the Congregation for the Doctrine of the Faith on the manner of proceeding. To that extent some distance is created. But the Congregation generally directs the bishop to conduct an administrative or judicial trial and the same problem arises.

Despite all these problems with the canonical system, the Church's most senior canon lawyer, Archbishop Julian Herranz, President of the Pontifical Council for the Interpretation of Legislative Texts, said in 2002 that canon law is perfectly capable of dealing with the problems of sexual abuse by clergy.[59] This is precisely the clericalist attitude that gave rise to the revival of privilege of clergy in the first place, with such disastrous effects on children.

Disciplinary Proceedings of Other Professions

Any organisation has the right to make its own rules and to discipline its members in accordance with those rules. But when the 'misconduct' also amounts to a serious crime, the right of the state to deal with that should be paramount. It is only when the state criminal procedures have been exhausted that an organization should be able to deal with the member's actions on the basis of its disciplinary rules.

Quite apart from any laws relating to misprision of felony, this is the system adopted by all professions in Australia and in most parts of the world. Allegations of a criminal misuse of trust funds by lawyers, sexual abuse of patients by doctors and other professionals are dealt with first by the criminal justice system. None of these professional bodies have rules that say that any information gathered by their investigators should not be disclosed to the police. Protecting the good name of the people involved in such proceedings does not require anything like pontifical secrecy—something which the canon lawyer, Fr John P Beal concedes. If a person's identity needs to be withheld for some good reason, the use of pseudonyms is effective, as many of the commissions of inquiry in various countries have demonstrated.

---

59. http://cf.americamagazine.org/content/article.cfm?article_id=1953   (Accessed 11 June 2013).

Disciplinary bodies for professions in Australia do not need a law to tell them to report any crimes to the police, because they are imbued with the culture of the state—the point made by Professor Parkinson and by the NSW Law Reform Commission in 1999 when recommending the abolition of S.316 of the *Crimes Act 1900* (NSW). On the other hand, so long as the Church thinks it is a law unto itself, there will be continuous problems.

Legislation that sets up professional disciplinary tribunals in modern democracies creates an exception to confidentiality to allow reporting crimes to the police. The *Legal Profession Act* (NSW) 2004 and the various state *Ombudsman Acts* require their investigators to observe confidentiality, but there is always an exception where allegations of crimes or other breaches of discipline arise.[60]

As already stated, that was the kind of simple exception to pontifical secrecy that the Vatican could have included in *Crimen Sollicitationis* in 1922 and 1962, in the *2001 Motu Proprio* and at the time of its revision in 2010. The omission of such an exception and the limited extent to which the Vatican will allow reporting is an indication of its deliberate intent to preserve privilege of clergy as much as it can, and wherever it can. It cannot be an oversight.

Because of different standards of proof in criminal and disciplinary matters, it is quite possible for a lawyer or doctor, for example, to be acquitted of a criminal charge, but still disciplined for professional misconduct over the same facts. That is entirely appropriate, and there is every reason for the Church to have a similar system. But that is not how the Church system has worked because of its secrecy provisions which prevented any civil prosecution from taking place.

Quite apart from issues of reporting criminal behaviour to police, civil society also has an interest in appropriate standards being applied by professional bodies because of the standard of proof for striking someone off a professional register is not as high as that required for a criminal prosecution. Numerous superior courts have said that the purpose of disciplinary proceedings is not to punish the offender, but to protect the public.[61]

---

60. *Legal Profession Act* 1974 (NSW) S.722(2)(f). There are also similar provisions in the Ombudsman Acts, for example, 26A *Ombudsman Act* 1973 (Victoria).
61. *Smith v New South Wales Bar Association* [1992] HCA 36; (1992) 176 CLR 256

But it is absurd to have a convoluted disciplinary system whereby a person can only be struck off the rolls of their profession if they consent to it. That is what canon law did, and the people in charge of it at the Vatican were aware of it, but did nothing about it, at least until 2001, and even then, in many cases, it seems to have been ineffective. Even with recent improvements to canonical procedures, the problem for Australian civil society is that the disciplinary rules for Catholic clergy are determined not by a local association that can be controlled by civil law, but by a foreign government. The *Australian Church Submission* acknowledges that any disciplinary action against priests has to be consistent with canon law, a point Professor Parkinson has consistently made.[62]

A secular society that respects the freedom of religion has an interest in seeing that priests (or rabbis, imams or pastors) who sexually assault children are not allowed to continue to practice, just as much as it has an interest in seeing that fraudulent lawyers, predatory psychologists and drug dealing doctors are struck off the register. The standards and procedures that should be applied are a matter for the religious organization, but if those standards are not satisfactory, it only has itself to blame if there is a public demand for the state to intervene.[63]

Since 2001, the Church has claimed that its disciplinary procedures have improved. Archbishop Hart of Melbourne, in evidence before the *Victorian Parliamentary Inquiry* was asked about the situation in 2013. He said that he had no power to dismiss priests, but could remove them from ministry and restrict their activities. If it is a serious matter, he can refer it to the Vatican and petition it to dismiss the priest, or he can take the matter to the pope directly. He said it is a 'much simpler' procedure now.[64]

(13 August 1992).

62. *Australian Church Submission,* 136, paragraph 34, http://dev.childabuseroyalcommission.gov.au/wp-content/uploads/2013/10/14.-Truth-Justice-and-Healing-Council.pdf (Accessed 12 October 2013).

63. Fr Frank Brennan, 'Church-State Issues and the Royal Commission', in *Eureka Street* 3 September 2013: 'Clearly, the Church itself cannot be left alone to get its house in order. That would be a wrongful invocation of freedom of religion in a pluralist, democratic society', www.eurekastreet.com.au (Accessed 3 September 2013).

64. http://www.parliament.vic.gov.au/images/stories/committees/fcdc/inquiries/57th/Child_Abuse_Inquiry/Transcripts/Catholic_Archdiocese_of_

Despite the simplifications to the procedure and the extensions of the limitation period, the legal principles relating to the dismissal of priests have not changed. The documents released by the Archdiocese of Milwaukee in 2013, the Gannon case in the State of Victoria, and the DS case in Lismore about which Bishop Jarrett gave evidence to the *Australian Royal Commission* would suggest that the requirements for dismissing a priest after 2001 are still not so 'simple'. Whether these cases are indications of a systemic problem or the occasional aberrations one might expect in any legal system is a matter that can only be resolved by independent assessment of the 4,400 cases that the Vatican has handled since 2001.

Melbourne_20-May-13.pdf p.16 (Accessed 18 June 2013).

Pope Benedict XVI

15

The Practical Application of Canon Law

The preceding chapters have dealt with both canon and civil law so far as it dealt with the sexual abuse of children, and the clash between the two legal systems, the so-called 'parallel' systems that were never parallel. Then we dealt with the clerical culture of secrecy and the avoidance of scandal that shaped canon law, and finally how ineffectual the canonical procedures were. This chapter provides a sample of cases that reveals the practical application of the principles of canon law and the culture that it both reflected and reinforced.

The consistent pattern of how canon law operated is illustrated by the 2004 study done by the John Jay College of Criminal Justice in New York, commissioned by the American bishops. Their report, entitled, 'The Nature and Scope of the Problem of Sexual Abuse of Minors by Catholic Priests and Deacons in the United States 2004' looked at some 4,000 priests involved in sexual abuse of minors, and it studied the extent of reporting to the civil authorities. Only fifteen percent were reported to the police by the victim, and a much smaller percentage were reported by a diocese or religious community. Only 217 were criminally charged.[1]

The Report examined 10,519 substantiated allegations against priests. Only 3.6% of the priests involved were removed from the ministry. Another 3.7% sought laicisation, 18.7% resigned or retired, and 26.3% had either died or were no longer in active ministry. That left some forty-eight percent who were reprimanded, given administrative leave, sent to spiritual retreats or treatment, suspended, or some other action taken.[2] And, as indicated earlier, in the thirty

---

1. http://www.jjay.cuny.edu/churchstudy/main.asp par 3.7 (Accessed 16 July 2013).
2. *Ibid,* paragraph 5.3.1.

year period covered by the Murphy Commission, there were only three Church trials of clergy sexual abusers in the Archdiocese of Dublin amongst the 102 cases examined where there was credible evidence of a criminal offence. And there was no serious reporting to the police by the Archdiocese until 2002 when Cardinal Connell decided to hand over some files to the Irish police.

The figures for non-reporting to the civil authorities and low levels of punishment under the Church processes are hardly surprising because of the restrictions imposed by canon law.

1971–1997 Bishop Ronald Mulkearns in Ballarat, Australia

Bishop Ronald Mulkearns of the Australian diocese of Ballarat in the State of Victoria had a doctorate in canon law and was one of the founders of the Canon Law Society of Australia and New Zealand. He was bishop of Ballarat from 1971 to 1997, and the first chairman of the Special Issues Committee set up by the Australian Catholic Bishops Conference to find a better way of dealing with sexually abusing priests.

Mulkearns knew of the serious allegations against two of his priests Gerald Ridsdale and David Ryan. He shifted Ridsdale to different parishes of his own diocese before he was transferred to Melbourne, Sydney and the United States.[3] Paul David Ryan was shifted to the United States for treatment where he continued to operate as a priest. He then returned to Melbourne and to Ballarat, where he continued to sexually abuse minors.[4] He was arrested and jailed in Australia in 2006. A number of his victims committed suicide. Mulkearns destroyed a number of documents, such as reports from psychologists.[5]

Mulkearns actions were consistent with *Crimen Sollicitationis* and the *1983 Code of Canon Law*. *Crimen Sollicitationis* determined the procedures for these allegations from the time he became bishop in 1971 until 1983 when the new *1983 Code of Canon Law* was promulgated, and the latter covered his time as bishop from 1983 to 1997.

3. http://brokenrites.alphalink.com.au/nletter/page116-ridsdale.html (Accessed 16 July 2013).
4. http://brokenrites.alphalink.com.au/nletter/page117-ryan.html (Accessed 16 July 2013).
5. Evidence of Bishop Connors, *Victorian Parliamentary Inquiry,*16, http://www. parliament.vic.gov.au/images/stories/committees/fcdc/inquiries/57th/Child_ Abuse_Inquiry/Transcripts/Catholic_Diocese_of_Ballarat_29-April-13.pdf (Accessed 24 May 2015).

- *Crimen Sollicitationis* in Clause 11 required him to observe the 'strictest confidentiality in any investigation of sexual abuse by his priests, preventing him from reporting these crimes to the police.
- Under the *1983 Code of Canon Law*, Canon 1395, the sexual abuse of children was a 'delict against morals' and the decree *Secreta Continere* of 1974 imposed pontifical secrecy on the allegations, investigation and trial of such matters.
- *Crimen Sollicitationis* Clause 42 provided that if the evidence of a crime is considered 'grave enough', but not yet sufficient to file a formal complaint, he was to admonish these priests 'paternally' and 'gravely' with a first or second warning, and to threaten them with a trial if a new accusation is brought.
- *Crimen Sollicitationis* in Clause 63 prevented the bishop from imposing the penalty of dismissal from the priesthood unless he showed 'no hope . . . of amendment'. In other words, the bishop's obligation under canon law was to try and 'cure' these clergy sexual abusers, and only if there was no hope of any change, could he dismiss the priest.
- Canon 1341 of the *1983 Code of Canon Law* says a bishop can only commence formal disciplinary proceedings against a priest after he is satisfied that 'fraternal correction or reproof', or 'any methods of pastoral care' cannot 'repair the scandal, restore justice, reform the offender'.
- *Crimen Sollicitationis* Clause 64 allows the bishop to shift the priest if 'it seems necessary either for the amendment of the delinquent, the removal of a near occasion [of sin], or the prevention or repair of scandal'.
- Canon 1741 allows a bishop to remove a pastor from a parish and to shift him elsewhere because of a 'loss of a good reputation among upright and responsible parishioners'.
- Clause 68 of *Crimen Sollicitationis* provides that if the priest is transferred to another diocese, even after an 'admonishment', then the new bishop is to be told of

the priest's record and legal status. Whether or not Mulkearns did this is another matter.

- Canon 489 of the *1983 Code of Canon Law* required the destruction of documents relating to clergy sexual abuse, kept in the secret archive of every bishop, after ten years, with only a brief summary of what occurred with the text of the final sentence being retained.[6] It is not clear from the evidence given by Bishop Connors to the *Victorian Parliamentary Inquiry* as to whether the destruction of psychology reports was part of the canonical ten year clean out, but his destroying them is consistent with the intent of the Canon. This contrasts with Canons 482 to 491 which require the bishop to preserve all documents regarding the diocese or parishes 'with the greatest care'

Mulkearns' actions not only followed the 'proper meaning of the words' in canon law, but the interpretations that the Vatican itself had placed on them.

The *Victorian Parliamentary Inquiry* Report concluded that the evidence showed that Mulkearns had dealt with complaints of sexual abuse in the strictest confidentiality and had destroyed documents in accordance with the policy laid down by *Crimen Sollicitationis*.[7]

1975: Cardinal Sean Brady

In 1975, the current Primate of Ireland, Cardinal Sean Brady (then Dr Brady) was involved in an investigation of a paedophile priest, Fr Brendan Smyth who had abused a boy, Brendan Boland. He

---

6. Canon 489 provides: §1. In the diocesan curia there is also to be a secret archive, or at least in the common archive there is to be a safe or cabinet, completely closed and locked, which cannot be removed; in it documents to be kept secret are to be protected most securely.
    §2. Each year documents of criminal cases in matters of morals, in which the accused parties have died or ten years have elapsed from the condemnatory sentence, are to be destroyed. A brief summary of what occurred along with the text of the definitive sentence is to be retained.

7. *Betrayal of Trust*, Report of *Victorian Parliamentary Inquiry*, 42 https://s3-ap-southeast-2.amazonaws.com/family-and-community-development-committee/Inquiry+into+Handling+of+Abuse_Volume+1_FINAL_web.pdf (Accessed 14 November 2013).

typed up the questions asked by a more senior priest and signed the complainant's statement. He did not report the matter to the police, and did not allow the boy's father who accompanied him to enter the room. The boy was sworn to secrecy. When Brady was told that other boys had been abused, he interviewed one of them and swore that boy to secrecy as well.[8]

Cardinal Brady refused to resign, despite demands that he do so. In swearing the boys to secrecy he was acting in accordance with the procedures laid down in Clause 13 of *Crimen Sollicitationis*. Monsignor Scicluna, the Promoter of Justice (prosecutor) for the Congregation for the Doctrine of the Faith, defended Brady, saying that he was just a 'note taker' and his only obligation was to pass on the information to Smyth's superiors who had the responsibility to take action.[9] Brady was more than a note taker. He was a thirty-six year old priest with a doctorate in canon law.[10]

Clause 11 of *Crimen Sollicitationis* required the 'strictest confidentiality . . . in all things and with all persons', with no exceptions for the police or civil authorities. The bishop to whom Fr Brady sent the report could not tell either the parents or the police, because to do so would make him liable for punishment for breaching canon law. Nor could Fr Smyth's superior in the Norbertine Order—he being someone who came to know about it by 'reason of his office'. It is not then surprising that the parents were not told in this case. This was not the inaction of some negligent or insensitive priest or bishop. It was the inaction of a bishop and his investigators following canon law to the letter—as you would expect from a man who had a doctorate in canon law. The prominent Irish canon lawyer, Monsignor Maurice Dooley confirmed that canon law prevented Brady from taking the information he obtained in the investigation to the Irish police.[11]

---

8. http://www.bbc.co.uk/news/uk-northern-ireland-17894419 (Accessed 9 February 2013).
9. http://www.bbc.co.uk/news/uk-northern-ireland-17921671 (Accessed 16 July 2013). http://www.belfasttelegraph.co.uk/news/local-national/republic-of-ireland/vatican-adds-voice-to-support-for-cardinal-brady-16153049.html (Accessed 3 February 2014), http://www.bbc.co.uk/news/uk-northern-ireland-17921673 (Accessed 2 May 2012).
10. http://www.armagharchdiocese.org/cardinal-brady/ (Accessed 14 July 2013).
11. http://www.fifavideos.com/Colm-OGorman-and-Monsignor-Maurice-Dooley-The-Last-Word-with-Matt-Cooper__F9wtljHDT-c.html at 5.56 (Accessed 16 July 2013).

Monsignor Scicluna significantly makes no mention of the obligation under Irish law at the time to report such crimes to the police. The statement by the Church that in 1975 'no state or Church guidelines for responding to allegations of child abuse existed in Ireland', was not correct. The Irish *Criminal Law Act* 1997 was passed on 22 April 1997, and came into effect three months later, on 22 July 1997, and it had the effect of abolishing the common law offence of misprision of felony.[12] When the Church investigation was taking place, it was still a criminal offence to withhold information from the civil authorities about a serious felony of sexually assaulting children. Misprision of felony had been part of the English common law system for 700 years, and it was not abolished in Ireland until some twenty-two years later. Canon 22, *Crimen Sollicitationis* and his oath of office required Brady to observe canon law, even if it involved breaching the civil law.[13]

Needless to say, Fr Brendan Smyth was shifted around where he continued to sexually assault children.[14]

1987: Cardinal Roger Mahony

Documents recently produced to an American court allege that in 1986/87 US Cardinal Roger Mahony and his top adviser on sexual abuse collaborated to hide from the civil authorities sex crimes committed by clergy as late as 1987, and further, advised certain priests not to return to Los Angeles in case they were arrested. Canon law did not require bishops to go to that extent, and this is a very good example of how law influences and deepens a culture.

In other instances, the documents express concern about whether to tell therapists of behaviour by priests if the therapists would be required to report what they knew to civil authorities—again with the idea that such documents might be subject to subpoena. This was

---

12. http://www.irishstatutebook.ie/1997/en/act/pub/0014/print.html#sec1 (Accessed 16 July 2013), http://www.independent.ie/opinion/analysis/change-in-the-law-means-there-is-now-no-criminal-offence-for-failure-to-report-crime-26031940.html (Accessed 16 July 2013), http://www.irishtimes.com/newspaper/opinion/2009/1207/1224260239925.html (Accessed 9 February 2013).
13. *Crimen Sollicitationis*, Clauses 11 & 12.
14. http://www.irishcentral.com/news/Cardinal-Sean-Brady-sued-over-church-sex-abuse-cover-up-96371739.html (Accessed 15 April 2013).

the same pattern of concern about which Fr Brian Lucas in Australia wrote his article in 1996 about the 'safety' of the Church's archives.[15]

Cardinal Mahony released a statement in January 2013, after the release of the documents, apologising for what he termed his 'naïve' belief that treatment could heal sexual abusers.[16] The real problem was canon law and the culture it reinforced. Canon law prevented him from taking the information to the police, and required him to adopt the 'pastoral and therapeutic' approach, to try and cure them, before subjecting them to any canonical investigation and trial. It was canon law that was 'naïve'.

1992: The 'Father F' Case

On Monday 2 July 2012, the Australian ABC *Four Corners* program *Unholy Silence* dealt with the failure of the Australian Church to report the sex crimes of a priest, identified on the program only as 'Father F'.[17] Persistent allegations had been made about the priest, and on 3 September 1992, three priests interviewed him.

In 2012, after the television program was shown, the Church appointed a retired Federal Court judge, Antony Whitlam QC to investigate. On 17 January 2013, Mr Whitlam published his report in which he found that despite receiving a series of allegations about F's behaviour, including a written report from 1990 suggesting he be sent for medical treatment, Bishop Kennedy of Armidale, who was then his bishop, did not pass this information on to Bishop Heather of the Parramatta diocese where he knew 'Father F' was working as a priest.[18] Again, this is the familiar pattern found by the Murphy Dublin Report where misunderstandings over the reach of pontifical secrecy were a cause of this kind of problem.

In regard to the three priests who interviewed 'Father F', two of them, Fr Brian Lucas and Fr John Usher did not recall the admissions made. Father Wayne Peters alleged in a report to Bishop Manning

---

15. http://www.lawlink.nsw.gov.au/lawlink/Special_Projects/ll_splprojects.nsf/vwFiles/Transcript_Day_15_-_TOR_2_-_24_July_2013.pdf/$file/Transcript_Day_15_-_TOR_2_-_24_July_2013.pdf , 1621

16. http://m.thetablet.co.uk/article/163741 (Accessed 9 February 2013).

17. 11 September 2012 http://www.abc.net.au/4corners/stories/2012/06/28/3535079.htm (Accessed 28 March 2013).

18. http://www.parra.catholic.org.au/ paragraph 168 (Accessed 9 February 2013).

that on 11 September 1992 'Father F' admitted to having sexually assaulted several boys. Mr Whitlam found that Fr Peters may have attributed admissions to 'Father F' that they did not share, a somewhat surprising conclusion, given that the best evidence of what was said, so far as the public is aware, was Fr Peter's letter sent shortly after the meeting. There may well have been other contemporary notes that justified such a finding, but these notes do not appear in Whitlam's report.[19] This was a private inquiry ordered by the Church, and it illustrates the problems of such private inquiries where the evidence is not available for scrutiny by the public.

It is not clear whether or not the three priests were conducting a preliminary inquiry under the *1983 Code of Canon Law*, or were acting informally as advisers to Bishop Manning as to what he should do. The evidence of Fr Brian Lucas at the Maitland-Newcastle Inquiry would suggest that he regarded his attempts to convince such priests to resign as outside the canonical system.[20] The reason for adopting such an approach was because canon law was 'unworkable' as a means of dealing with the problem.[21]

It appears from the evidence before Mr Whitlam that the strategy adopted by the three priests was to convince 'Father F' that he should agree to be suspended permanently and eventually to agree to be laicised. His faculties to operate as a priest had been removed.[22] In November 1992, he offered to 'resign from the priesthood', although at that stage he did not agree to laicisation.[23] In 2005, Father F finally agreed to accept voluntary laicisation.[24] But the whole procedure is yet another example of the shambles in canon law when it came to dismissing clergy sexual abusers. It took, in the end, thirteen years to finally dismiss 'Father F'. This case is another illustration that the

---

19. See also the comment on this by Fr Frank Brennan, in *Eureka Street,* 3 September 2013, http://www.eurekastreet.com.au/article.aspx?aeid=38146#.Ui5vaKt-8qQ (Accessed 10 September 2013).

20. http://www.lawlink.nsw.gov.au/lawlink/Special_Projects/ll_splprojects.nsf/vwFiles/Transcript_Day_15_-_TOR_2_-_24_July_2013.pdf/$file/Transcript_Day_15_-_TOR_2_-_24_July_2013.pdf, 1570 and 1632(Accessed 18 August 2013).

21. *Ibid,* 1570.

22. Whitlam Report http://www.parra.catholic.org.au (Accessed 9 February 2013), 17–34.

23. *Ibid*, paragraph 100.

24. *Ibid*, paragraph 139.

so called 'reforms' of 2001 might have overcome some of the earlier procedural difficulties, but they did not really change the canonical basis upon which a priest could be dismissed.

Fr Peters' letter also reflects the culture expressed both in *Crimen Sollicitationis*, and the *1983 Code of Canon Law*, that the most important issue in deciding to take action against a priest for sexual abuses against children was the 'scandal' it caused, and. Peters' wrote:

> There continued to be a **widespread scandal** in the Diocese of Armidale. Because of the **knowledge of the scandal**, it was not possible for an appointment in the Diocese of Armidale in the near future. Appointment to another diocese was also seen as impossible given that the whole matter of the allegation was an unresolved matter. Without resolution no recommendation could come from an appointment to another diocese from the Bishop of Armidale. **Such a recommendation could be seriously injurious to the Church** and the Diocese of Armidale in particular in the event of further criminal charges being made by the other boys involved without a previous clearance for appointment from competent psychiatric authority. As there is no statute of limitations on charges being brought in the matter of sexual abuse of children, the possibility always remains that one or some of the boys involved may bring criminal charges .
> . . **with subsequent grave harm to the priesthood and the Church** . . . [25] (my emphases).

The letter makes no mention of the harm done to the boys involved, two of whom committed suicide.[26] Fr Peter's letter reflects very well the philosophy and culture expressed by the Spanish canon lawyer Fr Aurelio Yanguas as far back as 1946, that the reason for secrecy in *Crimen Sollicitationis* was the protection of the Church's reputation.[27]

---

25. http://www.abc.net.au/4corners/documents/abuse2012/Letter_1992.pdf (Accessed 9 July 2013).

26. http://www.parra.catholic.org.au/ (Accessed 9 February 2013), paragraph 178. http://www.abc.net.au/4corners/stories/2012/06/28/3535079.htm (Accessed 16 July 2013).

27. John P Beal in 'The 1962 Instruction, *Crimen Sollicitationis*: Caught Red Handed or Handed a Red Herring?', in 41 *Studia Canonica* 199 at 233. http://www.vatican.

1993: The Fr Tony Walsh Case in Ireland

The *Murphy Dublin Report* found that in the thirty years period covered by the Commission's investigation into the Dublin Archdiocese, there were only three Church trials of priests for sex assaults on children, despite the 102 well founded allegations.[28] One of them was Fr Tony Walsh, a serial paedophile, who had made a name for himself as an Elvis impersonator, appearing on the Irish Television program, *The All Priests Show*. His case is also dealt with extensively in the documentary *Mea Maxima Culpa*.[29]

The Murphy Commission said this about Walsh:

> Fr (Walsh) is probably the most notorious child sexual abuser to have come to the attention of the Commission. The Commission is aware of more than 40 named people who have complained of child sexual abuse by him. He has admitted to abusing many others; while he may not use the term 'child sexual abuse', he has admitted to using children for sexual gratification once a fortnight over an eight-year period.[30]

The first complaints against him were in 1978, some fifteen years before any formal action was sought to be taken against him. This was hardly surprising. The Murphy Commission found that one of the most influential canon lawyers in the Dublin Archdiocese, Monsignor Sheehy considered that the penal aspects of canon law should rarely be invoked against priests. Monsignor Sheehy was correct. That is in

---

va/resources/Beal-article-studia-canonica41-2007-pp.199-236.pdf (Accessed 15 July 2013).

28. http://www.justice.ie/en/JELR/DACOI%20Fr%20Jovito%20published.pdf/Files/ DACOI%20Fr%20Jovito%20published.pdf, paragraph 1.28. (Accessed 15 July 2013). Paragraph 1.26 refers to two trials, but paragrah 4.6 suggest that there were three. It seems that there were in fact three, Fr Bill Carney, Fr Tony Walsh and Fr Patrick McGuirce. Because a criminal prosecution had been started against Walsh, he was given the pseudonym of 'Fr Jovito', in chapter 19 of the *Murphy Dublin Report*. In December 2010, he was sentenced to twelve years jail: http:// www.huffingtonpost.com/2010/12/17/tony-walsh-ireland-pedoph_n_798268. html (Accessed 16 July 2013).

29. At 50.20.

30. http://www.justice.ie/en/JELR/DACOI%20Fr%20Jovito%20published.pdf/Files/ DACOI%20Fr%20Jovito%20published.pdf (Accessed 15 April 2013), paragraph 19.2.

effect what *Crimen Sollicitationis* said. Sheehy also advised Archbishop Connell in 1990 that any attempt to dismiss Walsh was entering a 'canonical minefield'.[31] That was correct, as the subsequent history showed. And when another bishop suggested that they should inform the civil authorities, Sheehy said it was 'an outrageous suggestion'.[32] It was outrageous, because it involved breaching pontifical secrecy under canon law, which the bishops had sworn to uphold.

Archbishop Connell of Dublin, to his credit, was at least prepared to test the limits of canon law, even if he could not report criminal priests to the police. According to the *Murphy Dublin Report,* he was one of the first bishops in the world to initiate canonical trials in modern times.[33]

Connell was also the one who had a stand up argument with Cardinal Castrillón at a meeting between him and the Irish bishops in 1998 at Sligo, Ireland, over the issue of reporting clergy to the police—which Castrillón refused to countenance.[34] Connell's efforts in 1992/93 to dismiss Walsh—who, in 2010 was given a sentence of sixteen years jail—were frustrated by the Vatican.

Walsh appealed to the Vatican against the decision of the Irish canonical judges in 1993 to dismiss him. His appeal was successful and the dismissal was set aside. Instead, Walsh was required to stay in a monastery for ten years. The Vatican applied the Vatican Catch 22: Walsh could not be dismissed for paedophilia because he was a paedophile.[35] As it turned out, no monastery, understandably, wanted to have him.[36] So, he was still on the loose, and then committed another one of his crimes for which he was subsequently convicted and sent to jail.[37]

Cardinal Connell then appealed directly to Pope John Paul II, and Walsh was finally dismissed in 1996, the year that the Irish bishops

---

31. *Ibid*, paragraph 19.52.
32. *Ibid.*
33. *Ibid,* paragraph 4.65.
34. 'Unspeakable Crimes', 17 January 2011, http://www.rte.ie/tv/wouldyoubelieve/unspeakablecrimes.html (Accessed in January 2011, but the program has been archived by RTE).
35. http://www.justice.ie/en/JELR/DACOI%20Fr%20Jovito%20published.pdf/Files/DACOI%20Fr%20Jovito%20published.pdf (Accessed 15 April 2013), paragraph 4.80. An appeal by Fr Maguire against his dismissal was also upheld on this same ground.
36. *Ibid*, paragraph 4.74.
37. *Ibid*, paragarph 4.75.

drew up the *Framework Document* to allow them to report clergy sexual abusers to the police, and which the Vatican rejected because it conflicted with canon law and reporting a priest, even a serial paedophile, raised 'moral' issues.[38]

No wonder Cardinal Connell had a stand up argument with Cardinal Castrillón in 1998. The canonical system was hopeless, and despite this, the Vatican insisted that the Irish bishops not report these criminals to the police.

1994: Bishop Bede Heather and the St Gerard Majella Society

In 1994 there were allegations of sex crimes against some members of the St Gerard Majella Society, which was founded by Fr John Sweeney in 1958 to conduct religious classes for Catholic students in state high schools.[39] It recruited young men to become brothers, some being upgraded to priests. Investigating police approached Bishop Bede Heather of Parramatta, in the State of New South Wales, to hand over any documents relating to the allegations, including a report by Fr Rodger Austin, a canon lawyer appointed by Heather to investigate the matter. Bishop Heather allegedly refused. The police obtained a search warrant, and executed it at his presbytery and the archdiocesan offices, seizing documents. Three of the priests belonging to the Society, including its founder were sentenced to jail terms ranging from two to six years, and shortly before the sentencing of one of them, Bishop Heather quietly retired.[40] Any refusal to hand over the documents would have been in accordance with the secrecy provisions of canon law.

---

38. Letter from Archbishop Storero 31 January 1997, http://graphics8.nytimes.com/packages/pdf/world/Ireland-Catholic-Abuse.pdf?ref=europe http://www.nytimes.com/2011/01/19/world/europe/19vatican.html?_r=0 (Accessed 9 July 2013).
39. http://brokenrites.org.au/drupal/node/12.
40. Various aspects of the case were reported in some newspapers: *Sydney Daily Telegraph,* 19/7/1997, 13/11/1997; *Sydney Morning Herald,* 13/11/1997, 3/3/1998, 4/3/1998, 28/3/1998; *The Australian,* 23/12/1994, 13; *Sydney Sun-Herald,* 16/11/1997, 56 http://brokenrites.alphalink.com.au/nletter/page12.html (Accessed 16 July 2013).

1995: Fr Denis McAlinden

Fr Denis McAlinden was a serial paedophile in the Maitland-Newcastle diocese of Australia, who was shifted around whenever there were complaints about his activities.[41] Bishop Leo Clarke invited him to agree to laicisation, assuring him that his good name would be protected by the 'confidential nature' of the process.

Again, we have the extraordinary situation of a bishop asking a serial paedophile to agree to being dismissed—which, of course, would mean that he would no longer have a livelihood from the Church. Father Philip Wilson, now Archbishop Wilson of Adelaide and former President of the Australian Catholic Bishops Conference, interviewed two of McAlinden's victims in 1995 and took statements from them. No report was sent to the police.

Wilson was interviewed by the TV station Aljazeera and it was put to him by the interviewer:

> Interviewer: 'that concerns a lot of people that by somehow by having that knowledge and not reporting it to police that puts you in a position of being party to a concealment.'
> Wilson: 'Well, as I said, I took legal advise and that was their advice to me, and that is now a matter for investigation.'[42]

Whatever may be the proper interpretation of section 316 of the *New South Wales Crimes Act* of 1900 (and Wilson has the presumption of innocence whatever it is), like Father Brady (now Cardinal) in the Brendan Smythe case in Ireland in 1975, Wilson was performing the same canonical function as a notary. Both notaries had doctorates in canon law.[43] Pontifical secrecy prevented them from reporting any

---

41. McAlinden's case was examined by the *Maitland-Newcastle Inquiry*, http://www.lawlink.nsw.gov.au/lawlink/Special_Projects/ll_splprojects.nsf/pages/sisa_index (Accessed 16 July 2013).

42. http://www.aljazeera.com/programmes/101east/2013/04/2013410101055913509.html (Accessed 16 July 2013).

43. http://www.adelaide.catholic.org.au/our-people/archbishop-wilson/biography (Accessed 17 July 2013).

information they had obtained in canonical investiagtions to police. The dispensation for reporting where the civil law required it was only given to both countries in 2010. Canon 22 required them to follow canon law whenever it conflicted with civil law. Assuming that Wilson's legal advice was that he had no obligation under the civil law to report, as his response in the interview suggests, canon law prevented him from reporting even if he wanted to.

1996–1998: Fr Lawrence Murphy

The case of Fr Lawrence Murphy is a another example of the ineffectiveness of the canonical process because of the limitation period, and also because of the 'pastoral approach' insisted on by Cardinal Ratzinger's Congregation for the Doctrine of the Faith even as late as 1998.

Fr Murphy, the subject of the documentary *Mea Maxima Culpa,* had been accused of molesting as many as 200 deaf mute boys when he was in charge of St John's School for the Deaf in the Archdiocese of Milwaukee.[44] Murphy had taught at the school from 1950 to 1974, but was still a priest. Archbishop Weakland was Archbishop from 1977 to 2002. In the 1990s he received complaints from the victims that Murphy was still a priest, and no action had been taken against him. In 1993 Weakland tried to commence proceedings against Murphy but had to discontinue them because of the five year limitation period. The later extensions to the period did not operate retrospectively. Murphy's crimes had been 'extinguished' under canon law.

However, in 1995, Weakland received information from a victim that Murphy had also solicited sex in the confessional. This was a matter for the Congregation for the Doctrine of the Faith, and there was no limitation period.[45] Weakland conducted a preliminary

---

44. A summary of the matter is in the *New York Times* of 24 March 2010 http://www. nytimes.com/2010/03/25/world/europe/25vatican.html?pagewanted=all&_r=0 (Accessed 16 July 2013).

45. The Apostolic Constitution of John Paul II, *Pastor Bonus* of 28 June1988 gives jurisdiction to the Congregation for the Doctrine of the Faith: Article 52 — 'The Congregation examines offences against the faith and more serious ones both in behaviour or in the celebration of the sacraments which have been reported to it and, if need be, proceeds to the declaration or imposition of canonical sanctions in accordance with the norms of common or proper law.' Soliciting sex in the confessional was 'behaviour in the celebration of the sacraments' requiring

investigation, as he was required to do under Canon 1717, and on 21 December 1995 concluded under Canon 1341 that the matter could not be resolved by 'fraternal correction' or other 'ways of pastoral care'. He therefore decreed that under Canon 1718 the case should proceed to a judicial trial.

On 17 July 1996, Weakland wrote to Cardinal Ratzinger at the Congregation for instructions on how to proceed.[46] He did not receive any reply until nine months later on 24 March 1997 when Archbishop Bertone, the Secretary of the Congregation, advised Weakland that he could proceed under *Crimen Sollicitationis*. In the meantime, Weakland had decided to proceed with the trial anyway. On 10 December 1996, a formal canonical process was commenced, and Murphy notified.

On 12 January 1998 Murphy wrote to Cardinal Ratzinger, and said that in 1974, he resigned from the St John School for the Deaf because of accusations of sexual misconduct, and that he had retired to a family home in the Diocese of Superior with the permission of the Archbishop of Milwaukee at the time. He said that his ministry 'has never been restricted' and he used to help out in parishes from time to time when required. He did not deny the allegations, but said that there have been no further accusations against him since he left St John's in 1974. He said he was in poor health because of a stroke and all he wanted was to 'live out the time I have left in the dignity of my priesthood'.

On 6 April 1998, Archbishop Bertone, the Secretary of the Congregation for the Doctrine of the Faith wrote to Weakland, referring to the matters put to him by Murphy, including that he had 'repented of any past sins'. Archbishop Weakland had already considered the 'pastoral' approach required under Canon 1341 and had determined two and a half years earlier in December 1995 that a judicial trial was the only appropriate avenue. Bertone told Weakland to reconsider what 'pastoral methods' might be used to repair the scandal and restore justice.

---

canonical sanctions. Canon 1362§1 provided that there was no limitation period for such crimes reserved to that Congregation.

46. http://documents.nytimes.com/reverend-lawrence-c-murphy-abuse-case#document/p2 (Accessed 16 June 2013).

On 13 May 1998, Bishop Fliss (in whose Diocese of Superior, the trial was taking place because of Murphy's residence there) wrote to Bertone telling him that they had already considered all such pastoral avenues, and the only alternative was a judicial trial of Murphy.

As the American bishops were due to go to Rome at the end of the month for their five yearly visits to present reports on their dioceses (called *ad limina* visits), Weakland and Fliss went to see Bertone. It became clear from the file notes of the meeting that Bertone was not in favour of dismissing Murphy. He had repented of his sins and had not been in trouble since leaving St John's School for the Deaf. Weakland told Bertone that the deaf community was very angry about this serial abuse. He suggested that it would be inappropriate for Murphy to celebrate Mass for the deaf in Milwaukee, but he should be able to do so in the Diocese Superior where he was living. The outcome of the meeting was clear: the trial would have to be aborted, and if it proceeded and Murphy appealed, Rome would allow the appeal against his dismissal from the priesthood.

On 2 September 1998, Weakland wrote to Bertone telling him that Murphy died on 21 August of natural causes, and that despite Weakland's request that the funeral be private, Murphy had a full requiem Mass celebrated by a bishop, with an open casket with Murphy dressed in full liturgical vestments.

On 28 September 1998, Bertone replied, acknowledging the letter, saying the case is now closed and that he hoped the Church would be spared any undue publicity in the matter. The final irony of this case is that the story of the 200 deaf mute boys, abused over a period of twenty-four years by Father Lawrence Murphy became the subject of a critically acclaimed and Emmy award winning documentary, *Mea Maxima Culpa*, in which Archbishop Weakland himself told the story of his being frustrated by the Vatican in dismissing Murphy from the priesthood. Weakland himself by that time had resigned as Archbishop after admitting to having a homosexual affair. The bad publicity that the Vatican received over the Murphy case was more than due. The 'scandal' created by the Vatican's handling of the Murphy case became far worse than what Cardinals Bertone and Ratzinger could possibly have imagined.

On 19 March 2010, in his *Pastoral Letter* to the people of Ireland, Benedict XVI criticised the Irish bishops for their 'misguided tendency to avoid penal approaches' in the period 1975–2004, examined by the Murphy Commission. On 21 May 2010, when he rewrote the historical introduction to the *2001 Motu Proprio*, Benedict criticised the 'pastoral attitude' to misconduct, and those who thought that canonical processes were 'anachronistic'. There was no acknowledgement that the criticism applied above all to himself and the Congregation for the Doctrine of the Faith that he headed from 1981 until 2005, and of which Archbishop Bertone was secretary from 1995 to 2002.

2000 Fr Patrick Maguire in Ireland

Maguire was a serial paedophile against whom complaints had been made since 1975. Between that time and 1996, his superiors in the Colomban Fathers paid for rehabilitation and treatment, but to no avail. In 1998, in England, he was sentenced to 18 months imprisonment for sexual assault on two boys. He was sentenced to a further six years imprisonment in 2000 in Ireland for other sexual assaults on children. In September 2000, the Dublin Canonical Tribunal dismissed him from the priesthood. He appealed to Rome, which overturned the dismissal and substituted a suspension for a period of nine years. 'Catch 22': he had been diagnosed as a paedophile. Maguire was released from prison in 2003 and continued as a member of the Columban congregation. In 2004, he was charged again with indecent assault and sentenced to another three years imprisonment, suspended on his remaining under the supervision of the Columban congregation.[47]

Father Marcial Maciel

Another case showing the virtual impossibility of dismissing a serial sex abusing priest under canon law, and the conflicts of interest in the Church's own disciplinary processes was that of Fr Marcial Maciel. He was an extremely successful fundraiser for the Church, starting his own congregation of priests, the Legion of Christ, and opening up many seminaries. He managed a budget of $650m.[48] Detailed allegations had been sent to the Vatican in 1976, 1978 and 1979 about his sexual abuse of seminarians. Nothing happened. In

---

47. *Murphy Dublin Report*, Part 2, 16.1–16.75
48. *Mea Maxima Culpa* at 1:01.48

1998 eight former members of the Legion lodged complaints against him to Cardinal Ratzinger's Congregation for the Doctrine of the Faith. Maciel had the support of Cardinal Sodano who pressured Ratzinger not to prosecute him. Ratzinger told the Mexican bishop, Carlos Talavera, who had written to him at the behest of one of his victims, that a case could not be mounted against Maciel because he had helped the Church a lot, and was well loved by Pope John Paul II. He said the matter was ' very delicate'. Pope John Paul II honoured Maciel in a Vatican ceremony which entrusted the Legion with the administration of the Jerusalem Notre Dame Centre. The following week, Ratzinger authorized an investigation.[49] Yet, even when Ratzinger, as Benedict XVI did take action against Maciel, he did not report him to the police, nor was he dismissed from the priesthood. He was merely suspended, and asked to go to a monastery to lead 'a reserved life of prayer and penance'.[50] His 'monastery' was a house with a pool in a gated community in Jacksonville, Florida, bought for him by the Legion of Christ which he founded. He died there in 2008.[51]

22 June 2012: Monsignor Lynn

Monsignor Lynn from the Philadelphia diocese in the United States was convicted of a breach of state laws over the cover up of clergy sexual abusers. Lynn was in charge of investigating claims of sexual abuse by clergy from 1992 until 2004 on behalf of the Archbishop, Cardinal Bevilacqua.[52] These dates are significant because in December 2002, the American bishops were granted an exemption from the secrecy provisions of the *2001 Motu Proprio decree* to allow reporting of sexual abuse allegations to the civil authorities. In other words, for ten out of the twelve years in this job, there was no such exemption. Everything Lynn did was consistent with his following canon law. In

---

49. http://ncronline.org/news/accountability/money-paved-way-maciels-influence-vatican (Accessed 17 July 2013).
50. http://www.thetablet.co.uk/article/57 (Accessed 12 September 2013).
51. http://www.associationofcatholicpriests.ie/2013/02/legion-of-christs-deception-unearthed-in-new-documents-indicates-wider-cover-up/ (Accessed 16 July 2013).
52. http://www.nytimes.com/2012/06/23/us/philadelphias-msgr-william-j-lynn-is-convicted-of-allowing-abuse.html?pagewanted=all&_r=0 (Accessed 16 July 2013).

July 2012, Lynn was sentenced to three to six years jail for covering up the crimes he investigated.[53] His appeal was subsequently allowed on the basis that the statute, before its amendment, only applied to direct supervisors of children.[54]

Cardinal Bevilacqua, who was Archbishop of Philadelphia from 1988 to 2003, was not charged with any offence, having died in January 2012. Bevilacqua was unique amongst American clergy in having both doctorates in canon and civil law. He was also visiting Professor of Canon Law at the Immaculate Conception Seminary, New Jersey. He faithfully followed the secrecy provisions of canon law and his oath of office in not communicating to state authorities the information he had gathered relating to child sexual abuse. Monsignor Lynn did the same.[55] The civil law, at the time, did not make that a criminal offence.

These are a handful of cases showing the same consistent pattern throughout the world. The *Ryan, Murphy Dublin Report* and *Cloyne Report* in Ireland also reveal many examples of the same pattern.

The Murphy Commission said in relation to the Dublin Archdiocese,

> The Commission has no doubt that clerical child sexual abuse was covered up by the Archdiocese of Dublin and other Church authorities over much of the period covered by the Commission's remit. **The structures and rules of the Catholic Church facilitated that cover-up**. The state authorities facilitated the cover up by not fulfilling their responsibilities to ensure that the law was applied equally to all and allowing the Church institutions to be beyond the reach of the normal law enforcement processes. The welfare of children, which should have been the first priority, was not even a factor to be considered in the early stages. Instead the focus was on the avoidance of scandal and the preservation of

---

53. http://www.reuters.com/article/2012/07/24/us-usa-crime-church-idUSBRE86N12E20120724 (Accessed 16 July 2013).
54. http://www.pacourts.us/assets/opinions/Superior/out/J-A23005-13o%20-%201016613421853550.pdf?cb=1 (Accessed 26 December 2013).
55. http://www.nytimes.com/2012/02/02/us/anthony-j-bevilacqua-retired-cardinal-in-philadelphia-dies-at-88.html?_r=0 (Accessed 25 April 2013).

the good name, status and assets of the institution and of what the institution regarded as its most important members—the priests[56] (my emphasis).

The *Victorian Parliamentary Inquiry* came to the same conclusion after an extensive examination of the cover up of the crimes against children of numerous priests and religious in that state:

> This minimisation or concealment of the problem was due to a number of factors, including the structure of the Catholic Church and lack of accountability, the teachings of the Catholic Church, canon law, leadership policy and, to some extent, the understanding of the issue at the time. Church leaders' approach was motivated by a desire to protect the reputation of the Catholic Church and to 'cure' the offender . . . Various structures, laws and teachings of the Catholic Church contributed to the concealment of this issue from wider society and civil authorities. The manner in which the Catholic Church responded (or failed to respond) to complaints gave perpetrators the opportunity to commit further abuse.[57]

These cases are not isolated instances, and many more can be examined on the Bishop-accountability website, with the same pattern of no reporting to the police, very few dismissals from the priesthood and the use of the 'pastoral approach' that led to many more children being abused.[58] The attitude of the Vatican itself in dealing with these

---

56. *Murphy Dublin Report*, Part 1 http://www.justice.ie/en/JELR/DACOI%20 Part%201.pdf/Files/DACOI%20Part201.pdf (Accessed 25 April 2013) 1.15, 1.113 (Conclusion).

57. *Betrayal of Trust*, Report of the *Victorian Parliamentary Inquiry*, paragpah 7.5.6, page 193, and paragraph 7.6, 195 https://s3-ap-southeast-2. amazonaws.com/family-and-community-development-committee/ Inquiry+into+Handling+of+Abuse_Volume+1_FINAL_web.pdf (Accessed 14 November 2013).

58. http://www.bishop-accountability.org/ (Accessed 18 July 2013), and see *Betrayal of Trust*, Report of the *Victorian Parliamentary Inquiry*, paragraph 7.3.6, 172 https:// s3-ap-southeast-2.amazonaws.com/family-and-community-development- committee/Inquiry+into+Handling+of+Abuse_Volume+1_FINAL_web.pdf (Accessed 14 November 2013).

cases is further evidence that canon law meant what it said, and that bishops were following not only canon law, but the interpretation that the Vatican had placed on it.

Pope Francis

16

The Cardinals Defend the Privilege of Clergy

In English law, as we have seen, privilege or benefit of clergy (*Privilegium clericale*) was originally an agreement between the Church and the secular authority by which clergy would not be prosecuted for crimes before the state courts, and would only be tried in ecclesiastical courts in accordance with canon law.

The effect of the secrecy provisions of canon law was to create a de facto privilege of clergy for those accused of sex crimes against children, because if the state did not know about such crimes, then it had no evidence on which it could prosecute. The Church would use its own tribunals to determine guilt or innocence, and to impose its own punishments. Fr Thomas Doyle says that although the privilege of clergy is anachronistic in contemporary society, the attitude or mentality in clerical circles that clergy should only be accountable to the institutional church authorities is still active.[1]

This hankering for the power that the Church had during the medieval period can be seen from the vehemence with which senior Cardinals insisted on the right not to have to report paedophile clergy to the police. But their claims went even further than that. They claimed that all communications between bishops and priests were 'privileged', and no court had the right to demand production of any such documents, because this would be an interference with religious freedom.

1984: Letter from the Congregation for the Clergy to Archbishop Moreno

Archbishop Moreno of Tucson, Arizona had written to the Congregation for the Clergy in Rome, about disciplinary action

---

1. http://www.bishop-accountability.org/news2010/03_04/2010_03_12_Doyle_VeryImportant.htm paragraph 24 (Accessed 5 August 2013).

taken against a priest. The complaints against the priest did not include sexual assaults on minors, but things like drunkenness and womanising. But in relation to handing over his files to civil lawyers, the Congregation stated in a letter dated 31 January 1984,

> . . . under no condition whatever ought the afore-mentioned files be surrendered to any lawyer or judge whatsoever . . . The files of a Bishop concerning his priests are altogether private; their forced acquisition by civil authority would be an intolerable attack upon the free exercise of religion in the United States . . .[2]

Pontifical secrecy applied not just to the sexual abuse of minors, but to all 'delicts' under canon law which included the persistent breaching of the celibacy rule.[3] The letter indicates the attitude of the Vatican to handing over Church documents to civil authority, especially where pontifical secrecy applied. The whole idea that a bishop's files on his priests should somehow be protected against production to the state courts when no other organisation can resist their production is another indication of the belief in the Vatican that priests and bishops should be above the civil law. The Church in the United States has, for the last thirty years, been fighting for the right to keep its documents out of the hands of the courts. It will surprise no one that it has lost that fight.[4]

8 September 2001: Cardinal Castrillón's Letter to Bishop Pican

A court in the French city of Caen handed Bishop Pierre Pican, 66, a three-month suspended prison sentence for concealing knowledge that a priest in his diocese, the Rev René Bissey, had sexually assaulted a number of boys.[5] According to the report in the *New York Times*, the bishop regretted that the court's decision had set a precedent limiting the Roman Catholic clergy's right to keep 'professional secrets'.[6]

---

2. http://www.bishop-accountability.org/Vatican/Documents/1984_01_31_Oddi_to_Moreno_Priest_Files_R.pdf (Accessed 23 June 2013).
3. Canon 1395§1.
4. http://www.huffingtonpost.com/2013/01/30/la-catholic-church-abuse-files_n_2586028.html (Accessed 23 June 2013).
5. Pican was prosecuted under Article 434–3 of the French Penal Code: Pierre-Antoine Cals, French lawyer in private correspondence, September 2013.
6. http://www.nytimes.com/2001/09/08/world/world-briefing-europe-france-

Cardinal Castrillón, then Prefect of the Congregation for the Clergy, a canon lawyer with a doctorate in canon law, wrote to Bishop Pican in these terms

> Most Reverend Excellency I write to you as Prefect of the Congregation for the Clergy entrusted with aiding the Holy Father is his responsibility for the priests of the world. I congratulate you on not denouncing a priest to the civil authorities. You have acted wisely, and I am delighted to have a fellow member of the episcopate who, in the eyes of history and of other bishops, would prefer to go to prison rather than denounce his priest-son. For the relationship between priests and their bishop is not professional but a sacramental relationship which forges very special bonds of spiritual paternity . . . The bishop has other means of acting, as the Conference of French Bishops recently restated; but a bishop cannot be required to make the denunciation himself. In all civilised legal systems it is acknowledged that close relations have the possibility of not testifying against a direct relative . . . This Congregation, in order to encourage brothers in the episcopate in this delicate matter, will forward a copy of this letter to all the conferences of bishops . . . [7]

In a radio interview later, Cardinal Castrillón justified his actions, saying the late Pope John Paul II authorised him to send the letter.

> After consulting the Pope, I wrote a letter to the bishop, congratulating him as a model of a father who does not turn in his children.[8]

---

   bishop-won-t-appeal.html (Accessed 23 June 2013).
7. http://www.reuters.com/article/2010/04/15/us-pope-abuse-france-idUSLDE63E2H420100415 (Accessed 23 June 2013). http://blogs.reuters.com/faithworld/tag/castrillon-hoyos/ (Accessed 23 June 2013,)http://www.reuters.com/article/2010/04/15/us-pope-abuse-france-idUSLDE63E2H420100415 (Accessed 23 June 2013), http://www.eltiempo.com/archivo/documento/MAM-3925512 (Accessed 23 June 2013).
8. http://www.nytimes.com/2010/04/22/us/22priest.html?_r=0 (Accessed 23 June 2013), http://article.wn.com/view/2010/04/23/Colombia_Cardinal_Defends_Churchs_Abuse Policies_d/

The Vatican spokesman Fr Federico Lombardi SJ did not dispute the authenticity of the letter but said,

> how opportune it was to centralize treatment of Catholic sex abuse cases by clerics under the Congregation for the Doctrine of the Faith.[9]

Cardinal Castrillón, at the time, was not some cleric going off on a frolic of his own. He was the Prefect of the Congregation for the Clergy. Fr Lombardi implies that Cardinal Ratzinger (now emeritus Pope Benedict XVI), who was in charge of the Congregation for the Doctrine of the Faith had a different view of reporting clergy crimes to the police to his colleague, Cardinal Castrillón. The evidence shows that Ratzinger did not.

Geoffrey Robertson QC says that the proposal by Cardinal Castrillón to send out a copy of his letter to Bishop Pican

> . . . could be no clearer example of the Holy See deciding that its own law should trump the criminal law of another nation, or at least requiring its spiritual adherents—nationals of that other nation—to breach the law of the land.[10]

Cardinal Billé & Bishop Fihey on Bishop Pican's Case

Cardinal Castrillón was not alone in defending Bishop Pican. At his trial, the President of the French Catholic Bishops' Conference, Cardinal Louis Marie Billé, gave evidence at Pican's trial, and condemned the 'intellectual terrorism' of those who demanded that such crimes should always be reported. Bishop Fihey, who was also called to give evidence, spoke of 'the special relationship both fraternal and paternal that unites a priest to his bishop', implying that this was an excuse for not reporting.[11] Billé at the November 2001 French Bishops Conference said that the conviction of Pican was

---

9. http://news.bbc.co.uk/2/hi/europe/8624763.stm (Accessed 23 June 2013).
10. Geoffrey Robertson QC, *The Case of the Pope,* chapter 2, paragraph 53.
11. http://www.thetablet.co.uk/article/5114 (Accessed 16 July 2913).

an infringement by secular authorities of the norms of professional secrecy.[12]

February 2002 Archbishop Bertone's Interview with *30 Giorni*

In a February 2002 interview with the Italian journal *30 Giorni*, Archbishop Bertone, a canon lawyer with a doctorate in canon law, who was Secretary of the Congregation for the Doctrine of the Faith, and second in charge to Cardinal Ratzinger, said:

> 'In my opinion, the demand that a bishop be obligated to contact the police in order to denounce a priest who has admitted the offense of paedophilia is, perhaps, unfounded.' 'Naturally civil society has the obligation to defend its citizens. But it must also respect the `professional secrecy' of priests, as it respects the professional secrecy of other categories, a respect that cannot be reduced simply to the inviolable seal of the confessional. If a priest cannot confide in his bishop for fear of being denounced, then it would mean that there is no more liberty of conscience.'[13]

Archbishop Bertone probably had in mind the 1985 variation to the 1929 *Lateran Treaty* with Mussolini that provided that the clergy in Italy were not required to provide information to courts or other authorities that arose out of the 'ministry', and that this included communications with the bishop.[14] But he seems to have misunderstood the 'professional secrecy' of other professions, at least

---

12. Delaney, *Canonical Implications of the Response of the Catholic Church in Australia,* 69.

13. John L Allen, 30 May 2002, in *National Catholic Reporter,* http://natcath.org/NCR_Online/archives/053102/053102h.htm (Accessed 16 July 2913). See also http://www.guardian.co.uk/world/2005/apr/24/children.childprotection(Accessed 16 July 2913). Fr Thomas Doyle, http://reform-network.net/?p=3006 , paragraph 26. (Accessed 16 July 2913).

14. Agreement signed 3 June 1985 Article 4(4) http://www.vatican.va/roman_curia/secretariat_state/archivio/documents/rc_seg-st_19850603_santa-sede-italia_it.html (Accessed 14 December 2013).

in the English speaking world. Doctors, psychologists, counsellors etc. have obligations to keep confidential matters revealed to them by their patients. But they are obliged to answer questions, if required, in a Court of law about those disclosures, and they are obliged to produce to court on subpoena their records without the client's consent.

Even lawyers are obliged to produce their client's documents or their own advices to a court, but the client is entitled to claim 'privilege' on them where they are created or made for the purpose of the client receiving legal advice or for conducting litigation. If the court accepts that the particular document meets those criteria, then it will simply declare it 'privileged', and it cannot be used in any court proceedings as evidence. Other documents, such as transactional documents, or ones not created for advice or litigation do not have the benefit of such privilege.[15]

Archbishop Bertone's statement is a claim that clergy should be above the civil law—that they should enjoy the medieval 'privilege of clergy'.

29 April 2002: Archbishop Herranz Address to the Catholic University of Milan

Archbishop Julian Herranz (later Cardinal) was head of the Pontifical Council for the Interpretation of Legislative Texts, that is, he was the Church's most senior canon lawyer. In an address to the Catholic University of Milan, he said,

> When ecclesiastical authorities deal with these delicate problems, they not only must respect the presumption of innocence, they also have to honor the **rapport of trust, and the consequent secrecy of the office, inherent in relations between a bishop and his priest collaborators**," Herranz said. 'Not to honor these exigencies would bring damages of great seriousness for the church'[16] (my emphasis).

---

15. This is the legal position in Australia. The position in other countries may be slightly different.
16. http://natcath.org/NCR_Online/archives/053102/053102h.htm (Accessed 16 July 2913).

According to the journalist John L Allen Jr, Herranz had this to say about demands in the United States for the right for bishops to report clergy sex crimes to civil authorities,

> While recognizing the competence of civil authorities, Herranz expressed strong reservations about the application to the Catholic church of two hallmarks of American civil law—an obligation to report misconduct and monetary damages for institutional negligence.
>
> 'Given the emotional wave of public clamor,' Herranz said, 'some envision an obligation on the part of ecclesiastical authority to denounce to civil judges all the cases that come to their attention, as well an obligation to communicate to judges all the documentation from ecclesiastical archives.'
>
> Herranz rejected the idea. '**The rapport of trust and the secrecy of the office inherent to the relationship between the bishop and his priest collaborators, and between priests and the faithful, must be respected**'[17] (my emphasis).

Archbishop Herranz (later Cardinal Herranz) has a doctorate in canon law, as well as being Professor of Canon Law at the University of Navarra.

Needless to say, his position as head of the Pontifical Council for the Interpretation of Legislative Texts speaks of the attitude of the Vatican to reporting.[18] Herranz's words reflect exactly what was in *Crimen Sollicitationis*, the *1983 Code of Canon Law*, and since 2001 in the *Motu Proprio* with its pontifical secrecy—the bishop will be the judge of a priest who sexually assaults children under canon law, but the investigation that determines his guilt must be kept secret from the outside world because of the special relationship between them.

---

17. http://www.natcath.org/crisis/051702e.htm (Accessed 16 July 2913).

18. The Pontifical Council for the Interpretation of Legislative Texts interprets laws for the Church and publishes such laws with papal confirmation. 'The Council also examines the juridical aspects of the general decrees of episcopal conferences during the necessary review (recognitio) process'. Beal, Coriden & Green, *New Commentary on the Code of Canon Law*, 488.

16 May 2002: Cardinal Oscar Rodríguez Maradiaga News Conference

At a news conference on 16 May 2002, Cardinal Oscar Rodriguez Maradiaga of Honduras who was seen as a leading Latin American candidate to succeed John Paul II, and who is now one of the senior Cardinals appointed by Pope Francis I to reform the Curia, stated,

> Paedophilia is a sickness, and those with this sickness must leave the priesthood. But we must not move from this to remedies that are non-Christian. … For me it would be a tragedy to reduce the role of a pastor to that of a cop. **We are totally different, and I'd be prepared to go to jail rather than harm one of my priests**. I say this with great clarity. We must not forget that we are pastors, not agents of the FBI or CIA[19] (my emphasis).

It is important to understand what Cardinal Rodriguez and Cardinal Castrillón before him in September 2001 are saying. They are saying that they would prefer to go to jail than to report to the police a priest who had been sexually assaulting children.

18 May 2002: Fr Gianfranco Ghirlanda SJ in *La Civiltá Cattolica*

Fr Gianfranco Ghirlanda SJ was Dean of the Faculty of Canon Law at Rome's Gregorian University and a judge for the Apostolic Signatura, considered the Vatican's Supreme Court. He wrote an article for *La Civiltà Cattolica,* a journal considered quasi-official since it is reviewed by the Vatican's Secretariat of State prior to publication. Ghirlanda wrote:

> Certainly it does not seem pastoral behaviour when a bishop or religious superior who has received a complaint informs the legal authorities of the fact in order to avoid being implicated in a civil process **that the victim could undertake**[20] (my emphasis).

---

19. http://natcath.org/NCR_Online/archives/053102/053102h.htm (Accessed 18 February 2013).

20. *Ibid* and http://www.nytimes.com/2002/05/18/us/a-vatican-lawyer-says-bishops-

Fr Ghirlanda's reference to 'pastoral behaviour', is a direct reference to Canon 1341 of the *1983 Code of Canon Law* which says a bishop can only commence formal disciplinary proceedings against a priest after he is satisfied that 'fraternal correction or reproof', or 'any methods of pastoral care' cannot 'repair the scandal, restore justice and reform the offender'. In other words, quite apart from the specific requirements of pontifical secrecy, going to the police is also inconsistent with Canon 1341. Again, we have a very senior Vatican canon lawyer, and a member of its highest court insisting on the 'pastoral approach', which some eight years later, his colleague in the Curia, as Pope Benedict XVI, would condemn in the Irish bishops after the publication of the *Murphy Dublin Report* that covered the period 1975 to 2004. Those complaints of sexual abuse were dealt with by the Irish bishops using this 'pastoral approach' that senior Vatican officials insisted on, and which Benedict in 2010 hypocritically condemned.

Fr Murphy's case, involving the abuse of 200 deaf mute boys, is indicative of the absurdity of Ghirlanda's statement that it should be up to the victims to go to the police. He is suggesting that the deaf mute boys, under the care of the Church, should have been the ones to lodge a complaint. And the boys interviewed by Fr Brady (now Cardinal Brady) in 1975, when their parents were not told, and could not be told under *Crimen Sollicitationis*, should also have gone to the police even after Brady made them swear an oath of secrecy.

But the statement is even more absurd in the light of changes made to the *Graviora Delicta* or *Substantive Norms* in the 2010 revision of the *2001 Motu Proprio*. The revision expanded the matters to be dealt with secretly by the Congregation for the Doctrine of the Faith to those where a priest has sex with a person 'who habitually lacks the use of reason'. And the same comment can be made of the extension to include the possession of child pornography, whose victims, the children in the photos, would have no idea that the priest had them in his possession.

8 June 2002 Cardinal Schotte of Belgium interview with National Catholic Reporter

Before the US Bishops Conference in Dallas in 2002, the head of the Belgian Synod of Bishops expressed reservations about reporting

---

should-not-reveal-abuse-claims.html (Accessed 9 July 2013).

requirements being proposed by the American Bishops. John L Allen Jr states:

> Schotte expressed reservations about calls for quasi-automatic cooperation with the police and the courts. He said that in Belgium the bishops had successfully resisted demands to turn over their records about priests accused of misconduct, on the grounds that these are confidential Church documents.

It seems, however, that Schotte was mistaken. Allen adds that in the five cases of criminal actions against priests, the Church had to turn its files over each time. Nevertheless his words indicate clearly what Schotte considered *should* be the case—the privilege of clergy against ordinary legal processes[21]

July 2002, Cardinal Lehmann interview with *Der Spiegel*

In 2002 the Chairman of the German Bishops' Conference, Cardinal Lehmann, was asked by *Der* Spiegel whether or not the bishops reported allegations of clergy abuse to the civil authorities. He said that was not the bishops' role. They can 'motivate the culprit to self denunciation'.[22]

2002 and 2010: Monsignor Maurice Dooley

Monsignor Maurice Dooley was a senior Irish canon lawyer who was widely reported as expressing views in 2002 and 2010 that bishops could not report allegations and evidence that had gathered about clergy sexual abusers to the police without breaching canon law.[23] According to a report in the *Belfast Telegraph* of 20 March, 2010:

> Mgr Dooley's views were clearly no different in 2002 when he said: 'A bishop swears allegiance to canon law.

---

21. John L Allen: *All the Popes Men: The Inside Story of How the Vatican Thinks* (New York: Doubleday Image), 69.
22. http://www.spiegel.de/spiegel/print/d-22955262.html (Accessed 16 July 2013) (translation as appears in David Yallop's *Beyond Belief*,)
23. http://www.bishop-accountability.org/news2010/03_04/2010_03_18_IrishTimes_ViewOf.htm (Accessed 16 July 2013).

> If there was a real conflict, he would simply have to maintain canon law, even if there was a chance of going to jail ... A bishop's relationship with a priest was similar to that of a parent and child,' Fr Dooley said. 'As a parent, you are entitled to protect your child or even to conceal him from punishment'.[24]

Monsignor Dooley repeated that view in 2010 when he was interviewed over the matter of Cardinal Brady who was part of a canonical investigation of Fr Brendan Smyth, and did not report the serious allegations against Smyth to the police. Dooley said,

> He (Brady) got this information within a canonical procedure, the rules of which bound him not to reveal the matter to people outside the particular process, and that would involve the Gards (*the police*). Now if it was a matter of Fr Sean Brady as an ordinary public citizen and he saw someone abusing a child, he would be perfectly entitled to use that information personally[25] (my insertion).

Monsignor Dooley was correct. That is exactly what canon law required. Very few clergy did see children abused. They found out about it by carrying out investigations as they were required to do by canon law, by interviewing victims and other witnesses. That was the information they could not take to the police. And, as we have seen, his views were in agreement with what senior Curia Cardinals and senior Vatican canon lawyers were saying.

One of the interesting things about these statements from senior members of the hierarchy around 2002 is that they occurred right at the time when the American bishops were trying to get the Vatican to approve reporting clergy sexual abusers to the police. After the *recognitio* was granted to the United States in December 2002, there was not a whimper from them. The first cracks in the wall of the de

---

24. http://www.theinquiry.ca/Dooley_200310.hide.php (Accessed 10 June 2013).

25. http://www.fifavideos.com/Colm-OGorman-and-Monsignor-Maurice-Dooley-The-Last-Word-with-Matt-Cooper__F9wtljHDT-c.html at 5.56 (Accessed 16 July 2013).

facto privilege of clergy had appeared. Court cases, especially in the United States, were revealing a consistent pattern of cover up. The cat was out of the bag. There was no point in denying it anymore. Something had to change. Reporting in some form or another had to be accepted, and the real question was to determine how little reporting the Church could get away with.

The Americans were not the only ones trying to convince the Vatican that it should allow reporting of clergy crimes to the police. The Irish bishops tried to do it in 1996 and the British bishops in 2001. The pragmatic Australians had thrown in the towel. There was no point in banging heads against a brick wall. Like tax lawyers, they went looking for loopholes in canon law.

17

Bishop's Conferences:
Sexual Abuse Protocols and the Vatican

Australia
1996: *Towards Healing*

In the 1980s, the Australian bishops were faced with the problem that the canonical disciplinary system was 'unworkable' for dealing with priests who sexually assaulted children.[1] In 1988, the Australian Catholic Bishops Conference set up a 'Special Issues Committee' to establish a protocol where allegations of a criminal nature were made against priests and religious. In 1990, they came up with a protocol that, among other things, required bishops and religious superiors to abide by any laws relating to compulsory reporting. Cardinal George Pell said at the *Victorian Parliamentary Inquiry* that the 'Special Issues Committee' was set up by the Australian bishops in 1988 because:

> . . . there were no protocols and no procedures in the archdiocese before that. In 88 people were trying to come to grips with this and they put into place . . . Then nationally they drew up some rudimentary protocols in 92. I suppose it was a recognition that things had not been handled well and we needed to do better.[2]

---

1. Evidence of Fr Brian Lucas before the *Maitland-Newcastle Inquiry* http:// www.lawlink.nsw.gov.au/lawlink/Special_Projects/ll_splprojects.nsf/vwFiles/ Transcript_Day_15_-_TOR_2_-_24_July_2013.pdf/$file/Transcript_Day_15_-_ TOR_2_-_24_July_2013.pdf , 1570.36 (Accessed 18 August 2013).
2. http://www.parliament.vic.gov.au/images/stories/committees/fcdc/ inquiries/57th/Child_Abuse_Inquiry/Transcripts/Catholic_Archdiocese_of_ Sydney_27-May-13.pdf, 6.7 (Accessed 16 July 2013).

There was a protocol, and there was a procedure in place: *the 1983 Code of Canon Law* and its secrecy decreed by *Secreta Continere*. It provided for no reporting to the police, a five year limitation period, a requirement to use 'pastoral' methods prior to taking any canonical action, that is, to try and 'cure' the priest, an impossibly complicated system for dismissing a priest if those 'pastoral' methods failed, and the possibility of an appeal to Rome where the Vatican 'Catch 22' defence was likely to let him off. The canonical protocol also gave the victim the right to bring a 'contentious action' for damages, as part of a penal trial, but as penal trials were effectively impossible, there could be no claims for damages.[3] Things 'had not been handled well' because bishops were following canon law, as they were required to do under their oath of office.

Fr Brian Lucas was involved in the Special Issues Committee, and was looking for ways of getting around canon law by using an informal process, which generally involved trying to convince the priest to resign.[4] In places like the State of New South Wales where there was a civil law duty to report, the canonical prohibition on reporting could be evaded by referring victims onto a priest who would organise counsellors for them, and that priest or the counsellors did the reporting. Counselling was not part of any canonical investigation.[5]

---

3. Canon 1729.
4. Evidence of Fr Brian Lucas before the *Maitland-Newcastle Inquiry* http:// www.lawlink.nsw.gov.au/lawlink/Special_Projects/ll_splprojects.nsf/vwFiles/ Transcript_Day_15_-_TOR_2_-_24_July_2013.pdf/$file/Transcript_Day_15_-_ TOR_2_-_24_July_2013.pdf , 1570.36 (Accessed 18 August 2013). Lucas denied that he was involved in the preliminary investigation under canon law in interviewing the priest and witnesses: 1648. http://www.lawlink.nsw. gov.au/lawlink/Special_Projects/ll_splprojects.nsf/vwFiles/Day_22_-_9_ September_2013.pdf/$file/Day_22_-_9_September_2013.pdf, 2361 (Accessed 11 September 2013).
5. Lucas often worked with Fr John Usher who had a background in social work. Allegations of clergy sexual abuse came to his attention informally or through a referral from a bishop, but he was only authorised to organise counselling for the victim. He or the counsellors used to refer the complaints to the police, as was required by New South Wales law, but often his involvement occurred after the police were already involved. On limited occasions, he was asked to speak to the accused cleric at the request of a bishop for the purpose of giving the bishop advice, but he was not involved in taking statements from them (paragraph 51) https://cdn.fairfaxregional.com.au/transcriptsinquiry/Exhibit%20226%20 Statutory%20Declaration%20of%20Monsignor%20Usher.pdf (Accessed 10 September 2013), http://www.lawlink.nsw.gov.au/lawlink/Special_Projects/

In 1994, Bishop Geoffrey Robinson was appointed by the Australian Bishops to prepare an official response to clerical sexual abuse of children.[6] He was not finding it an easy task. At a public meeting he said he was 'not happy with the levels of support' he was receiving from Rome. On 7 August 1996, he received an official letter from the Congregation for Bishops rebuking him for criticism of the 'magisterial teaching and discipline of the Church', and that the matter had been reported to the pope. He was told that the relevant documents would be forwarded on to the Congregation for the Doctrine of the Faith, which deals with matters of heresy.[7]

As a result of his committee's discussions, the first *Towards Healing* document was created which required reporting where the civil law required it. Archbishop Pell of Melbourne did not sign up to *Towards Healing* and created his own protocol called *The Melbourne Response.*

The original 1996 version of *Towards Healing* had provision for clergy to step aside pending determination of an accusation against them, while acknowledging the presumption of innocence.[8] The provisions and procedures of canon law had to be kept in mind.[9] As the Irish Murphy Commission found, there were canonical difficulties about making a priest step aside pending resolution of such allegations.[10] It was also one of the matters which the Vatican steadfastly refused to change in their discussions in 2002 with the American bishops over the Dallas Charter.

Towards Healing in 1996 provided that all Church personnel should comply with mandatory reporting requirements for child sexual abuse that exist in some states or territories.[11] Complainants

---

ll_splprojects.nsf/vwFiles/Day_22_-_9_September_2013.pdf/$file/Day_22_-_9_September_2013.pdf p. 2361 (Accessed 11 September 2013).

6. Geoffrey Robinson, *Confronting Power and Sex in the Catholic Church* (Melbourne: John Garrett Publishing, 2007), 20.

7. *Ibid.*

8. http://www.parliament.vic.gov.au/images/stories/committees/fcdc/inquiries/57th/Child_Abuse_Inquiry/Submissions/Catholic_Church_in_Victoria_Appendix_1_Part_B.pdf Annexure 8 clause 24, and clause 6.2, page 11. (Accessed 31 March 2013).

9. *Ibid*, clause 1.4 of the footnotes on page 6.

10. *Murphy Dublin Report*, Part 1 http://www.justice.ie/en/JELR/DACOI%20Part%201.pdf/Files/DACOI%20Part%201.pdf) paragraphs 4.47–4.50. (Accessed 25 April 2013).

11. http://www.parliament.vic.gov.au/images/stories/committees/fcdc/inquiries/57th/Child_Abuse_Inquiry/Submissions/Catholic_Church_in_

were to be told of their right to take the matter to the police, and state or territory laws regarding the reporting of knowledge of a criminal offence had to be observed.[12] In applying the *Towards Healing* provisions, the bishops had to keep in mind the 'penal and procedural provisions of the Code of canon law'.[13] On the one hand there was an unenforceable 'gentleman's agreement' amongst the bishops to obey the civil law by reporting to the police where the law so required, and on the other, there was a prohibition under canon law that prevented them from doing so.

If there was a finding against the accused either in a civil court or through the *Towards Healing* assessment, clerics and religious were to take administrative leave pursuant to Canon 1722.[14] If the Church authorities were satisfied that the accused was guilty of sexual abuse, he could be asked to voluntarily return to the lay state, or formal processes for dismissal could be commenced under Canons 1717–1731.[15] As we have already seen, the chances of that formal process succeeding were virtually zero. According to the Storero letter, the very fact of the priest being reported to the police would be regarded by the Vatican as sufficient to nullify the canonical process.

The extraordinary thing is that not only were there the so called two 'parallel' systems of canon law and civil law to deal with clergy sexual abuse, but there was a third 'parallel system' under *Towards Healing* whose reporting provisions were unenforceable under civil law, and they conflicted with canon law.

As the Vatican Response to the Irish Foreign Minister pointed out, every bishop is the governor of his own diocese, and the only

---

Victoria_Appendix_1_Part_B.pdf Annexure 8 clause 4.3, on page 9 (Accessed 31 March 2013).

12. *Ibid*, clause 5.3, 5.4.1, on page 10.

13. Clause 1.4.

14. *Ibid*, clause 9.1.2, on page 15. Canon 1722 allows for suspension from the ministry during the course of a canonical investigation and trial, but it does not apply to the preliminary investigation: John P Beal, James A Coriden and Thomas J Green, *New Commentary on the Code of Canon Law*, 1812. The provision therefore conflicted with canon law because such suspension could only take place once a canonical trial has commenced after a preliminary investigation. That position was rectified in the 2010 revision of the *2001 Motu Proprio*. But at this time, the whole thrust of *Towards Healing* seems to have been to find a way around canon law.

15. *Ibid*, clause 9.2, on page 15.

constraint on him is canon law. So even though bishops might have signed up to *Towards Healing*, they were prohibited by canon law to follow its procedures for reporting, so long as it did not have Vatican approval to become canon law for the particular region. But neither was *Towards Healing* enforceable under civil law as a contract because of a lack of consideration. In addition, as priests had not signed the document, they could not be forced to take administrative leave under civil law, or indeed do anything as required by *Towards Healing*. The suspension of a priest under Canon 1722 could only be imposed after the preliminary inquiry has been completed and a canonical trial commenced. If priests were asked to take 'administrative leave', they could simply ignore it under both civil and canon law. As one Australian bishop told me, the Vatican regarded it as no more than a piece of paper, and so long as it had not received a *recognitio* under canon law, that is all it was.

Professor Patrick Parkinson, writing in 2003, pointed out that this is an unacceptable situation, and that one of the main problems with these protocols was that they were not consistent with canon law. If a priest was disciplined under their provisions, he simply appealed to Rome and the decision overturned.

> The complaints procedure has been grafted onto existing processes, or created alongside existing processes, but without having any formal standing in the rules of the Church . . . The lack of consistency between the complaints procedure and the law of the Church has been a problem in the Catholic Church in Australia . . . . . As a consequence, the best intentions of the Church leadership in Australia concerning the removal of offenders from ministry have not always been achieved.[16]

Parkinson says that a new version of *Towards Healing* was brought out in 2000 with the aim of bringing it in line with canon law. The following clause was added:

---

16. Patrick Parkinson, *Child Sex Abuse and the Churches: Understanding the Issues* (Sydney: Aquila Press, 2003). The problem of clergy being 'disciplined' in accordance with *Towards Healing* and then having the decision overturned in Rome because *Towards Healing* was inconsistent with canon law is also mentioned by Delaney, *Canonical Implications of the Response of the Catholic Church in Australia,* xi and footnote 3.

The procedures for determining the future ministry
of a priest or religious shall be consistent with the
requirements of canon law.[17]

That did not solve anything, because the conflicts between *Towards
Healing* and canon law still existed.

In 2010, the conflict between *Towards Healing* and canon law over
'administrative leave' was resolved under the 2010 revision of the *2001
Motu Proprio*. The priest can be asked to stand down immediately the
allegation is made.[18] However, there are still problems over reporting
to the police.

The *2001 Motu Proprio*, as revised in 2010 still requires a bishop
to carry out a 'preliminary investigation' under Canon 1717. Under
Towards Healing, an 'assessor' is to be appointed under Clause 40
to 'investigate the facts'. Canon 1717 only requires a preliminary
investigation to be done by 'a suitable person', and does not have
to be a priest. In November 2002, the Australian Catholic Bishops
Conference stated that an assessment under its *Towards Healing*
protocol would be the preliminary investigation under Canon
1717 where the allegation is denied.[19] Any report by the assessor is
covered by pontifical secrecy, making it a breach of canon law for
the bishop or the assessor to report that information to the police at
least up until the dispensation in 2010.[20] But the dispensation itself
is limited to where there is a civil law requiring reporting. All states
have that provision relating to children at risk, but only the State of

17. Clause 42.4. A footnote then refers to Canons 1720–1728, 1740–1747, 1041 and
    1014.
18. Article 19, http://www.vatican.va/resources/resources_norme_en.html (Accessed
    5 August 2013).
19. *Australian Church Submission* to the *Australian Royal Commission*: http://dev.
    childabuseroyalcommission.gov.au/wp-content/uploads/2013/10/14.-Truth-
    Justice-and-Healing-Council.pdf, 91, paragraph 57.
20. In his report to the *Maitland-Newcastle Inquiry*, Dr Rodger Austin said at
    paragraph 27 that ' . . . *Towards Healing* is not ecclesiastical law, and does not in
    any way affect the obligations a Bishop has in canon law in respect of allegations
    of sexual abuse committed by a priest.' Unless a bishop instigates two independent
    investigations, the appointment of the assessor was his preliminary inquiry.
    http://www.lawlink.nsw.gov.au/lawlink/Special_Projects/ll_splprojects.nsf/
    vwFiles/Transcript_Day_20_-_TOR_2_-_31_July_2013.pdf/$file/Transcript_
    Day_20_-_TOR_2_-_31_July_2013.pdf, Exhibit 209 page 2214.

New SouthWales has it for historic abuse. In other states, if bishops reported historic abuse, they were breaching canon law.

Towards Healing had a series of revisions in 2000, 2003, and 2010, which undoubtedly improved its operation in other matters, such as counselling, help for victims etc. The current *Towards Healing* document goes further than requiring compliance with civil laws relating to reporting.[21] It provides for reporting of all crimes. If the complainant does not wish to report, the Church authorities will still report the matter, but without any details that might identify the complainant.[22] Both the Irish bishops in their 1996 *Framework Document*, and the American bishops in their original 2002 *Dallas Charter,* wanted the right to report to the police irrespective of whether or not there was a law requiring reporting. In both cases, the Vatican rejected the idea. The 2010 dispensation and the 2011 Levada guidelines allow reporting only when the local law requires it.

Towards Healing was always going to be beset with problems so long as it had never become part of the canon law applicable to Australia, for reasons already set out by Professor Parkinson. This was also one of the concerns of the Cumberlege Commission in the United Kingdom where there were national protocols about reporting to the police that did not have the *recognitio* of the Vatican.[23] The same problems of compliance occurred in the United States when the United States Catholic Bishops Conference resolved in 1992 to relieve a priest of his duties if an allegation was supported by sufficient evidence. They also required reporting the matter if the law required it. As the resolution had not become canon law under canon 455 it was often ignored.[24]

---

21. *Towards Healing* as at 27 March 2013, Clause 34.6 and 37.5. http://www.catholic.org.au/index.php?option=com_docman&task=cat_view&gid=38&Itemid=395 (Accessed 6 April 2013).

22. *Ibid*, Clause 37.4. 'In the case of an alleged criminal offence, if the complainant does not want to take the matter to the police, all Church personnel should nonetheless pass details of the complaint to the Director of Professional Standards, who should provide information to the Police other than giving those details that could lead to the identification of the complainant.'

23. http://www.cathcom.org/mysharedaccounts/cumberlege/report/downloads/CathCom_Cumberlege2.pdf (Accessed 18 February 2013).

24. Nicholas Cafardi, 'Another Long Lent: The Abuse Crisis Resurfaces in Philadelphia', http://www.commonwealmagazine.org/another-long-lent (Accessed 4 June 2013).

The *Cloyne Report* in Ireland demonstrates what happens when there were conflicting decisions of the Irish Catholic Bishops Conference and directions from Rome. Bishop Magee signed up to the *Framework Document* which required reporting to the police, but he clearly did not agree with it. Neither did his canon law adviser, Monsignor O'Callaghan. The result was that sometimes matters were reported and sometimes they were not.[25] Legal obligations have to be clear and enforceable, and if they are not, people will do as they like—even in the Church.

There is currently no publically available information about how often bishops reported clergy sexual crimes in the State of New South Wales in accordance with *Towards Healing*.[26] If it is found that allegations were not always reported there is a very good explanation: since *Towards Healing* never received the *recognitio* of the Vatican, the secrecy provisions of *Secreta Continere* and the *2001 Motu Proprio* still applied. If bishops did report, they commendably found ways of evading canon law or simply defied it.[27]

1996 *The Melbourne Response*

When misprision of felony was abolished in the State of Victoria in 1981, it was not replaced by the equivalent of S.316 of the *Crimes Act 1900* (NSW). In Victoria there was no general obligation on bishops to report information about clergy sexual abuse of children to the civil authorities.

Archbishop Pell of Melbourne did not sign up to the *Towards Healing* protocol, and in October 1996 instead created his own response that is known as *The Melbourne Response*. It has no provision

---

25. http://www.justice.ie/en/JELR/Cloyne_Rpt.pdf/Files/Cloyne_Rpt.pdf paragraph 1.22ff (Accessed 9 February 2013).

26. Fr John Usher at the *Maitland-Newcastle Inquiry* says that he reported a number of complaints to the police or child welfare authorities, but it appears that he was doing this as part of an informal group of priests who were working with victims, rather than as part of any direction from the bishop to conduct a preliminary inquiry under canon law. https://cdn.fairfaxregional.com.au/transcriptsinquiry/Exhibit%20226%20Statutory%20Declaration%20of%20Monsignor%20Usher.pdf (Accessed 10 September 2013).

27. *Ibid.* The bishop, arguably, was still in breach of canon law by informing Fr Usher of the allegation to enable him to report to the police, because the allegations themselves were subject to pontifical secret under *Secreta Continere*.

for reporting to the Victorian Police, but it says that it would encourage complainants to take their allegations to the police.[28] There is some dispute about how seriously that was done.[29]

Quite apart from the prohibition imposed by the *1983 Code of Canon Law* and the *2001 Motu Proprio*, *The Melbourne Response* with its 'no reporting' is in line with views expressed in 1997 by Cardinal Castrillón, the Prefect of the Congregation for Clergy to the Irish bishops, and to statements made by the Secretary of the Congregation for the Doctrine of the Faith, Archbishop Bertone in 2002, and other senior Church leaders that bishops should not report clergy sexual abusers to the civil authorities.

Archbishop Pell was a member of the Congregation for the Doctrine of the Faith from 1990 to 2000 and he had meetings with Cardinal Ratzinger once every twelve to eighteen months during that period.[30] It is difficult to believe that he was unaware of the thinking of Cardinals Ratziner and Castrillón, Archbishop Bertone and the Roman Curia, on the issue of reporting to police. At the *Victorian Parliamentary Inquiry*, speaking about his meetings in Rome as a member of that Congregation, he said that the people in Rome from 1996 onwards were aware of *The Melbourne Response* and were 'pleased with it'. [31]

That was perfectly understandable—*The Melbourne Response* had no provision for Church authorities to report clergy sexual abusers to the police.

There was no requirement whatsoever on bishops to report clergy sexual abuse in the State of Victoria. Misprision of felony had been abolished in 1981, and the mandatory welfare reporting laws did not apply to clergy. Prior to 2010, *Towards Healing* only required reporting

---

28. http://www.cam.org.au/Portals/0/Documents/Melbourne-Response-2012-brochure.pdf (Accessed 16 July 2013).

29. Geoffrey Robertson QC, *The Case of the Pope*, chapter 1 paragrpah 42. David Marr in 'The Prince, Faith, Abuse and George Pell', in *Quarterly Essay*, 51 (September 2013), electronic copy at 46%, says that documents produced by O'Callaghan to the *Victorian Parliamentary Inquiry* showed that only about ten victims our of more than 300 went to the police after first seeing O'Callaghan.

30. http://www.parliament.vic.gov.au/images/stories/committees/fcdc/inquiries/57th/Child_Abuse_Inquiry/Transcripts/Catholic_Archdiocese_of_Sydney_27-May-13.pdf, page 21.1(Accessed 16 July 2013).

31. *Ibid*, 23.

where the law required it. Pell and the three other Victorian bishops could comply with pontifical secrecy, and not breach the civil law by failing to report. The *Victorian Parliamentary Inquiry* found that this is exactly what they did—they reported none of the 611 cases.[32]

The Melbourne Response also reflected canon law in its attempt to avoid 'scandal'. In an interview with Richard Carleton on *Sixty Minutes* in 2002 dealing with the paedophile activities of Fr Gerard Ridsdale, Pell, who by then had become Archbishop of Sydney, admitted that the victims had to swear to observe secrecy in return for the limited compensation that the scheme offered. He said that if the victims did not want to use *The Melbourne Response*, they could 'go to the courts'. But, he said, many do not want the publicity and 'of course, it is shameful for the Church'.[33] But another good reason for not wanting to go to court was the legal difficulty of suing a Church which in law did not exist, as Cardinal Pell would later establish in the *Ellis* case.

The Melbourne Response Compensation Package

The Melbourne Response provided for compensation to be fixed by an 'independent' Commission which was funded by the Church, but it was not allowed to award more than $50,000 (since increased to $75,000) on compensation payouts. Cardinal Pell tried to justify this scheme on the basis that it was the same amount of money paid by state government to the victims of crime.[34]

The big difference is that the Church's structure is an unincorporated association whose clergy either take vows of poverty as members of a religious order, or whose every need is provided for by the Church, and are not likely to have assets to meet a judgment. Cardinal Pell conceded this in his evidence when he said that 'most priests are not well off'.[35] On the other hand, it is very rare for a large

---

32. *Betrayal of Trust*, Report of the *Victorian Parliamentary Inquiry*, paragraph 7.3.6, page 170.

33. http://sixtyminutes.ninemsn.com.au/article.aspx?id=8630762, 12.45ff (Accessed 16 July 2013).

34. http://www.parliament.vic.gov.au/images/stories/committees/fcdc/inquiries/57th/Child_Abuse_Inquiry/Transcripts/Catholic_Archdiocese_of_Sydney_27-May-13.pdf, 16.5 (Accessed 23 June 2913).

35. *Ibid*, 40.8

association with enormous assets not to be incorporated. Likewise, the state itself is a legal entity that can always be sued. Those who are injured by the servants or agents of such corporations and the state can always sue them as legal entities. They are not restricted to suing the abusing employee who may well be in jail, or the general manager, or the premier at the time, both of whom might well be dead and their estates distributed, or are alive but have no assets. As much as Pell likes to claim that the Church is on a level playing field, it is not. It is in a very privileged position to avoid having to pay compensation. The *Roman Catholic Church Property Trust Act* 1936 (NSW) was amended in 1986 to allow the Trustees to engage in any activity of a natural person, in addition to holding of property.[36] But it does not oblige them to do so, and if they keep these activities separate, then the Church will continue to enjoy the immunity provided by the *Ellis* decision.

The James Hardie Company in Australia was facing massive claims from mesothelioma victims as a result of its mining and distributing asbestos. It used legal means to shift its assets offshore, thus insulating its assets from those claims. It is not suggested that the Church has done this (it could not anyway, because most of its assets are in real estate), but it has the opportunity to hide behind its status as an unincorporated association, and to keep its activities in appointing and supervising priests separate from the activities of the trust. The end result is exactly the same: the assets are protected from claims.

The Brilliant Business Move

Lawyers acting for victims have always been aware of the difficulty of 'going to the courts' to recover compensation from the Church, the alternative that Cardinal Pell said the victims always had. In the *Ellis case*, Ellis sued Pell who was then the Cardinal Archbishop of Sydney, and the archdiocesan trustee for damages arising out of sexual abuse by a Sydney priest. Pell's lawyers argued that the Church did not exist in law, that Pell was not responsible for the sins of his predecessors in Sydney, and that Ellis was restricted to suing the abusing priest or the former Archbishop of Sydney, Cardinal Freeman, both of whom

---

36. *Roman Catholic Church Trust Property (Amendment) Act 1986*. Assented to 18.12.1986.

were dead, and their estates distributed.[37] Ellis would be wasting his time to sue their estates.

Father Frank Brennan SJ is critical of the defence raised in the case on Pell's behalf:

> The Church should not give any appearance of hiding behind the corporate veil. Justice demands that present church leaders agree to satisfy any judgment debt against their predecessors or their deceased predecessors' estates when there is an allegation of past failure to supervise or adequately investigate a sexual predator in the ranks. Any damages should be paid from church assets.[38]

The canon lawyer, Dr Roger Austin goes further than that and says canon law does recognise this demand of justice. A bishop is obliged under canon law to take responsibility for the legal liabilities of his predecessor.[39] According to Dr Austin, a bishop is a 'corporation sole' under canon law. He succeeds to the property of his predecessor and incurs his liabilities. The English common law recognised a bishop as a 'corporation sole' up until the Reformation, but then the concept withered away in favour of the modern idea that a corporation can only be created by statute. There have been some cases in the United States where bishops have been found to be a 'corporation sole', and

---

37. *John Ellis v Pell and the Trustees of the Roman Catholic Church for the Diocese of Sydney* [2006] NSWSC 109, [2007] NSWCA 117, http://www.austlii.edu.au/cgi-bin/sinodisp/au/cases/nsw/NSWCA/2007/117.html?stem=0&synonyms=0&query=Ellis%20near%20Pell (Accessed 25 October 2013).

38. Fr Frank Brennan, 'Church-State Issues and the Royal Commission', in *Eureka Street*, 3 September 2013: http://www.eurekastreet.com.au/article.aspx?aeid=38146#.Ui5vaKt-8qQ (Accessed 10 September 2013). The term, 'hiding behind the corporate veil', usually refers to an individual or organisation escaping responsibility by using a $2 company which it would be useless to sue. The Church has done the opposite. It hides behind the fact that it is not incorporated, so that no one bears responsibility for the crimes or torts of predecessors who have died.

39. Affidavit of the canon lawyer, Dr Rodger Austin filed in the *Ellis case* http://www.parliament.vic.gov.au/images/stories/committees/fcdc/inquiries/57th/Child_Abuse_Inquiry/Right_of_Reply/John_Ellis_Appendix_A.pdf, paragraphs 3 and 4 (Accessed 18 August 2013).

liable for the torts of their predecessors, but in each case, their status as a 'corporation sole' was created by statute.[40]

Canon law has no standing in civil law, and Pell was entitled to take the point in the New South Wales courts. If Dr Austin is correct, it is indeed an extraordinary irony that the archbishop of Sydney could avoid liability under civil law by defying his own Church's canon law. The result was that the civil court was then precluded from even examining whether the abuse had taken place or what damage had been suffered by John Ellis.

The outcome of the *Ellis case* was inevitable because, unlike in many parts of the United States, Catholic Church dioceses in Australia are not incorporated, and under the *Roman Catholic Church Trust Property Act* 1936 *(NSW)*, the Church's assets can be insulated against claims.[41] In the case of the Archdiocese of Sydney, the court found that the trustee was not involved in the appointment or supervision of priests, and therefore the corporate trustee which holds billions of dollars in Church assets cannot be liable.

Cardinal Pell revealed in his evidence to the *Victorian Parliamentary Inquiry* that not only did he and the Church property trustee corporation waive their entitlement to 'in excess of' $500,000 in party/party costs for a case that went all the way to the High Court of Australia, but the Church also paid Ellis $500,000 in compensation.[42] John Ellis concedes that the Sydney Archdiocese paid for the 'gap' in his ongoing psychiatric therapy, and for him to have a holiday, and for some urgent repairs to his house.[43] The Church would not have

---

40. *Trustees of the Roman Catholic Church v Ellis* and anor [2007] NSWCA 117 (24 May 2007) Per Mason P at 152-181 http://www.austlii.edu.au/cgi-bin/sinodisp/au/cases/nsw/NSWCA/2007/117.html?stem=0&synonyms=0&query=Ellis%20near%20Pell (Accessed 25 October 2013).

41. http://www.austlii.edu.au/au/legis/nsw/num_act/rcctpa1936n24440.pdf?stem=0&synonyms=0&query=Roman%20near%20Catholic%20near%20property (Accessed 23 June 2013).

42. http://www.parliament.vic.gov.au/images/stories/committees/fcdc/inquiries/57th/Child_Abuse_Inquiry/Transcripts/Catholic_Archdiocese_of_Sydney_27-May-13.pdf, 35.8 (Accessed 23 June 2013).

43. http://www.parliament.vic.gov.au/images/stories/committees/fcdc/inquiries/57th/Child_Abuse_Inquiry/Right_of_Reply/John_Ellis_Right_of_Reply.pdf (Accessed 10 August 2013).

paid a cent on his behalf if it really thought that he was like Potiphar's wife, making a bogus claim. What was the point of defending the case on that legal point? Why did not Pell and the trustee let Ellis prove his claim and his damage if he could, and let the court decide the appropriate amount of compensation under the law of the land, a policy that the diocese of Maitland-Newcastle and the Jesuits had adopted?[44]

The decision in this case sent some very clear messages to all the victims of clergy sexual abuse and their lawyers in Australia: they were limited to suing the sex abusing priest who could either be dead or in jail, but in any event unlikely to have assets even if alive. And even if the victim could sue the bishop in negligence, the bishop is also unlikely to be 'well off', as his every need is looked after by the Church. The Church's insurance policy did not cover the situation where the bishop was negligent, that is, where he had prior knowledge of the abuse by the particular priest.[45]

Another message was that the victim's only alternative in the Archdiocese of Melbourne was to accept the limit of $50,000 (later $75,000) and to sign a secrecy agreement. If the victim went to court then the case would be strenuously defended.[46]

In the other dioceses where *Towards Healing* operates, the victim would have to negotiate an agreement with the Church from a position of severe disadvantage. As any lawyer experienced in settlement negotiations and mediations knows, the outcome is always dependent on the assessment by both parties of the likely result of the dispute going to court. If the plaintiff does not have solid legal grounds against the defendant, the end result of any settlement negotiations is often the payment of what Australian lawyers call 'go away money'. In Australia it is measured by the difference between

44. David Marr 'The Prince, Faith, Abuse and George Pell', in *Quarterly Essay,* 51 (September 2013), electronic copy at 57%.
45. http://www.parliament.vic.gov.au/images/stories/committees/fcdc/inquiries/57th/Child_Abuse_Inquiry/Submissions/Catholic_Church_Insurance.pdf, 4 (Accessed 10 August 2013). http://www.parliament.vic.gov.au/images/stories/committees/fcdc/inquiries/57th/Child_Abuse_Inquiry/Transcripts/Catholic_Church_Insurance_30-April-13.pdf (Accessed 10 August 2013)..
46. *Ibid.* David Marr 'The Prince, Faith, Abuse and George Pell', in *Quarterly Essay,* 51 (September 2013), electronic copy at 32%.

the party/party costs (that is, the costs that the successful defendant can recover from the plaintiff) and the solicitor/client costs (the costs based on the defendant's cost agreement with its lawyer).

A good example of this is the *Ellis case* itself. The Archdiocesan corporate trustee and Pell (Pell was also a defendant) offered John Ellis $30,000 through *Towards Healing* to settle the case before he started legal action, that being a reasonable assessment of the amount that the trustee and Pell would have been out of pocket if the matter went to a successful hearing and cost them $100,000. As it turned out the trustee and Pell invested some $756,000 paying their lawyers to fight the case because it went all the way to the High Court.[47] Ironically, this was even more than the amount for which Ellis had offered to settle the case at the beginning. Pell and the trustee accepted that they could only recover some $500,000 of those costs from Ellis. In other words, they were out of pocket some $250,000 anyway, even though they won the case.[48] That is the 'go away money' difference, which in this case was much higher than usual because the case went all the way to the High Court.

An illustration of how the outcome of negotiations is dependent on the strength of the legal claim is the case of two abused brothers in the diocese of Green Bay, Wisconsin. The diocese was incorporated, so any *Ellis* type of defence was not available. The Supreme Court of Wisconsin in 1995, in an earlier case, had held that the diocese was not vicariously liable for the abuse of a priest. The brothers were offered $5,000 'go away money'—their claim was on very shaky ground. They declined the offer. In a subsequent decision, the same Supreme Court of Wisconsin said that if a bishop wilfully shifted a paedophile priest around, then the diocese was liable. The brothers were able to establish that in court, and the jury awarded them $700,000. The

47. Submission in Reply of John Ellis to the *Victorian Parliamentary Inquiry,* http://www.parliament.vic.gov.au/images/stories/committees/fcdc/inquiries/57th/Child_Abuse_Inquiry/Right_of_Reply/John_Ellis_Right_of_Reply.pdf par 4, 5 (Accessed 10 August 2013).

48. Submission in reply, John Ellis http://www.parliament.vic.gov.au/images/stories/committees/fcdc/inquiries/57th/Child_Abuse_Inquiry/Right_of_Reply/John_Ellis_Right_of_Reply.pdf and http://www.parliament.vic.gov.au/images/stories/committees/fcdc/inquiries/57th/Child_Abuse_Inquiry/Right_of_Reply/John_Ellis_Appendix_B_C__D.pdf (Accessed 10 August 2013).

Church succeeded on an appeal because of a problem with one of the jurors, and a new trial was ordered. There were then negotiations between the parties to settle the matter. The diocese settled for the $700,000.[49]

Towards Healing suffered from the same problems as *The Melbourne Response* and the philosophy behind it was identical, even if its practical application was different. The victim had no choice but to accept the amount offered by the very institution that had betrayed them, or go to court against an opponent that had almost unlimited resources.[50]

Even assuming that the Church had paid out $500,000 for Ellis's therapy and other benefits, it is an illustration of why there has been so much dissatisfaction over both *The Melbourne Response* and *Towards Healing*. Apart from anything else, sexual abuse is an abuse of power, and because the Church can hide behind its lack of legal status, the victims are forced to go cap in hand to ask for favours from the institution that had failed them.

The Los Angeles Archdiocese, with a population of 4.6m Catholics has paid out some $700m in compensation to victims of clerical sexual abuse, at a cost of $152 per Catholic. [51] The Melbourne Archdiocese has a Catholic population of 1.06m, and has paid out $10.5m through its *The Melbourne Response* at a cost of a little under $10 per Catholic.[52] On the Los Angeles figures, the Melbourne Archdiocese would have paid out $160m. The Sydney Archdiocese has half the number of Catholics than Melbourne (577,000), because of the splitting off of the Parramatta and Broken Bay dioceses in 1986.[53] On the Los Angeles figures, the Sydney Archdiocese would have paid out $87.7m. The Victorian bishops' submission, *Facing the Truth* quotes the 2004 John Jay study in the United States about the incidence of child sexual abuse amongst priests (three to six per cent), and claims

49. http://ncronline.org/news/accountability/settlement-surprises-wisconsin-plaintiffs.
50. David Marr 'The Prince, Faith, Abuse and George Pell', in *Quarterly Essay*, 51 (September 2013), at 30% (Accessed 22 September 2013).
51. http://www.la-archdiocese.org/Pages/default.aspx (Accessed 23 June 2013) http://www.reuters.com/article/2013/03/13/us-usa-church-abuse-idUSBRE92B15D20130313 (Accessed 23 June 2013).
52. http://www.cam.org.au/Church-in-Melbourne/Facts (Accessed 25 August 2013).
53. http://www.sydneycatholic.org/about/who_we_are.shtml (Accessed 24 June 2013).

that the figures for Australia are similar.[54] The figures presented to the *Victorian Parliamentary Inquiry* by Professor Patrick Parkinson of the incidence of abuse amongst Catholic clergy being six times higher than all other religious denominations put together, suggests that the Australian figures are significantly higher.[55] Even accepting that the Victorian Church is correct, the amount paid out in compensation is minuscule compared to the Los Angeles figures.

The benefit of the *Ellis* decision accrues for every diocese in Australia, because the law is much the same. Similar *Roman Catholic Property Trust Acts* are in every state, with no significant difference between them, and the common law on unincorporated associations is the same. The Catholic population of Australia, according to the 2011 census was 5.439m.[56] On the Los Angeles figures, the cost to the Church in Australia would be in the order of $827m, as against an amount of $54m based on the Melbourne figures.

Damages awards in the United States are higher than in Australia, but not that much higher. Part of the reason they appear higher is that lawyers' fees are taken out of the verdict. Lawyers' fees in Australia are treated as a separate figure, are separately negotiated or assessed, and do not appear in the verdict amount. But even if you take into account higher compensation figures in the United States, the saving to the Australian Church by not incorporating, and keeping the property affairs of the trust separate from the appointment and supervision of priests has been huge.

---

54. http://www.parliament.vic.gov.au/images/stories/committees/fcdc/ inquiries/57th/Child_Abuse_Inquiry/Submissions/Catholic_Church_in_ Victoria.pdf, 15 (Accessed 24 June 2013), and http://www.parliament.vic.gov.au/ images/stories/committees/fcdc/inquiries/57th/Child_Abuse_Inquiry/Right_ of_Reply/Right_of_Reply_Francis_Moore.pdf (Accessed 10 August 2013).

55. http://www.parliament.vic.gov.au/images/stories/committees/fcdc/ inquiries/57th/Child_Abuse_Inquiry/Transcripts/Prof_Patrick_Parkinson_19- Oct-12.pdf , 2 (Accessed 24 June 2013). See also, Professor Patrick Parkinson: 'The Smith Lecture 2013: Child Sexual Abuse and the Churches: A Story of Moral Failure?', where he quotes research saying that abuse by males in the general population is between one and two per cent, but research by Professor Des Cahill found that in a particular Australian seminary, the abuse was 3.7% of those ordained between 1940 and 1966 and 5.4% of those ordained between 1968 and 1971) .http://smithlecture.org/sites/smithlecture.org/files/downloads/ lecture/smith-2013-transcript.pdf (Accessed 25 October 2013).

56. http://pro.catholic.org.au/pdf/E-%20News%20Bulletin%201.pdf (Accessed 24 June 2013).

The benefits of the *Ellis* defence must have left many a businessman gobsmacked with admiration at the business acumen of the Archbishops of Sydney who kept the property affairs of the Church corporate trustee separate from the appointment and supervision of priests, and then went to court to prove that the structure worked to protect its assets from the claims of victims. Not only that, the case operated as a precedent that lower courts must follow. One has already done so.[57] It has saved the Church in Australia hundreds of millions of dollars, at the expense of victims.

Despite all this, Cardinal Pell in his evidence before the *Victorian Parliamentary Inquiry* said

> . . . I have always been on the side of victims.[58]

And,

> I have tried to be prudent with money, but my record shows that I have acted compatibly with the general standards of the community, and I have tried to be generous.[59]

By 'general standards of the community', he was referring to the amount paid out by Australian state governments to all victims of crime, in circumstances where the state has no control or supervision of the criminals whatsoever, unlike the Church's control over its priests in terms of a seven year training period and constant monitoring and supervision, including through canon law.

At the *Victorian Parliamentary Inquiry*, Cardinal Pell was asked about a conversation he had with Sir Richard McGarvie (1926–2003) a former Victorian Supreme Court Judge and Governor of the State of Victoria that he mentioned in a speech he gave on 29 July 2011 entitled 'Authentic Catholicism and Cafeteria Catholicism'.

---

57. Hoeben J in *PAO v Trustees of the Roman Catholic Church for the Archdiocese of Sydney and Ors;* [2011] NSWSC 1216 (19 October 2011) followed the Ellis case in dismissing another claim against the trustees.

58. http://www.parliament.vic.gov.au/images/stories/committees/fcdc/inquiries/57th/Child_Abuse_Inquiry/Transcripts/Catholic_Archdiocese_of_Sydney_27-May-13.pdf, 4 (Accessed 22 June 2013).

59. *Ibid*, 16 (Accessed 22 June 2013).

He said in that speech that McGarvie told him that he had to take some 'decisive action', because 'the scandals would bleed us to death year after year'. Pell denied that McGarvie was talking about money but about 'our position in the community'.[60] The Church's material position in the community has certainly benefited by the Church being unincorporated and by the court declaration that it is entitled to avoid liability because of it.

There is a further problem that victims face in recovering compensation, and that is the extent to which a bishop can be vicariously liable for the criminal acts of his priests. There is a difference of view between the Australian High Court and superior courts in the United Kingdom and Canada with the latter moving closer to what is a strict liability for injuries done to children under the care of institutions. Despite statements by the Australian High Court that there is no strict liability under Australian law, it is difficult to see in the cases much practical difference.[61] Any doubts about the matter can be removed by legislation.

Even if some people in the Church think it has been generous in its settlements, the amount of compensation is effectively at its discretion, and not fixed by an independent third party, based on principles set out in the law. This problem can be fixed by legislation to make the Australian Church property trusts strictly liable.[62] For some, that might seem a radical move, but Australia has done that before.

Prior to 1886, injured workers were denied any possibility of claiming compensation from their employers because of what was termed 'the voluntary assumption of risk', that is, the worker knew that when he took a job in a coal mine, there was always the chance

---

60. *Ibid*, 9.
61. Fr Frank Brennan SJ, 'Church-State Issues and the Royal Commission', in *Eureka Street*, 3 September 2013, http://www.eurekastreet.com.au/article.aspx?aeid=38146#.Ui5vaKt-8qQ (Accessed 10 September 2013). In Australia it does not take much to prove negligent supervision where a child is injured. A few seconds inattention is enough: Kieran Tapsell, 'Turning the Negligence Juggernaut', in *Australian Law Journal*, 76 (2002): 581.
62. The *Victorian Parliamentary Inquiry* Report recommends changes to the law that would make institutions with the care of children vicariously liable for the criminal assaults of their employees or agents, and that the Ellis defence be abolished by some form of compulsory incorporation and the provision of insurance: XlVI, https://s3-ap-southeast-2.amazonaws.com/family-and-community-development-committee/Executive+summary+%26+recommendations.pdf)

that the roof would fall in on him. In 1886, the government of the State of Queensland introduced the first workers compensation legislation in the English speaking world that eventually became a system of strict liability for work place injuries. The end result of that legislation was much improved safety regimes in the workplace. Most other developed countries in the world followed suit. It would not be surprising that the disquiet and anger created by the *Ellis* defence will lead to laws creating a strict liability for sexual or indeed any other abuse of children in Australia, by people connected with institutions (and not just the Church), and this itself will go a long way to ensuring that adequate systems are put in place to minimise the chance of it happening again.

In the end, Cardinal Pell might have done for the world, what Scrooge eventually did for Christmas, made it a happier place for children.

The Flaws in the Australian Protocols

Towards Healing and *The Melbourne Response* suffered from the systemic flaw of trying to do a bit of everything to solve the issues raised by clergy sexual abuse, and ended up doing none of it very well:

- They tried to deal with the clash between canon law's requirement of secrecy and the civil law's requirement of reporting. In those states where there was no requirement to report, there was no conflict. But in the State of New South Wales, there was, until 2010, when the Vatican provided a dispensation from pontifical secrecy, provided such reporting took place before any canonical trial. After 2010, *Towards Healing* required the bishops (other than in the State of New South Wales) to breach canon law by reporting even when there was no legal requirement to do so, thus creating conflicts with their oath of office. In the case of *The Melbourne Response* it meant that the Church was advising the victim to go to the police where the Church has a conflict of interest in giving that advice.
- They tried to provide a system of compensation outside the civil justice system. In the case of *Towards Healing*,

it was a system of negotiation and mediation where the victim was at a severe disadvantage because of the structure of the Church. *The Melbourne Response* had compensation fixed by an independent Commissioner whose independence was limited by a ceiling figure, and where the victim suffered the same severe legal disadvantage if he wished to take the alternative of going to Court.

- They tried to provide medical, psychiatric and counselling services which made the victims still dependent on the institution that had already abused its power over them.
- They tried to create a disciplinary system for priests because of the established failure of canon law to do so, but that system clashed with canon law.

On the relationship with the civil law, the Victorian Deputy Police Commissioner Ashton, on 18 October 2012, told the *Victorian Parliamentary Inquiry*,

> I think the following analogy is telling when one examines why there is in fact a need for any sort of process within the Catholic Church system for dealing with child sexual abuse. If a stranger were to enter the grounds of a church and rape a child, then that rape would be immediately reported to the police and action expected. But if that stranger happened to be a member of the clergy, such as a priest, the matter under the current experience would not be reported. If that stranger is a member of the clergy, then a special process is wrapped around him which discourages the victim from complaining to police, seeks to ensure that the offending clergy member is not only not prosecuted and jailed but never included on the sex offenders register and never adversely recorded on future working-with-children checks.[63]

---

63. http://www.parliament.vic.gov.au/images/stories/committees/fcdc/inquiries/57th/Child_Abuse_Inquiry/Transcripts/Victoria_Police_19-Oct-12.pdf (Accessed 5 March 2013).

The issues of reporting to the police and compensation to victims can only be resolved by changes to civil law. The problem of the discipline of priests can only be solved by changes to canon law to create a viable and respected disciplinary system, which it certainly has not provided over the last ninety years.

Ireland

1996 The Irish Bishops Forward *Framework Document* for Comment by the Vatican

On 4 January 1996, the Irish bishops forwarded to the Vatican the *Framework Document* which outlined their proposals for dealing with sexual abuse of children by clergy, including proposals for mandatory reporting to the civil authorities of all complaints about sexual abuse, irrespective of whether the law required them to report or not, and irrespective of whether the victim was then an adult or not.[64]

The *Cloyne Report* stated that *recognitio* was sought for the document which would have given it the status of canon law for Ireland, but the approval was not forthcoming.[65]

The response came from the Papal Nuncio, Archbishop Storero in a letter dated 31 January 1997.

> The Congregation for the Clergy has attentively studied the complex question of sexual abuse of minors by clerics and documents entitled 'Child Sexual Abuse : Framework for a Church Response', published by the Irish Bishops Advisory Committee.
>
> The **Congregation wishes to emphasize the need for this document to conform to the canonical norms presently in force.**

---

64. Paragraph 2.2.3 'In all instances where it is known or suspected that a child has been, or is being, sexually abused by a priest or religious the matter should be reported to the civil authorities. Where the suspicion or knowledge results from the complaint of an adult of abuse during his or her childhood, this should also be reported to the civil authorities.' http://www.bishop-accountability.org/reports/1996_Irish_Catholic_Bishops_Advisory_Committee_Framework.pdf, paragraph 2.2.1(Accessed 19 May 2013).

65. http://www.justice.ie/en/JELR/Cloyne_Rpt.pdf/Files/Cloyne_Rpt.pdf para 4.21 (Accessed 16 July 2013).

The text, however, contains **procedures and dispositions which appear contrary to canonical discipline and which, if applied, could invalidate the acts of the same Bishops who are attempting to put a stop to these problems**. If such procedures were to be followed by the Bishops and there were cases of eventual hierarchical recourse lodged at the Holy See, the results could be highly embarrassing and detrimental to those same Diocesan authorities.

In particular, the situation of 'mandatory reporting' gives rise to serious reservations of both a moral and a canonical nature.

. . . the procedures established by the Code of Canon Law must be meticulously followed under pain of invalidity of the acts involved if the priests so punished were to make hierarchical recourse against his Bishop[66] (my emphases).

The letter came from the Papal Nuncio on behalf of the Congregation for the Clergy, whose Pro-Prefect at the time was Cardinal Castrillón, (1996–2006). At this time, the Congregation for the Clergy dealt with issues of clergy sexual abuse of children.[67]

The canonical reservations about 'mandatory reporting' were the requirements to observe pontifical secrecy, and the requirement to adopt 'pastoral' methods of dealing with sex abusing priests.

The 'moral reservations' referred to must relate to what Cardinal Castrillón said in his meeting in 1998 with the Irish bishops that bishops had to be 'fathers' to their priests and not 'policemen', and in his letter to Bishop Pican in September 2001 that there was a 'sacramental' relationship between a bishop and his priests.

The latter part of the letter contains an implied threat, described by the *Murphy Dublin Report* as follows:

---

66. http://graphics8.nytimes.com/packages/pdf/world/Ireland-Catholic-Abuse. pdf?ref=europe, http://www.nytimes.com/2011/01/19/world/europe/19vatican. html?_r=0 (Accessed 9 July 2013).
67. Nicholas Cafardi, 'The Scandal of Secrecy: Canon Law and the Sexual-abuse Crisis', in *Commonweal*, 21 July 2010, http://commonwealmagazine.org/ scandal-secrecy (Accessed 27 May 2013).

> Monsignor Dolan's view was that this placed the bishops
> in an invidious position because, if they did seek to
> operate the Framework Document, then any priest
> against whom disciplinary or penal measures were
> taken had a right of appeal to Rome and was most likely
> to succeed. The bishops, on the other hand, were not in
> a position to strengthen the Framework Document by
> enacting it into law. It was his view that the only way a
> bishop could properly proceed canonically was with the
> accused priest's co-operation.[68]

This was no empty threat. The experience of appeals to Rome
suggested that the Vatican appeal courts were more concerned with
procedural niceties than the substance of the matter.[69]

1998/1999 Cardinal Castrillón Meets with the Irish Bishops

In 1998, according to the Irish Television program, *Would You Believe*,
'*Unspeakable Crimes*', Cardinal Castrillón met with the Irish bishops
at Sligo in Ireland.[70] The Archbishop of Dublin, Cardinal Desmond
Connell insisted on the right to report clergy sexual abusers to the
police. But Cardinal Castrillón disagreed saying that it was Vatican
policy to defend the rights of the accused priest. Bishop Michael Smith
was interviewed on the program, and he said that the Colombian
cardinal and the officials in his congregation did not seem to take on
board the fact that there was criminality involved, and they regarded
it as a moral issue between the individual priest and bishop. At a later
meeting to discuss the letter, one of the Irish bishops made a note:

> We have received a mandate from the Congregation for
> the Clergy asking us to conceal the reported crimes of a
> priest.[71]

And indeed they had been so asked.

---

68. http://www.justice.ie/en/JELR/DACOI%20Fr%20Jovito%20published.pdf/Files/
    DACOI%20Fr%20Jovito%20published.pdf, paragraph 7.14 (Accessed 7 May
    2013).
69. Cafardi, *Before Dallas,* 38.
70. 17 January 2011, http://www.rte.ie/tv/wouldyoubelieve/unspeakablecrimes.html
    (Accessed January 2011, but since archived by RTE).
71. http://www.cinews.ie/article.php?artid=8053 (Accessed 16 July 2013).

According to the program at a later meeting in Rome in 1999 between Castrillón and the Irish bishops, the meeting is reported to have ended in 'uproar' as Castrillón told the Irish bishops to be 'fathers to your priests, not policemen'.

Cardinal Connell Breaches Pontifical Secrecy

Cardinal Desmond Connell of Dublin came in for his fair share of criticism at the Murphy Commission but he did earn a few brownie points for trying to use the canonical processes on two occasions to dismiss clergy child sexual abusers. He acted against the advice of one of the most powerful canonists in the Archdiocese, Monsignor Sheehy, who considered that the penal aspects of canon law should rarely be invoked.[72]

Monsignor Sheehy was right. That is what *Crimen Sollicitationis* and the *1983 Code of Canon Law* required. Dismissing a priest was an absolute last resort when there was no hope of reforming him. One of the priests involved in these trials was Fr Tony Walsh, the Elvis impersonator and serial paedophile. As we have seen, even these efforts were frustrated by the Vatican, and required Connell to make a direct personal appeal to the pope.

Cardinal Connell is not a canon lawyer, and he freely admitted that he left all such matters to others so qualified.[73] But he knew enough about canon law to be concerned about the secrecy imposed. In late 1995, the year before the *Framework Document* was adopted by the Irish Catholic Bishops Conference, he handed over to the police the names of seventeen priests, against whom complaints were made. It wasn't a complete disclosure as the Murphy Commission found there were twenty-eight.[74] Nevertheless, it was a start. The Murphy Commission also found that in 2002, he handed over some diocesan files, but he was concerned that in doing so, he was breaching his ordination oath.[75] He tried to explain that on the basis of some special

---

72. http://www.justice.ie/en/JELR/DACOI%20Part%201.pdf/Files/DACOI%20 Part%201.pdf, , paragraph 1.26 (Accessed 16 July 2013).

73. http://www.justice.ie/en/JELR/DACOI%20Part%201.pdf/Files/DACOI%20 Part%201.pdf , paragraph 4.21.

74. *Ibid,* paragraph 5.15(Accessed 16 July 2013).

75. *Ibid,* paragraph 3.46.

confidentiality between priest and bishop, but his ordination oath said nothing about that. It required him to follow canon law which imposed pontifical secrecy on allegations of sexual abuse by priests.[76]

Handing over any files in 2002 took some courage on Cardinal Connell's part because he had been reminded by Cardinal Castrillón in the Storero letter of 1997, and at two meetings one in Sligo, Ireland in 1998 and again in 1999 in Rome that giving this information to the police breached canon law. In addition, around this time, there was a barrage of strong statements from his fellow Cardinals in 2001/2002 that it was not the bishop's role to report clergy sexual abusers to the police—and in the case of two Cardinals, one of them the Prefect of the Congregation for Clergy, Castrillón, saying that bishops should be prepared to go to jail rather than do that.

Cardinal Connell served as a member of the Congregation for the Doctrine of the Faith for twelve years from 1992 to 2004 under Cardinal Ratzinger, and it was during those years that he also had his disagreements with Cardinal Castrillón from the Congregation for the Clergy about reporting. He was unsuccessful in convincing the Vatican that bishops should be able to report all allegations of sexual abuse to the police.

2005: The *Our Children, Our Church* Guidelines on Child Abuse

In 2005, the Irish Bishops' Conference adopted a new set of guidelines called *Our Children, Our Church 2005*. This document also provided for all allegations of child abuse to be taken to the civil authorities, including historic abuse.[77] The *Murphy Dublin Report* said that it did not receive a *recognitio* by the Vatican, and was left 'without legal status under canon law'.[78] This was not surprising. The only inference that can be drawn from the behaviour of the Vatican in its dealings with the protocols from the United States, Great Britain, Australia and Ireland, is that it was only prepared to countenance the minimum reporting to the civil authorities that would keep bishops out of jail. This is also the standard set in the Levada Guidelines.

---

76. Canon 833 http://www.vatican.va/roman_curia/congregations/cfaith/documents/rc_con_cfaith_doc_1998_professio-fidei_en.html (Accessed 16 July 2013).
77. *Cloyne Report*, paragraph 4.50–4.55, http://www.justice.ie/en/JELR/Cloyne_Rpt.pdf/Files/Cloyne_Rpt.pdf (Accessed 9 February 2013).
78. http://www.justice.ie/en/JELR/DACOI%20Part%201.pdf/Files/DACOI%20Part%201.pdf paragraph 3.42 (Accessed 16 July 2013).

The lack of Vatican approval of these protocols means that they are seriously compromised. Bishops were not obliged to obey, and some of the Irish bishops may have refused to do so, on the grounds that Monsignor Dooley outlined in 2002, that it was in breach of canon law.[79]

2009: The *Safeguarding Children* Document

In 2009, a new set of guidelines was drawn up, *Safeguarding Children, Standards and Guidance Document for the Catholic Church in Ireland*, commissioned and produced in February 2009 by the National Board for Safeguarding Children in the Church. All allegations were to be referred to the Irish Police or the Health Board, irrespective of any legal requirement to do so.[80]

A Vatican press release of 31 May 2010 referred to the 'norms' contained in this document, which would tend to suggest that it had been approved by the Vatican.[81] Likewise the *Summary of Findings of the Apostolic Visitation* also referred to these norms'.[82] But there is no indication on the Vatican website that the document had ever been approved, so as to become part of the local canon law pursuant to Canon 455. At most, Ireland had the benefit of a dispensation from pontifical secrecy in an instruction from the Congregation for the Doctrine of the Faith, referred to in the Vatican's 2010 Guide to 'lay persons and non-canonists' of 12 April 2010, to comply with any local laws requiring reporting.

On 12 November 2010, the Vatican sent out a press release at the beginning of the 'Apostolic Visit to Ireland', which was effectively a private Vatican investigation of the situation in Ireland. If any new or old allegations of abuse were to arise during the course of that investigation, the release said that Church authorities had to

---

79. http://www.bishop-accountability.org/news2010/03_04/2010_03_18_
IrishTimes_ViewOf.htm (Accessed 16 July 2013).

80. http://www.catholicbishops.ie/wp-content/uploads/images/stories/cco_
publications/Safeguarding/safeguarding_children_standards.pdf, 55, 60, 62, 77,
84 and 87 (Accessed 16 October 2013).

81. http://www.vatican.va/resources/resources_comunicato-irlanda-2010_en.html.
(Accessed 9 February 2013).

82. http://www.vatican.va/resources/resources_sintesi_20120320_en.html
(Accessed 25 March 2013).

comply with any civil and ecclesiastical laws relating to reporting.[83] At the time this 2010 press release was issued, there were no civil law requirements to report, and the only 'ecclesiastical law' was that of pontifical secrecy and the requirement to report to the Vatican, imposed by the revised *2001 Motu Proprio.*

In 2012, the *Criminal Justice (Withholding of Information on Offences Against Children and Vulnerable Persons) Act* 2012 was passed, making it an offence not to report information about the exploitation of 'vulnerable persons'.[84] Once that Act was passed, the Vatican dispensation from pontifical secrecy applied, (subject to the qualification about canonical trials mentioned by Fr Lombardi) and bishops were able to report those matters without breaching canon law.

Great Britain
2001 Lord Nolan's Report to the British Bishops

In September 2000 the British bishops engaged Lord Nolan, a recently retired member of the House of Lords, to prepare two reports.[85] The effect of the reports was to recommend openness and reporting to the police, and prosecution of offenders.[86]

Lord Nolan said that if any difficulties with canon law over his recommendations emerged, he trusted that Church authorities would deal with them "responsively".[87] That turned out to be wishful thinking. The Catholic Bishops Conference of England and Wales adopted Lord Nolan's Final Report.[88]

Cardinal Levada in an interview in the *New York Times* 26 March 2010, in speaking about the Dallas Charter said that a number of other

---

83. http://www.vatican.va/resources/resources_irlanda-inizio-visita-2010_en.html (Accessed 16 October 2013).

84. http://www.irishstatutebook.ie/2012/en/act/pub/0024/print.html (Accessed 19 May 2013).

85. http://www.cathcom.org/mysharedaccounts/cumberlege/finalnolan2.htm (Accessed 16 July 2013).

86. Summarised by Lord Rees-Mogg in *The Times*, on 30 March 2010 http://www.timesonline.co.uk/tol/comment/columnists/william_rees_mogg/article7079471.ec (Accessed August 2012).

87. http://www.cathcom.org/mysharedaccounts/cumberlege/finalnolan2.htm, paragraph 2.3.1(Accessed 16 July 2013).

88. http://www.cathcom.org/mysharedaccounts/cumberlege/report/downloads/CathCom_Cumberlege2.pdf, paragraph 2.2(Accessed 16 July 2013).

countries had adopted similar protocols, including Great Britain.[89] What he did not say in that interview is that while the revised Dallas Charter received the *recognitio* of the Vatican on 8 December 2002 to become the particular canon law for the United States, the adoption of the Nolan Report by the Catholic Bishops Conference of England and Wales in November 2001 had not been given a *recognitio* by the Vatican, at least not by 2007.[90] There still seems to be no sign of it on the Vatican website.

The Cumberlege Commission in 2007 reviewed the Nolan Report in which it criticised the lack of implementation of the Report, and noting that there were conflicts with canon law. One of its recommendations was for a *recognitio* by the Vatican, similar to what had occurred after the Dallas Charter for the United States.[91] The importance of the *recognitio* is that once approval had been given to the proposals for reporting clergy sex crimes to the police, there was no longer any conflict between canon and civil law. Great Britain, however, has the same problem that all Australian states other than New South Wales have. Misprision of felony was abolished in 1967, and it has no mandatory reporting requirements, even for children at risk.[92]

It was useless having a local proposal for reporting which conflicted with canon law, and which had not been approved as an exception by Rome, because then each bishop was placed in a position of conflict as to whether or not they should report. The Commission made exactly the same point that Professor Parkinson did about *Towards Healing*, a disciplinary system and protocol system for protecting children that does not have the support of canon law, is seriously defective.

89. http://www.vatican.va/resources/resources_card-levada2010_en.html (Accessed 18 February 2013).
90. http://www.rcdow.org.uk/cardinal/default.asp?content_ref=259 (Accessed 18 February 2013) See also Cardinal Levada's speech to the 'Symposium on Sex Abuse at the Pontifical Gregorian University' on 6 February 2012. The only *recognitio* that he mentions is that of the United States.
91. http://www.cathcom.org/mysharedaccounts/cumberlege/report/downloads/CathCom_Cumberlege2.pdf (Accessed 18 February 2013).
92. *Criminal Law Act* 1967. *A v Hayden (ASIS case)* [1984] HCA 67; (1984) 156 CLR 532 (6 November 1984) per Mason J paragraph 7, http://www.guardian.co.uk/society/2012/nov/09/uk-ireland-report-child-abuse (Accessed 15 July 2013) http://www.change.org/en-GB/petitions/educationgovuk-introduce-law-requiring-adults-working-with-children-to-report-alleged-abuse-mandatenow (Accessed 21 August 2013).

The United States

1987–2002: The United States Bishops' Attempts to Change Canon Law

In the late 1980s when the first court cases commenced in the United States against priests, bishops had two specific problems in dealing with the sexual abuse of children: the prohibition on reporting to the police and Pope John Paul II's changes to canon law that made it virtually impossible to dismiss a priest. Nicholas Cafardi has written:

> It is truly ironic that, just as the clergy child sexual crisis began to mushroom in the mid-1980, the bishops of the United States (and throughout the world for that matter) lost three highly effective ways to deal with priests who had sexually abused children.[93]

A long series of negotiations continued with the Vatican to try and improve the situation, but without any success. Cardinal Bernardin said that while the Curia officials listened, they did not appreciate fully the situation.[94]

These words were echoed by Cardinal Pell at the *Victorian Parliamentary Inquiry* when describing his meetings in Rome during the 1990s as a member of the Congregation for the Doctrine of the Faith that the Congregation for the Clergy 'did not get it'.[95] But it was not just the Congregation for the Clergy. The view expressed by the Vatican through Archbishop Geraldo Agnello, Secretary for the Congregation for Divine Worship (the Congregation then dealing with voluntary laicisation) in 1993 was that the Vatican's main concern was that a simplification of the laicisation process 'might not adequately protect the rights of priests and the value of the sacrament of ordination'[96]

The American bishops then looked for other means in the *Code of Canon Law* to remove clergy sexual abusers by using Canon

---

93. Cafardi, *Before Dallas*, 63.
94. *Ibid*, 66.
95. http://www.parliament.vic.gov.au/images/stories/committees/fcdc/inquiries/57th/Child_Abuse_Inquiry/Transcripts/Catholic_Archdiocese_of_Sydney_27-May-13.pdf, 21.8 (Accessed 16 July 2013).
96. Cafardi, *Before Dallas*, 67.

1740 which allowed the removal of parish priests if their ministry had become 'harmful' and 'ineffective', but the Vatican rejected that remedy as well, as being 'insufficiently sensitive to the rights of clerics'.[97] Again, we have statements from the Vatican that reflected the extremes of clericalism. The ontological change brought about by ordination was far more important than the ruined lives of children sexually abused by priests. Clericalism had triumphed, and the victims were children.

In 1994, the Vatican finally agreed to some of the American requests. They agreed to increase the age for sexual abuse from sixteen to eighteen years, but that provision was not to be retrospective.[98] Many of the claims of sexual abuse against priests involved boys and girls between the ages of sixteen and eighteen. The lack of retrospectivity meant that these priests could not be dismissed.[99] The Vatican also agreed to extend the limitation period, but it was not to be in all cases, so that some canonical crimes that had been extinguished stayed extinguished.[100] The former Vatican chief prosecutor, Monsignor Charles Scicluna in 2006 wondered why the Church had not returned to the situation before 1983 when there was no limitation period at all.[101]

The extraordinary thing about these long drawn out negotiations was that the American bishops were simply asking for the right to go back to the situation that existed before the introduction of the *1983 Code of Canon Law*, which had effectively emasculated any possibility of dealing effectively with clergy sexual abusers, either through canonical trials or through suspensions.

And even with the extension to the limitation period being granted in 1994, 'pastoral and therapeutic' solutions were still required under

---

97. *Ibid*, 69, quoting John P Beal in 'At the Cross Roads of Two Laws: Some Reflections on the Influence of Secular Law on the Church's Response to Clergy Sex Abuse in the United States', in *Louvain Studie,s* 25 (2000).

98. Rescript of the Secretariat of State 24 April 1994 Prot. 346.053.

99. Cafardi, *Before Dallas*, 73.

100. Secretary of State, April 25 1994, rescript, protocol No 346.053, quoted in Cafadi, *Before Dallas,* at 74, footnote 94..

101. Charles Scicluna 'The Procedure and Praxis of the Congregation for the Doctrine of the Faith regarding *Graviora Delicta*' (2006): 'Experience has shown that a term of ten years is inadequate for these types of cases and that it would be desirable to return to the former system in which these delicts were not subject to prescription at all.' http://www.vatican.va/resources/resources_mons-scicluna-graviora-delicta_en.html (Accessed 14 June 2013).

Canon 1341 before any penal provisions could be invoked. The Vatican 'Catch 22' defence was still available, and the Vatican refused to reform the appeals process which provided that the sentence of the diocesan court was suspended pending the appeal to Rome. And, there was still no provision for suspending a priest pending the outcome of a preliminary inquiry. It was not surprising that, even after the extension of the limitation period in 1994, there were still very few canonical trials.[102]

The American bishops then collectively tried to introduce a uniform protocol, requiring reporting of all complaints to the police. One of the difficulties was that the United States Catholic Bishops Conference had no authority under canon law to bind any particular bishop, unless it became part of canon law through a *recognitio* by the Vatican.[103] The Vatican was soon bludgeoned into reality by the multi-million dollar law suits being brought by victims against the Church.

The American Bishops' 'Difficult Sales Job'

On April 23–24, 2002 an extraordinary meeting was held in the Vatican between the Roman Curia cardinals and the leadership of the United States Catholic Conference of Bishops to discuss the sexual abuse crisis in that country.[104] Not all American bishops shared Cardinal Castrillón's view that reporting clergy sexual abusers to the police meant that they were acting like policemen or FBI agents. Cardinal James Stafford said that it was not a matter of a bishop acting as a policeman, but of being a pastor of everyone, and that included the victims of sexual abuse. Yet Stafford acknowledged that if the US bishops adopted a strong policy on cooperation with the police, they 'may face a difficult sales job in Rome'. [105]

The difficulty of that 'sales job' soon became apparent after the Dallas Conference of the American Bishops, two months later. It seems that they were facing the same difficulties as the Irish had in 1996 in trying to get approval for reporting clergy child sex crimes to

---

102. Cafardi, *Before Dallas*, 74.
103. Canon 455§4.
104. John L Allen, *All the Popes Men*, 66.
105. John L Allen, *National Catholic Reporter*, 31 May 2002, http://www.natcath.org/crisis/053102h.htm (Accessed 18 February 2013).

the civil authorities. The Australian bishops had abandoned the idea of getting approval and tried to devise ways of evading canon law.

The Dallas Conference of American Bishops and Cardinal Re's Letter

At the Dallas Conference of American bishops held in June 2002, the bishops wanted to have the right to report clergy sexual abuse crimes to the civil authorities, irrespective of whether or not the law required it, and submitted a proposal to Rome.[106] There were a number of other proposals, such as a zero tolerance approach to sexual abuse, suspension of priests pending investigation, the role and powers of lay review boards, and due process for accused priests that potentially involved conflicts with the *1983 Code of Canon Law*.[107] But the right to report to the civil authorities involved a conflict with pontifical secrecy provisions of the *2001 Motu Proprio*.

Cardinal Re, then Prefect of the Congregation for Bishops sent them a letter on 14 October 2002. This acknowledged the efforts of the American bishops to protect minors, but said:

---

106. http://old.usccb.org/ocyp/charter.pdf, Article 4 (Accessed 17 August 2013). The original Dallas Charter provided in Article 4: 'Dioceses/eparchies are to report an allegation of sexual abuse of a person who is a minor to the public authorities. Dioceses/eparchies are to comply with all applicable civil laws with respect to the reporting of allegations of sexual abuse of minors to civil authorities and cooperate in their investigation in accord with the law of the jurisdiction in question. Dioceses/eparchies are to cooperate with public authorities about reporting cases even when the person is no longer a minor. In every instance, dioceses/eparchies are to advise victims of their right to make a report to public authorities and support this right.' The Charter was revised and approved by the Vatican on 1 January 2006. See also Thomas Green *Critique of the Dallas Charter*, http://natcath.org/NCR_Online/documents/Greencritique. htm (Accessed 21 July 2013). Article 4, paragraph B. B. 'Is reporting in cases where no minor is involved civilly necessary? This is a civil law question about which I am unsure. However, if there is no civil obligation to report, why should we do so as long as we proceed canonically where appropriate?' Green was querying the requirement in the original proposals to report if there is no civil law requirement to do so where the victim is now an adult. The Vatican ultimately adopted Green's argument.

107. Thomas Green, *Critique of the Dallas Charter*, http://natcath.org/NCR_Online/ documents/Greencritique.htm (Accessed 21 July 2013), John L Allen, *All the Popes Men*, 69-70%

> . . . the 'Norms' and 'Charter' contain provisions
> which in some aspects are difficult to reconcile with
> the universal law of the Church . . . Questions also
> remain concerning the concrete manner in which the
> procedures outlined in the 'Norms' and 'Charter' are
> to be applied in conjunction with the requirements
> of the Code of Canon Law **and the *Motu proprio***
> ***Sacramentorum sanctitatis tutela*** (AAS 93, 2001,
> 787)[108] (my emphasis).

Since Cardinal Re specifically mentioned the difficulty of reconciling the proposals with the *2001 Motu Proprio*, he must have had in mind its requirements for pontifical secrecy and the proposal to allow reporting to the civil authorities. All of the other potential conflicts with the 'universal law of the Church' involved the *1983 Code of Canon Law*. That he was thinking about pontifical secrecy was confirmed by the compromise that was reached in Rome to the effect that an exception would only be made for where the local law required reporting.

October 2002 American Delegation of Bishops Goes to the Vatican

On 26 March 2010, Cardinal Levada, who later became the Prefect of the Congregation for the Doctrine of the Faith from 2005 to 2012 under Pope Benedict XVI, gave an interview with the *New York Times* in which he described being part of a delegation to see Cardinal Ratzinger after the receipt of the letter from Cardinal Re.[109] He said that because the norms developed by the 2002 Dallas Charter 'intersected with existing canon law, they required approval before

---

108. http://www.boston.com/globe/spotlight/abuse/documents/vatican_response_101802.htm (Accessed 16 July 2013), http://www.vatican.va/resources/resources_card-levada2010_en.html (Accessed 16 July 2013).
109. http://www.vatican.va/resources/resources_card-levada2010_en.html (Accessed 3 July 2013). John L Allen, *All the Popes Men* at 70%, John L Allen says that those representing the Vatican were Herranz, Bertone, Castrillón and Monterisi. The US delegation included Cardinal George, Archbishops Levada and Bishops Doran and Lori.

being implemented as particular law for our country'. He said that Cardinal Ratzinger and his canonical experts gave them a 'sympathetic understanding' of the problems the American bishops faced. One problem was the fact that some American states had misprision of felony laws requiring reporting of clergy sex crimes to the civil authorities, contrary to the requirements of pontifical secrecy.

The 'parallel' systems of canon and civil law were not so parallel after all. One does not have to be a fly on the wall to know what finally convinced Cardinals Ratzinger and Archbishop Bertone: American cardinals and bishops would be going to jail unless they were allowed to report where the law required it. But the Vatican was only prepared to allow the minimum reporting to keep bishops out of jail, and the American bishops accepted the compromise.

The Dallas proposals had originally provided for the priest to go on leave as soon as the allegation was made, but this was also rejected by the Vatican, which insisted on this only applying after the preliminary investigation.[110] The bishops still did not have the right to stand down a priest once the allegation had been made, as they had under the *1917 Code of Canon Law*.

December 2002: Reporting to Police Approved for the United States

The new norms were approved by the Vatican on 8 December 2002, with limited rights to report to the civil authorities. They became a particular law for the United States only:

> 11. The diocese/eparchy **will comply with all applicable civil laws with respect to the reporting of allegations of sexual abuse of minors to civil authorities** and will cooperate in their investigation. In every instance, the diocese/eparchy will advise and support a person's right to make a report to public authorities[111] (my emphasis).

---

110. http://www.vatican.va/roman_curia/congregations/cbishops/documents/rc_con_cbishops_doc_20021216_recognitio-usa_en.html#top   paragraph 6 (Accessed 17 July 2013) John L Allen, *All the Popes Men,* at 70%, point 3, *Recognitio*, Article 6.

111. http://www.vatican.va/roman_curia/congregations/cbishops/documents/rc_

If the Church wanted to avoid bishops going to jail, it had no choice but to cooperate where subpoenas had been issued, or where civil laws required reporting. But if there were no laws requiring reporting, and the police did not have any information about the crimes, there was no obligation to report anything, and pontifical secrecy forbade it. If the police did not know about the allegations, there would be no search warrants, no subpoenas and no trials in the civil courts. The privilege of clergy would continue where possible.

con_cbishops_doc_20021216_recognitio-usa_en.html (Accessed 9 February 2013). The norms were revised in 2005, but this clause remains the same: http:// old.usccb.org/ocyp/2005EssentialNormsFinalHighlighted.pdf (Accessed 30 September 2013). The Canadian Protocol, 'From Pain to Hope', has a similar clause requiring reporting only where the civil law requires it: http://www.cccb. ca/site/images/stories/pdf/orientations-diocesan_protocols.pdf, paragraph 2.3 (Accessed 30 September 2013).

18

The Defence of the Vatican and Pope Benedict XVI

In 2005, Cardinal Josef Ratzinger who was in charge of administering *Crimen Sollicitationis* from 1981 to 1983, and was responsible for drawing up the *2001 Motu Proprio*, was elected Pope, and became Benedict XVI. Not long after his election, allegations started to appear in the media, such as the BBC Panorama Program, *Sex Crimes and the Vatican* of 1 October 2006, that Benedict was directly involved in the cover up of clergy sexual abuse through his position as Prefect of the Congregation for the Doctrine of the Faith. A major campaign started to defend the Pope, the Vatican and canon law.

The first tactic in the campaign was to assert that *Crimen Sollicitationis* only dealt with soliciting sex in the confessional, and did not deal with sexual abuse of children.

The second was to say that *Crimen Sollicitationis* and the *1983 Code of Canon Law* were never intended to stop reporting to the civil authorities, and that pontifical secrecy applied only to the Church's 'internal procedures'.

The third tactic was to put all the blame on the bishops, and to deflect it away from the six popes who, from 1922, introduced and reinforced the policy of cover up.

Crimen Sollicitationis Did Not Deal with Clergy Sexual Abuse of Minors

In 2006, the BBC Panorama Program, *Sex Crimes and the Vatican* alleged that Pope Benedict XVI was in charge of enforcing secrecy about sex crimes of clergy on children, as laid down in *Crimen Sollicitationis*.[1] The program alleged that the cover up was not just a

---

1. http://vimeo.com/654677 (Accessed 12 September 2013).

case of isolated instances, sadly mishandled, but a Vatican policy of cover up.

On 2 October, 2006, the British Catholic News Agency announced that the Catholic Bishops Conference of England and Wales intended making a formal protest to the BBC about the program. According to Archbishop Nichols of Birmingham, *Crimen Sollicitationis* was 'not directly concerned with child abuse at all, but with the misuse of the confessional'. It described the documentary as an 'unwarranted, prejudiced attack on a revered world religious leader', and that it misrepresented the two documents and 'uses them misleadingly to connect the horrors of child abuse to the person of the pope'.[2]

The statement of Archbishop Nichols that *Crimen Sollicitationis* 'was not directly concerned with child abuse at all' is contradicted by the 2010 revised historical introduction to the Norms of the *2001 Motu Proprio* itself, which said:

> The norms concerning the '*crimen pessimum*' also extended to the heinous crime of sexual abuse of prepubescent children and to bestiality.[3]

In April 2008, the BBC dismissed the complaint finding:

> The programme had accurately reported the effect of the 1962 and 2001 documents, in that the documents ensured that allegations of child sexual abuse by priests were bound by secrecy within the Catholic Church.[4]

Canon Law Did Not Prevent Reporting to the Police

As we have seen, canon law is different to the common law, in that the canonical courts do not determine the meaning of a text, but the Vatican itself does, through the pope, the Pontifical Council for the Interpretation of Legislative Texts and the Vatican Congregations.

---

2. http://www.catholicnewsagency.com/news/uk_bishops_angered_by_bbc_attack_on_pope/ (Accessed 16 July 2013).
3. http://www.vatican.va/resources/resources_introd-storica_en.html (Accessed 5 August 2013).
4. http://www.bbc.co.uk/bbctrust/assets/files/pdf/appeals/esc_bulletins/2008/feb.txt (Accessed 16 July 2013).

Further clarification can come from the opinions of canon law scholars, which are the equivalent of non-binding court decisions for lawyers in the common law system.[5] The highest authorities in the Church, Cardinals Castrillón and Bertone, and two of the Vatican's most senior canon lawyers, Archbishop Herranz, and Fr Gianfranco Ghirlanda SJ indicated either directly or indirectly that bishops were prohibited from reporting to the police the information they received through their investigations under canon law.

Despite these statements, a series of Church spokesmen from about 2007 onwards started to assert that the secrecy provisions of canon law applied only to the Church's 'internal procedures' and were not intended to impede any police investigation of breaches of the civil law.

On 7 December 2009, soon after the publication of the *Murphy Dublin Report*, a prominent Irish priest, Fr Sean McDonagh wrote a letter to the Irish Times, commenting on calls for some Irish bishops to resign. He said that the *2001 Motu Proprio* had encouraged bishops to commit criminal offences by not reporting clergy crimes to the police, and, perhaps in a moment of prescience, wondered if Pope Benedict should also resign.[6] The former Prime Minister of Ireland, Garrett Fitzgerald had also stated that the Irish bishops considered that the secrecy provisions prevented them from going to the police.[7] *The Murphy Dublin Report* had found that the obligation of secrecy/confidentiality for participants in the canonical process could undoubtedly inhibit reporting sexual abuse to the civil authorities.[8]

On 10 December 2009, the Irish Catholic Bishops Conference, through its spokesman, Martin Long of the Catholic Communications

5. Edward Peters, 'Lest Amateurs Argue Canon Law: A reply to Patrick Gordon's brief against Bp Thomas Daily', in *Angelicum* 83 (2006): 121–142.http://www.canonlaw.info/a_gordon.htm (Accessed 3 July 2013), between footnotes 34 and 35..

6. http://www.alliancesupport.org/news/archives/003257.html (Accessed 16 July 2013).

7. http://www.irishtimes.com/newspaper/letters/2009/1222/1224261109324.html (Accessed January 2013). Martin Long, letter to the *Irish Times* 10 December 2009 http://www.irishtimes.com/newspaper/letters/2009/1210/1224260419632.html (Accessed January 2013).

8. *Murphy Dublin Report* Part 1 http://www.justice.ie/en/JELR/DACOI%20Part%201.pdf/Files/DACOI%20Part%201.pdf paragraph 4.82 (Accessed 16 July 2013).

Centre in Ireland, wrote to the *Irish Times*, saying that the secrecy provisions of canon law only applied to the 'internal disciplinary procedures' of the Church, and were not intended to frustrate or undermine any civil investigation or prosecution.[9]

On 20 March 2010, Monsignor Scicluna, the Vatican prosecutor for the Congregation for the Doctrine of the Faith in an interview with the British Catholic magazine, *The Tablet*, said:

> The norms on sexual abuse were never understood as a ban on denouncing [the crimes] to the civil authorities.[10]

On 25 March 2010, Fr Federico Lombardi SJ, the Vatican spokesman, issued a statement on the notorious Fr Lawrence Murphy who sexually assaulted some 200 deaf mute boys in the United States. In the course of discussing this he said,

> . . . Indeed, contrary to some statements that have circulated in the press, neither *Crimen* nor the *Code of Canon Law* ever prohibited the reporting of child abuse to law enforcement authorities.[11]

On 25 June, 2010, according to the *National Catholic Reporter*, the canon lawyer, Fr John P Beal called the secrecy requirements that stop participants talking about the proceedings after the case is over, a 'stupid law'. Then he said.

> Pontifical secrecy does not prevent Catholic officials from reporting sexual abuse to civil authorities, Beal said. It applies only to internal church proceedings.[12]

Beal has previously stated in his *Studia Canonica* article that pontifical secrecy prevented such officials revealing 'everything that they learned as part of the penal process' and which they did not discover by other

9. Martin Long, letter to the *Irish Times* 10 December 2009 http://www.irishtimes. com/newspaper/letters/2009/1210/1224260419632.html (Accessed January 2013).

10. http://www.thetablet.co.uk/article/14451 (Accessed 30 April 2013).

11. http://www.zenit.org/article-28746?l=english (Accessed 25 June 2013).

12. http://ncronline.org/news/vatican/vatican-secrecy-keeps-victims-accused-dark (Accessed 22 July 2013).

means. He also said that it prevented a bishop from informing anyone that the priest had been found innocent or guilty.[13]

On 15 July 2010, Fr Federico Lombardi explained the 2010 revision of the *2001 Motu Proprio* and he referred to cooperating with the civil authorities as provided for in the Guide for "lay persons and non-canonists". He said that such cooperation had to be done:

> . . . in good time, not during or subsequent to the canonical trial.[14]

Then four days later, on 19 July 2010 he said,

> The revised norms maintain the imposition of 'pontifical secret' on the church's judicial handling of priestly sex abuse and other grave crimes, which means they are dealt with in strict confidentiality.[15]

On 21 July 2010, Nicholas Cafardi, wrote:

> But that's all the secrecy requirement covers: the internal church legal process, not the crime itself. It does not prevent victims, their families, or even church officials from reporting a civil crime to the civil authorities or to the media.[16]

Three out of four of the Church's most respected canon lawyers, plus the Vatican spokesman, Fr Lombardi, and the Irish bishops' spokesman, had confirmed that pontifical secrecy applied to all information obtained in the Church's internal proceedings. The

13. John P Beal: 'The 1962 Instruction *Crimen Sollicitationis*: Caught Red Handed or Handed a Red Herring?', in 41 *Studia Canonica* 199 at 212 and 233. http://www.vatican.va/resources/Beal-article-studia-canonica41-2007-pp.199-236.pdf (Accessed 3 July 2013).

14. http://www.vatican.va/resources/resources_lombardi-nota-norme_en.html (Accessed 21 July 2013).

15. http://www.catholicnews.com/data/stories/cns/1002901.htm (Accessed 6 March 2013) http://en.radiovaticana.va/storico/2010/07/16/vatican%E2%80%99s_revised_rules_on_sexual_abuse_of_children/in2-408723 (Accessed 25 August 2013).

16. Nicholas Cafardi, 'The Scandal of Secrecy: Canon Law and the Sexual-abuse Crisis', in *Commonweal*, 21 July 2010, http://commonwealmagazine.org/scandal-secrecy (Accessed 27 May 2013).

statement of Monsignor Scicluna is ambiguous. Church officials who saw a priest sexually abusing a child were not prevented by pontifical secrecy from going to the police. But those, whose knowledge came from their involvement in the 'internal church legal process', could not report that to the police, or indeed to anyone. The vast bulk of information that the Church had about the sex crimes of its priests against children was obtained through 'the internal church legal process': its preliminary inquiries under Canon 1717 and any subsequent judicial or administrative trial.[17]

And as to suggestions that it was not the intention of the Vatican to frustrate or undermine any civil investigation or prosecution, there would be no such investigation or prosecution to be frustrated or undermined if the police did not know about the allegations.

In 2008, Rev Gerald Vosen wrote a book about his account of his canonical trial. Bishop Robert Morlino of Maddison told Catholics to destroy or return the book, because even buying the book could be in breach of the pontifical secret and 'may result in a canonical crime being declared on the individual involved'.[18] That stance by Bishop Molino is in accord with what Frs John P Beal, Federico Lombardi and Professor Cafardi said about pontifical secrecy applying to the canonical investigation and trial.

When information or a document is covered by 'pontifical secrecy', the Church's 'Top Secret' classification, it immediately raises the question: who can or can't be told? Saying that the information only applies to 'internal church proceedings' does not answer that

---

17. In the State of New South Wales where there was an obligation to report all cases of sexual abuse to the police, Church officials found a way around canon law that would have done any tax avoidance accountant proud. The bishop would refer the victim to Fr John Usher, a social worker, for counselling. He or another counsellor would then report the matter to the police. Counselling was not part of the 'internal church process' laid down under canon law. The New South Wales Church officials should be given full credit for their creativeness in finding a way around pontifical secrecy. https://cdn.fairfaxregional.com.au/transcriptsinquiry/Exhibit%20226%20Statutory%20Declaration%20of%20Monsignor%20Usher.pdf (Accessed 10 September 2013). http://www.lawlink.nsw.gov.au/lawlink/Special_Projects/ll_splprojects.nsf/vwFiles/Day_22_-_9_September_2013.pdf/$file/Day_22_-_9_September_2013.pdf, 2361 (Accessed 11 September 2013), Canon 1425.

18. http://ncronline.org/news/vatican/vatican-secrecy-keeps-victims-accused-dark (Accessed 22 July 2013). http://www.catholicculture.org/news/headlines/index.cfm?storyid=1387 (Accessed 22 July 2013).

question. The reports of papal legates, and information obtained officially with regard to the appointment of cardinals, bishops and papal legates are also covered by pontifical secrecy under the decree *Secreta Continere*.[19] They are also 'internal Church' matters, or to use Fr Lombardi's words below, 'exclusively concern the Church'. But that does not mean that they can be communicated to the local shopkeeper, the town gossip or the police.

The appropriate and logical way in any coherent legal system is to allow such reporting by means of an exception, written into the canons, and not stuck away in some public relations pamphlet for 'laypersons and non-canonists', which has no standing in canon law. It was not difficult to draft. All it needed to say was:

> The strictest confidentially (or pontifical secrecy) is to be observed in all things and to all persons except for the purposes of reporting the matter to the civil authorities.

But quite apart from the plain words of canon law, the overwhelming evidence is that the highest officials in the Roman Curia, including Cardinals Castrillón (Congregation for Clergy), Archbishop Bertone (Congregation for the Doctrine of the Faith), and Cardinal Re (Congregation for Bishops), as well as other Cardinals, and Archbishops, bishops and the Church's senior canon Lawyers, interpreted *Crimen Sollicitationis, Secreta Continere* and the *1983 Code of Canon Law*, and the *2001 Motu Proprio* to mean that canon law forbade bishops and anyone involved in the investigation from reporting to the civil authorities—and that is the way, according to all of them, it should be.

Monsignor Scicluna, in that same 2010 interview with *The Tablet* said that since 2001, when all complaints had to be sent to Cardinal Ratzinger's Congregation for the Doctrine of the Faith, 3,000 cases had been dealt with, some of them from countries with misprision of felony type laws.[20] In 2012, the number had risen to more than 4,000.[21] The terms of the *2001 Motu Proprio* were that the matter was

---

19. http://www.tutorgigpedia.com/ed/Pontifical_secret (Accessed 25 June 2013).
20. http://www.thetablet.co.uk/article/14451 (Accessed 30 April 2013).
21. http://blogs.voanews.com/breaking-news/2012/02/08/vatican-prosecutor-denounces-deadly-culture-of-silence/ (Accessed 16 July 2013). On 17 January

to be reported to the Congregation, and it would instruct the bishop how to proceed. In the thirteen years since that was in force, and despite all the allegations of cover up, and statements by the Vatican in 2010 that there should be cooperation with the civil authorities, it has not produced one instance of where it has instructed the bishop to report the matter to the civil authorities, or where it has reported the matter itself. That is not to say it has not, but it is surprising that it has not produced such evidence to support its contention that the Congregation for the Doctrine of the Faith does give that instruction, particularly in the face of international criticism.

In December 2013, the United Nations Committee for the Rights of the Child asked the Vatican to provide data relating to abuse cases it has dealt with. On 5 December 2013, the Vatican initially refused, but on 16 January 2014, Archbishop Tomasi told the Committee that they would 'consider it'.[22] On 17 January, 2014, some figures were produced in a spreadsheet about complaints and dismissals from 2005 on. The information did not contain any information of whether any of these crimes had been reported to the civil authorities.[23]

Long before any allegations of a cover up through canon law of clergy sexual abuse, the Spanish canon Lawyer, Fr Aurelio Yanguas SJ wrote an article in 1946, in which he said that only by taking 'swift, decisive and secret action' before these crimes reach the civil courts that the Church could be spared the humiliation of having priests in the public dock as sex offenders.[24] Perhaps if canon law had provided for 'swift' and 'decisive' action to dismiss clergy sexual abusers from

---

2014, the Vatican released figures for 2011 and 2012. There were an additional 418 new cases of allegations of abuse of minors made in 2012: http://ncronline. org/blogs/ncr-today/anatomy-now-you-see-it-now-you-dont-vatican-denial (Accessed 21 January 2012). The earlier report of 4,000 was made on 12 February 2012, so it is highly likely that the 418 cases was in addition to those.

22. http://www.theglobeandmail.com/news/world/un-rights-committee-grills-vatican-over-its-handling-of-child-sex-abuse/article16370203/ (Accessed 17 January 2014).

23. http://worldnews.nbcnews.com/_news/2014/01/17/22340073-pope-benedict-defrocked-400-priests-in-2-years-report?lite (Accessed 17 January 2014).

24. 'De crimine pessimo et competentia S. Officia relate ad illud', in *Revista Espanola de Derecho Canonico*. 1(1946): 427–439. John P Beal: 'The 1962 Instruction: Crimen Sollicitationis: Caught Red Handed or Handed a Red Herring?', in 41 *Studia Canonica* 199 at 228ff. http://www.vatican.va/resources/Beal-article-studia-canonica41-2007-pp.199-236.pdf (Accessed 16 July 2013).

the priesthood, it might also have prevented many more children from being abused.

Bishops throughout the world understandably interpreted canon law to mean that they could not take these allegations to the police. The *Murphy Dublin Report* stated:

> Most officials in the Archdiocese were, however, greatly exercised by the provisions of canon law which deal with secrecy. It was often spoken of as a reason for not informing the Gardaí about known criminal offences.
>
> A similar 'culture of secrecy' was identified by the Attorney General for Massachusetts in his report on child sexual abuse in the Boston Archdiocese. In the case of that diocese, as in the case of Dublin, secrecy 'protected the institution at the expense of children'.[25]

The *Victorian Parliamentary Inquiry* Report, *Betrayal of Trust,* states that the extent to which the Church in Australia followed the secrecy provisions of canon law is not known. But, it said:

> . . . given the clergy's obligations to be obedient, and the Church's hierarchical structure, the Committee believes it is reasonable to think that Church members followed the instruction. At the very least, the instruction would have been highly influential. This could partly explain why an apparent policy of concealment continued for the next thirty years. Certainly, the instruction would have provided comfort to those who were reluctant to attract public embarrassment or expose fellow religious to criminal prosecution by reporting their offending. It probably also increased perpetrators' sense of freedom to act, and let them assume that their Church would protect them if their crimes were detected.[26]

---

25. *Murphy Dublin Report* Part 1 http://www.justice.ie/en/JELR/DACOI%20 Part%201.pdf/Files/DACOI%20Part%201.pdf, paragraph 1.27, 1.28 (Accessed 16 July 2013).

26. *Betrayal of Trust*, Report of the *Victorian Parliamentary Inquiry*, paragraph 1.3, page 11, https://s3-ap-southeast-2.amazonaws.com/family-and-community-

The pattern was the same, all over the world. History has shown that the Church through secrecy under canon law was very successful in keeping its sex abusing clerics out of the civil courts.

At the *Victorian Parliamentary Inquiry*, Archbishop Hart of Melbourne was questioned about *Crimen Sollicitationis*. He initially said that confidentiality was for the protection of the child, but he was then asked about the obligation to report such crimes to the police. He admitted that there was 'too much' confidentiality in an attempt to preserve the reputation of the Church.[27]

Archbishop Hart was then asked about a predecessor, the late Archbishop Little, Archbishop of Melbourne from 1975 to 1996, who kept no records of allegations against two notorious clergy sexual abusers. He agreed that in failing to keep records, Archbishop Little was covering up 'the foulest crime' but he said that the person ultimately responsible was Little himself. It was then put to him that his 'riding instructions from Rome were strict confidentiality'. Hart admitted that that was what *Crimen Sollicitationis* required, and that he assumed that Little abided by the rules.[28]

Archbishop Little was Archbishop of Melbourne from 1974 to 1996, when he was succeeded by Bishop George Pell. From 1974 until 1983, his instructions from Rome came from *Crimen Sollicitationis*, which, as has been shown, made it virtually impossible to dismiss a sex abusing priest. From 1983 to 1996, his instructions came from the *1983 Code of Canon Law* which made it even harder because of the five year limitation period. And both documents required him to observe pontifical secrecy in relation to the information that he obtained when he conducted inquiries about the allegations. The Church's 'Top Secret' classification through *Secreta Continere* prevented him from revealing that information to the police, even if he wanted to.

Fr Frank Brennan SJ has written that Archbishop Little's cover up of sexual assaults against children was:

development-committee/Inquiry+into+Handling+of+Abuse_Volume+1_ FINAL_web.pdf.

27. http://www.parliament.vic.gov.au/images/stories/committees/fcdc/ inquiries/57th/Child_Abuse_Inquiry/Transcripts/Catholic_Archdiocese_of_ Melbourne_20-May-13.pdf p. 11 (Accessed 18 June 2013).

28. *Ibid*, 12–13 and 35.

. . . devastating news for those of us who thought Frank Little to be a kind, compassionate, considerate, prayerful leader of his flock. And he was…But he was part of an institution infected with clericalism to the extent that he was unable to see how inappropriate it was to place children at risk with known or strongly suspected paedophiles who happened to be priests. And the hierarchical structure was such that the cry of the children and their families was not heard, believed or heeded.[29]

Canon law reflected that clericalism when *Crimen Sollicitationis* was promulgated in 1922 requiring all complaints of sexual abuse to be dealt with in strict confidentiality. The clericalism was entrenched with subsequent decrees in 1962, 2001 and 2010 confirming it. Archbishop Little may well have been a kindly leader of his flock, but he had also sworn an oath to follow canon law, even if it meant breaching civil law, which, until 1981, required such crimes to be reported in the State of Victoria. His first loyalty was to the pope and to canon law under his oath of office. The *Victorian Parliamentary Inquiry* accepted that in acting as he did, he was following Church policy as laid down in canon law.[30]

---

29. Frank Brennan, 'Church-State Issues and the Royal Commission', in *Eureka Street*, 3 September 2013. http://www.eurekastreet.com.au/article.aspx?aeid=38146#. Ui5vaKt-8qQ (Accessed 10 September 2013).
30. *Betrayal of Trust*, Report of the *Victorian Parliamentary Inquiry*, paragraph 7.3.3, 166 https://s3-ap-southeast-2.amazonaws.com/family-and-community-development-committee/Inquiry+into+Handling+of+Abuse_Volume+1_FINAL_web.pdf (Accessed 14 November 2013).

Pope Pius XI

Pope Pius XII

19

Benedict's *Pastoral Letter*: Blame the Bishops

Pope John Paul II died on 2 April 2005, and on 19 April 2005, Cardinal Ratzinger was elected Pope and took the name, Benedict XVI. The allegations against him personally for his role in the cover up started to intensify, and the Vatican spokesmen had their time cut out for them with all the revelations from Ireland. The new Vatican cover up policy—on the role of canon law and the popes—had already started with responses to programs like the *BBC Panorama Program* of 2006. But that was just a television program. Now they had to deal with the findings of judicial inquiries.

On 20 May 2009, the Ryan Report on the abuse of children in Irish institutions was published. On 26 November 2009, the *Murphy Dublin Report* was published. It criticised canon law and the Vatican for facilitating the cover up of child sexual abuse in the Archdiocese of Dublin.[1]

Now the second cover up received Pope Benedict's *imprimatur* ('let it be published') with his *Pastoral Letter* to the People of Ireland. In fact the second cover up had more than an *imprimatur*. Benedict wrote the script himself.

Pope Benedict XVI's *Pastoral Letter* to the People of Ireland

In his *Pastoral Letter* to the people of Ireland of 19 March 2010, Pope Benedict XVI made no mention of his own role, or the role of any other member of the Roman Curia or the role of canon law in the cover up.

---

1. *Murphy Dublin Report*, Part 1 http://www.justice.ie/en/JELR/DACOI%20 Part%201.pdf/Files/DACOI%20Part%201.pdf1.15,1.113 (Conclusion).(Accessed 25 April 2013).

In paragraph 11 addressing the bishops, the pope said,

> It cannot be denied that some of **you and your predecessors failed, at times grievously, to apply the long-established norms of canon law to the crime of child abuse.** Serious mistakes were made in responding to allegations. **I recognize how difficult it was to grasp the extent and complexity of the problem, to obtain reliable information and to make the right decisions in the light of conflicting expert advice. Nevertheless, it must be admitted that grave errors of judgement were made and failures of leadership occurred. All this has seriously undermined your credibility and effectiveness.** I appreciate the efforts you have made to remedy past mistakes and to guarantee that they do not happen again. **Besides fully implementing the norms of canon law in addressing cases of child abuse, continue to cooperate with the civil authorities in their area of competence**[2] (my emphasis).

Rather than having given the *Murphy Dublin Report* 'careful study', and being 'deeply disturbed and distressed by its contents', as the Vatican Press Release of 11 December 2009 solemnly announced, Benedict's response suggested that he had never read it. His failure to acknowledge the real source of the problem was extraordinary.

In 1988, as Prefect of the Congregation for the Doctrine of the Faith, he himself had complained to Cardinal Castillo Lara about the unworkability of the 'long-established norms of canon law', and he wanted a simpler procedure. He was overruled. He must have known of the complaints that the American bishops had raised with the Vatican about the five year limitation period which made it impossible to dismiss even serial sexual abusers. Nothing was done to help the Irish bishops until at least eight years later in 1996 when the Vatican agreed to extend the period for them. The rest of the world had to wait another five years.

---

2. http://www.vatican.va/holy_father/benedict_xvi/letters/2010/documents/hf_ben-xvi_let_20100319_church-ireland_en.html (Accessed 16 July 2013).

He was also aware that *Crimen Sollicitationis* and the *1983 Code of Canon Law* required a 'pastoral approach', that is, to try and cure the priest before taking proceedings to dismiss him. This is exactly what the Irish bishops were doing, and were roundly criticised by the Murphy Commission for doing so. The American canon lawyer, Nicholas Cafardi, after quoting numerous opinions of American canon lawyers about the *1983 Code of Canon Law* says that there was nearly unanimous opinion that canon law regarded it as improper to start penal proceedings to dismiss a priest except as a last resort. Canon law insisted that the first response of a bishop was to try and cure the priest.[3]

Yet, in his letter, Benedict said,

> The programme of renewal proposed by the Second Vatican Council was sometimes misinterpreted and indeed, in the light of the profound social changes that were taking place, it was far from easy to know how best to implement it. **In particular, there was a well-intentioned but misguided tendency to avoid penal approaches to canonically irregular situations** (my emphasis).

Even assuming that all the world's canon lawyers had misunderstood Canon 1341, the problem was that when the bishops tried to subject abusive priests to a judicial trial (the only way they could be dismissed), they were frustrated by the Vatican, and by Cardinal Ratzinger's Congregation for the Doctrine of the Faith, which insisted on this 'pastoral approach'. There could be no starker examples of this approach than the cases of two of the Church's worst serial paedophiles, Fr Tony Walsh and Fr Lawrence Murphy. The Vatican allowed an appeal from Walsh against his dismissal, and Archbishop Bertone effectively told Archbishop Weakland to discontinue a judicial trial against Murphy and to apply the 'pastoral approach'. And Benedict's behaviour in the case of Fr Marcial Maciel is even starker. Bearing in mind that in the canonical system the authority on interpretation is the Vatican itself, the very clear message coming from the Vatican was the avoidance of 'penal approaches to canonically irregular

3. Cafardi, *Before Dallas*, 20–21.

situations'. If there was a 'misguided tendency', Josef Ratzinger, both as Cardinal and as Pope, and his colleagues in the Curia, were doing the misguiding.

Then Benedict blamed the Irish bishops for their

> ... misplaced concern for the reputation of the Church and the avoidance of scandal, resulting in failure to apply existing canonical penalties.

Canon law, for which he as pope is solely responsible, was and is riddled with a misplaced concern for the reputation of the Church, and the avoidance of scandal. The whole idea of pontifical secrecy without an exception for reporting these crimes to the police was designed to avoid scandal.

But worse than that, Cafardi also points out that while Ratzinger in 1988 tried to have a speedier canonical process, in 2001, when he got what he wanted, he and his Congregation for the Doctrine of the Faith were doing the delaying.[4]

The documents produced to a Court in the United States by the Archdiocese of Milwaukee in 2013 provide ample evidence for Cafardi's assertion. Even when the priest convicted of child sexual abuse agreed to be dismissed, the process which should have been a rubber stamping, sometimes took as long as six years.[5]

The Vatican has not always been that slow to respond to requests. In 2007 Cardinal Timothy F Dolan, then the Archbishop of Milwaukee requested permission from the Vatican to move nearly $57 million of Church assets into a cemetery trust fund. He advised the Vatican that it would provide 'an improved protection of these funds of any legal claim and liability'. He obtained approval within six weeks of the request.[6] Dolan has denied that the move was to protect Church assets from litigation commenced by the victims of clergy child

---

4. Nicholas Cafardi *Loose Canons: Ratzinger, Church Law & the Sexual-Abuse Crisis* http://www.commonwealmagazine.org/loose-canons (Accessed 4 June 2013).
5. The case of Fr John A O'Brien http://www.andersonadvocates.com/documents/Key_Milwaukee_Documents/Lacization_All.pdf (Accessed 2 July 2013).
6. http://www.nytimes.com/2013/07/02/us/dolan-sought-vatican-permission-to-shield-assets.html?pagewanted=1&_r=1&hp   and   http://www.andersonadvocates.com/documents/Key_Milwaukee_Documents/Trust_Transfer_2.pdf (Accessed 2 July 2013).

sexual abuse. Whatever the motivation, that was the effect because in January 2014, the Archdiocese of Milwaukee filed for bankruptcy in the face of claims by victims. The transactions suggest that the Vatican is more concerned about looking after the dead than the living.

The canonical system for dealing with clergy sexual abusers, as described by the Murphy Reports, the canon lawyers, Doyle, Cafardi and Beal, and the bishops, Robinson, Gumbleton, Weakland, Michael Smith, Malone, Pell, Hart and others can only be described as a fiasco. That is not to say that the bishops, including the Irish ones, were above criticism. They deserved to be criticised for failing to defy canon law, and failing to report these allegations to the police for investigation.

Benedict's *Pastoral Letter* outlined the Vatican strategy to deal with the furore arising from the findings of the Commissions: blame the bishops and don't mention any of the other telling criticisms in the Murphy report; keep canon law and the popes and their Vatican Curia advisers out of it.

At the very least Benedict could have acknowledged the serious mistake of the secrecy provisions of canon law that prevented reporting these crimes to the police, the standards that canon law had imposed for dismissing priest sexual abusers, and the hopelessness of the 'therapeutic model' that was enshrined in both *Crimen Sollicitationis* and the *1983 Code of Canon Law*.

But this latest application of *bella figura* did not stop with the Vatican and its Pope and Curia. It spread to the whole Church, even to the Irish bishops, and, as we shall see, even to Australia. Bishop Robinson points out that Peter, the first pope was not above criticism and had to answer for his actions.[7]

> Today, on the contrary, the pope is held to be above criticism, is not answerable to the Church and must be protected and defended in every way possible."[8]

And the way in which he was to be protected and defended was for the bishops to take the rap over the cover up, and not to point the finger at the Vatican, the pope or canon law. The documentary *Mea Maxima Culpa* shows the current primate of Ireland, Cardinal Brady, taking the rap. He read out Benedict's *Pastoral Letter* in a Church:

---

7. Acts 11:1–18.
8. Geoffrey Robinson *Confronting Power and Sex in the Catholic Church*, 123.

> To us bishops he (Pope Benedict) says, we must admit
> that great errors of judgment were made and failures of
> leadership occurred, which have seriously undermined
> your credibility and effectiveness. [9]

The RTE Irish television reporter, Mick Peelo says he spoke to one
Irish bishop after the pope's letter:

> He was so angry. He said, 'How dare he blame us. Show
> me where we didn't follow canon law. Canon law was
> the problem'.[10]

And indeed it was, and still is. And this bishop's anger was perfectly
understandable. *The Dublin Murphy Report* has many examples of
the frustration of the Irish bishops who wanted to do something
about clergy sexual abusers, but were thwarted by canon law and the
Vatican.

Archbishop Martin of Dublin Blames the Irish Bishops

Archbishop Martin who replaced Cardinal Connell as Archbishop of
Dublin has been rightly praised for taking an active role in dealing
with clergy sexual abuse, and in handing over the Archdiocese's
files to the Murphy Commission. He has also made some pertinent
criticism of clericalism within the Church.[11] However, in one matter,
he has shown himself to be a company man *par excellence*.

In keeping with the Vatican strategy of blaming the bishops and
deflecting attention away from canon law, the Vatican and the Popes,
Archbishop Martin called for the resignation of several bishops. Some
did so. On 5 September 2011 he excoriated his fellow Irish bishops
for the cover up, and again did not mention canon law or Benedict's
responsibility as an influential member of the Roman Curia and as
pope.[12] He did mention the Storero letter, but said that it did not stop
the Irish bishops from approving the *Framework Document*. No, it
did not, because the *Framework Document* was approved before the

---

9.   At 58.07.
10. At 58.35.
11. http://www.catholicbishops.ie/2013/04/24/address-archbishop-diarmuid-martin-russo-family-lecture/ (Accessed 15 May 2013).
12. http://www.zenit.org/article-33357?l=english (Accessed 16 July 2013).

Storero letter. Besides, the *Framework Document* did not just deal with reporting to the police. It also dealt with education, promotion of awareness, support for alleged victims, and the creation of an advisory panel to include lay experts in the field of child protection to advise the bishop of each diocese.[13] None of those things were forbidden by canon law, and could be applied and improved over the years without needing the consent of the Vatican. But the one thing that was central to the cover up and the continuing attacks on children was the requirement of pontifical secrecy.

Archbishop Martin made no mention of this, made no mention of the terms of *Crimen Sollicitationis*, or even of secrecy imposed by *Secreta Continere* and the *1983 Code of Canon Law*, or of the rejection by the Vatican in January 1997 of the contents of the *Framework Document* on reporting, and the continued barrage of statements from Vatican Curia cardinals and canon lawyers, particularly in 2001 and 2002 stating that it was not the bishop's role to report clergy sexual abusers to the civil authorities. In the face of this barrage, it is hardly surprising that the bishops, who had sworn allegiance to the pope and to canon law, acted accordingly, and did not report the allegations to the police.

Prior to his appointment as Archbishop of Dublin, Martin spent his whole professional life as Vatican bureaucrat and diplomat.[14] It is difficult to believe that he was unaware of the Vatican decrees on pontifical secrecy and the policy statements about reporting to police coming from the Vatican. Pontifical secrecy did, after all, apply to 'reports by papal legates' of which he must have seen and written many.

The Victorian Bishops Blame Their Predecessors

Bishops blaming their predecessors became a kind of blood sport for current and former Victorian bishops at the *Victorian Parliamentary Inquiry*. Ronald Mulkearns was bishop of Ballarat from 1971 to 1997, and he routinely shifted around clergy sexual abusers, Gerald Ridsdale and David Ryan.

---

13. http://thedublinreview.com/ferns-report (Accessed 16 July 2013).
14. http://www.dublindiocese.ie/content/biography-archbishop-diarmuid-martin (Accessed 14 July 2013).

On 29 April 2013, his successor, Bishop Connors said Mulkearns 'effectively facilitated' child sexual abuse, and was 'very naïve'. Connors' successor, Bishop Bird said Mulkearns made 'terrible mistakes'.[15] Bishop Mulkearns was and did all of that, but there is a reason for his acting as he did. Everything he did reeked of *Crimen Sollicitationis*, and the *1983 Code of Canon Law*. And that is exactly what one would have expected of a bishop who was a canon lawyer, had a doctorate in canon law and was one of the founders of the Canon Law Society of Australia and New Zealand.

Bishop Bird said,

> (Mulkearns) believed the accepted opinion at the time that dismissal was not the first option, but that a person might be referred for treatment in the hope they would correct their behaviour. It proved to be a terrible mistake, and I accept that.[16]

It was not just 'the accepted opinion'. It was canon law. Dismissal wasn't the first option because canon law said it was not. Mulkearns' interpretation of Canon 1341 was no different to that of the Vatican. Mulkearn's 'terrible mistake' was also canon law's mistake. It was canon law that 'effectively facilitated child sexual abuse', to quote Bishop Connors, as much as it was Bishop Mulkearns.

On 27 May 2013, Cardinal George Pell, formerly Archbishop of Melbourne and now Archbishop of Sydney gave evidence before the *Victorian Parliamentary Inquiry*. Pell was questioned about how his predecessor from 1974 to 1996, Archbishop Little, had dealt with a priest named Baker. In 1978 a family complained to the Church about Baker's behaviour with their son. Little transferred Baker to another parish where he continued to abuse children. Baker pleaded guilty to sixteen counts of indecent assault and one of gross indecency,

---

15. http://www.parliament.vic.gov.au/images/stories/committees/fcdc/inquiries/57th/Child_Abuse_Inquiry/Transcripts/Catholic_Diocese_of_Ballarat_29-April-13.pdf, 10, 14 (Accessed 20 May 2013), and see the finding in *Betrayal of Trust*, Report of the *Victorian Parliamentary Inquiry* to that effect, paragraph 7.3.6, 174, https://s3-ap-southeast-2.amazonaws.com/family-and-community-development-committee/Inquiry+into+Handling+of+Abuse_Volume+1_FINAL_web.pdf (Accessed 14 November 2013).
16. *Ibid*, 5.

involving eight boys, aged ten to thirteen, over a twenty-year period between 1960 and 1979. He was given four years jail.[17] Pell's explanation for this was that Little 'didn't know how to deal with it'.[18] But he did. Canon law prevented him from going to the police, and it was impossible under canon law to dismiss such a priest.

It was put to Cardinal Pell that the structures of the Church facilitated child sexual abuse. He denied the structures had anything to do with it and said the responsibility was that of the bishops and religious superiors in their 'mistaken decisions' or 'inactivity'. When asked what their responsibility was, he said:

> Some people are inclined to say, 'That's the province of Rome'. No, the responsibility lies with us to deal with these things.[19]

Well, it was Rome's 'province', because the cover up was dictated by canon law. And as the Murphy Commission found, the structures and rules of the Church facilitated the cover up. Canon law was the structure for the cover up, and still is.

Bishop Connors said that when Fr Paul David Ryan was imprisoned, both he and Bishop Mulkearns had visited him in prison to sign a consent petition for dismissal from the priesthood, which Ryan refused to do.[20] This is as absurd as the President of the Law Society visiting a lawyer in prison for stealing his clients' money, begging him to sign a document agreeing to be struck off the Rolls, because the legal procedures to disbarment are so convoluted that it is impossible to strike him off without his consent. It is even more absurd if the lawyer was on the Law Society payroll and agreeing to be struck off would result in a loss of his income.

---

17. http://brokenrites.alphalink.com.au/nletter/page137-baker.html (Accessed 22 June 2013).
18. http://www.parliament.vic.gov.au/images/stories/committees/fcdc/inquiries/57th/Child_Abuse_Inquiry/Transcripts/Catholic_Archdiocese_of_Sydney_27-May-13.pdf, 13.5 (Accessed 22 June 2013).
19. http://www.parliament.vic.gov.au/images/stories/committees/fcdc/inquiries/57th/Child_Abuse_Inquiry/Transcripts/Catholic_Archdiocese_of_Sydney_27-May-13.pdf, 30.6 (Accessed 24 June 2013).
20. http://www.parliament.vic.gov.au/images/stories/committees/fcdc/inquiries/57th/Child_Abuse_Inquiry/Transcripts/Catholic_Diocese_of_Ballarat_29-April-13.pdf, 18 (Accessed 20 May 2013).

Despite the best efforts of the Victorian bishops to blame their predecessors it failed to convince the *Victorian Parliamentary Inquiry*. In referring to the criticisms of both Archbishop Little and Bishop Mulkearns by their successors, it said:

> The Committee found, however, that while this suggests that personal errors of judgement were made, it is unfair to allow the full blame to rest with these individuals, given that they were acting in accordance with a Catholic Church policy.[21]

The situation in the State of Victoria was not unique. It was part of a consistent pattern throughout the whole world, and that could only have been possible within a legal framework laid down by canon law.

---

21. *Betrayal of Trust*, Report of the *Victorian Parliamentary Inquiry*, paragraph 7.3.3, 166 https://s3-ap-southeast-2.amazonaws.com/family-and-community-development-committee/Inquiry+into+Handling+of+Abuse_Volume+1_FINAL_web.pdf (Accessed 14 November 2013).

20

The Cloyne Report In Ireland

The *Cloyne Report* of 13 July 2011 arose from an investigation by the Murphy Commission of clergy sexual abuse and its concealment in the diocese of Cloyne.[1] The publication of the report resulted in an unprecedented breach between the Irish Republic and the Vatican.

The *Cloyne Report* found that Bishop John Magee, formerly a private secretary to three popes, had misled a previous inquiry and his own advisors by creating two different accounts of a meeting with a priest suspected of abusing a child, one for the Vatican and the other for diocesan files. He advised his staff that statements to the Irish police should be 'minimal', and he 'put out an erroneous view' about a report. He held three different versions of one meeting in diocesan files.[2] The *Cloyne Report* found that between 1996 and 2005, the diocese failed to report nine out of fifteen complaints made against priests, which 'very clearly should have been reported', and that while the dioceses ostensibly supported child protection procedures, it was 'never genuinely committed to their implementation'.[3]

The Vatican Withdraws its Nuncio

The *Cloyne Report* referred to the Storero letter criticising the *Framework Document* and its mandatory reporting provisions. The *Cloyne Report* put it fairly diplomatically,

---

1. http://www.justice.ie/en/JELR/Cloyne_Rpt.pdf/Files/Cloyne_Rpt.pdf, paragraph 1.48.
2. http://www.rte.ie/news/2011/0713/cloynetracker.html (Accessed 16 July 2013). http://www.justice.ie/en/JELR/Pages/Cloyne_Rpt (Accessed 16 July 2013) paragraphs 1.48, 9.84-85, 1.40 & 21.27.
3. *Ibid*, paragraph 4.88.

There can be no doubt that this letter greatly strengthened the position of those in the Church in Ireland who did not approve of the *Framework Document* as it effectively cautioned them against its implementation.[4]

The Irish Foreign Minister, Mr Ian Gilmore was not so diplomatic. He called in the Papal Nuncio to Ireland, Archbishop Leanza, and on 14 July 2011 handed him a note which said, amongst other things,

> Frankly, it is unacceptable to the Irish Government that the Vatican intervened to effectively have priests believe they could in conscience evade their responsibilities under Irish law.[5]

The Irish Prime Minister's Speech to Parliament

On 20 July 2011, the Irish Prime Minister, Enda Kenny, a Catholic, was even less diplomatic and made a pointed attack on the Vatican in the Irish Parliament accusing the Vatican of interfering in Irish domestic affairs. The Vatican had refused to cooperate with the Murphy commissions, claiming sovereign immunity.

> It's fair to say that after the Ryan and Murphy Reports Ireland is, perhaps, unshockable when it comes to the abuse of children. But Cloyne has proved to be of a different order. Because for the first time in Ireland, a report into child sexual-abuse exposes an attempt by the Holy See, to frustrate an Inquiry in a sovereign, democratic republic . . . as little as three years ago, not three decades ago.
> And in doing so, the Cloyne Report excavates the dysfunction, disconnection, elitism . . . the narcissism that dominate the culture of the Vatican to this day.
> The rape and torture of children were downplayed or 'managed' to uphold instead, the primacy of the institution, its power, standing and 'reputation'.

---

4. http://www.justice.ie/en/JELR/Cloyne_Rpt.pdf/Files/Cloyne_Rpt.pdf paragraph 4.22 (Accessed 5 April 2013).
5. http://www.vatican.va/resources/resources_risposta-gilmore_20110903_en.html (Accessed 5 April 2013).

And at the end of his speech, Kenny said,

> Cardinal Josef Ratzinger said: 'Standards of conduct appropriate to civil society or the workings of a democracy cannot be purely and simply applied to the Church.'
>
> As the Holy See prepares its considered response to the Cloyne Report, as Taoiseach, I am making it absolutely clear, that when it comes to the protection of the children of this State, the standards of conduct which the Church deems appropriate to itself, cannot and will not, be applied to the workings of democracy and civil society in this republic.
>
> Not purely, or simply or otherwise. Children . . . first.[6]

In addition, the Irish Parliament passed a motion that it

> . . . deplores the Vatican's intervention which contributed to the undermining of the child protection framework and guidelines of the Irish State and the Irish Bishops.

On 25 July 2011, the Vatican recalled the Papal Nuncio 'for consultations'.

This was an extraordinary situation with a blistering attack on the Vatican by the Catholic Prime Minister of a county that was once called by Cardinal Montini, the future Pope Paul VI, 'the most Catholic country in the world'.[7] Then the Papal Nuncio was withdrawn, a formal diplomatic way of saying that the relationship is somewhat unhappy. But what was even more extraordinary was the Vatican's formal response because the most important part of it was simply not true, and other parts misleading.

The Formal Vatican Response to the Irish Minister for Foreign Affairs

On 3 September 2011, the Vatican published its 11,000 word formal response.[8] It mentions *Crimen Sollicitationis* and the *2001 Motu*

---

6. http://www.rte.ie/news/2011/0720/cloyne1.html (Accessed 16 July 2013). See also *Mea Maxima Culpa* at 59.31.
7. http://www.catholicworldreport.com/Item/1065/ireland_stand_up.aspx#. Umor5au4YqQ (Accessed 15 October 2013).
8. http://www.vatican.va/resources/resources_risposta-gilmore_20110903_

Proprio in general terms, but there is not one word about the secret of the Holy Office or pontifical secrecy. It was as if they never existed.

The response explained that the *Framework Document* was not the work of the Irish Catholic Bishops Conference, but only of an advisory committee, and as such it could not receive a *recognitio* from Rome under canon law. However, it went on to say,

> However, the lack of *recognitio* would not of itself prevent the application of the *Framework Document* in individual Dioceses. Despite the fact that the *Framework Document* was not an official publication of the Conference as such, each individual Bishop was free to adopt it as particular law in his Diocese and apply its guidelines, **provided these were not contrary to canon law** (my emphasis).

And there's the rub because that is exactly what the Storero letter was pointing out in reference to the proposal for mandatory reporting. The proposals for mandatory reporting were contrary to canon law—and they were, on any reading of *Crimen Sollicitationis, Secreta Continere,* the *1983 Code of Canon Law* and the *2001 Motu Proprio.*

The Vatican Response then purports to clarify what the canonical difficulties were in relation to reporting:

> It should be borne in mind that, without ever having to consult the Holy See, every Bishop, is free to apply the penal measures of canon law to offending priests, and has never been impeded under canon law from reporting cases of abuse to the civil authorities.

Again, we have another example of 'mental reservation'. If it refers to the bishop having first hand evidence of abuse, that he caught a priest *in flagrante delicto*, in bed with an altar boy, it is true. If it refers to what he found out in the course of a canonical investigation, it is false. If the Vatican statement means that bishops could reveal what they had discovered in their inquiries they were required

en.html (Accessed 16 July 2013).

to carry out under canon law, then it flies in the face of the plain words of *Crimen Sollicitationis, Secreta Continere* and the *1983 Code of Canon Law*, and the *2001 Motu Proprio*. It is also contrary to the repeated statements of the Church's senior Roman Curia cardinals, Archbishops and canon lawyers, and the way *Crimen Sollicitationis* was applied in practice. And in support of its statement, the Response quotes another letter from Cardinal Castrillón of 12 November 1998, as if it really supported its assertion about the bishops never being impeded from reporting.

> I also wish to say with great clarity that the Church, especially through its Pastors (Bishops), should not in any way put an obstacle in the legitimate path of civil justice, **when such is initiated by those who have such rights**, while at the same time, she should move forward with her own canonical procedures, in truth, justice and charity towards all[9] (my emphasis).

In other words, no obstacle should be put in the path of the victims to go to the police (ignoring of course, that under *Crimen Sollicitationis* they would have be sworn to secrecy). But that has never been the issue. The issue was the obligation under civil law for bishops to report under the misprision of felony laws where they then still existed. This letter says nothing about that, and Cardinal Castrillón's other public statements made it clear that bishops should be prepared to go to jail rather than to report one of their paedophile priests to the police.

The Vatican Response then continued,

> In 1996, apart from cases relating to misprision of felony, the reporting of incidents of child sexual abuse to either the relevant health board or the Irish police was not mandatory. Furthermore, misprision of felony was

---

9. Cardinal Castrillón had his supporters in Ireland. Monsignor Callaghan from the diocese of Cloyne thought that the matter of reporting should be left to the victim, as reporting to the police interfered with the Church's 'pastoral approach' to the question of sexual abuse. *Murphy Dublin Report*, Part 1 http://www.justice.ie/en/JELR/DACOI%20Part%201.pdf/Files/DACOI%20Part%201.pdf paragraph 4.74ff. (Accessed 7 May 2013).

removed from the Irish Statute Book by the *Criminal Justice Act* of 1997.[10]

Child sexual abuse was invariably a felony—reporting was always mandatory. Misprision of felony was removed from the Irish Statutes by the *Criminal Law Act* 1997 of 22 April 1997, coming into effect three months, later on 22 July 1997.[11] At the time the Storero letter was written on 31 January 1997, there was mandatory reporting under the misprision of felony law. The Vatican response did not mention the date in 1997, when misprision of felony was abolished, giving the impression that it was abolished at the time the Storero letter was written.

Three months earlier, on the 20th of July 2011, the Vatican spokesperson, Fr Federico Lombardi, seemed unaware of the date of the repeal of misprison of felony. In reference to the Storero letter he said.

> Moreover, there is absolutely nothing in the letter that is an invitation to disregard the laws of the country', Father Lombardi added. 'The objection the letter referred to regarded the obligation to provide information to civil authorities ('mandatory reporting'), it did not object to any civil law to that effect, **because it did not exist in Ireland at that time** (and proposals to introduce it were subject to discussion for various reasons in the same civil sphere)[12] (my emphasis).

The statement that such a law 'did not exist' in Ireland as at 31 January 1997 was incorrect. The proposals under discussion were to require some professionals in a confidential relationship to report, similar

---

10. http://www.vatican.va/resources/resources_risposta-gilmore_20110903_en.html (Accessed 16 July 2013).

11. http://www.irishstatutebook.ie/1997/en/act/pub/0014/print.html#sec1 (Accessed 16 July 2013). After the abolition, failure to report only became an offence if there was a benefit in return, as in the United Kingdom and all Australian States, other than NSW: http://www.independent.ie/opinion/analysis/change-in-the-law-means-there-is-now-no-criminal-offence-for-failure-to-report-crime-26031940.html (Accessed 16 July 2013).

12. http://www.zenit.org/article-33112?l=english(Accessed 16 July 2013).

to the proposals for mandatory 'welfare' reporting to child welfare authorities in Australia for children at risk. That had nothing to do with the obligation to report under the existing misprision of felony law at the date of the Storero letter. The instruction from Cardinal Castrillón through Archbishop Storero was an instruction to breach Irish law in the case of allegations of sex crimes against children by priests.

Needless to say, as often happens with this exotic dance called diplomacy, a new Papal Nuncio to Ireland was appointed, but the Irish Government made a further gesture of displeasure by announcing in November 2011 the closure of its embassy in Rome, and that its ambassador to the Vatican would be situated in Dublin.

Pope John XXIII

Pope Paul VI

21

Some Theological Problems With Facing The Truth

Pope Benedict XVI had an excellent opportunity with his *Pastoral Letter* to the people of Ireland to come clean, acknowledge that the whole policy of secrecy from 1922 onwards was a disaster, and that the Church's own attempts to deal with its clergy sexual abusers through the use of its Church procedures were hopelessly ineffective, causing many more children to be abused than would otherwise have occurred. But he made no apology for the state of canon law, the buck for which stops at the popes.

Benedict's predecessor, Pope John Paul II, apologised for some of the Church's sins of the past—the Inquisition, the execution of John Hus, the treatment of Galileo, the burning of witches, the Church's anti-Semitism and the Muslims killed in the crusades.[1] But it seems that it takes between 200 and 500 years for an apology to appear out of the glacier, and it is always for the misdeeds of long forgotten leaders.[2]

The theological problem at the root of reluctance to apologise for present misdeeds at the highest level of the Church has a lot to do with what Bishop Geoffrey Robinson calls 'creeping infallibility'.

---

1. http://www.guardian.co.uk/world/2000/mar/13/catholicism.religion (Accessed 14 July 2013), http://www.catholicaustralia.com.au/page.php?pg=austchurch-popes17h (Accessed 14 July 2013).
2. With the election of Francis, perhaps the glacier pace might quicken. In 2012, he issued an apology as head of the Argentine Catholic Bishops Conference for the complicity of the Church with the military regime in the 1970s. However, it remains to be seen if he will apologise for the actions of his predecessors as pope in relation to the clergy sexaul abuse cover up. It is one thing to blame bishops. It is quite another to criticise the Vicars of Christ. http://www.washingtonpost.com/national/on-faith/vatican-defends-pope-francis-actions-during-argentinasdirty-war/2013/03/15/070f5324-8db5-11e2-adca-74ab31da3399_story.html Accessed 15 July 2013).

The Church sees itself as the direct descendant of the faith community established by Jesus Christ, and the bishops are the successors of the twelve apostles under the leadership of St Peter, the first Pope.[3] Jesus Christ is the Son of God, the second person of the Trinity and the creator of the universe. The Church continues Jesus Christ's redemptive work for mankind. The pope, as head of the Church, is the Vicar of Christ, and the Church is guided by the Holy Spirit. The declaration of the infallibility of the pope by the First Vatican Council in 1870 was initially limited to his solemn declarations on faith and morals, such as the doctrine of the assumption of the Blessed Virgin into heaven.

But Bishop Robinson in his book, *Confronting Power and Sex in the Catholic Church* refers to an increasing trend to extend those limits, so that if a teaching is repeated enough by a pope, it becomes infallible.[4] Typical examples these days are the teaching on contraception, homosexuality and women priests. It is not hard to find conservative Catholic websites declaring that the Church's teaching on contraception and homosexuality are infallible.[5] But in the case of women priests, the infallibility suggestion comes from the Vatican itself.[6] This 'creeping infallibility' stems from a belief that the Church, led by the popes is guided by the Holy Spirit, and therefore Popes are unlikely to make mistakes if they repeat themselves often enough on matters of faith and morals. It is an understandable conclusion that derives from a belief that the Church was founded by 'Almighty God' to guide humanity along the straight and narrow.

While a policy to create a de facto medieval privilege of clergy is not a doctrine of the Church, it is an example of a policy that stemmed from the Vicars of Christ—all six of them since 1922 (not counting John Paul I). Two of those popes, who had the most to do with the reinforcement of secrecy and the system of clergy privilege, John XXIII (who reissued *Crimen Sollicitationis* in 1962) and John Paul II

---

3. *Facing the Truth* paragraph 4.1
4. At page 121.
5. http://www.zenit.org/en/articles/germain-grisez-on-humanae-vitae-then-and-now (Accessed 15 July 2013) http://www.ewtn.com/library/christ/confatal.txt. See also http://ncronline.org/news/vatican/long-simmering-tension-over-creeping-infallibility (Both accessed 15 July 2013).
6. http://www.nytimes.com/1995/11/19/world/vatican-says-the-ban-on-women-as-priests-is-infallible-doctrine.html (Accessed 15 July 2013).

(who issued the *2001 Motu Proprio*) were canonized as saints on the 27th of April 2014. In 1974, Pope Paul VI issued *Secreta Continere* that again imposed pontifical secrecy on clergy sex crimes against children. Benedict XVI, as Cardinal Ratzinger, advised Pope John Paul II to confirm pontifical secrecy in the *2001 Motu Proprio*, and Benedict himself, in 2010, not only confirmed it, but even extended it to priests having sex with intellectually disabled adults.

The Church, under the guidance of the Holy Spirit, ended up creating a policy that significantly increased the damage to the 'little children'—a crime which Jesus said deserved a millstone around the neck, and being thrown into the sea.[7] It is one thing to apply that curse to the clergy sexual abusers, or even slack and lazy bishops. It is quite another to apply it to the Vicars of Christ for designing the system in the first place, and then continually reinforcing it throughout their pontificates. The second cover up is perfectly understandable, because the truth strikes at the very heart of Catholic doctrine.

Bishop Geoffrey Robinson writes in his book, *For Christ's Sake*,

> . . . the entire response of the Church to the scandal of sexual abuse has taken place in an atmosphere that the pope cannot have been wrong in any matter that involved papal energy and prestige. This has had a crippling effect on the entire response. Abuse has called into question papal prestige in a way that few other things have, and it is manifestly impossible to give an adequate response while maintaining that the Pope (and, therefore the Church) cannot have been wrong in his response or in any of the facts that underlie the scandal.[8]

Hence, we have Pope Benedict's *Pastoral Letter* to the people of Ireland, blaming everyone except himself, his predecessors and colleagues in the Roman Curia.

But there is another problem with 'facing the truth', and that is the problem of scandal, and the feared loss of faith and membership of the Church as a result of it.[9] The 'scandal' of priests sexually attacking

---

7. Mark 9:42.
8. (Melbourne: John Garratt publishing, 2013), 119
9. http://www.parliament.vic.gov.au/images/stories/committees/fcdc/

children was bad enough, but there is clear evidence not only of a cover up, but that cover up being ordered and directed by the Vatican. The theological problem of popes making mistakes is the only real explanation for the reluctance to face the truth. Protecting popes and canon law from criticism comes at the price of honesty.

And so, we have seen the Vatican adopting the practice of 'mental reservation' in its responses to allegations about canon law enforcing the cover up.

And while many of the Irish bishops were prepared to tell the Murphy Commission that the secrecy provisions of canon law prevented them from going to the police, many of them simply fell on their swords when criticised by Pope Benedict in his *Pastoral Letter*. Cardinal Pell also came closer to criticising the Vatican by saying that the Congregation for the Clergy 'did not get it'. But the bishops' reluctance to criticise openly the Vicar of Christ himself is understandable because of the oath of loyalty to the pope that bishops take at ordination, and by the whole belief system that says the pope is 'God's Vicar'. The system requires them to take the rap if the Pope, the man pre-eminently responsible, will not, and then blames them.

Bishop John Magee studied theology in Rome and spent most of his professional life as a priest there, from 1969 to 1987, being private secretary to Pope Paul VI, John Paul I and John Paul II, and Papal Master of Ceremonies from 1982 to 1987, until his appointment as Bishop of Cloyne in February 1987. He, more than anyone, would have known of the attitudes that prevailed in the Vatican over exposing priests to the civil courts. He kept two sets of records with one account for the Vatican, and another for those who would come to his diocesan offices with a subpoena or search warrant from a civil court. He said he took advice from a solicitor who told him that the communications between a priest and bishop were 'privileged'— advice which the solicitor, unsurprisingly, denied ever giving.[10] This idea that there was some sort of 'privilege' in communications– between a bishop and a priest, that can resist a legitimate claim for production by the State, reflects very much the claims of senior cardinals and Roman Curia canon lawyers made during the period

inquiries/57th/Child_Abuse_Inquiry/Transcripts/Catholic_Archdiocese_of_Melbourne_20-May-13.pdf, 9 (Accessed 18 June 2013).

10. http://www.justice.ie/en/JELR/Cloyne_Rpt.pdf/Files/Cloyne_Rpt.pdf, paragraph 21.14–21.19 (Accessed 5 April 2013).

1984–2002 that the Church and its priests and bishops should be above the law. While Magee paid lip service to the *Framework Document*, he was slack about implementing it in Cloyne so far as reporting to the police was concerned.

The *Cloyne Report* found Magee and his assistant, Monsignor O'Callaghan, misled Mr Ian Elliott of the *National Board for Safeguarding Children in the Catholic Church* which had been set up by the Irish Catholic Bishops Conference to establish best practice relating to child protection policies and procedures. They tried to hide the fact that they had communicated Fr Caden's admission of sexual abuse to the Vatican.[11] It is obvious where Bishop Magee's loyalties were. Confidentiality prevented him from reporting the priest's admission to the police, but not to the Vatican. At the *Cloyne Inquiry*, he took the rap for everything, never once pointing the figure at canon law, or his bosses and colleagues in the Vatican, and then quietly retired on his Church pension. The good and faithful servant had done well.

The only people prepared to speak out are the few 'turbulent priests', Bishop Geoffrey Robinson, Archbishop Weakland, and former bishops Pat Power and William Morris, Fr Thomas Doyle OP and Fr Sean McDonagh, and Fr Frank Brennan SJ, and any number of former priests.

The bishops' reluctance to speak out is also understandable for other reasons. In 1996 threats of disciplinary action were made against Bishop Geoffrey Robinson for merely telling victims at a meeting where several journalists were present, that he was 'not happy with the level of support we are receiving from Rome'.[12]

Even more serious is the case of Bishop William Morris of Toowoomba. According to Fr Frank Brennan SJ, his dismissal by Pope Benedict XVI was contrary to the principles of natural justice.[13] Morris's 'crime', as described by Brennan was discussing having married clergy and ordaining women. He was sacked, not for ordaining a woman or a married woman, but 'inviting a conversation about it'.[14]

---

11. *Ibid*, 21.79.
12. Geoffrey Robinson *Confronting Power and Sex in the Catholic Church* (Melbourne: Joh Garratt), 21.
13. http://www.eurekastreet.com.au/article.aspx?aeid=26378 (Accessed 16 July 2013).
14. *Ibid*.

Likewise, none of the Irish bishops were prepared to go on camera to say what happened at their meeting with Cardinal Castrillón in 1998 where he bluntly told them, as one bishop put it to a reporter, to hide clergy criminals from the police. However, at the *Victorian Parliamentary Inquiry,* cracks were appearing in the edifice with Archbishop Hart's oral evidence, even if his joint submission with the three other bishops, in *Facing the Truth* was straight down the party line. And Cardinal Pell in his oral evidence was at least prepared to criticise a Vatican congregation, and admit that the confidentiality imposed by canon law was 'inappropriate'.

Whether Pope Francis will make a difference to this situation is a matter still to be seen. One of the advantages of having a government based on an absolute monarchy is that the monarch can do what he likes—as John XXIII did when he called the Second Vatican Council to the apoplectic opposition of Cardinal Ottaviani and the then reactionary Roman Curia. Despite Pope Francis' important and much admired gestures on many issues since being elected, his instructions to his delegates to the United Nations Committee for the Rights of the Child, in January 2014, dealt with in the next chapter, do not create hopes for optimism.

22

The United Nations Committee on the Rights of the Child Report

On 16 January 2014 Bishop Scicluna, the former Vatican Chief Prosecutor gave evidence before the United Nations Committee for the Rights of the Child on behalf of the Vatican, and said,

> It is not the policy of the Holy See to encourage cover-ups. Only the truth will help us move on to a situation where we can start being an example of best practice.[1]

Scicluna was asked by Committee members why Church policy did not provide that in 'all cases these crimes should be reported', and not just where there were reporting laws. His answer was that every local Church has the duty to educate people about their rights and to 'empower' them.[2] In other words, he was repeating Cardinal Castrillón instruction in his November 1998 letter to the Irish bishops that it was up to the victims to report the matter to the police, not the Church, even if, after the Pope Benedict's 2010 'reforms', the victims 'habitually lack the use of reason'. But apart from that, the Church has a conflict of interest in advising complainants about their rights to report to the police, particularly in view of its concern about 'scandal', its theological teaching of the father/son relationship between a bishop and a priest, and its history of cover up.

The Vatican's response shows that despite all the spin that everything has changed, the crux of the problem has not. Pontifical secrecy will remain wherever the Church can get away with it. The

1. http://www.treatybodywebcast.org/ (Viewed 16 January 2014).http://www.nytimes.com/2014/01/17/world/europe/un-sex-abuse-panel-questions-vatican-officials.html?_r=0 (Accessed 21 January 2014).
2. Ibid.

dispensation to allow limiting reporting reveals where the Vatican's true priorities lie: keeping bishops and priests out of jail, rather than the welfare of children. In November 2009, the *Murphy Dublin Report* pointed out that the focus of the Church then was:

> . . . the avoidance of scandal and the preservation of the good name, status and assets of the institution and of what the institution regarded as its most important members—the priests.[3]

Nothing has changed.

On 31 January 2014, the United Nations Committee on the Rights of the Child handed down its *Concluding Observations on the Second Periodic Report of the Holy See.*[4] The UN Committee noted that some of the rules of canon law are not in conformity with the provisions of the Convention on the Rights of the Child, and it recommended a comprehensive review of canon law to ensure compliance.[5] It accused the Vatican of adopting 'policies and practices which have led to the continuation of the abuse by and the impunity of the perpetrators.' It noted the practice of covering up known sexual abusers and transferring them to other institutions under Church control. It said that despite the fact that the Church has full control of these personnel under canon law, it had declined to provide the UN Committee with information about the outcome of the canonical procedures against them.[6] It accused the Vatican of allowing the vast majority of abusers to escape criminal prosecution by its use of its confidential disciplinary proceedings, and that,

> Due to a code of silence imposed on all members of the clergy under penalty of excommunication, cases of child sexual abuse have hardly ever been reported to the law enforcement authorities in the countries where

---

3. *Murphy Dublin Report* Part1 http://www.justice.ie/en/JELR/DACOI%20
    Part%201.pdf/Files/DACOI%20Part%201.pdf (Accessed 25 April 2013) 1.15,
    1.113 (Conclusion).
4. http://tbinternet.ohchr.org/Treaties/CRC/Shared%20Documents/VAT/
    CRC_C_VAT_CO_2_16302_E.pdf (Accessed 6 February 2014).
5. *Ibid*, paragraph, 8, 13.
6. *Ibid*, paragraph, 43.

such crimes occurred. On the contrary, cases of nuns and priests ostracized, demoted and fired for not having respected the obligation of silence have been reported to the Committee as well as cases of priests who have been congratulated for refusing to denounce child abusers, as shown in the letter addressed by Cardinal Castrillón Hojos to Bishop Pierre Pican in 2001.[7]

The Committee also noted that reporting to national law enforcement authorities has never been made compulsory and was expressly rejected by the Storero letter of 1997. It also noted that in many cases, the Holy See has refused to cooperate with judicial inquiries.[8]

On 7 February 2014, the Vatican responded through its spokesman, Fr Federico Lombardi, and once again the impression was given that the Church's left hand did not know what its right was doing. Lombardi gratuitously accused the UN Committee of having written the report before hearing the Vatican's response.[9] He claimed that the Committee did not understand 'the Holy See's responsibilities', which had to be a reference back to his claim of 5 December 2013, that those responsibilities were limited to the thirty-one children of the Swiss Guards and others who resided in the Vatican City.[10] But on 16 January 2014, the Vatican's delegates, Archbishop Tomasi and Bishop Scicluna, when fronting the Committee in Geneva, accepted its international responsibility for child abuse by reason of its control under canon law.[11] On 17 January 2014, they even produced some

---

7. *Ibid*, paragraph, 43(d).
8. *Ibid*, paragraph 43(e).
9. http://www.news.va/en/news/fr-lombardi-sj-note-on-childrens-rights-committee (Accessed 16 February 2014).
10. http://www.news.com.au/world/vatican-denies-legal-responsibility-for-catholic-child-abuse/story-fndir2ev-1226775551025 (Accessed 16 February 2014) Ivor Roberts: 'UN report: who speaks for the Church?', in *The Tablet*, 5 February 2014 p.13 (Accessed 16 February 2014)
11. The Vatican bulletin dated 16 January 2014, containing its periodic report on the Rights of the Child, confirmed its ratification of the Convention on the Rights of the Child. It contains this passage acknowledging its responsibility beyond the Vatican City: ' . . . the Holy See as the central organ of the Catholic Church has formulated guidelines to facilitate the work of the local Churches to develop effective measures within their jurisdiction and in conformity with canonical legislation.' http://press.vatican.va/content/salastampa/it/bollettino/

figures on how many priests had been dismissed since 2005 for child sexual abuse out of the more than 4,000 the Vatican had been investigating since 2001. These priests were not abusing the children of the Swiss Guards.

Fr Lombardi criticised the Committee for paying more attention to 'certain NGOs, the prejudices of which against the Catholic Church and the Holy See are well known' and for 'going beyond its powers' by attempting to interfere in the moral and doctrinal positions of the Catholic Church regarding contraception, abortion, and its vision of 'human sexuality'.

Fr Lombardi said nothing about the central criticism of the United Nations Report: pontifical secrecy over the Church's investigations of clergy sexual abuse of children. The Church's response to the United Nations Report followed the script written for it by Benedict XVI in his *Pastoral Letter* to the people of Ireland: when pontifical secrecy is raised, do not admit it, do not deny it, say nothing about it, and create a distraction.

Pope Francis has made many important and much admired gestures since being elected, but his instructions to his delegates to the United Nations Committee for the Rights of the Child in Geneva are deeply disappointing. Thomas C Fox, the publisher of the *National Catholic Reporter* wrote on 21 January 2014,

> Despite Pope Francis' heartfelt expressions of lament over priest sex abuse last week, the Geneva hearing suggests to date he does not understand the full magnitude of the related sex abuse issues, or, if he does, is yet unwilling or incapable of responding to it.[12]

pubblico/2014/01/16/0032/00067.html (Accessed 16 February 2014).

12. http://ncronline.org/blogs/ncr-today/much-stake-francis-vatican-sex-abuse-moves (Accessed 30 January 2014).

23

The Australian Royal Commission

On 12 November 2012, the Australian Prime Minister, Julia Gillard, announced the setting up of a *Royal Commission into Institutional Responses to Child Sex Abuse* involving all Churches and institutions that had the care of children. On 11 January 2013, she announced the Commission's terms of reference.[1] In broad terms, the Commission is to inquire into the appropriate responses of institutions, with the need to focus on systemic issues, and to make recommendations for changes to laws, policies and systems for the better protection of children from sexual abuse. The Commission started its hearings on 16 September 2013.

On 12 November 2012, the Australian Catholic Bishops Conference issued a press release promising cooperation with the *Australian Royal Commission*, repeating the line that there is a greater awareness of sexual abuse in the broader community, but denying there was any systemic problem of it in the Church. It said that the criticisms of the Church centered on what happened twenty years ago, and that major procedural changes have since been introduced and implemented:

> It is unacceptable, because it is untrue, to claim that the Catholic Church does not have proper procedures, and to claim that Catholic authorities refuse to cooperate with the police.[2]

The 'major procedural changes' in 2001 did not seem to help in the Archdiocese of Melbourne's attempt to deal with Fr Desmond

---

1. http://www.childabuseroyalcommission.gov.au/our-work/terms-of-reference/ (Accessed 24 December 2013).
2. http://mediablog.catholic.org.au/?p=1364 (Accessed 5 March 2013).

Gannon that started in 1993. Archbishop Hart was still trying to get the Vatican to dismiss him in 2012. And the Vatican still insists that the only amount of cooperation with police it will allow is just enough to keep bishops out of jail. Otherwise pontifical secrecy applies to any information it gains about sex abusing clergy through its canonical investigations. This is a serious *systemic* problem that is peculiar to the Church.

On 12 December 2012, the Australian Catholic Bishops Conference announced that it had set up the *Truth, Justice and Healing Council,* headed by a group of distinguished lay men and women whose functions were to cooperate with the Commission, explore the truth, and to identify system institutional failures that have impeded the protection of children.[3] Archbishop Hart, the Chairman of the Australian Catholic Bishops Conference says that the Church recognised it needed a 'sophisticated and coordinated response'.[4]

The *Truth Justice and Healing Council* did not get off to a good start. Its Chief Executive Officer Francis Sullivan acknowledged that there have been 'cover ups'. But on 3 April 2013, on the Australian ABC's *7.30 Report* he was asked what steps the Church should take if one of its teachers reported to Church authorities that he suspected that a priest was sexually abusing children at their school. He said it was up to the teacher to report it, and not the Church authorities.[5]

This answer reflects the whole clerical culture, expressed in the pontifical secrecy of canon law, that it is not the Church's role to report allegations of clergy sexual abuse to the police for investigation. It is an answer that repeats the words of Cardinals Castrillón, Bertone, Herranz, Rodriguez, Schotte, Lehmann and Billé plus the Dean of Canon Law at the Gregorian University in Rome, Professor Ghirlanda given ten years earlier to the same question. It is the answer enshrined in *The Melbourne Response,* and it is the whole basis for the secret revival of privilege of clergy and the appalling mess that the Church created for children: it is not the Church's responsibility to report to

---

3.   http://mediablog.catholic.org.au/?p=1489 (Accessed 16 July 2013).

4.   http://cathnews.co.nz/2012/12/14/church-in-aust-forms-truth-justice-and-healing-commission/ (Accessed 16 July 2013).

5.   http://www.abc.net.au/news/2013-04-03/justice-mcclellan-opens-royal-commission/4608378 (Accessed 6 April 2013).

the civil authorities. It is up to the victims even if, since the 'reforms' of 2010, they 'habitually lack the use of reason'.

On 22 April 2013, Francis Sullivan addressed the St Thomas More Forum in Canberra. He admitted that the abuse had been terrible and that there had been cover ups. But, he said, the Church, like the rest of society has been on a learning curve, and things are much better now than they were twenty years ago, but of course, there is always room for improvement, etc etc. He made no mention of the current conflict between canon law and *Towards Healing* where there is no civil law obligation to report to the police, and no mention that the Vatican has not approved *Towards Healing* under Canon 455 to make it part of canon law for Australia.[6]

In its submission to the *Australian Royal Commission* of 30 September 2013, the Australian Church acknowledged that sexual abuse was a crime under both criminal and canon law, and that in some cases those in positions of authority covered up what they knew of the facts, moved perpetrators, enabling them to offend again, or failed to report to the police when they should have.[7] It acknowledged that this was 'indefensible'. There was no mention that all of this occurred in conformity with canon law for which the Pope alone is responsible.

On 3 October 2013, Francis Sullivan said that the *Australian Church Submission* to the *Australian Royal Commission* was 'the most comprehensive document ever produced by the Church dealing with child sexual abuse. It is a warts-and-all history going back decades'. But the biggest wart of all, canon pontifical secrecy and the continuing existence of unsatisfactory canons in the code dealing with the discipline of priests is not mentioned in this history.[8]

In his concluding remarks to the Thomas More Forum, Francis Sullivan said that the Australian community 'has been kept in the

6. http://www.tjhcouncil.org.au/media/32495/130622-Speech-St-Thomas-More-Forum-Francis-Sullilvan-copy.pdf (Accessed 15 Janury 2014).

7. http://www.childabuseroyalcommission.gov.au/wp-content/uploads/2013/10/15.-Truth-Justice-and-Healing-Council1.pdf page 1 (Accessed 25 November 2013).

8. David Marr: 'Catholic Church Admits Grave Faults in Dealing with Australian Abuse Victims', http://www.theguardian.com/world/2013/oct/03/catholic-church-grave-faults-abuse (Accessed 29 October 2013).

dark for too long'.[9] Indeed it has, and it is still being kept in the dark about the role of canon law in these systemic failures, and that it was not just the result of some universal incompetence or bad faith on the part of individual bishops.

Sullivan also said that this period was a crucial one in the Church's history. In 1986, Raymond Mouton, a lawyer working with Fr Thomas Doyle to develop a protocol for dealing with the clergy sexual abuse problem, told a meeting of canon lawyers in Washington:

> The Church . . . cannot credibly exert moral authority in any area where the public perceives it as incapable of maintaining moral authority internally.[10]

And moral authority does not come from covering up the role of canon law, the popes and the Roman Curia in the debacle.

The Vatican's Attitude to Public Inquiries

Cardinal Pell at the *Victorian Parliamentary Inquiry* said he was assured by a 'senior Vatican official', that all documents would be available to the *Australian Royal Commission,* provided that an approach was made 'through the appropriate channels, recognising that the Holy See is an independent country'.[11] If the Vatican does honour that assurance, then this will be a new development.

During the Murphy Commissions in Ireland, the Vatican refused to hand over its documents relating to issues of clergy sexual abuse of children, claiming sovereign immunity. The instructions given by *Crimen Sollicitationis* were that any reports by investigators were to be sent to the bishop, and no copy kept. This practice of not keeping copies still occurs in Vatican practice, as can be seen by the report of Archbishop Chaput into Bishop William Morris of Toowoomba in 2007. Chaput had been sent by the Vatican to investigate the

---

9. http://www.tjhcouncil.org.au/media/32495/130622-Speech-St-Thomas-More-Forum-Francis-Sullilvan-copy.pdf (Accessed 24 June 2013).
10. Michael D'Antonio, *Mortal Sins: Sex, Crime and the Era of Catholic Scandal* (St Martin's Press 2013), 44
11. http://www.parliament.vic.gov.au/images/stories/committees/fcdc/inquiries/57th/Child_Abuse_Inquiry/Transcripts/Catholic_Archdiocese_of_Sydney_27-May-13.pdf, 22.4 (Accessed 23 June 2013).

complaints about Morris, and he prepared a report. When Morris asked to see a copy, Chaput replied that he did not have a copy anymore because he had sent the report in hard copy and electronic copy to the Vatican and then destroyed his own, that being 'what he was supposed to do'.[12]

The issue over Bishop Morris was mainly over his attitude to women priests, but if this is still the practice, it means that there are relevant documents kept at the Vatican, but there are no copies that can be subpoenaed in Australia.[13]

Canon law itself requires the destruction of documents relating to clergy sexual abuse, kept in the secret archive of every bishop after ten years, with only a brief summary of what occurred with the text of the final sentence being retained.[14]

The willingness of the Vatican to hand over relevant documents will be the litmus test for how much the Vatican itself is prepared to 'cooperate' with civil authorities—the advice which Benedict XVI himself gave to the Irish bishops in his *Pastoral Letter*, but which the Vatican did not honour at the Murphy Commission in Ireland.

The Murphy Commission in Ireland asked the Papal Nuncio to Ireland to 'submit to it any information which you have about the matters under investigation'. The Commission accepted that it had no power to compel the Papal Nuncio. The Vatican replied that the Nunciature did not handle such matters and said that such cases were 'the responsibility of local ecclesiastical authorities'.[15]

Once again, there was a reply from the Vatican that reeked of 'mental reservation'. The Murphy Commission received its terms of reference for the Cloyne diocese investigation on 31 March 2009, and it was required to inquire into all complaints received by the diocese in the period 1 January 1996 to 1 February 2009.[16]

For the period 1996 to May 2001, what the Vatican said about cases of sexual abuse being handled by the local ecclesiastical authorities was correct. But for the eight year period after 2001, it

---

12. http://ncronline.org/news/vatican/forced-retirement-message-all-bishops-morris-says (Accessed 15 July 2013).
13. *Ibid.*
14. Canon 489.
15. http://www.justice.ie/en/JELR/Cloyne_Rpt.pdf/Files/Cloyne_Rpt.pdf paragraphs 21.18 and 2.11. (Accessed 5 April 2013).
16. *Ibid*, paragraph 1.2.

was misleading. Under Article 13 of the *2001 Motu Proprio*, where a bishop had undertaken a preliminary inquiry into an accusation of sexual abuse, the results of that inquiry had to be sent to the Congregation for the Doctrine of the Faith through the Nunciature, and the Congregation would tell the bishop how to proceed, or would tell him that the Congregation itself would handle the matter from then on. Article 14 provided that where the matter is directly referred to the Congregation without a preliminary investigation, the Congregation itself would carry that out.

In other words, in those situations, the 'responsibility' was not that of the 'local ecclesiastical authorities', but of the Vatican itself through the Congregation for the Doctrine of the Faith. The Commission found that Bishop Magee did refer a number of cases directly onto the Congregation, something of which the Vatican must have been aware at the time of writing this letter through its Papal Nuncio.[17] It would have been more correct to say that after 2001 the Congregation for the Doctrine of the Faith 'determined the handling of cases of sexual abuse in Ireland', and that the Vatican had such documents.

Communications between the Vatican and the Australian bishops are relevant to 'the adequacy and appropriateness of the responses by institutions, and their officials', within the terms of reference of the *Australian Royal Commission*. Whether or not the Vatican lives up to the promise by the 'senior Vatican official' to produce all its documents is a matter to be seen.

The Current Systemic Issues Created by Canon Law

The 2010 revision of the *2001 Motu Proprio* represents current canon law. It requires any complaint of sexual abuse of children, of the intellectually disabled and of possession of child pornography by clergy to be reported to the Congregation for the Doctrine of the Faith which will then instruct the bishop how to proceed. Pontifical secrecy still applies to any allegation and any information gathered by bishops from their preliminary or later proceedings, and, unless there is a local law requiring reporting, the bishop is prohibited from reporting those matters to the police.

---

17. *Ibid*, paragraph 3.40.

On 3 May 2011, the Vatican asked bishops conferences to present it with guidelines for dealing with sexual abuse by clergy. Once approved under Canon 455, those guidelines then become canon law for the area covered by the Bishops Conference, in the same way as the American guidelines developed after the Dallas Charter in 2002 became canon law for the United States. Like the dispensation given in 2010, those guidelines only provide for an exception to pontifical secrecy where the local law requires reporting.

The proposed changes do not affect the 'systemic issue' of pontifical secrecy when there is no law requiring reporting. If the local law does not require reporting, then pontifical secrecy will ensure that the inadequate parallel system of law—the 'privilege of clergy'—will continue, and where punishment is not jail, but spiritual exercises, restrictions on performing the liturgy and at the most dismissal. There is already evidence that this will happen in Italy and in other countries that lack 'misprision of felony' laws.

In May 2012, the Italian Bishops Conference developed its guidelines in accordance with the direction from Cardinal Levada of 3 May 2011. It announced that it had no obligation to report clergy crimes against children to the civil authorities because the terms of the 1929 Concordat between the Vatican and Italy specifically provides that there is no obligation on a bishop to report 'illicit' acts.[18]

According to those reports, the Italian bishops said that they would co-operate with civil authorities where a police investigation is ongoing or where a penal proceeding has been opened according to Italian state law. But if the police don't know about the allegations, then they will be told nothing. The Italian bishops' stand is correct from the point of view of canon law at present and as it is proposed to be amended, because pontifical secrecy will still apply where there is no legal obligation to report. The de facto 'privilege of clergy' and its inadequate system of ecclesiastical justice will continue in Italy, and in every other country in the world where there are no laws requiring reporting of historic abuse. These include the United States, Canada, the United Kingdom, New Zealand and Australia (other than NSW).

---

18. http://www.irishtimes.com/newspaper/world/2012/0525/1224316664040.html (Accessed 9 February 2013).
http://www.belfasttelegraph.co.uk/news/world-news/bishops-not-obliged-to-report-sexual-abuse-to-police-28753674.html (Accessed 9 February 2013).

The only Australian state that has laws to overcome the systemic issue of pontifical secrecy is NSW with its S.316 of the *Crimes Act 1900 (NSW)* and the provisions of the *Ombudsman Act 1974*.[19] S.316 of the *Crimes Act 1900 (NSW)* needs to be reviewed by the Royal Commission in the light of the criticism by the NSW Law Reform Commission that its reach is uncertain.[20] The *Ombudsman Act 1974* needs to be reviewed because activities of clergy involved in 'pastoral work', such as visiting families, do not seem to be covered by it.

A particular concern now arises from the 2010 'reforms' of canon law that apply pontifical secrecy to allegations against priests of sexually abusing intellectually disabled people. The recommendation of the NSW Law Reform Commission about intellectually disabled people is not to have mandatory reporting backed up by criminal sanctions, but by 'policies' adopted by government departments and service providers.[21] The problem that this recommendation has for cases involving Catholic clergy is that a policy is not a 'law' requiring reporting. Pontifical secrecy will still apply.

The position in all other States regarding reporting of children at risk is similar to the State of Victoria, except that the mandatory reporting laws apply to clergy in the Northern Territory, and arguably in South Australia and the Australian Capital Territory.

The simplest solution would be for Pope Francis to change canon law to remove any requirement of pontifical secrecy for any canonical crime that is also a crime against civil law, anywhere in the world. But, he is showing very little inclination to do so. Even if he did change canon law, civil society would still have to deal with the cultural inertia that creates reluctance in Church authorities to report where they are not obliged by law to do so. The Church is not the only institution that has covered up sexual abuse, even if it is one of those rare ones that has enshrined the cover up in its own internal laws.

---

19. The *Ombudsman* Acts of the other Australian State and Territories do not have any equivalent of Part 3A of the NSW Act.

20. http://www.lawlink.nsw.gov.au/lrc.nsf/pages/r93chp3 (Accessed 14 February 2013). See also: Lesley Townsley, 'Conceal or Reveal', in *Public Space, Journal of Law and Social Justice* http://epress.lib.uts.edu.au/journals/index.php/publicspace/article/view/537 (Accessed 5 March 2013).

21. http://www.lawreform.lawlink.nsw.gov.au/agdbasev7wr/lrc/documents/pdf/report_93.pdf, 3.7 (Accessed 16 July 2013).

Uncertainty about Pontifical Secrecy under the 2010 Vatican Reforms

When the Vatican spokesman, Fr Federico Lombardi explained the proposals to change canon law on 15 July 2010, he introduced an element of uncertainty into how pontifical secrecy will still operate. He said that reporting to the civil authorities should take place, 'in good time, not during or subsequent to the canonical trial'.[22] This seems to suggest that despite the existence of the dispensation or a *recognitio* under Canon 455 of Bishops Conference protocols, pontifical secrecy will still apply once the preliminary investigation or the judicial trial starts.

The Vatican position on this needs to be clarified because such a limitation is objectionable, because it means that bishops and those associated with the canonical tribunal could not disclose to the police further evidence of the same or other crimes that are uncovered during the course of the preliminary investigation and penal trial, for example, that an accused priest had also murdered one of his victims. Since the canonical procedure is an investigative one, it is to be expected that if the Congregation for the Doctrine of the Faith, in accordance with Article 13 of the *2001 Motu Proprio*, instructs the bishop to continue with a penal trial, there will be further evidence produced.[23] If what Fr Lombardi says is taken literally, pontifical secrecy applies to that further evidence.

A response that the bishop or tribunal members could apply for a further dispensation from the Vatican is also objectionable, because it would mean that the Vatican, a foreign state, would be interfering in the proper affairs of another country once again by preventing its bishops and priests from acting in according with a clear moral obligation to report in those circumstances. This is precisely the

---

22. http://www.vatican.va/resources/resources_lombardi-nota-norme_en.html (Accessed 21 July 2013). Amongst the documents produced by the Archdiocese of Milwaukee the decision of the judicial tribunal in the case against Fr Knighton, the following note appeared at the bottom of the definitive sentence of 27 July 2007: 'Be it known to all that this case is explicitly subject to the pontifical secret (Art 25, Graviora Delicta . . .); this applies to all information, processes and decisions associated with this case' *(Secreta Continere, February* 4, 1974(AAS 66 1974, pages 89-92.)http://www.andersonadvocates.com/documents/Key_Milwaukee_Documents/Lacization_All.pdf (Accessed 2 July 2013).

23. Delaney, 161

kind of interference of the Vatican in the affairs of another country that the Irish Foreign Minister and Prime Minister so trenchantly condemned after the *Cloyne Report*. Any State legislation must make it clear that the obligation to report applies irrespective of whether it arises 'during or subsequent to a canonical trial', and the Vatican, as a foreign State should be formally asked to drop pontifical secrecy under canon law for all matters which are also crimes under civil law.

The Irish Legislation

The Irish *Criminal Justice (Withholding of information on offences against children and vulnerable persons) Act* 2012 provides a precedent for Australian wide legislation. It requires reporting of any abuse of a "vulnerable person", and not just children. That legislation also protects the privacy of the victim who does not want the abuse reported.[24] The extension of this requirement to report in the case of 'vulnerable' people is necessary because of the extension of pontifical secrecy to cases of clergy assaulting those with an intellectual disability.

On 11 October, 2012, the Victorian Church offered to support changes in legislation by having clergy listed amongst the people required to report under the welfare reporting legislation, that is, where children are currently at risk.[25] In *Facing the Truth*, the Victorian bishops indicated that they would support legislation requiring all offences to be reported to the police while preserving the privacy of those who do not want to report.[26] The *Victorian Parliamentary Inquiry* Report, *Betrayal of Trust,* recommended changes to the Victorian *Crimes Act* to restore misprision of felony where child abuse was involved.[27] Uniform legislation throughout

24. http://www.irishstatutebook.ie/2012/en/act/pub/0024/print.html (Accessed 19 May 2013).
25. http://www.sandhurst.catholic.org.au/index.php/news-a-events3/news2/item/649-media-release-catholic-church-in-victoria-backs-mandatory-reporting-for-clergy-and-reporting-to-police (Accessed 16 February 2013).
26. http://www.parliament.vic.gov.au/images/stories/committees/fcdc/inquiries/57th/Child_Abuse_Inquiry/Submissions/Catholic_Church_in_Victoria.pdf, at 16.5 (Accessed 6 April 2013). http://www.cam.org.au/Portals/45/Documents/factsheets/Fact-Sheet-15_Reform-for-reporting-to-police.pdf (Accessed 7 August 2013).
27. *Betrayal of Trust*, Report of the *Victorian Parliamentary Inquiry*, XXXVIII https://s3-ap-southeast-2.amazonaws.com/family-and-community-development-

Australia along the lines of the Irish legislation would go a long way to prevent another cover up happening again.

The Canonical Disciplinary System

The 'reforms' initiated by the then Cardinal Ratzinger in 2001 were widely lauded by the Church press which painted him as the great reformer who was really doing more than anyone else about the sexual abuse problem.[28] In comparison with other people in the Vatican, he was, but that is using a baseline at the bottom of the barrel. When you analyse the *2001 Motu Proprio*, and its 2010 revision, little more was achieved than restoring the simplified method of administrative dismissal abolished by Pope John Paul II in 1980, and allowing priests to be placed on administrative leave prior to the preliminary hearing.[29] The *2001 Motu Proprio* created the possibility of some degree of uniformity by requiring all complaints to be sent to the Congregation to the Doctrine of the Faith, but this was often the practice anyway under *Crimen Sollicitationis* and the *1983 Code of Canon Law*.[30]

The central problems of the Church's disciplinary system are:

- The limitation period did not exist prior to the *1983 Code of Canon Law*. The *2001 Motu Proprio* extended the five year period, as did the 2010 revision, but even having any limitation period was worse than what existed before 1983.

committee/Inquiry+into+Handling+of+Abuse_Volume+1_FINAL_web.pdf (Accessed 14 November 2013).

28. http://northlandcatholic.blogspot.com.au/2010/07/did-pope-benedict-xvi-drop-ball-on.html (Accessed 21 October 2013) http://www.cbc.ca/news/world/former-pope-benedict-defends-sex-abuse-record-1.1866637 (Accessed 21 October 2013).

29. According to Monsignor Scicluna in 2013, 60% of all cases are dealt with by the administrative procedure. http://ncronline.org/news/accountability/canon-lawyers-hear-church-prosecutor-sex-abuse-cases (Accessed 27 October 2013).

30. *Crimen Sollicitationis* required the bishop to notify the Vatican about the allegations, and any appeals went to the Congregation for the Doctrine of the Faith. The Lawrence Murphy case illustrates how Archbishop Weakland in 1998 (prior to the *2001 Motu Proprio*) wrote to the Congregation seeking directions—even approval—for starting a judicial trial against Murphy.

- The Vatican 'Catch 22' defence: a priest cannot be dismissed for paedophilia because he is a paedophile. Canon 1321 which embodies this defence still stands in the Code unchanged. There is nothing in the *2001 Motu Proprio* or its revision in 2010 that modifies it.
- The 'pastoral approach', contained in Canon 1341 has not been changed. Monsignor Charles Scicluna in 2006 stated that this Canon applies and has not been affected by the *2001 Motu Proprio*.[31]
- The standard of proof for dismissal of a priest under Canon 1608 is 'moral certitude', a standard that appears to be the equivalent of the criminal standard of proof under Australian, English and United States law. [32] That has not changed under the reforms. Further, where a matter is referred to the pope for an ex officio dismissal under the norms of the *2001 Motu Proprio*, the guilt of the cleric has to be 'beyond doubt and well documented'.[33] This is an even higher standard than that required for criminal cases in civil law.

---

31. http://www.vatican.va/resources/resources_mons-scicluna-graviora-delicta_en.html

32. Beale and others in the *New Commentary on the Code of Canon Law*, on page1716 state:
'moral certitude is distinguished from absolute certitude on the one hand, and probability on the other. Pope Pius XII gave the classic description of moral certitude in an address to the Roman Rota on January 10, 1942. To reach moral certitude, judges must be able to exclude the probability of error, but are not held to the impossible and paralysing standard of excluding all possibility or error'. Delane, 186, quotes Pope Pius XII saying that moral certainty involves on *the* 'positive side by the exclusion of well-founded or reasonable doubt, [and] on the negative side it does admit the absolute possibility of the contrary.' This would appear to be the criminal standard of proof under English law. In fairness, it should be said that where allegations of a serious nature are made in disciplinary proceedings under civil law, a higher standard is required than mere balance of probabilities: Professor Patrick Parkinson: 'The Smith Lecture 2013: Child Sexual Abuse and the Churches – a Story of Moral Failure?' http://smithlecture. org/sites/smithlecture.org/files/downloads/lecture/smith-2013-transcript.pdf, 11 (Accessed 25 October 2013).

33. Monsignor Scicluna: *The Procedure and Praxis of the Congregation for the Doctrine of the Faith regarding Graviora Delicta* http://www.vatican.va/resources/resources_mons-scicluna-graviora-delicta_en.html.

In any respectable legal system, where a particular law is found to be defective or inadequate, the legislature will change the wording of the law so that those involved in enforcing and applying it know that they have to act differently. At the *Australian Royal Commission*, Archbishop Coleridge of Brisbane said that the Vatican is 'neuralgic' about changing the canons and prefers to change their 'interpretation'. He said that the Vatican can suffer from a 'lack of coordination' in such matters.[34]

The *2001 Motu Proprio* simplified the procedures for dismissing a priest, but it did not change the standards for dismissal that had to be applied by those simplified procedures.

In his 2010 historical introduction to the revised *2001 Motu Proprio*, Pope Benedict criticised the 'pastoral attitude' and that 'the bishop was expected to 'heal' rather than 'punish'. But this was and is the 'proper meaning of the words' of Canon 1341, and one that was interpreted that way by the world's canon lawyers and by the Vatican itself. If Pope Benedict wanted those applying canon law to act differently, the terms of Canon 1341 needed to be changed, or at least that it be made abundantly clear that the words 'reform the offender' in Canon 1341 did not apply in the future to the sexual abuse of children. But the words have not been changed, and it has not been made clear that 'reform the offender' in Canon 1341 does not now apply to child sexual abusers. *Bella figura*—the reluctance to admit a mistake—might well be behind this, but the effect is to turn the oldest continuing legal system in the Western world into Humpty Dumpty law, with words meaning so many contradictory things at the whim of the one who has the power.[35]

34. http://www.childabuseroyalcommission.gov.au/wp-content/uploads/2013/08/Transcript-RC_IRCSA_Day-026_11-Dec-2013_Public pdf 2740–2741 (Accessed 12 December 2013).
35. Lewis Carroll, *Alice in the Looking Glass*:
    When I use a word, Humpty Dumpty said in a rather scornful tone, 'It means just what I choose it to mean, neither more nor less'.
    'The question is,' said Alice, 'whether you can make words mean so many things'.
    'The question is,' said Humpty Dumpty, 'which is to be master—that's all'.

    All legal systems do make words mean whatever the legislature wants them to mean by the use of fictions, for example, for the purposes of the Motor Vehicle

The end result is that despite all the claims that everything changed after 2001, it is not surprising that there seems little change at all. When asked at the *Victorian Parliamentary Inquiry*, why it took 18 years to dismiss Fr Desmond Gannon, Archbishop Hart said steps had been taken as early as 1993 to remove Gannon's faculties, but Rome required 'absolute certitude as to what took place' for dismissal.[36] Gannon had been sentenced four times (in 1995, 1997, 2000, and 2009) for sexual crimes against children, but this was not enough to satisfy the need for 'absolute certitude' by the Vatican.[37] It is little wonder, as Hart said, that there were few dismissals up until 2002.[38] But it seems that Hart was having the same problems having him dismissed after 2002. In 2012, Hart wrote to the Vatican, saying that steps taken to dismiss Gannon would be seen as 'inadequate and a cause of scandal for the faithful'.[39] The Vatican declined to dismiss him because of his 'extreme age'. In 2006, when Bishop Jarrett of Lismore reported a serial sexual abuser to the Vatican under the *2001 Motu Proprio*, he received a reply from the Vatican two years later imposing a punishment of saying Mass for the victims every Friday and living a life of 'prayer and penance' in a comfortable presbytery.[40]

Act, a horse might be included in the definition of a motor car. But when they do that, they make it absolutely clear that this is what they are doing. Likewise a nation's highest courts might decide that previous interpretations of a law by the same court were wrong, but they make it quite clear that they have changed their mind. They never try to hide the mistake or the change of mind. Honesty and integrity are hallmarks of any decent legal system. *Bella figura* only corrupts it.

36. http://www.parliament.vic.gov.au/images/stories/committees/fcdc/inquiries/57th/Child_Abuse_Inquiry/Transcripts/Catholic_Archdiocese_of_Melbourne_20-May-13.pdf, 9(Accessed 18 June 2013).

37. Transcript Hart, *Victorian Parliamentary Inquiry* http://www.parliament.vic.gov.au/images/stories/committees/fcdc/inquiries/57th/Child_Abuse_Inquiry/Transcripts/Catholic_Archdiocese_of_Melbourne_20-May-13.pdf, 8–9 (Accessed 18 June 2013), and *Betrayal of Trust*, Report of the *Victorian Parliamentary Inquiry*, Table 7.4, 192 https://s3-ap-southeast-2.amazonaws.com/family-and-community-development-committee/Inquiry+into+Handling+of+Abuse_Volume+1_FINAL_web.pdf (Accessed 14 November 2013).

38. *Ibid*, transcript Hart, 8–9.

39. *Ibid*.

40. *Australian Royal Commission* http://www.childabuseroyalcommission.gov.au/wp-content/uploads/2013/12/Transcript-RC_IRCSA_Day-032_19-Dec-2013_TBC_Public.pdf 3392.36 (Accessed 20 December 2013).

The Australian bishops were not the only ones to have had this kind of problem, even after the so called 'reforms' of 2001. The recently released Milwaukee documents suggest that the Vatican still had this reluctance to dismiss even when the priest was a serial paedophile and requested voluntary laicisation.[41]

On 23 September 2003, Archbishop Dolan of Milwaukee wrote to Cardinal Josef Ratzinger requesting the laicisation of Fr John A O'Brien who pleaded guilty to a charge of sexually abusing a seventeen year old boy, and against whom there were other allegations. O'Brien signed a letter agreeing to voluntary laicisation. Nothing happened for two years, despite Dolan continually requesting a reply. When he finally did get a reply on 6 September 2005, the Congregation said the impossibility of returning to the ministry was not sufficient reason, and that O'Brien's letter must contain an admission of guilt and 'a sincere expression of remorse', before it could be passed on to the pope for approval. The plea of guilty before a civil court was apparently not sufficient proof. The laicisation decree came through on 3 April 2009, five and a half years after it was requested.[42]

Then there are the three other cases where the priests did not agree to voluntary laicisation, and where Archbishop Dolan requested permission to conduct a penal administrative or judicial trial to dismiss them. The Vatican then asked Dolan to try to convince the priests to submit to voluntary laicisation despite the fact that they had refused prior requests, and hardly showed remorse.[43] The Vatican was still insisting on this 'pastoral' approach by asking Dolan to try to convince the priests to agree to voluntary laicisation, rather than

---

41. http://www.andersonadvocates.com/documents/Key_Milwaukee_Documents/Lacization_All.pdf (Accessed 2 July 2013). It should be stated that these are documents produced by the victim's lawyer, Jeffrey Anderson, and one might have expected him to have highlighted the worst cases. If it is suggested that they are not a representative sample, the solution is simple: the Vatican should open its files to an independent assessment. The Congregation for the Doctrine of the Faith has dealt with 4,000 cases since 2012. These twelve cases create concerns about whether the Vatican culture had changed at all. See also Nicholas Cafardi: *Loose Cannons: Ratzinger, Church Law & the Sexual-Abuse Crisis* http://www.commonwealmagazine.org/loose-canons (Accessed 3 June 2013).
42. http://www.andersonadvocates.com/documents/Key_Milwaukee_Documents/Lacization_All.pdf (Accessed 2 July 2013).
43. *Ibid.* In the cases of Frs Wagner, Benham and Lanser.

impose on them the Church's version of a 'dishonourable discharge'. Cardinal Francis George was right—if you want to change a culture, you have to change the law. But if the law is not changed (as Canon 1341 has not been), one has to expect that Vatican bureaucrats will continue to interpret the law as they always had.

24

A Greek Tragedy: Not Facing The Truth

In October 2012, after the publication of figures showing some forty suicides of clergy sexual abuse victims, the Victorian Parliament started its inquiry.[1] The four Victorian Catholic dioceses, Melbourne, Ballarat Sale and Sandhurst, and religious orders operating within the state put in a submission. Its title, *Facing the Truth,* starts off with a quote from the highly respected nineteenth century English Cardinal, John Henry Newman, recently beatified by the Church.

> Let us take things as we find them: let us not attempt to distort them into what they are not. We cannot make facts. All our wishing cannot change them. We must use them.

It then proceeds to ignore his advice by failing to mention the most significant factor in the whole clergy sexual abuse story, not only in Australia, but throughout the world: *Crimen Sollicitationis.* It claims that the submission focuses on the 'broader and systemic implications of abuse' but then fails to mention the document that since 1922, more than anything else, created the systemic framework for the cover up.

On 30 September 2013, the Australian Church released its submission in response to Issues Paper Number 2 of the *Australian Royal Commission*, regarding *Towards Healing.*[2] Section 10 entitled

---

1. http://www.theage.com.au/victoria/churchs-suicide-victims-20120412-1wwox. html . (Accessed 16 July 2013). For the terms of reference and the submissions, see http://www.parliament.vic.gov.au/images/stories/committees/fcdc/ inquiries/57th/Child_Abuse_Inquiry/Final_FCDC_CAinROs_Submission_ Guide.pdf (Accessed 16 July 2013)
2. http://www.childabuseroyalcommission.gov.au/wp-content/ uploads/2013/10/15.-Truth-Justice-and-Healing-Council1.pdf, 1 (Accessed 25

'Dealing with the Accused' discusses canon law at length, but nowhere is there any mention of *Crimen Sollicitationis*. The *2001 Motu Proprio* is mentioned, but there is no mention of pontifical secrecy applying to the cases of sexual abuse of children by clergy.

Both submissions follow the Vatican script, written by Pope Benedict XVI in his *Pastoral Letter* to the people of Ireland: acknowledge that the abuse occurred, apologise to the victims, acknowledge that the response of bishops has been slow and inadequate, but like Basil in *Fawlty Towers* telling his non German guests not to mention the War: don't mention the role of the Pope or the Vatican in the cover up, and if you have to mention canon law, choose some part of it that has little to do with the real issue.

Both submissions have chapters dealing with 'emerging' or 'developing' awareness of sexual abuse issues, suggesting that child sexual abuse was some sort of hidden problem that the whole world, including the Church, had only just discovered.[3] There was a better awareness from about the 1960s onwards of the damage done to victims by child sexual abuse, and that it was more widespread than was earlier thought, but that is all.[4]

Sexual abuse is a new name for an old crime—sexually assaulting children. There is nothing new about it, either in society or in the Church. Except in a few cultures, it has always been severely condemned and punished. It is only in recent years that the Church has claimed that it and society have been on a 'learning curve'. The Church made the same claim to the the inquiry into the Archdiocese of Dublin, the Murphy Commission. They rejected it.[5] So did the *Victorian Parliamentary Inquiry* Report, *Betrayal of Trust*, which

---

November 2013).

3. *Facing the Truth*, chapter 5. http://www.parliament.vic.gov.au/images/stories/committees/fcdc/inquiries/57th/Child_Abuse_Inquiry/Submissions/Catholic_Church_in_Victoria.pdf (Accessed 6 April 2013), paragraph 1, *TJHC* Submission par 5.2 http://dev.childabuseroyalcommission.gov.au/wp-content/uploads/2013/10/14.-Truth-Justice-and-Healing-Council.pdf (Accessed 3 October 2013).

4. http://www.aifs.gov.au/nch/pubs/issues/issues1/issues1.html (Accessed 2 October 2013).

5. *Murphy Dublin Report*, Part 1 http://www.justice.ie/en/JELR/DACOI%20Part%201.pdf/Files/DACOI%20Part%201.pdf (Accessed 7 May 2013) par 1.14

noted that if there was a lack of awareness of the extent of the sexual abuse of children within society, the Church contributed to it by actively concealing it within its own ranks.[6]

Bishops in the United States, Canada and elsewhere have claimed to be unaware of the serious nature of clergy sexual abuse and its impact on victims, but the historical record shows that this is not true. They may not have been aware of the scientific nature of the sexual disorders of these priests or the clinical descriptions of the impact on victims, but they always knew it was criminal and damaging. The 2004 John Jay College survey shows that the American bishops were well aware of the problem as far back as the 1950s, and consistently mishandled it.[7]

Religious Orders and Congregations within the Church have arisen historically in response to a particular social problem. In 1947, Fr Gerald Fitzgerald saw that there were serious enough alcohol and sexual problems within the clergy in the United States to justify founding a separate religious congregation called the Servants of the Paraclete. Fitzgerald had consistently recommended a zero tolerance approach for priests who sexually assaulted children, because of their tendency to recidivism. He told the hierarchy that such clergy should be immediately dismissed from the priesthood. He did this in letters to American bishops and to the Vatican, and to Pope Paul VI with whom he discussed the matter in 1963.[8] Yet, the Church spin is that it only started 'learning' about the extent of the abuse in the late 1970s. What it then learned is that there was an explosion of child sexual abuse amongst clergy in the 1960s and 1970s, that it fell away in the

---

6. *Betrayal of Trust, Victorian Parliamentary Inquiry* Final Report, executive summary page XXVIII and paragraph 7.3, page 157 https://s3-ap-southeast-2. amazonaws.com/family-and-community-development-committee/Executive+s ummary+%26+recommendations.pdf (Accessed 13 November 2013).

7. Thomas Doyle, *Affidavit in the case of Jane Doe v Oblates of Mary Immaculate, District Court Bexar County Texas, Cause No. 2006CI09725, January 2008,* paragraph 51,52 http://reform-network.net/?p=1464 (Accessed 6 May 2013).

8. *Ibid,* paragraph 48 for a list of letters sent by Fitzgerald, and http://ncronline. org/news/accountability/bishops-were-warned-abusive-priests (Accessed 19 May 2013), Michael D'Antonio: *Mortal Sins* at 299. And see http://ncronline. org/news/accountability/disagreement-why-abuse-warnings-were-ignored (Accessed 9 July 2013).

subsequent decades, and that the psychological damage of sexual abuse was greater than perhaps earlier thought.[9]

For 1500 years, the Church at its highest and most respected levels recognized that the punishments that it could impose under canon law, such as dismissal from the clerical state, were not sufficient to deal with sexual abuse amongst the clergy. As early as the fourth century, St Basil of Caesarea recognized that priests who abused children should be jailed, and even when released should be closely supervised. The inadequacy of canonical punishments was recognized by Bede the Venerable in the seventh century in England, by the founder of canon law, Gratian, by decrees of Pope Celestine III, Pope Innocent III in the twelfth century, of Pope Leo X in 1514, of Pope St Pius V in 1568, of the third, fourth and fifth Lateran Councils, and of the Council of Trent in 1551, all of which required the offender to be handed over to the civil authorities. The Vatican itself in the eighteenth century showed a 'zero tolerance' approach to the sexual abuse of minors by refusing to reinstate a priest who had been found committing such a crime.

But not everyone in the Church agreed with this attitude, and the clericalist school of thought that considered priests were specially marked by God, that they should be treated differently to other mortals, and that scandals needed to be covered up, was always lurking beneath the surface. Just when and why the Church's official attitude changed between the eighteenth century and *Crimen Sollicitationis* in 1922 is beyond the scope of this book, but there is no doubt that the clericalism and theology that preached the special status of priests had gained the upper hand in the Church by that time. It was not secular society that had changed its attitude to the appropriate way to treat clergy who sexually abused children. It was the Church, and it was only in the last 200 years and especially in the last 90 since 1922.

The Church's real 'learning curve' started when groups of bishops in Ireland, the United States, Britain and Australia in the late 1980s realised that canon law, which prevented reporting clergy sex crimes to the police, and was useless for dismissing them from the priesthood, was a disaster, and led to more attacks on children. These

---

9. http://www.parliament.vic.gov.au/images/stories/committees/fcdc/
    inquiries/57th/Child_Abuse_Inquiry/Submissions/Catholic_Church_in_
    Victoria.pdf paragraph 5.4.1 (Accessed 6 April 2013).

bishops developed 'protocols' that either tried to change canon law for their regions (the Irish, Americans and British), or used creative ways to get around it (the Australians). The Vatican, regrettably, still 'does not get it' with its continued insistence on pontifical secrecy.

The two submissions defend the efforts made by the Australian Church in *Towards Healing* and in *The Melbourne Response*. They fail to mention that *The Melbourne Response* was far more in tune with Vatican thinking at the time, that is, of bishops not reporting clergy crimes to the police, than was *Towards Healing* which required it. The *Australian Church Submission* concedes that the early attempts to create a protocol from 1988 onwards were directed to disciplinary measures for accused priests, rather than the needs of victims.[10] What it fails to mention is that the need to do something about those disciplinary issues arose because canon law on the subject was 'unworkable'. This was the reason that Fr Brian Lucas was trying to get rid of priests outside the canonical system by convincing them to agree to voluntary laicisation.[11]

The *Australian Church Submission* describes how various principles for dealing with priests accused of the sexual abuse of children were developed over the years, including 'convicted or admitted paedophiles are never to be reappointed to pastoral ministry', that the Church 'would not tolerate sexual abuse and that it would cooperate with police and victims', 'no one should be permitted to exercise a public ministry if doing so presents an unacceptable risk of abuse to children or young people'.[12] No attempt is made to explain how these principles are consistent with canon law, and particularly with its requirements for pontifical secrecy, and to reform the offender.

The *Australian Church Submission* mentions the meeting in Rome between Bishops Robinson and Wilson and the Vatican in 2000 over the issue of sexual abuse.[13] It mentions that Bishop Robinson subsequently provided a report that stated that the permanent

---

10. *Australian Church Submission*, page 76, paragraph 44, http://dev. childabuseroyalcommission.gov.au/wp-content/uploads/2013/10/14.-Truth-Justice-and-Healing-Council.pdf (Accessed 12 October 2013).
11. http://www.lawlink.nsw.gov.au/lawlink/Special_Projects/ll_splprojects.nsf/ vwFiles/Transcript_Day_15_-_TOR_2_-_24_July_2013.pdf/$file/Transcript_ Day_15_-_TOR_2_-_24_July_2013.pdf, 1570 and 1632(Accessed 18 August 2013).
12. *Ibid*, 78, paragraph 55, 78, paragraph 60, page 88, paragraph 35(o)
13. *Ibid*, 90, paragraph 50.

removal of a priest required a judicial process and could only be taken in a 'small proportion of cases' because of the limitation period.[14] The *Australian Church Submission* failed to mention that both bishops were highly critical of the Vatican's attitude to the sexual abuse problem and to the obstacles imposed by canon law, Bishop Robinson asking: 'Why was the Vatican so many years behind?'[15] It still is.

On 26 July 1990, Dr Nicholas Tonti-Filippini, a Catholic ethicist advised the Australian bishops:

> For the sake of the Church, reasonable suspicion of a crime must be reported to the authorities. Any attempt to contain it within an in-house investigation and management risks bringing the Church into disrepute.[16]

It took the Australian bishops twenty years to write that into *Towards Healing* in 2010. The Australian Catholic Bishops Conference passed a resolution in 2003 to require reporting irrespective of the requirements of civil law.[17] But this was not written into *Towards Healing* until January 2010 because:

---

14. *Ibid*, 90, paragraph 50–57.
15. *New York Times*, 1 July 2010: http://www.nytimes.com/2010/07/02/world/europe/02pope.html?pagewanted=all&_r=0 (Accessed 12 October 2013).
16. http://www.lawlink.nsw.gov.au/lawlink/Special_Projects/ll_splprojects.nsf/vwFiles/Transcript_Day_16_-_TOR_2_-_25_July_2013.pdf/$file/Transcript_Day_16_-_TOR_2_-_25_July_2013.pdf, 1744-45 (Accessed 28 July 2013).
17. *Towards Healing* 2010 par 37.4. In the previous versions, 2003 at paragraph 37 did not require the Church to report, except where it was 'mandatory': 37.2, 37.3. *Facing the Truth*, Appendix 1A. http://www.parliament.vic.gov.au/images/stories/committees/fcdc/inquiries/57th/Child_Abuse_Inquiry/Submissions/Catholic_Church_in_Victoria_Appendix_1_Part_A.pdf (Accessed 15 August 2013). The same was true of the 2000 version (Appendix 1B), and the original 1996 version, paragraph 4.3, *Facing the Truth*, Appendix 1B, http://www.parliament.vic.gov.au/images/stories/committees/fcdc/inquiries/57th/Child_Abuse_Inquiry/Submissions/Catholic_Church_in_Victoria_Appendix_1_Part_B.pdf (Access 15 August 2013). The Australian Catholic Bishops Conference in 2003 had accepted reporting irrespective of a law requiring it, but it was not written into the document until 2010, because it was only relevant to New South Wales because of S.316 *Crimes Act NSW* 1900, *Australian Church Submission* to the *Australian Royal Commission*, http://dev.childabuseroyalcommission.gov.au/wp-content/uploads/2013/10/14.-Truth-Justice-and-Healing-Council.pdf, paragraph71 (Accessed 3 October 2013).

. . . the proposal was specific to the regulatory context of New South Wales, and a broader approach might be required."

That was code for: only the State of New South Wales is obliged to report historic abuse, why should the dioceses in the other states have to report? It reflects the comments of the American canon lawyer, Fr Thomas Green on the original proposals of the Dallas Charter that required reporting of all allegations to the police, irrespective of a legal obligation to do so: ' . . . if there is no civil obligation to report, why should we do so as long as we proceed canonically where appropriate?'.[18] That was the stance taken by the Vatican in the negotiations over the Charter that it ultimately approved, and it reflects the clericalism in Archbishop Herranz's claim in 2002, that the Church has all the 'necessary tools' to deal with clergy sexual abuse and that it is not the role of bishops to report child sexual abuse by priests unless they are forced to by the civil law.

It is significant that the Australian bishops put off this recommendation at its next meeting after the Vatican had approved the revised Dallas Charter for the United States, restricting reporting to where local laws required it. The Vatican attitude was clear: reporting will only be allowed where bishops might otherwise be going to jail. Neither submission acknowledges that reporting where there is no legal requirement to do so conflicts with canon law.

The chickens have now come home to roost, as Dr Tonti-Filippini predicted. The *Victorian Parliamentary Inquiry* Report, *Betrayal of Trust,* that examined the responses of the dioceses of Melbourne, Ballarat, Sale and Sandhurst, the last three of which were signatories of *Towards Healing*, found,

> No representatives of the Catholic Church directly reported the criminal conduct of its members to the police. The Committee found that there is simply no justification for this position.[19]

---

18. *Critique of the Dallas Charter* http://natcath.org/NCR_Online/documents/ Greencritique.htm, Article 4, paragraph B. B. (Accessed 21 July 2013).

19. *Betrayal of Trust*, Report of the Victorian Parliamentary Committee, paragraph 7.3.6, page 170 https://s3-ap-southeast-2.amazonaws.com/family-and-community

There was no justification, but there was a reason: canon law prohibited reporting unless, since 2010, there was a civil law requiring it. None existed in the State of Victoria.

Facing the Truth claims:

> Since 2001, the Holy See, in consultation with Episcopal Conferences and individual bishops, and following careful examination of the various aspects of the issue of the sexual abuse of children, has continued to modify the relevant canonical legislation and procedures to make them easier to apply, more effective and expeditious.[20]

It fails to mention that the central plank of the cover up, pontifical secrecy, is still part of canon law, and that in 2010, the Vatican expanded its scope to include cases of sexual abuse of those who 'habitually lack the use of reason'.

As to making the Church's canonical procedures for disciplining priests, 'easier to apply, more effective and expeditious', there has been no change to the Vatican 'Catch 22' defence in Canon 1321. Nor has there been any change to Canon 1341 requiring the 'pastoral approach'. Indeed, the Vatican's *Guide to Understanding Basic CDF Procedures* provides that where the accused priest has admitted to his crimes and has 'accepted a life of prayer and penance', his public ministry will be restricted and it is only if he violates those conditions that he may be dismissed. The Archdiocese of Milwaukee documents suggest that the best that could be said for the 2001 reforms is that the standard for dismissing a sex abusing priest had changed from 'impossible' to 'difficult'. The Gannon case in the State of Victoria is another good example of that difficulty.

Quite apart from a mistaken view of the Church's own history, both submissions are selective when it comes to canon law and to the systemic problems that it caused. The most important document in the modern history of the Church's response to sexual abuse by clergy, *Crimen Sollicitationis*, originally issued in 1922 and reissued in 1962, is never mentioned.

-development-committee/Inquiry+into+Handling+of+Abuse_Volume+1_ FINAL_web.pdf (Accessed 14 November 2013).
20. *Facing the Truth*, paragraph 5.9.

Facing the Truth contains a nine page chronology from 1961 to 2012, of 'Significant Developments Internationally and in Australia Both in the Church and Civil Society'. The 'significant developments' listed are some 150 pieces of legislation, both civil and canonical, and reports and documentaries dealing with child sexual abuse.[21] The chronology starts in 1961 with Dr H Kempe's paper on 'battered child syndrome' in the USA, and then ignores the 1962 reissue of *Crimen Sollicitationis*. Some of the entries it regards as 'significant' enough to include were the 1983 *Irish Social Workers Conference on Incest* and the 1999 *Report on Abuse in the Gwynedd and Clwydd Council Areas* (Wales).

Yet the document that had the most profound effect on child abuse by priests throughout the whole Catholic world, in every Catholic diocese, the reissue of *Crimen Sollicitationis* in 1962 that represented canon law from 1962 to 1983 at the height of figures for the abuse of children, is not even mentioned. Nor is it mentioned in the *Australian Church Submission*.

Both submissions mention the *2001 Motu Proprio* and its 2010 revision, where *Crimen Sollicitationis* is mentioned a total of five times in the historical introductions.[22] Archbishop Hart, one of the signatories to *Facing the Truth*, certainly knew about it when questioned by the members of the *Victorian Parliamentary Inquiry*.[23] It is difficult to believe that the failure to mention the central document that formed the legal framework for the coverup from 1922 until 1983 was an oversight.

One of the most significant systemic problems that prevented the Australian Church from dismissing sex abusing priests was the five year limitation period imposed by the *1983 Code of Canon Law*. There is a brief mention of the problems of the limitation period in the *Australian Church Submission*, by reference to its allowing very few canonical proceedings to be brought against sex abusing priests.[24]

---

21. *Ibid*, 131
22. http://www.vatican.va/resources/resources_introd-storica_en.html (Accessed 5 August 2013).
23. http://www.parliament.vic.gov.au/images/stories/committees/fcdc/inquiries/57th/Child_Abuse_Inquiry/Transcripts/Catholic_Archdiocese_of_Melbourne_20-May-13.pdf , 10 (Accessed 18 June 2013).
24. http://dev.childabuseroyalcommission.gov.au/wp-content/uploads/2013/10/14.-Truth-Justice-and-Healing-Council.pdf Section 6, paragraph 53(a)Annexure D,

Neither submission mentions the fact that the American bishops spent six years negotiating with the Vatican to try and get the five year limitation period extended, and that it was finally granted in 1994, but only for the United States.[25] In 1996, the five year period was extended for Ireland, but no mention is made that it was not extended to Australia.[26] It took thirteen years from the time the American bishops first pointed out the problem with the five year limitation period for the Vatican to agree to provide an extension for the whole Church in 2001, and even then the extension was inadequate.

Facing the Truth does mention the *1983 Code of Canon Law* in the main body of the submission, and provides a detailed explanation of how it functions. After providing an eighteen page survey of civil legislation and Church responses in the United States, Canada, Ireland, New Zealand, and the United Kingdom on child sexual abuse by clergy, *Facing the Truth* then says that Canon 1395 §2 deals with sexual abuse of children.

It says nothing about the devastating effect that other canons of the *1983 Code of Canon Law* had on the capacity of the Church to deal with clergy sexual abusers. In its survey, the Victorian Church sets out the measures taken to reform such priests in different countries, but makes no mention of the fact that Canon 1341 made that necessary, and prevented canonical proceedings to dismiss such priests being initiated until it was clear those measures had failed. And the failure was established by further abuse.

---

page 172, paragraph 75 (Accessed 3 October 2013).

25. Nicholas Cafardi, 'The Scandal of Secrecy: Canon Law and the Sexual-abuse Crisis', in *Commonweal*, 21 July 2010, http://commonwealmagazine.org/ scandal-secrecy (Accessed 27 May 2013) The *Australian Church Submission* does mention that the United States bishops recognized the limitation problem that prevented taking action against priests under canon law, but made no mention of the difficulties of trying to extend it: Annexure D, paragraph 72: http://dev. childabuseroyalcommission.gov.au/wp-content/uploads/2013/10/14.-Truth-Justice-and-Healing-Council.pdf (Accessed 3 October 2013).
    http://www.vatican.va/resources/resources_introd-storica_en.html

26. *Ibid.* The *Australian Church Submission* mentions that Bishop Geoffrey Robinson reported to the Australian Catholic Bishops Conference in 2000 that judicial proceedings to dismiss a priest could only be taken in a 'small proportion of cases' because of the limitation period. http://dev.childabuseroyalcommission. gov.au/wp-content/uploads/2013/10/14.-Truth-Justice-and-Healing-Council. pdf, 90 paragraph 53(a) (Accessed 3 October 2013).

Nowhere in either submission is there any mention of the secret of the Holy Office or pontifical secrecy that was imposed from 1922 to the present time. It is as if it never existed and was never part of canon law which bishops swore to obey on their ordination. It was only when he was questioned by the *Victorian Parliamentary Inquiry,* that Archbishop Hart admitted that *Crimen Sollicitationis* imposed 'strict confidentiality', and that there was 'too much' of it.[27]

The Victorian Church's summary of the *Murphy Dublin Report* follows to the letter the strategy of Pope Benedict XVI in giving the impression that all the Murphy Commission did was damn the Irish bishops for not following the rules of canon law, and that canon law had nothing to do with the problem. They quote Benedict XVI's statement through a Vatican press release prior to the *Pastoral Letter:*

> The Holy See takes very seriously the central issues raised by the Report, including questions concerning **governance by local Church leaders**, with the ultimate responsibility for the pastoral care of children[28] (my emphasis).

There is no mention of the central issue of governance by the Vatican through canon law, and the failure of the Vatican Congregations to dismiss priest criminals. *Facing the Truth* cherry picks findings of the *Murphy Dublin Report* and the *Cloyne Report* that criticised the behaviour of the Irish bishops or Irish State, but ignores the Commission's criticisms of the Vatican and canon law.

> The Archdiocese of Dublin's priorities in dealing with cases of child sexual abuse at least until the mid 1990s were the maintenance of secrecy, the avoidance of scandal, the protection of the reputation of the Church, and the preservation of its assets. All other considerations, including the welfare of children and justice for victims were seen as less important. The

---

27. http://www.parliament.vic.gov.au/images/stories/committees/fcdc/ inquiries/57th/Child_Abuse_Inquiry/Transcripts/Catholic_Archdiocese_of_ Melbourne_20-May-13.pdf, 13 (Accessed 18 June 2013).
28. *Ibid,* 5.6.3, Vatican Press Release 11 December 2009.

Archdiocese did not implement its own canon law rules and did its best to avoid the application of the laws of the state.[29]

All of that is true, but the Dublin bishops were not the only ones concerned with secrecy and scandal. The *1983 Code of Canon Law* is riddled with concerns about 'scandal' (mentioned twenty-eight times) and 'secret' or 'secrecy' (thirty-five times). The whole point of pontifical secrecy was the avoidance of scandal.

The Victorian Church submission ignores the Murphy Commission's conclusion that:

> The Commission has no doubt that clerical child sexual abuse was covered up by the Archdiocese of Dublin and other Church authorities . . . **The structures and rules of the Catholic Church facilitated that cover-up**[30] (my emphasis).

It makes no mention of the Murphy Commission's findings that Church officials from the Dublin Archdiocese felt that they could not report these crimes to the police because of the secrecy provisions.[31] And they were right. That is what canon law said, whether it was *Crimen Sollicitationis* or the *1983 Code of Canon Law* and *Secreta Continere* or the *2001 Motu Proprio.*

The *Australian Church Submission* ignores these findings of the *Murphy Dublin Report* and says:

> There is nothing in the 1983 Code that is in conflict with any applicable civil law obligations relating to the reporting of allegations of child sexual abuse.[32]

29. *Murphy Dublin Report* Part 1 http://www.justice.ie/en/JELR/DACOI%20Part%201.pdf/Files/DACOI%20Part%201.pdf (Accessed 7 May 2013) paragraph 1.15.
30. *Ibid,* paragraph 1.113.
31. *Ibid,* paragraph 1.27.
32. *Australian Church Submission,* page 132 paragraph 10 http://dev.childabuseroyalcommission.gov.au/wp-content/uploads/2013/10/14.-Truth-Justice-and-Healing-Council.pdf (Accessed 12 October 2013).

The *1983 Code* is not the only source of canon law. *Secreta Continere* and the *2001 Motu Proprio* are also canon law, but are not part of the *Code*. Until 2010, when the dispensation was given to allow reporting where there was an applicable civil law, canon law did conflict with civil law in the State of New South Wales, and in other states where 'children at risk' were involved. Likewise, there is still a conflict if Fr Lombardi's comments on 15 July 2010 are a reflection of canon law because it will mean that after a canonical trial starts, pontifical secrecy will prevent any reporting to the civil authorities of evidence presented to that trial.

The Victorian Church chronology mentions the Irish *Framework Document* of 1996, but makes no mention of what the Vatican said about its proposals for mandatory reporting to the police in the letter of 31 January 1997 from the Papal Nuncio, Archbishop Storero. There is no mention of what the Murphy Commission said about the influence of that letter on the cover up in both the *Murphy Dublin Report* and the *Cloyne Report*.[33] There is no mention of the impossible position that the Storero letter placed the Irish bishops— if they reported these crimes to the police, the Vatican threatened that it would allow appeals from any canonical procedures that were brought against the priest sexual abuser, quite apart from what might have happened to them for breaching canon law.[34]

There is no mention of the chaos that pontifical secrecy caused in other ways. As the Murphy Commission found, sometimes people who should have known about the allegations against the priest, did not.[35] There is no mention of the confusion in canon law as to whether a bishop could suspend a priest pending an investigation.[36]

---

33. *Murphy Dublin Report*, Part 1 http://www.justice.ie/en/JELR/DACOI%20 Part%201.pdf/Files/DACOI%20Part%201.pdf paragraphs 7.13 and 6.14. (Accessed 7 May 2013).
 http://www.justice.ie/en/JELR/Cloyne_Rpt.pdf/Files/Cloyne_Rpt.pdf, 4.21 and 4.22. (Accessed 7 May 2013).

34. http://www.justice.ie/en/JELR/DACOI%20Fr%20Jovito%20published.pdf/Files/ DACOI%20Fr%20Jovito%20published.pdf paragraph 7.14 (Accessed 7 May 2013).

35. http://www.justice.ie/en/JELR/DACOI%20Part%201.pdf/Files/DACOI%20 Part%201.pdf paragraph 1.64 (Accessed 25 April 2013).

36. *Murphy Dublin Report*, Part 1 http://www.justice.ie/en/JELR/DACOI%20 Part%201.pdf/Files/DACOI%20Part%201.pdf paragraphs 4.47–4.50. (Accessed 25 April 2013). This was also one of the conflicts with canon law that Cardinal

The *Australian Church Submission* states that the adoption of *Towards Healing* was a breakthrough:

> The process was adopted by the Church in Australia in deliberate preference to relying solely on canon law processes, which are not victim-focused and are mainly concerned with dealing with accused persons.[37]

It was not a matter of 'solely relying on canon law' when it came to dismissing sexually abusing priests from the priesthood. They could not rely on it at all. There was no attempt to explain why the Australian bishops had no choice but to convince clergy sexual abusers to agree to be suspended or dismissed.

Neither submission makes mention of the barrage of public and private statements from senior cardinals and canon lawyers from 1997 to 2002, asserting that it was not the role of bishops to report clergy sexual abusers to the police, and that to do so was, in some ways, immoral, and the influence that must have had on bishops worldwide. There is no mention of the letter of 8 September 2001 of Cardinal Castrillón, the Prefect of the Congregation for the Clergy to Bishop Pican congratulating him for breaching the French civil law in not reporting a paedophile priest to the police, and advising that he was sending a copy of his letter to all the bishops of the world to 'encourage' them how to behave—don't report clergy sexual abusers to the police and go to jail if need be.

The Vatican's approval of the US Bishops Charter arising from the 2002 Dallas proposals, giving them a limited exception to pontifical secrecy is mentioned in both submissions. But there is no mention of the fact that *Towards Healing* was never given a *recognitio* by the Vatican to create an exception to allow reporting as part of canon law applicable to Australia, and the reasons why it was pointless asking for one—the Vatican did not approve of bishops reporting any clergy sex crimes to the police until 2010 when it gave a limited dispensation, and it does not approve of the current *Towards Healing* requirement for reporting without a law requiring it.

Re mentioned in his 2002 letter to the American bishops over their proposals for administrative leave pending preliminary investigations.

37. http://dev.childabuseroyalcommission.gov.au/wp-content/uploads/2013/10/14.-Truth-Justice-and-Healing-Council.pdf, 16, paragraph 36 (Accessed 3 October 2013).

Cardinal Levada's 2011 guidelines for Bishops Conferences are mentioned in the *Facing the Truth* chronology, but there is no mention in either submission of the fact that under these guidelines, pontifical secrecy will still apply unless there is a local law requiring reporting. The submission does mention the fact that, apart from the State of New South Wales, there is no law in Australia requiring reporting of allegations by adults of being abused by priests as children—more than ninety-nine per cent of all cases, if the figures for *The Melbourne Response* are an indication generally.

The Victorian Church does make a recommendation that Victorian law be changed to make it mandatory that all allegations of sexual abuse be reported to the police. Such reporting laws are advisable because of cultural inertia, and because the Church is not the only institution that has been covering up sexual abuse. However, if pontifical secrecy still applies after the commencement of a canonical trial, there will still be a conflict between canon and civil law.

Three of the four Victorian dioceses, Sale, Sandhurst and Ballarat had signed up to *Towards Healing* in 1996, but they did not report any of the 307 complaints since that time to the police. This is hardly surprising. Victorian law did not require them to do so. *Towards Healing* until 2010 only required reporting when there was such a law. And pontifical secrecy still prevents them from reporting any such information when there is no such law.[38]

Facing the Truth goes on to say:

> The Church acknowledges that prior to the introduction of the *Melbourne Response* and *Towards Healing*, it did not respond appropriately to some allegations of criminal conduct. This was a mistake. The mistake was compounded because the manner in which the Church dealt with the allegations was sometimes ineffective. With great regret, the Church acknowledges that there have been instances in the past where further abuse

---

38. The Melbourne Archdiocese dealt with 304 cases http://www.parliament.vic. gov.au/images/stories/committees/fcdc/inquiries/57th/Child_Abuse_Inquiry/ Right_of_Reply/Right_of_Reply_P._OCallaghan_Part_1.pdf (Accessed 9 May 2013).

> could have been prevented by more effective action
> against offenders . . .[39]

It was a mistake, but it was canon law's mistake, and the ineffectiveness of the response was created by canon law. Bishop Connors and Cardinal Pell in their oral evidence continued to blame the predecessor bishops as if canon law had no relevance whatsoever.[40]

The *Australian Church Submission* of 11 October 2013 to the *Australian Royal Commission* concedes that some in positions of authority concealed and covered up clergy sexual abuse and that this behaviour was indefensible.[41] There is no mention that canon law underpinned this behaviour.

The Victorian Church in their submissions to the *Victorian Parliamentary Inquiry* and the Australian Church in their submission, the *Australian Church Submission*, to the *Australian Royal Commission* have meticulously followed the lead laid down by Pope Benedict XVI in his *Pastoral Letter* to the Irish People: blame negligent bishops, and make no mention of the role of canon law, the Roman Curia or any of the popes; do not, under any circumstances, suggest that the Vicars of Christ had anything to do with it.

At the *Victorian Parliamentary Inquiry* on 30 April 2013, the former bishop of Ballarat, Peter Connors, one of the signatories to *Facing the Truth* and the current one, Bishop Bird, poured the bucket over their predecessor, Ronald Mulkearns, and accepted that the Australian bishops had made terrible mistakes.

When asked by the Deputy Chairman of the Committee, Frank Maguire, at what level should the church take responsibility for the systemic failure, Bishop Connors who led the diocese from 1997 until late 2012 replied,

---

39. *Facing the Truth*, paragraph 16.6.
40. Peter Connors http://www.parliament.vic.gov.au/images/stories/committees/fcdc/inquiries/57th/Child_Abuse_Inquiry/Transcripts/Catholic_Diocese_of_Ballarat_29-April-13.pdf p.26 Cardinal Pell http://www.parliament.vic.gov.au/images/stories/committees/fcdc/inquiries/57th/Child_Abuse_Inquiry/Transcripts/Catholic_Archdiocese_of_Sydney_27-May-13.pdf, 30.6 (Accessed 24 June 2013).
41. http://www.childabuseroyalcommission.gov.au/wp-content/uploads/2013/10/25.-Truth-Justice-and-Healing-Council.pdf paragraph 6 & 7. (Accessed 1 November 2013).

> As a group of bishops, I think the bishops have accepted
> that we have failed terribly in the past, and that will
> come out in this inquiry and also in the forthcoming
> royal commission.[42]

The bishops failed as a group when they obeyed canon law, and
became part of the world wide pattern of cover-up. Popes Pius XI,
Pius XII, John XXIII, Paul VI, John Paul II and Benedict XVI, and
Cardinals Ratzinger (later Benedict XVI), Castrillón, Re, Bertone,
Herranz, Sodano, and all the others in the curia who presided over
the mess that was canon law really did effectively facilitate child
sexual abuse by prohibiting bishops from reporting to the police, and
by relying on their own disciplinary system in canon law that was
nothing but a shambles.

Every bishop before ordination is required to take an oath of
loyalty to the Pope, the source of all canon law.[43] The good and faithful
servants in Australia have done well. *Bella figura* is alive and thriving
in the Antipodes. And that is disappointing because the Australian
Church since the 1990s had shown considerable courage and at times
ingenuity in trying to find a way around the morass that canon law
had laid for them in dealing with sexual abuse. That courage has now
gone out the window by their failing to face the truth about the six
popes who since 1922 orchestrated the coverup through canon law.

Two and a half thousand years ago, Sophocles wrote one of the
most famous plays ever written, *Oedipus the King*. It is still performed
regularly somewhere in the world. Gabriel García Márquez, in his
autobiography, described it as the perfect play. It is the story about
a man who kills his father and marries his mother. Sigmund Freud
thought that this is what every male child wants to do. The popularity
of the play does not arise from Freud's fantasies, or because of its
dealing with deeply held taboos, but from its description of the
painful path of everyman finding out about himself and what he has
done.

When he was young, Oedipus was involved in a fight, and in that
fight, he kills his father and later marries a woman who turns out to

---

42. *Ibid*, Bishop Connors at 26.
43. Bishop   Geoffrey   Robinson: http://bishopgeoffrobinson.org/usa_lecture.htm
    (Accessed 23 August 2013).

be his mother. But Oedipus did not know that the man he had killed was his father and the woman he married was his mother. The play is about his finding this out, of his struggle to face up to the mounting evidence, and finally having to accept the appalling truth. It is so painful that he blinds himself.

Over the last thirty five years, the world has been treated to a real life performance of the unfolding of another Greek tragedy, of an Oedipus in reverse. Not of a man who painfully discovers the truth about himself and bravely accepts it, but of a man who has known the truth for some time about what he and his colleagues have done, and refuses to face up to it. This Oedipus sat not on the throne of Thebes, but on the throne of St Peter. And his deliberate blinding of himself does not occur at the end of the play, but at the beginning.

Josef Ratzinger knew right from the start of his being appointed as Prefect for the Congregation for the Doctrine of the Faith that he was part of the Roman Curia that was administering, confirming and entrenching a system of privilege of clergy that not only protected clergy sexual abusers from going to jail, but that led to further sex attacks by them on children. Before becoming Prefect of the Congregation for the Doctrine of the Faith in 1981, as Archbishop of Munich, he had agreed to shift a priest sexual abuser of children, Fr Peter Hullerman to his own diocese in Munich, so that he could receive psychiatric treatment. His Vicar General took responsibility for returning the priest to pastoral duties, contrary to the advice of his psychiatrist, where the priest then attacked more children. The police were never notified of the allegations against Hullerman, but Archbishop Ratzinger knew about them—he chaired the meeting when the transfer was agreed to.[44]

And even if Josef Ratzinger wasn't fully aware in 1981 that these priests were generally recidivists, and that canon law was incapable of dealing with the problem, it must have slowly dawned on him from his twenty-five years as a senior member of the Roman Curia and the requests for voluntary laicisation that were coming past his desk, many of them from convicted paedophiles. He even complained in 1988 about the complexities of the procedures for dismissing sex

---

44. http://www.spiegel.de/international/germany/sex-abuse-scandal-did-archbishop-ratzinger-help-shield-perpetrator-from-prosecution-a-684970.html (Accessed 27 April 2013).

abusing priests by means of a canonical trial. If he ever had any doubts about these things, the Murphy Dublin Report dispelled them. The Vatican announced in a press release of 11 December 2009, that His Holiness had given it 'careful study', and that he was 'deeply disturbed and distressed by its contents'[45]

But he chose to stay blind to the facts, and instead of being honest with himself, as the original Oedipus had been, he criticized the Irish bishops in his 2010 *Pastoral Letter* to the Irish people, for what he, his predecessors and Curia colleagues, had ordered them to do through canon law. Had he acknowledged the truth and apologised, had he abolished pontifical secrecy for canonical crimes that are also crimes under civil law, and required bishops to report such crimes to the police, irrespective of whether they were required to do so or not, most fair minded people would have accepted that everyone—even popes—can make mistakes. But instead of doing that, he wrote the script for the campaign to cover up his own involvement and that of his Roman Curial colleagues and his predecessors. Even in his retirement, he denied having anything to do with the cover up.[46] Whatever Josef Ratzinger's other admirable qualities, honesty is not amongst them.

The fact that priests were sexually assaulting children was bad enough, but through canon law since 1922, six popes and their Roman Curial advisers allowed so much more damage to be done to the 'little children'—a crime which the Church's own founder thought was so bad that those involved should have millstones put around their necks and be thrown into the sea.[47]

---

45. Vatican Press Release 11 December 2009. http://www.vatican.va/resources/resources_irish-bishops-dec2009_en.html (Accessed 19 May 2005).

46. http://www.abc.net.au/news/2013-09-24/former-pope-benedict-denies-cover-up-of-child-abuse-in-church/4979082 (Accessed 25 September 2013).

47. Mark 9:42.

Pope Benedict XVI

Pope John Paul II

Index of Subject

Index of Names

CPSIA information can be obtained
at www.ICGtesting.com
Printed in the USA
FFHW021728291018
49005090-53269FF